CORELDRAW! 3
MADE EASY

Emil & Sybil Ihrig
and
Martin & Carole Matthews

Osborne **McGraw-Hill**

Berkeley New York St. Louis San Francisco
Auckland Bogotá Hamburg London Madrid
Mexico City Milan Montreal New Delhi Panama City
Paris São Paulo Singapore Sydney
Tokyo Toronto

Osborne **McGraw-Hill**
2600 Tenth Street
Berkeley, California 94710
U.S.A.

For information on translations or book distributors outside of the U.S.A., please write to Osborne **McGraw-Hill** at the above address.

CorelDRAW! 3 Made Easy

1234567890 DOC 998765432

ISBN 0-07-881-838-9

Publisher
Kenna S. Wood

Acquisitions Editor
Elizabeth Fisher

Associate Editor
Scott Rogers

Editorial Assistant
Hannah Raiden

Technical Editor
Michael Katz

Project Editor
Wendy Rinaldi

Copy Editor
Michael Katz

Proofreader
Jeff Barash

Indexer
Phil Roberts

Computer Designer
VersaTech Associates

Cover Designer
Compass Marketing

CONTENTS

ACKNOWLEDGMENTS

A number of people are responsible for this Third Edition of *CorelDRAW! Made Easy*. John Cronan and Bill Loyd are responsible for updating a large number of the chapters. Erik Paulsen wrote the chapter on CorelCHART!. Osborne/McGraw-Hill once again assembled a superb team to produce the book under the able direction of Elizabeth Fisher and with the capable assistance of Scott Rogers and Wendy Rinaldi. The original authors, Emil and Sybil Ihrig of VersaTech Associates not only produced a wonderful initial book but also did a tremendous job of almost overnight page composition for this edition, with the expert help of Galen Bancroft. All of these people put out a considerable amount of effort in a short period of time to produce an excellent product. Their effort and the results are greatly appreciated.

INTRODUCTION

Since its initial release in January of 1989, CorelDRAW! has become the most talked-about graphics software package for IBM-compatible PCs. It's easy to understand why the program has received many major industry awards and received so much favorable attention. Quite simply, no other drawing software offers so many powerful drawing, text-handling, autotracing, color separation, and special effects capabilities in a single package. CorelDRAW! 3 continues this tradition by adding roll-up windows, full color editing, a new Help facility, text entry on a drawing, a thesaurus and a spelling checker, and Object Linking and Embedding (OLE). If this isn't enough, CorelDRAW! 3 also has added three new applications: CorelCHART!, a full-featured charting package; CorelSHOW!, a presentation package; and CorelPhoto-Paint!, a painting and photo retouching package.

About This Book

CorelDRAW! 3 Made Easy is a step-by-step training guide to CorelDRAW! that leads you from elementary skills to more complex ones. Each chapter contains hands-on exercises that are richly and clearly illustrated so that you can match the results on your computer screen.

This book makes few assumptions about your graphics experience or computer background. If you have never used a mouse or worked with a drawing package, you can begin with the exercises in the early chapters and move forward as you master each skill. On the other hand, if you have experience in desktop publishing, graphic design, or technical illustration, you can concentrate on the chapters that cover more advanced features or features that are new to you. Even the basic chapters contain exercises that stimulate your creativity, however, so it is worth your while to browse through each chapter in order to gain new design ideas.

How This Book Is Organized

CorelDRAW! 3 Made Easy is designed to let you learn by doing, regardless of whether you are a new, intermediate, or advanced user of CorelDRAW!. You begin to draw right away, and as the book proceeds, you continue to build on the skills you have learned in previous chapters.

The organization of this book is based on the philosophy that knowing how to perform a particular *task* is more important than simply knowing the location of a tool or menu command. The body of the book therefore contains step-by-step exercises that begin with basic drawing skills and progresses to advanced skills that combine multiple techniques. The appendixes at the end of the book contain handy reference material that you can turn to when you need to review what you have learned.

The organization of each chapter will help you locate quickly any information that you need to learn. Each section within a chapter begins with an overview of a particular skill and its importance in the context of other CorelDRAW! functions. In most chapters, every section contains one or more hands-on exercises that allow you to practice the skill being taught.

NOTE: The exercises in this book were designed with a VGA display adapter and screen driver in mind. If the screen driver that you installed for Windows has a lower or higher resolution (for example, EGA or 800 X 600), you may need to adjust viewing magnification or rulers for some of the exercises.

Conventions Used in This Book

CorelDRAW! 3 Made Easy uses several conventions designed to help you locate information quickly. The most important of these are:

✦ Terms essential to the operation of CorelDRAW! appear in *italics* the first time they are introduced.

✦ The first time an icon or tool in the CorelDRAW! toolbox or interface is discussed, it appears as a small graphic beside the text; for example, the Pencil tool.

✦ You can locate the steps of any exercise quickly by looking for the numbered paragraphs that are indented from the left margin.

✦ Names of keys appear as small graphics that look similar to the actual keys on your computer's keyboard (for example, Ctrl).

✦ Text or information that you must enter using the keyboard appears in **boldface**

CHAPTER

1

GETTING ACQUAINTED WITH CORELDRAW!

Welcome to CorelDRAW!. You have selected one of the most innovative and advanced graphics tools available for the IBM personal computer. CorelDRAW! will sharpen your creative edge by allowing you to edit any shape or character with ease and precision, fit text to a curve, autotrace existing artwork, create custom color separations, explore calligraphic "pens" and fountain fills, and more. You can combine CorelDRAW!'s features to achieve many different special effects, such as placing a line of text or an object in perspective; folding, rotating, or extruding a line of text or an object; blending two lines of text or two objects; and creating mirror images, masks and 3-D simulations. CorelDRAW! makes these and other capabilities work for you at speeds far surpassing those of other graphics programs.

To support your creative and technical endeavors, CorelDRAW! has a large number of fonts and clip art libraries at your disposal. If the more than 150 fonts provided with CorelDRAW! fail to meet your needs, you can use the WFNBOSS utility (provided with version 1.1 or later) to access thousands of commercial fonts. Your software also supplies over 3000 symbols and over 750 clip art images, and you can obtain thousands more from industry vendors.

If you haven't installed CorelDRAW!, turn to Appendix A before continuing with this chapter.

Starting CorelDRAW!

To start CorelDRAW!, first turn on your computer. Next, you may or may not need to start Windows. If you do *not* automatically load Windows, use the first two instructions below for that purpose. If you already have Windows up on your screen, skip to the paragraph following the second step.

1. Change to the drive and directory of the hard disk in which you have installed Windows. If you are not in the correct drive, you need to change the drive by typing the drive letter followed by a colon. For example, type **c:** and press Enter. To then change the directory to the Windows directory, type **cd windows** or **cd** *yourname*, if you have named the directory something else, and press Enter.

2. Type **win** and press Enter to start Windows. After an introductory screen and a few seconds, the Program Manager window appears on the screen, as shown in Figure 1–1.

Depending on how you or someone else last left Corel on your computer, the Corel Graphics window (representing the group of Corel Graphics) may be open, as shown in Figure 1–1, or you may see an icon at the bottom of the Program Manager window. If you don't see an

1

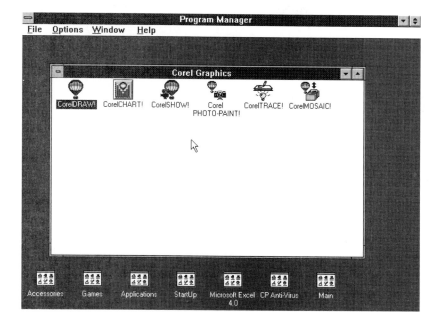

The Program
Manager
window with
the Corel
Graphics group
window open
Figure 1–1.

open window with the title "Corel Graphics," look for an icon with
that name, like the one on the left. If you don't see either the Corel
Graphics window or icon, open the Window menu and look there.

3. *Click* on "Window" in the menu bar of the Program Manager
    window (with your mouse, place the mouse pointer on top of the
    word "Window" and press and release the left mouse button). The
    Window menu should open and look like this:

```
Window
  Cascade                Shift+F5
  Tile                   Shift+F4
  Arrange Icons
  √ 1 Corel Graphics
    2 Microsoft Excel 4.0
    3 Main
    4 CP Anti-Virus
    5 Accessories
    6 StartUp
    7 Applications
    8 Wordperfect
    9 Games
```

4. If you see "Corel Graphics" in the Window menu, click on it (place the mouse pointer on top of the phrase "Corel Graphics" and press and release the left mouse button). Your Corel Graphics group window should open.

CAUTION: If you don't see "Corel Graphics" in the Window menu you need to turn to Appendix A and install CorelDRAW!. Do that now and then return here.

If "Corel Graphics" is an icon, open it now.

5. *Double-click* on the Corel Graphics group icon (place the mouse pointer on the icon and press and release the left mouse button twice in rapid succession). The Corel Graphics group window should open.

6. To start CorelDRAW!, double-click on the CorelDRAW! application icon (place the mouse pointer on the icon and press and release the left mouse button twice in rapid succession).

After a moment, an information screen is displayed, then the CorelDRAW! screen appears.

The CorelDRAW! Screen

You will see references to the various screen components of CorelDRAW! many times throughout the book. Take a moment now to familiarize yourself with these terms and their functions within the program. Figure 1–2 shows the location of each screen component.

Window Border   The Window border marks the boundaries of the CorelDRAW! window. By placing your mouse pointer on and dragging the border, you can scale this window. Refer to your *Microsoft Windows User's Guide* for full details on how to scale a window.

Title Bar   The title bar shows the name of the program you are working in and name of the currently loaded image. All files in

1

CorelDRAW! format have the file extension .CDR directly after the filename. When you first load CorelDRAW!, the screen hasn't been saved yet, so the title bar reads "UNTITLED.CDR."

Minimize Button   You will find the minimize button at the upper-right corner of your screen. Click on this button to turn the CorelDRAW! window into an icon—a small picture of a balloon. When running as an icon, CorelDRAW! frees up memory that you can use to run another application. To restore CorelDRAW! to its previous size, position the mouse over the icon, and double-click.

Maximize Button   If you want to make the CorelDRAW! window fill the entire screen, click on the maximize button located next to the minimize button. This button then turns into the restore button as shown in Figure 1–2. You can return the CorelDRAW! window to its previous size by clicking on this button once more.

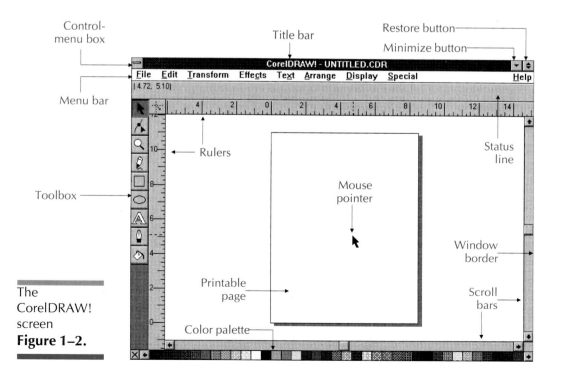

The CorelDRAW! screen
Figure 1–2.

Control-Menu Box You can use the Control-menu box as another easy way to move, minimize, maximize, or otherwise change the size of the CorelDRAW! program window. To use the Control-menu box, simply click on the small bar inside the box, or press Alt - Spacebar and the Control menu will appear. Select the command you want by clicking on it. When you have finished, click anywhere outside the Control menu to close it. The Control menu is a Windows feature that is not needed by CorelDRAW!.

Menu Bar The menu bar contains nine menus that you pull down by clicking on one of the menu names. See the section "The CorelDRAW! Menus" later in this chapter for a brief summary of the command options in each menu.

Status Line The status line contains a rich source of information about the image you have on your screen. When you first load CorelDRAW!, this line contains only a pair of numbers—the coordinates of the mouse pointer. When you are drawing or editing images, however, it displays information such as number, type, and dimensions of objects you select and the distance you travel when moving these objects. The exact nature of the information displayed depends on what you are doing at the time. The status line offers invaluable aid to technical illustration or to any work that requires precision.

Printable Page Area You create your images in the printable page area. The exact size of the page depends on the printer or other output device that you installed when you set up Microsoft Windows, as well as on the settings you choose through the Page Setup command in the File menu. When you first load CorelDRAW!, the screen displays the total printable page area. Once you learn about magnification in Chapter 5, you can adjust the area of the page that is visible at any one time.

Scroll Bars The scroll bars are most useful when you are looking at a magnified view of the page. Use the horizontal scroll bar to move to the left or right of the currently visible area of the page; use the vertical scroll bar to move to an area of the page that is above or below the currently visible area. You will find more information on how to use the scroll bars in Chapter 6.

Rulers   The horizontal and vertical rulers that appear in Figure 1–2 may not appear on your screen. These are optional and must be specifically turned on by selecting Show Rulers from the Display menu. A dashed line in each ruler shows you where the mouse pointer is. You can see such lines at about 4.7 on the horizontal ruler and about 5.1 on the vertical ruler. These are the same as the coordinates in the status line. The rulers allow you to judge the relative sizes and placements of objects quickly and accurately.

Color Palette   The color palette at the bottom of the CorelDRAW! window in Figure 1–2 allows you to apply shades of gray on a monochrome screen or shades of gray and colors on a color monitor. Like the rulers, the color palette can be turned on or off in the Display menu. In CorelDRAW!, shading and color can be applied to either a character's or object's outline or its body.

Toolbox   The toolbox contains tools that carry out the most important and powerful drawing and editing functions in CorelDRAW!. Click on a tool icon to select a tool. The tool icon now appears on dark grey background. Other changes to the screen or to a selected object may also occur, depending on which tool you have selected. For a brief explanation of the function of each tool, see the section, "The CorelDRAW! Toolbox," later in this chapter.

With a basic understanding of the screen elements, you can get around the CorelDRAW! window easily. The next three sections of this chapter explore three types of interface elements—menus, dialog boxes, and tools—in greater depth.

The CorelDRAW! Menus

When you pull down a menu, some commands appear in boldface, while others appear in gray. You can select any command that appears in boldface, but commands in gray are not available to you at the moment. Commands become available for selection depending on the objects you are working with and the actions you perform on them.

This book is a tutorial rather than a reference manual. As such, it organizes information about CorelDRAW! according to the task you want to perform and not by menu. You'll learn to use program menus by working with particular functions of CorelDRAW!. This section briefly describes the major purposes of each menu. These menus are shown in Figure 1–3.

The File Menu   The File menu in Figure 1–3(a) is similar in all Windows applications. Most of the commands in the File menu do not apply to the process of drawing. Instead, they cover program functions that deal with entire files at a time or with running the program as a whole. Examples of such functions are loading, saving, importing, exporting, and printing a file, as well as inserting an object and exiting CorelDRAW!.

The Edit Menu   The Edit menu in Figure 1–3(b) is also similar to other Windows applications. Use the commands in this menu to copy, cut, and paste objects or images, to undo the last action you performed, to copy or change attributes or objects and text, and to manage links with other applications.

The Transform Menu   The commands in the Transform menu, shown in Figure 1–3(c), allow you to edit the shape of selected objects and text. A more direct way to perform these functions is to use the Pick or Shaping tools, which you'll learn about in Chapter 6 through 9.

The Effects Menu   The Effects menu, shown in Figure 1–3(d) allows you to place text or an object in an envelope and then shape that envelope—make text to an object appear to be in perspective or extruded. It also allows you to blend two lines of text or two objects. A more detailed discussion will be presented in Chapter 16. The Effects menu also introduces a new convenience to CorelDRAW!, the roll-up window. A roll-up window, or just "roll-up," is a dialog box that remains on the screen either at its normal size or "rolled-up" in a minimized window. The roll-up will be fully discussed in the next section.

The Text Menu   The Text menu shown in Figure 1–3(e) is new to CorelDRAW! 3 and now combines the text commands from other menus in one location. New features available on the Text menu include a text roll-up, a spelling checker and thesaurus, and a dictionary of hyphenation possibilities.

1

a)
File	
New	
Open...	Ctrl+O
Save	Ctrl+S
Save As...	
Import...	
Export...	
Insert Object...	
Print...	Ctrl+P
Print Merge...	
Print Setup...	
Page Setup...	
Exit	Ctrl+X

b)
Edit	
Undo	Alt+Bksp
Redo	Alt+Ret
Repeat	Ctrl+R
Cut	Shift+Del
Copy	Ctrl+Ins
Paste	Shift+Ins
Paste Special...	
Delete	Del
Duplicate	Ctrl+D
Copy Style From...	
Edit Text...	Ctrl+T
Select All	
Edit Object...	
Links...	

c)
Transform	
Move...	Ctrl+L
Rotate & Skew...	Ctrl+N
Stretch & Mirror...	Ctrl+Q
Clear Transformations	

d)
Effects	
Edit Envelope	▸
Clear Envelope	
Copy Envelope From...	
Add New Envelope	
Edit Perspective	
Clear Perspective	
Copy Perspective From...	
Add New Perspective	
Blend Roll-Up...	Ctrl+B
Clear Blend	
Extrude Roll-Up...	Ctrl+E
Clear Extrude	

e)
Text	
Text Roll-Up...	Ctrl+2
Character...	
Frame...	
Fit Text To Path...	Ctrl+F
Align To Baseline	Ctrl+Z
Straighten Text	
Spell Checker...	
Thesaurus...	
Extract...	
Merge-Back...	

f)
Arrange	
Layers Roll-Up...	Ctrl+1
Align...	**Ctrl+A**
To Front	Shift+PgUp
To Back	Shift+PgDn
Forward One	PgUp
Back One	PgDn
Reverse Order	
Group	Ctrl+G
Ungroup	Ctrl+U
Combine	Ctrl+C
Break Apart	**Ctrl+K**
Separate	
Convert To Curves	Ctrl+V

g)
Display	
Snap To Grid	Ctrl+Y
Grid Setup...	
✓ Snap To Guidelines	
Guidelines Setup...	
Snap To Objects	
✓ Show Rulers	
✓ Show Status Line	
Show Color Palette	▸
Edit Wireframe	Shift+F9
Refresh Window	Ctrl+W
✓ Show Bitmaps	
Show Preview	F9
Preview Selected Only	

h)
Special	
Create Pattern...	
Create Arrow...	
Preferences...	Ctrl+J

i)
	Help
Contents	F1
Using Help	
Search for Keywords	
About CorelDRAW!...	

The CorelDRAW! menus **Figure 1–3.**

The Arrange Menu   The commands in the Arrange menu, shown in Figure 1–3(f), all have to do with the relative placement of objects within an image. Select the commands in this menu to move a selected object or group of objects to the forefront or background of an image, to combine, group, ungroup, or break apart selected objects, and to align objects and text. Additionally, CorelDRAW! 3 has added a layering feature which allows you to construct your drawings in multiple overlays. You will find more details about the Arrange menu commands in Chapter 6.

The Display Menu   The Display menu in Figure 1–3(g) has one very clear function: to help you customize the user interface and make the CorelDRAW! screen work the way you do. Use the commands in this menu to display or hide the rulers and the status line, to set up grids for precision drawing, and to choose whether and how to display fully accurate, WYSIWYG (What-You-See-Is-What-You-Get) previews of your images.

The Special Menu   The Special menu in Figure 1–3(h) has two main functions. First, you can use the Special menu to create patterns and line endings. Second, it lets you fine-tune many different program parameters using the Preferences command. Discussions about these options, which apply to a wide range of functions, appear in their respective contexts.

The Help Menu   The Help menu, shown in Figure 1–3(i), is a new feature provided by CorelDRAW! 3 which allows access to an enormous wealth of online help features including a glossary and reference library. Through the Contents button you can choose help topics which cover the screen, commands, tools, and keyboard, and which also explain how to perform certain functions, as you can see in Figure 1–4.

There are two other ways in which you can get help. First, by pressing F1, the Help Contents option is displayed, giving you the same eight categories of help that are available directly from the menu. The second method provides *context-sensitive* help. By pressing and holding down Shift followed by pressing F1, the mouse pointer changes to a question mark and arrow, as shown here:

1

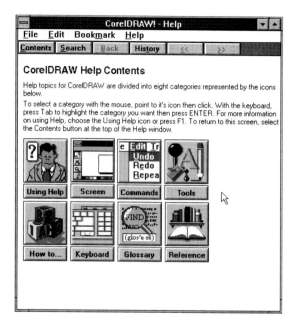

CorelDRAW! -
Help Contents
Figure 1–4.

You can then click on a menu command or screen item and a help
window will be displayed providing information on that particular
subject.

The final option on the Help menu, "About CorelDRAW!," displays
information on the current version of CorelDRAW! and other useful
information on the number of objects and groups that are open, and
on the available disk space on your C drive.

Dialog Boxes

Some menu commands are automatic: Click on them, and CorelDRAW!
performs the action immediately. Other commands are followed by
three dots (an ellipsis), indicating that you must enter additional
information before CorelDRAW! can execute the command. You enter
this additional information through dialog boxes that pop up on the
screen when you click on the command. This section introduces you to
the look and feel of typical dialog boxes in CorelDRAW! and the new
roll-up window.

Square *checkboxes* in a dialog box offer you choices that are not mutually exclusive, so you can select more than one option simultaneously. Check boxes behave like light switches; you turn them on or off when you click to select or deselect them. When you turn on or enable an option in a check box, an "X" fills it. When you turn off or disable the option, the "X" disappears.

The larger rectangles in a dialog box are *command buttons*. When selected, a command button is highlighted temporarily, and usually CorelDRAW! performs the command instantly. When you click on a command button that has a label followed by an ellipsis, you open another dialog box that is nested within it.

A rectangle that contains numeric entries and that is associated with up and down scroll arrows is a *numeric entry box*. You can change the numeric values in three ways. To increase or decrease the value by a single increment, click on the up or down arrow, respectively. To increase or decrease the value by a large amount, press and hold the mouse button over one of the scroll arrows. You can also click on the value itself to select it, erase the current value, and then type in new numbers.

Rectangles containing units of measurement represent *variable unit boxes* that are valid only for the associated option and dialog box. Click on the variable unit box as many times as necessary to change the unit of measurement you prefer.

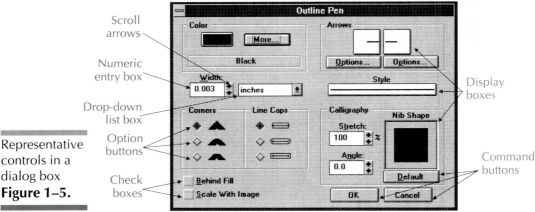

Representative controls in a dialog box
Figure 1–5.

single increment, click on the up or down arrow, respectively. To increase or decrease the value by a large amount, press and hold the mouse button over one of the scroll arrows. You can also click on the value itself to select it, erase the current value, and then type in new numbers.

Rectangles containing units of measurement represent *variable unit boxes* that are valid only for the associated option and dialog box. Click on the variable unit box as many times as necessary to change the unit of measurement you prefer.

Some dialog boxes contain *display boxes* that show you just how your current selection will look after you exit the dialog box. You do not perform any action on the display box itself; instead, its contents change as you change your selections in the dialog box.

Figure 1–6 shows an example of a dialog box that contains different types of controls. Use the *text entry boxes* available in some dialog boxes to enter strings of text. Depending on the dialog box involved, text strings might represent filenames, path names, or text to appear in an image. To enter new text where none exists, click on the text entry box and type the text. To edit an existing text string, click on the string, then use the keyboard to erase or add text. You will become familiar with the specific keys to use as you learn about each type of text entry box.

The *list boxes* within a dialog box list the names of choices available to the user, such as filenames, directory and drive names, or typestyle names. Click on a name in the list box to select it.

Scroll bars accompany text entry boxes or list boxes when the contents

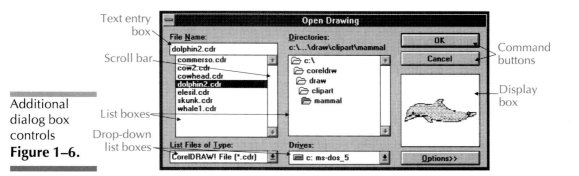

Additional dialog box controls
Figure 1–6.

of those boxes exceed the visible area in the dialog box. You can use the scroll bar to access the portions of the list that are outside of the currently visible area. To move up or down one name at a time, click on the up or down arrow of the scroll bar, respectively. To move up or down continuously, press and hold the mouse button over the up or down arrow of the scroll bar. Alternatively, you can click on the scroll bar itself, drag the scroll box, or press (Pg Up) or (Pg Dn) to move up or down the list box in large increments.

Some options in a dialog box appear in gray, indicating that you cannot select them at the moment. On the other hand, a command button within a dialog box may appear in boldface, indicating that you can select it, and also may have a bold outline around it. This command button represents the default selection. You can simply press (Enter) to activate that selection, exit the dialog box, and return to your graphic. The OK command button is normally the default. The OK button accepts and processes the entries you made in the dialog box. You can leave most dialog boxes without changing any settings by clicking on the Cancel button or pressing (Esc).

You will learn more about operating within dialog boxes in the context of each chapter in this book. The following section will acquaint you with the toolbox, the portion of the interface most vital to the operation of CorelDRAW!.

Roll-up Windows

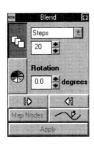

Roll-up windows, which are new to CorelDRAW! 3, are a special form of dialog box that you can keep on the screen to allow faster access to the features provided in the window. Once you've chosen a roll-up from a menu, you can choose any of the offered features and watch them take effect. You can also move the roll-up by dragging its title bar. After you've completed a task, you then have the choice of either keeping the roll-up on the screen in its full size or rolling up the window to its minimized size by clicking on the arrow in the upper-right corner, as shown here:

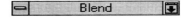

More than one roll-up can be kept on your screen at a time. A convenient way to display one or more minimized roll-ups is to choose the Arrange or Arrange All option from the roll-up's Control menu, located on the upper-left corner of the roll-up window. When chosen, Arrange (one roll-up) or Arrange All (multiple roll-ups) moves the minimized windows into a single column starting in the upper-right or upper-left corner of the full CorelDRAW! window.

You can also remove any roll-up from the screen by double-clicking its Control-menu box, or by selecting Close from its Control menu.

The CorelDRAW! Toolbox

One of the features that makes CorelDRAW! so easy to work with is the economy of the screen. The number of tools in the CorelDRAW! toolbox (Figure 1–7) is deceptively small. Several of the tools have more than one function, and nested submenus *fly out* when you select them. This method of organization reduces screen clutter and keeps related functions together.

The tools in the CorelDRAW! toolbox perform three different kinds of functions. Some allow you to draw objects, others let you edit the objects you have drawn, and a third group permit you to alter the appearance of the screen so that you can work more efficiently. This section describes each tool briefly in the context of its respective function.

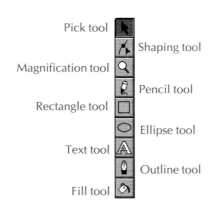

The
CorelDRAW!
toolbox icons
Figure 1–7.

Drawing Tools

CorelDRAW! allows you to create or work with nine different types of objects as shown in Figure 1–8. Because you use the same tools and techniques for some of the objects, however, there are actually only five different *classes* of objects. These classes, and the kinds of objects you can design in each, are

✦ Lines, curves, and polygons

✦ Rectangles and squares

✦ Ellipses and circles

✦ Text

✦ Bitmapped (pixel-based) images imported from a scanner or paint program

Does nine seem like a small number? Professional artists and graphic designers know that basic geometrical shapes are the building blocks on which more elaborate images are constructed. After you "build" an object using one of the four drawing tools, you can use one or more of the editing tools in the CorelDRAW! toolbox to reshape, rearrange, color, and outline it.

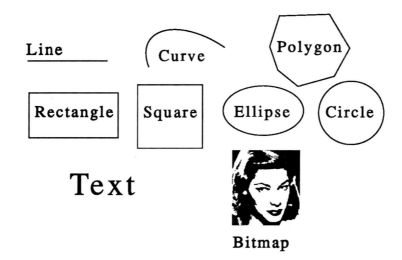

The nine types
of objects
Figure 1–8.

1

The four drawing tools—the Pencil tool, the Rectangle tool, the Ellipse tool, and the Text tool—are all you need to create eight of the nine object types in CorelDRAW!. You work with the last object type, a bitmapped image, after importing it. (See Chapters 14 and 18 for a fuller discussion of this subject.)

The Pencil Tool   The Pencil tool is the most basic drawing tool in the CorelDRAW! toolbox. This single tool allows you to create lines, curves, curved objects, and polygons. The Pencil tool can be changed from a single-mode freehand drawing instrument to a more sophisticated dual-mode instrument using Bézier lines and curves. Freehand mode is the default and is used for less precise work. Bézier mode is selected from the two-icon fly-out menu. Click on the Pencil tool, hold the mouse button down, and two icons, one for each drawing mode, are displayed as shown on the left. Bézier mode is used for smooth, precise curves, that remain so even when magnified or distorted.

Chapter 2 guides you through a series of exercises that teach you all the basic CorelDRAW! skills for using this tool in both modes.

To select the Pencil tool, press F5 or click on the Pencil icon once, and then move the mouse pointer in to the white space on the page. When you select this tool, the mouse pointer takes the shape of a crosshair, the Pencil tool icon becomes highlighted, and the message "Drawing in Freehand mode..." or for Drawing in Bézier mode..." appears on the status line.

The Rectangle Tool   The Rectangle tool lets you draw rectangles and squares. You'll create your own rectangles and squares in Chapter 3. To round the corners of a rectangle, however, you need to use the Shaping tool, one of the editing tools in the CorelDRAW! toolbox.

To select the Rectangle tool, press F6 or click on the Rectangle icon once, and then move the mouse pointer into the white space on the page. The Rectangle icon becomes highlighted, the mouse pointer becomes a crosshair, and the message "Rectangle..." appears in the status line.

The Ellipse Tool   The Ellipse tool allows you to design ellipses and perfect circles. You can learn more about using the Ellipse tool in Chapter 3.

To select the Ellipse tool, press F7 or click on the Ellipse icon once, and then move the mouse pointer into the white space on the page. The Ellipse icon becomes highlighted, the mouse pointer becomes a crosshair, and the message "Ellipse..." appears in the status line.

The Text Tool   The Text tool contains a two-icon fly-out menu for choosing between text or symbols. The text mode gives you access to more than 150 Corel Systems fonts and to thousands of other commercial fonts as well. The symbol mode provides access to CorelDRAW!'s extensive symbol library. Chapter 4 teaches you how to enter text in CorelDRAW!.

To select the Text tool, press F8 or click on the Text icon once, and then move the pointer into the white space on the page. the Text icon becomes highlighted, the mouse pointer becomes a crosshair, and the message "Text..." or "Symbol..." appears in the status line.

TIP: If you "scribbled" on the page while trying out any of the drawing tools, clear the screen before proceeding. To do this, click on the File menu name and select the New command. A dialog box appears with the message:

```
UNTITLED.CDR Has Changed, Save Current Changes?
```

Select the No command button to exit the message box and clear the screen.

Editing Tools

Once you have created objects on a page with the drawing tools, you use a different group of tools to move, arrange, reshape, and manipulate the objects. The editing tools include the Pick tool, the Shaping tool, the Outline tool, and the Fill tool.

The Pick tool   The Pick tool is really two tools in one. In the *select mode*, you can select objects in order to move, arrange, group, or combine them. In the *transformation mode*, you can use the Pick tool to rotate, skew, stretch, reflect, move, or scale a selected object. This tool

1

does not let you change the basic shape of an object, however. Chapters 6 and 7 introduce you to all the functions of the Pick tool.

The Shaping Tool   The Shaping tool allows you to modify the shape of an object. Use this tool to smooth or distort any shape, add rounded corners to rectangles, convert a circle into a wedge or arc, modify a curve, or kern individual characters in a text string. Chapters 8 and 9 cover the basics of using this tool.

The Outline Tool   The Outline tool, like the Pick tool, functions in more than one way. Use the Outline tool and its associated fly-out submenu to choose a standard or custom outline color, or to create a custom outline "pen" for a selected object. Chapter 11 and 12 instruct you in the use of this tool.

The Fill Tool   Use the Fill tool and its associated fly- out submenu to select a standard or custom fill color for selected objects or text. As you'll learn in Chapter 13, your options include custom colors, POSTSCRIPT screens, fountain fills, and POSTSCRIPT textures.

Tools for Customizing the CorelDRAW! Screen

The third group of tools helps you customize the CorelDRAW! interface so that it works the way you do. Only one of these tools, the Magnification tool, is visible in the CorelDRAW! toolbox. The Magnification tool and its associated fly-out menu let you control just how much of your picture you will view at one time. Use this tool when you need to work on a smaller area in fine detail, or when you need to zoom in or out of a picture. Chapter 5 will discuss the Magnification tool and its fly-out menu in more detail.

Quitting CorelDRAW!

Now that you are familiar with the screen components, exit CorelDRAW! and return to the Program Manager. You can use the mouse, the keyboard and mouse, or the keyboard alone to quit CorelDRAW!.

Using the mouse, double-click on the Control-menu box in the upper-left corner, or display the File menu by moving the mouse pointer to the File menu name and then click once. Then, select the Exit command by clicking on it once.

Using both mouse and keyboard, display the File menu by clicking on the menu name. Then, with the File menu displayed, press ⊠.

Using the keyboard alone, you can either press ⒜ⓛⓣ–Ⓕ to display the File menu and then type ⊠ or press Ⓒⓣⓡⓛ–⊠.

If you have attempted to draw during this session, a screen message like the one shown here appears:

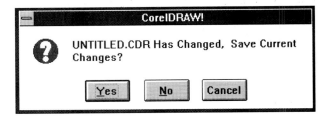

Select the No command button to abandon your changes.

If you are like most CorelDRAW! users, you will want to begin drawing immediately. This book encourages you to draw. In Chapter 2 you will use the Pencil tool to begin drawing lines and curves.

C H A P T E R

2

DRAWING AND WORKING WITH LINES AND CURVES

The Pencil tool *is the most versatile tool in the CorelDRAW! toolbox. By using this tool in two different modes, you can create both straight and curved lines, and from these simple building blocks you can construct an almost infinite variety of polygons and irregular shapes. Work through the exercises in this chapter to become thoroughly familiar with this most basic CorelDRAW! tool.*

Freehand vs. Bézier Mode

The Pencil tool has two modes of drawing: *Freehand* mode, where curves mirror the movements of your hand on a mouse, and Bézier mode, where curves are precisely placed between two or more points you identify. Drawing straight lines is very similar in the two modes, but drawing curves is very different. In the remaining sections of this chapter, Freehand mode, the default, will be discussed first, and then Bézier mode.

Drawing Straight Lines

In the language of the CorelDRAW! interface, *line* refers to any straight line, while the term *curve* refers to curved lines, irregular lines, and closed objects you create with such lines. Drawing a straight line requires that you work with the mouse in a different way than when you draw a curved or irregular line. To draw a straight line in CorelDRAW!,

1. Load CorelDRAW! if it isn't running already.

2. Position the mouse pointer over the Pencil tool icon and click once. The pointer changes to a crosshair and the Pencil tool icon becomes darkened.

3. Position the crosshair pointer at the point where you want a line to begin. This can be anywhere inside the printable page area.

4. Press *and immediately release (click)* the left mouse button, and then move the crosshair pointer toward the point where you want to end the line. A straight line appears and extends as far as you move the crosshair pointer, as in Figure 2–1. You can move the line in any direction, or make the segment longer or shorter.

5. When you have established the length and direction you want, complete the line by clicking and releasing the mouse button. As Figure 2–2 shows, a small square *node* appears at each end of the line to show that the line is complete and can be selected for further work.

6. Press Del to clear the line off the screen.

2

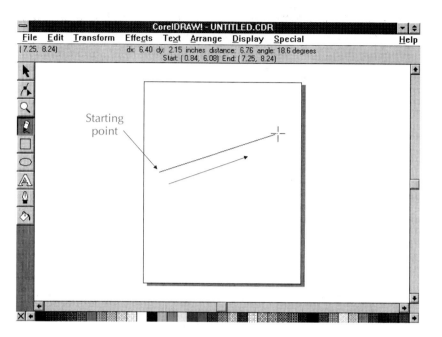

Extending a
straight line
Figure 2–1.

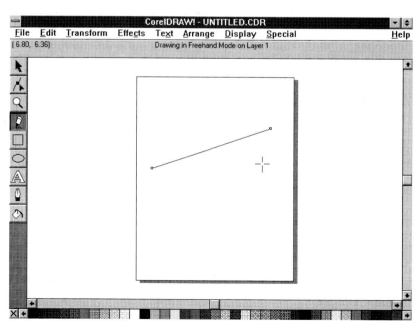

Nodes on a
completed line
Figure 2–2.

Tip: When you begin to draw a line, be sure to release the mouse button as soon as you press it. If you continue to hold down the mouse button while drawing, you create a curve instead of a straight line.

Using the Status Line to Improve Precision

Chapter 1 introduced you briefly to the status line and its potential for helping you draw with precision and accuracy. In the next exercise, pay attention to the useful information that appears on the status line.

1. With the Pencil tool still selected, begin another line by clicking the mouse button at a point about halfway down the left side of the page. The coordinates on the left side of the status line should be *about* 1.0, 5.5 (absolute precision is not important).

2. Move the mouse toward the right side of the page. Don't click a second time yet.

3. Notice that as soon as you clicked once and began to move the mouse, a message appeared on the status line as shown here:

Look more closely at the status line. It includes the following information about the line you are drawing:

dx   The *dx* code refers to the *x-coordinate* or horizontal location of your line on the page relative to the starting point. The number following this code identifies how far your line has traveled (in other words, its distance) from that starting point along the X or horizontal axis. A positive number (one with no minus sign in front of it) indicates that you are extending the line to the right of the starting point, while a negative number indicates reverse.

2

dy   The *dy* code refers to the *y-coordinate* or vertical location of your line on the page relative to the starting point. The number following this code identifies how far your line has traveled (in other words, its distance) above or below that starting point along the Y or vertical axis. A positive number indicates that you are extending the line above the starting point, while a negative number indicates that you are extending it below the starting point.

inches   The unit of measurement for the current *dx* and *dy* position indicators appears on the status line as well. The CorelDRAW! default is inches, but you can change it to millimeters or picas and points using the Grid Setup command in the Display menu. You'll gain experience with the grid later in this chapter.

distance   The number following this text indicates the length of your line relative to the starting point.

angle   The number following this text indicates the angle of the line relative to an imaginary compass, where 0 degrees is at the 3 o'clock position, 90 degrees is at the 12 o'clock position, 180 degrees is at the 9 o'clock position, and 90 degrees is at the 6 o'clock position.

Start and End   The pairs of numbers following each of these items represent the coordinates of the start and end points of the line.

4. Choose an end point for the line and click again to freeze the line in place. Note that the status line indicators disappear as soon as you complete the line, just as they did in Figure 2–2.
5. Press ⌦(Del) to delete the line before going further.

As you may have noticed, information appears on the status line only when you are performing some action on an object. This information makes CorelDRAW! especially powerful for applications requiring great precision, such as technical illustration.

Erasing Portions of a Line

In the following exercise, you'll practice erasing part of a line that you have extended but not completed. You can always backtrack and shorten a line in CorelDRAW!, as long as you have not clicked a second time to complete it.

1. With the Pencil tool still selected, choose a starting point for another line.

2. Move the pointer downward and to the right until the *dx* indicator reads about 5.00 inches and the *dy* indicator reads about -1.00 inches, as in the example in Figure 2–3.

3. Without clicking the mouse button a second time, backtrack upward until the *dx* indicator reads 4.00 inches. Notice that the line you have drawn behaves flexibly and becomes shorter as you move the mouse backward.

4. Click a second time to freeze the line at *dx* 4.00 inches.

5. Before going any further, delete the line by pressing Del.

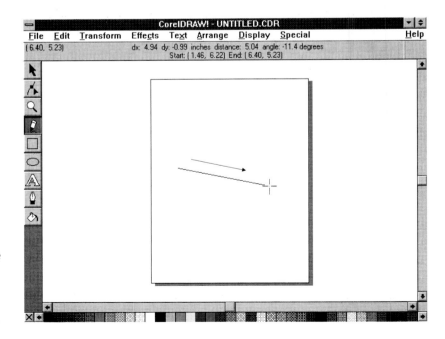

Extending a line
using the status
line indicator
Figure 2–3.

Constraining a Line to an Angle

You need not rely on the status line alone seeking to control the precision of your drawing. You can also use the Ctrl key while drawing to *constrain* (force) a line to an angle in increments of 15 degrees. In the following exercise, you'll create a series of seven straight lines this way.

1. With the Pencil tool still selected, press *and hold* Ctrl and click the mouse button to choose a starting point for the line.

2. Release the mouse button, but continue holding Ctrl as you extend the line outward and downward from the starting point. Try moving the line to different angles in a clockwise direction; as the angle indicator in the status line shows, the line does not move smoothly but instead "jumps" in increments of 15 degrees.

3. Now, extend the line straight outward, so that the angle indicator on the status line reads 0 degrees. While still holding down Ctrl, click the mouse button a second time to freeze the line at this angle.

4. Release Ctrl. (Remember always to click the mouse *before* you release Ctrl. If you release Ctrl first, the line doesn't necessarily align to an angle.)

5. Draw six more lines in the same way, each sharing a common starting point. Extend the second line at an angle of 15 degrees, the third at an angle of 30 degrees, the fourth at an angle of 45 degrees, the fifth at an angle of 60 degrees, the sixth at an angle of 75 degrees, and the seventh at an angle of 90 degrees. When you are finished, your lines should match the pattern shown in Figure 2–4.

Clearing the Screen

Before going any further, clear the screen of the lines you have created so far.

1. Click on the File menu to pull it down.

2. Select the New command.

3. A message box appears with the message:

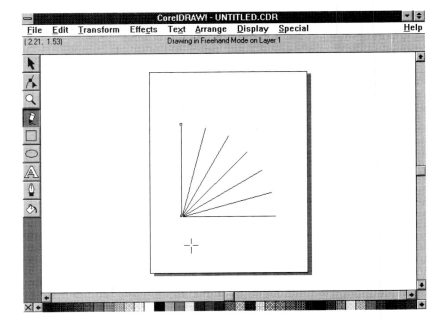

Constraining
lines to angles
in 15-degree
increments
Figure 2–4.

```
UNTITLED.CDR Has Changed, Save Current Changes?
```

Click on the No command button to exit the message box and
clear the screen. The Pick tool in the tool box is highlighted by
default, just as when you first loaded CorelDRAW!.

Drawing Multisegment Lines

With CorelDRAW!, you can easily draw several straight lines in
sequence so that each begins where the previous one left off. Use this
technique both for drawing open-ended line figures and for
constructing polygons. In the present exercise, you will construct a
series of peaks and valleys.

1. Select the Pencil tool using a shortcut—press the F5 function key.
   Then click to choose a line starting point. Extend a line upward
   and to the right.

2

2. When you reach the desired end point for the line, freeze it in place with a *double click* rather than a single click of the mouse button.

3. Move the mouse downward and to the right, without clicking again. The flexible line follows the crosshair pointer automatically.

4. Double-click again to freeze the second line in place.

5. Continue zig-zagging in this way until you have created several peaks and valleys similar to those in Figure 2–5.

6. When you reach the last valley, click once instead of twice to end the multisegment line.

7. Press Del to clear the screen before proceeding.

 TIP: If you make a mistake drawing, you can erase the last line segment you completed in one of two ways. You either press Alt - Backspace or select the Undo command in the Edit menu. Don't press Del when drawing a multisegment line, or you will erase all of the segments you have drawn so far.

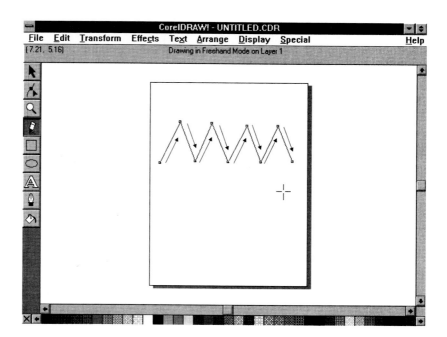

Drawing
multisegment
lines
Figure 2–5.

Drawing a Polygon

A *polygon* is a closed two-dimensional figure bounded by straight lines. You create polygons in CorelDRAW! by drawing multisegment lines and then connecting the end point to the starting point. In the following exercise, you'll create a polygon figure like the one in Figure 2–6.

1. Draw the first line, double-clicking at the line end point so that you can continue drawing without interruption.

2. Draw four additional lines in the same way, following the pattern in Figure 2–6. End the last line segment with a single click at the point where the first line segment began.

Did your last line segment "snap" to the beginning of the first? Or does a small gap remain between them? If you can still see a small gap, don't worry. In the section "Joining Lines and Curves Automatically" later in this chapter, you'll learn how to adjust the level of sensitivity at which one line will join automatically to another. If your lines did snap together to form an enclosed polygon, it will fill with a solid black color

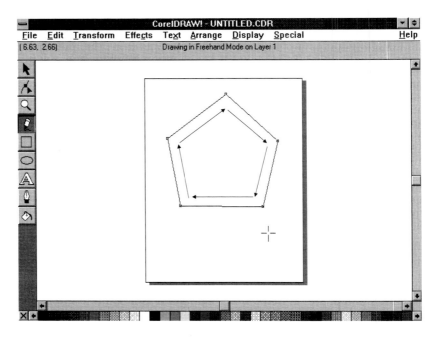

Drawing a
polygon
Figure 2–6.

if the standard defaults are set. For now, clear the screen and begin the next exercise.

Straight Lines in Bézier Mode

2

The Bézier mode of drawing is to identify end points or *nodes* and place lines or curves between them. Therefore, drawing straight lines in Bézier mode is very similar to drawing straight lines in Freehand mode. Try it next and see for yourself.

To use Bézier mode:

1. Select Bézier mode by pointing on the Pencil tool and pressing and holding the mouse button down until the pencil fly-out menu appears like this:

2. Click on the Bézier tool, the rightmost of the two icons on the fly-out menu.

Your status line should now include the words "Drawing in Bézier Mode..."

Drawing Single Lines in Bézier Mode

Now draw a single line segment as you did earlier in Freehand mode.

1. Click on a starting point in the middle left of the page, immediately release the mouse button (if you hold down the mouse button, CorelDRAW! will think you are drawing a curve), and move the mouse pointer to the upper right of the page.

Notice that the starting point is a solid black square. This starting point is a *node*, a point on a line that is used to define the line. When you start the line, the starting point is selected and is therefore black. Also, there is no line connecting the starting point and the mouse pointer, and no information in the status line except the coordinates of the mouse pointer. A line does not appear and there is no information in the status line because a Bézier line is not defined until you have placed at least two nodes.

2. Click on an end node. A straight line is drawn between the two nodes as shown in Figure 2–7, and information now appears in the status line. The line segment, however, is called a "curve."

Drawing a Polygon in Bézier Mode

Unlike Freehand mode, you can continue to add line segments after clicking on an end node only once in Bézier mode. Do that next to build a polygon (your screen should still be as you left it after drawing the first Bézier line segment).

1. Click on two more nodes, one toward the lower right and the other toward the lower left. Lines will be added connecting the nodes.

2. Position the mouse pointer on top of the original starting node

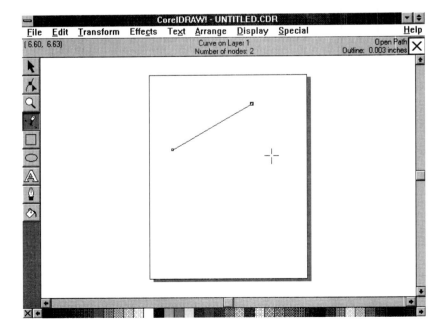

Bézier straight
line segment
Figure 2–7.

and click one final time. The result is a four-sided polygon like the one shown in Figure 2–8. If your sides join to form a polygon, and you still are using the standard defaults, your polygon will fill with a solid black color.

As you can see, there are many mechanical similarities between Freehand and Bézier drawing of straight lines. The results are virtually the same, but the screen looks very different during the creation of the lines. For straight lines there is little reason to use Bézier over Freehand.

Like Freehand mode, you can move the mouse pointer in any direction, including backward, over the path already traveled to "erase" the object *before* clicking on a node. After clicking on a node you can use Undo (either Alt - Backspace or choose Undo from the Edit menu) to erase the previous line (or curve) segment. If you want to delete the entire object (line or polygon) while it is still selected (you can see all of the nodes), press Del.

If you want to draw two or more Bézier line segments that are not connected, press the Spacebar twice, then draw your second line.

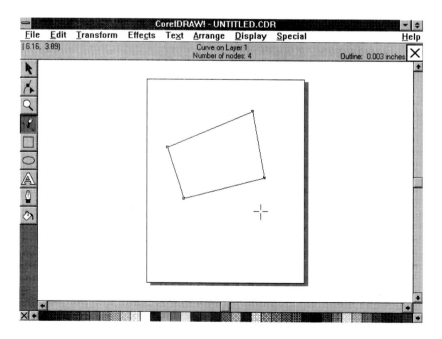

Bézier polygon
Figure 2–8.

3. Press Del to clear your drawing. To return to Freehand mode, click on the Bézier Pencil tool and hold the mouse button until the fly-out menu appears.

Now, you can either release the mouse button and click on the Freehand tool, or, you can continue holding the mouse button down and drag the mouse pointer to the Freehand tool and then release the mouse button. You are returned to your drawing, in Freehand mode, ready to begin working with curves.

Drawing Curves

The Pencil tool has a twofold purpose in CorelDRAW!; you can use it to draw curved or irregular lines as well as straight lines. This section introduces you to the basics of drawing a simple curve, closing the path of a curve to form a closed curve object, and erasing unwanted portions of a curve as you draw.

To draw a simple curve:

1. Select the Pencil tool (in Freehand mode) if it is not still selected.

2. Position the crosshair pointer at the point on the page where you want a curve to begin and then press *and hold* the mouse button. The Start and End coordinates appear on the status line.

3. Continue to hold the mouse button *and drag* the mouse along the path where you want the curve to continue. Follow the example in Figure 2–9.

4. Upon completing the curve, release the mouse button. The curve disappears momentarily while CorelDRAW! calculates exactly where it should go. Then the curve reappears with many small square nodes, as in Figure 2–10. Note that when you have finished, the words "Curve on Layer 1" and the number of nodes appears in the middle of status line and the message "Open Path" appears at the right side of the status line. "Open Path" indicates that you have drawn a curved line, not a closed figure.

5. Press Del or select the Undo command in the Edit menu to clear the curve you have just drawn.

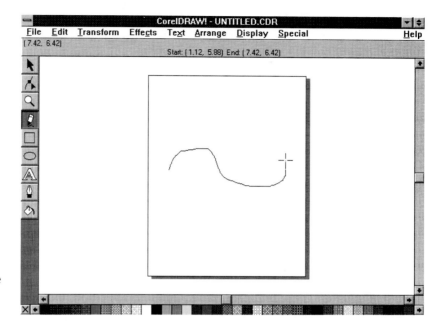

Drawing a curve
Figure 2–9.

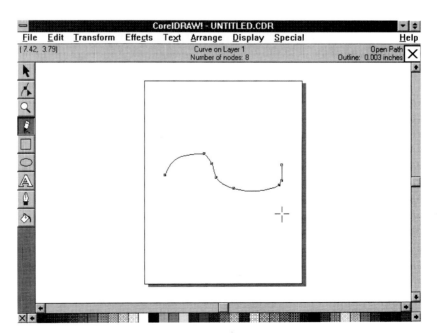

A complete
curve with
nodes
Figure 2–10.

TIP: To draw a straight line, click and release the mouse button. To draw a curve, press and hold the mouse button and drag the mouse along the desired path.

Erasing Portions of a Curve

Should you make a mistake while drawing a curve, you can backtrack and erase what you have drawn, as long as you have not yet released the mouse button. You use (Shift) to erase the portion of a curve that you no longer want.

1. Begin another curve by pressing and holding the mouse button over the point at which you want the curve to start.

2. Drag the mouse as desired. Do not release the mouse button yet.

3. While still holding down the mouse button, press and hold (Shift) and backtrack over as much of the curve as you wish to erase.

4. After you have erased a portion of the curve, release (Shift) and continue to draw by dragging the mouse in the desired direction.

5. Release the mouse button to finalize the curve. Delete the curve by pressing (Del).

6. Clear the screen by selecting New from the File menu. Do not save your changes.

Drawing Multisegment Curves

Just as you drew multisegment lines, you can also draw multisegment curves. You can join two successive curves together automatically if the starting point of the second curve is within a few pixels of the end point of the first curve.

1. Select a starting point for the first curve and begin dragging the mouse.

2. Complete the curve by releasing the mouse button. Do not move the mouse pointer from the point at which your first curve ends.

3. Draw the second curve and complete it. The second curve should "snap" to the first.

If the two curved lines didn't snap together, you moved the pointer farther than five pixels away before starting the second curve. Don't worry about it at this point. CorelDRAW! has a default value of five pixels distance for automatic joining of lines and curves. In the "Joining Lines and Curves Automatically" section of this chapter, you will learn how to adjust the sensitivity of this AutoJoin feature.

Closing an Open Path

When you drew your first curve, the message "Open Path" appeared at the right side of the status line. This message indicates that your curved line is not a closed object, and therefore that you cannot fill it with a color or pattern (see Chapter 13). You can create a closed curve object with the Pencil tool, however. Refer to Figure 2–11 to create a closed outline of any shape for this exercise. You'll draw this shape as a single curve.

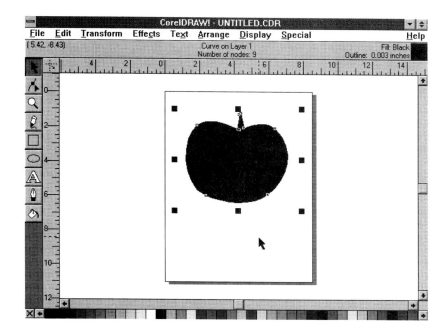

Drawing a
closed curve
object
Figure 2–11.

1. Before beginning the exercise, select New from the File menu to clear the screen. When a message box appears and asks whether you want to save your changes, select No.

2. Select the Pencil tool (Freehand mode).

3. Start the curve about midway across the page area.

4. Continue dragging the mouse creating the closed shape. Your drawing doesn't have to look exactly like the one in Figure 2–11. If you make a mistake, press Shift, backtrack and erase the portions of the curve that you do not want.

5. When you return to the point at which you began, make sure you are over your starting point and then release the mouse button. After a second the object reappears as a solid black shape.

Note that the message in the middle of the status line now reads "Curve" and the number of nodes. At the right side of the status line, the message "Fill:Black" appears, followed by a representation of a solid black color. This indicates that you now have a closed curve object and that it is filled with the default color, black.

Full Color vs. Wireframe Modes

In the last exercise and in the two previous polygon exercises, it was noted that the polygon would fill with solid black color when and if the polygon was closed and if the default settings were still in effect. In CorelDRAW! 3, the default drawing mode is *full color mode*, meaning that you can see the full color of an object as you are working on it. In versions of CorelDRAW! prior to 3, you could only see an object's color in what was called "preview mode" and you could not actually draw in this mode. In earlier versions, all work was done in *wireframe mode* where you could see only an object's outline and therefore not its color. Although by default all work in CorelDRAW! 3 and on is done in full color mode, you can switch to wireframe mode when it is beneficial to work with an object's outline. You do this by choosing Edit Wireframe from the Display menu. You can return to full color mode by again choosing Edit Wireframe to turn it off.

Drawing Curves in Bézier Mode

2

If you are like most people, drawing smooth curves in Freehand mode is very difficult, if not impossible. Of course, as you'll see in Chapter 8, CorelDRAW!'s Shaping tool allows you to clean up messy artwork very quickly. As an alternative, though, the Bézier mode of drawing allows you to draw smooth curves to start with—after a little practice.

The principle of Bézier drawing is that you place a node, set a pair of control points that determine the slope and height or depth of the curve, and then place the next node. The method is to place the crosshair where you want a node, press and hold the mouse button while you drag the control points until you are satisfied with their positioning, release the mouse button, and go on and do the same thing for the next node. When you have two or more nodes, curves appear between them reflecting your settings. This is very different from Freehand mode drawing and will take some getting used to. Dragging the mouse with the button depressed moves the control points in two dimensions and only indirectly identifies the path of the curve. Understanding how to handle control points, though, will help you use the Shaping tool in Chapter 10.

The only way to really understand Bézier drawing is to try it.

1. Clear your screen by selecting New from the File menu and choosing No in answer to the Save Changes message.

2. Momentarily hold the mouse button while clicking on the Pencil tool to open the Flyout menu, and then select the Bézier mode icon.

3. Move the mouse pointer to where you want to start the curve and press and hold the left mouse button.

4. Move the mouse in any direction while continuing to hold the left mouse button and you should see the *control points* appear—two small black boxes and dashed lines connecting them to the larger node, as shown here:

There are three principles involved in moving the mouse to set the control points:

◆ Begin by dragging a control point in the direction that you want the curve to leave the node.

◆ Drag the control point away from the node to increase the height or depth of the curve and drag the control point toward the node to decrease the height or depth.

◆ Rotate the control points about the node to change the slope of the curve. The slope follows the rotational increment of the control point.

5. Drag the control point out away from the node toward 2 o'clock and swing it in an arc about the node. Notice how the two points move in opposite directions. Continue to hold the left mouse button.

6. Drag the control point in toward the node until it is about a half inch away from the node and swing it until that control point you clicked on is pointing at 2 o'clock. Your node should look like this:

7. Release the mouse button and move the mouse pointer to where you want the second node to be—about two inches to the right and in line with the first node.

8. Again press and hold the left mouse button to set the node.

9. Drag the control point toward 5 o'clock so it is about a half inch away from the node.

10. Release the mouse button. A curve segment is drawn between the two nodes that should look like this:

11. Move the mouse pointer and press and hold the mouse button to set a third node about an inch below and in the middle of the first two nodes.

12. Drag the control point so it is about a quarter of an inch to the left of node, at 9 o'clock.

2

13. Release the mouse button. A second curve segment will appear as shown here:

14. Move the mouse pointer until it is on top of the first node you set and press and hold the mouse button.

15. Drag the control points until they are about a half inch away from the node and the top control point is aimed at 2 o'clock, like this:

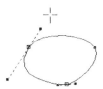

16. Release the mouse button. A third curve segment appears completing a curved triangle, which will be filled with solid black in full color mode.

Practice drawing other Bézier objects. Notice how moving the control points both in and out from the node and in an arc around the node can radically change the curve segment to its left (behind the node) and to a lesser extent, the curve segment to the right (ahead of the node). Also, notice how the number of nodes can affect the finished object. As a general rule the fewer nodes the better, but there are some minimums.

A continuous curve like a circle should have a node every 120 degrees or three nodes on a circle like this:

A curve that changes direction like a sine wave needs a node for every two changes in direction, as shown here:

A curve that changes direction in a sharp point (called a *cusp*) needs a node for every change in direction like this:

17. Return to Freehand mode by opening the Pencil tool fly-out menu, and choosing the Freehand mode icon, as before.

Increasing Precision

CorelDRAW! has three features that aid in precision drawing in addition to the mouse pointer coordinates and the other line and curve data displayed in the status line. These are an adjustable grid that underlays the drawing surface and assists in aligning points and objects, a pair of rulers to give you a visual reference to where you are, and the ability to place nonprinting guidelines on the page for purposes of alignment.

The grid and the guidelines can optionally be given a magnet-like property that causes points or objects that are placed near them to be drawn to them. These are called *Snap To Grid* and *Snap To Guidelines*.

2

The Snap To property can be turned on and off, like the rulers, through the Display menu. You can also turn the Snap To Grid on and off by pressing (Ctrl)–(Y). The Display menu also provides access to Setup dialog boxes for Grids and Guidelines. The Grid Setup dialog box allows you to display the grid on the screen (as a series of faint dots) and, if so, to determine the horizontal and vertical spacing of the grid. The Grid Setup dialog box also allows you to turn the Snap to Grid property on and off by clicking on its checkbox. The Guidelines Setup dialog box allows you to place guidelines with a very high degree of precision. You can also place guidelines by dragging them out of either ruler and placing them by visually aligning them in the opposite ruler.

This section shows you how to use the rulers and the grid to draw with greater precision. Guidelines will be used and discussed further in a later section.

Setting the Grid and Displaying Rulers

You will next make several changes to the settings for the grid and turn on the Snap To property. Then you will turn on the display of both the grid and the rulers.

1. Select the New command from the File menu to clear the screen of the shape you drew in the last exercise and don't save any changes.

2. Select the Grid Setup command from the Display menu. The dialog box in Figure 2–12 appears. The settings in your software may be different from the ones in the figure.

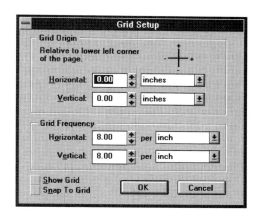

The Grid Setup
dialog box
Figure 2–12.

3. Adjust both horizontal and vertical grid frequencies to 16.00 per inch, if necessary. To change the value in the numeric entry box, press and hold the mouse button over the up or down scroll arrow until the number changes to 16.00. Alternatively, you can click on the numeric value itself and type in the new number. To change the unit of measurement in the rectangular units box, just click on it until the word "inch" appears.

4. Click on Show Grid to turn on its display and then adjust the Grid Origin so the Vertical position of the lower-left corner is at 11 inches. (Some versions of CorelDRAW! use the upper-left corner as the point of reference, in which case a vertical position of 0 is correct.)

5. Look at the Snap To Grid checkbox. If no check mark appears in front of it, select it to make the grid active. If a check mark already appears in front of it, you don't need to do anything. Click on OK to save these settings and close the dialog box.

6. Reopen the Display menu and notice that the Snap to Grid option now has a checkmark next to it, showing the feature is turned on.

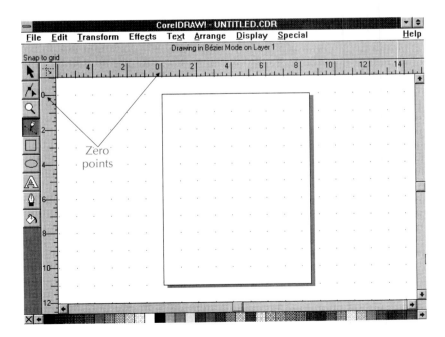

Displaying the rulers

Figure 2–13.

7. Choose the Show Rulers command from the Display menu. Since you have set the grid size to inches, the rulers will also display in inches, as in Figure 2–13. Notice that the zero point for both the horizontal and vertical rulers begins at the upper-left corner of the page area, as shown by the pointer arrow in the figure. This is a convenient way to set the rulers so that you can measure everything relative to that corner.

Joining Lines and Curves Automatically

CorelDRAW! has a feature called AutoJoin which causes lines and curves to "snap" together automatically when their end points are separated by a preset number of *pixels* (the smallest element on a screen—the "dots" with which everything is built). You can adjust the threshold number of pixels through the Preferences command in the Special menu.

Literal joining of two end points is important because CorelDRAW! classifies an object as being either *open* or *closed*. If an object is open, you cannot fill it with a color or shade. Try out the AutoJoin feature and then change the AutoJoin threshold and see the effect.

1. Select the Pencil tool (Freehand mode), then move the crosshair pointer to a point 1 inch to the right of the zero point on the horizontal ruler and 2 inches below the zero point on the vertical ruler. Notice that as you move the mouse, dotted "shadow" lines in each ruler show you the exact location of your pointer.

2. Click once at this point to begin drawing a line. The parameters in the status line appear.

3. Using the rulers and the status line to help you, extend the line 4 inches to the right. The *dx* and distance parameters on the status line should read 4.0 inches, as in Figure 2–14. Click a second time to freeze the line in position. Notice how both the grid display and the grid's Snap To feature help you do this.

4. Move the crosshair pointer exactly 1/4 inch to the right of the end point of the line. Use the rulers to help you.

5. Press and hold the mouse button at this point and drag the mouse to form a squiggling curve.

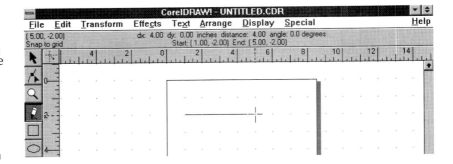

Extending a line (dx=4.00 inches, distance=4.00 inches)
Figure 2–14.

6. Release the mouse button to complete the curve. If you began the curve 1/4 inch or more to the right of the line end point, the curve remains separate from the line and does not snap to it, as in Figure 2–15. In order to make a curve snap to a line automatically at this distance, you'll need to adjust the AutoJoin threshold value in the Preferences dialog box. (You'll become familiar with this process in the next section.)

7. Select the New command from the File menu to clear the screen before proceeding. Do not save any changes.

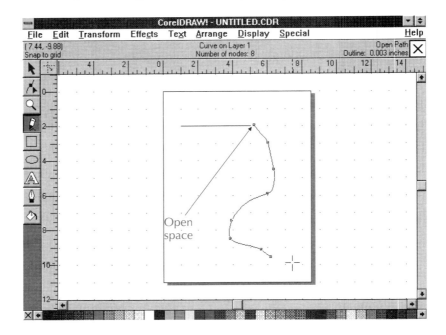

Curve failing to snap to a line (AutoJoin value too low)
Figure 2–15.

Adjusting the AutoJoin Threshold

The AutoJoin feature determines how far apart (in pixels) two lines or curves have to be for them to join together automatically. If the setting in the Preferences-Curves dialog box is a small number, such as 3 or less, lines snap together only if you draw with a very exact hand. Use this lower setting when you want to *prevent* lines from joining accidentally. If your technique is less precise, you can set the AutoJoin threshold value to a number higher than 5 pixels so that lines will snap together even if you don't have a steady hand.

1. Select the Curves option from the Preferences command in the Special menu. The Preferences-Curves dialog box in Figure 2–16 appears. The default setting for the features in this dialog box is 5 pixels. You'll use some of the other settings later on, when you learn skills for which these settings are useful. For now, concern yourself only with the AutoJoin setting.

2. Set the AutoJoin value to 10 pixels by clicking several times on the up scroll arrow.

3. Select OK twice to save the new value and return to the drawing.

4. Now you can redraw the line and make the curve snap to it. With the Pencil tool selected in Freehand mode, redraw a straight line as you did in steps 7 through 9 of the previous section.

5. Move the crosshair to a point 1/4 inch to the right of the end point of the line and then press and hold the mouse button to begin drawing a curve.

AutoJoin in the Preferences - Curves dialog box

Figure 2–16.

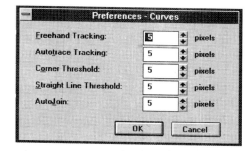

6. Drag the mouse and draw the squiggling curve as you did in step 5 of the previous section.

7. Release the mouse button. This time, the curve joins automatically to the line, as shown in Figure 2–17.

8. Select New from the File menu to clear the screen before going further.

The AutoJoin feature has other uses in addition to allowing you to connect lines and curves. You can also use it to accomplish the following:

✦ Join lines to lines or curves to curves.

✦ Add a curve or line to the end of an existing curve, line, or object that you have selected.

✦ Create closed curve objects and polygons by starting and ending a curve (or a series of line segments) at the same point.

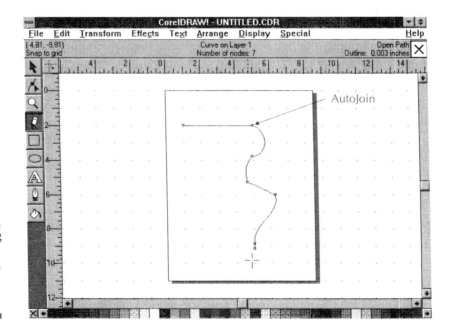

Curve snapping
to a line
(AutoJoin value
high)
Figure 2–17.

Creating a Drawing Using Lines, Curves, and Polygons

2

You have learned to create all of the simple objects—line, curve, closed curve, and polygon—that you can make with the Pencil tool. In this exercise, you'll bring together all of the skills you have learned by drawing a kite that consists of lines, curves, and a polygon. Use Figures 2–19 through 2–26 as a guide to help you position the start and end points of the lines and curves.

1. Turn on the rulers and show the grid (if they do not appear onscreen already) by selecting Show Rulers from the Display menu and Show Grid from the Grid Setup dialog box reached from the Display menu.

2. Also from the Display menu, select Snap to Guidelines and Edit Wireframe. You have now turned on all of CorelDRAW!'s precision enhancement features.

Guidelines, nonprinting lines placed on a drawing by either dragging on a ruler or via a dialog box, are used like the grid to align objects in a drawing. Guidelines have two major benefits over the grid: They can be placed anywhere, not just on a ruler mark and, since they are continuous dotted lines, they provide a better visual reference than the grid dots. When a guideline is near a grid line, the guideline always takes priority. This allows you to place a guideline very near a grid line and have objects on a drawing retroactively—turning on Snap To Grid, for example, will not move objects already on the drawing.

Since the drawing you are doing here only uses major ruler coordinates, you could very easily do it without guidelines. Use the guidelines anyway to see how they work and to use them as a visual reference.

3. With any tool, from any point on the horizontal ruler at the top of the drawing area, drag a horizontal guideline down to 7 inches below the zero point on the vertical ruler. (Move the mouse pointer to the horizontal ruler, press and hold the left mouse button while moving the mouse pointer and the dotted line that appears, down to 7 inches; then release the mouse button.) You'll see that the Snap To Grid helps you align the guideline. Your screen should look like this as you are dragging the guideline:

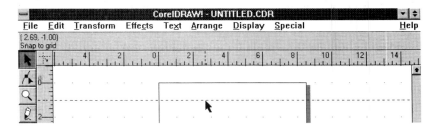

4. As you did in step 3, drag two more horizontal guidelines down to 3 inches and 1 inch, respectively, below the zero point on the vertical ruler.

If you misplace a guideline, move the mouse pointer to it, press and hold the left mouse button until a four-headed arrow appears, then drag the line into proper position. You can drag a guideline off the page to get rid of it. Also, you can double-click on a guideline and get the Guideline Setup dialog box. From there you can move a guideline precisely or delete it.

5. Again like step 3, drag three vertical guidelines to the right from the vertical ruler and place them at 6, 4, and 2 inches to the right of the zero point on the horizontal ruler.

   When you are done placing all of the guidelines, your screen should look like the one shown in Figure 2–18.

6. Select the Pencil (Freehand mode) tool.

7. Move to a point 2 inches to the right of the zero point on the horizontal ruler and 3 inches below the zero point on the vertical ruler and then click once to start a line.

8. Extend the line upward and to the right until you reach a point 4 inches to the right of the horizontal zero point and 1 inch below the vertical zero point. Use the status line information to help you and refer to Figure 2–19. Double-click and release the mouse button at this point. With the intersections of the guidelines at each of these points, the lines you are drawing jump to these points if you get anywhere near them.

9. Extend the next line segment downward and to the right as shown in Figure 2–20, until you reach a point 6 inches to the right of the

2

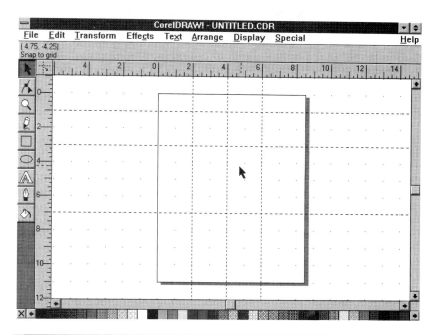

Guidelines in
place
Figure 2–18.

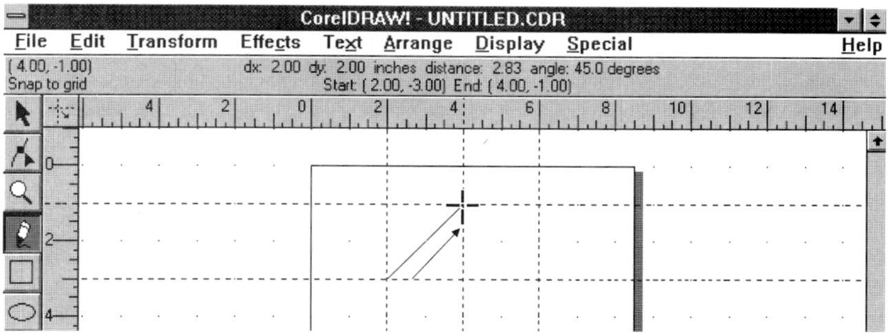

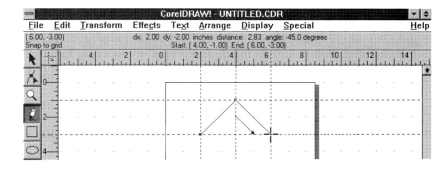

Drawing a kite:
the first line
segment
Figure 2–19.

Drawing a kite:
the second line
segment
Figure 2–20.

horizontal zero point and 3 inches below the vertical zero point. Double-click at this point to add on another line segment.

10. Extend another line segment horizontally to the left until you reach the starting point. Double click at this point. The last line segment will connect to the first line segment and form a triangle, as shown in Figure 2–21.

11. From this point, extend another line segment downward and to the right until you reach a point 4 inches to the right of the horizontal zero point and 7 inches below the vertical zero point, as shown in Figure 2–22. Double-click at this point to complete this segment.

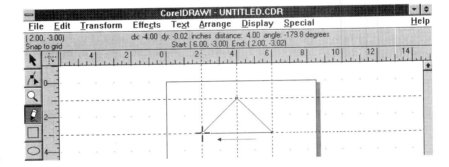

Drawing a kite: the third line segment
Figure 2–21.

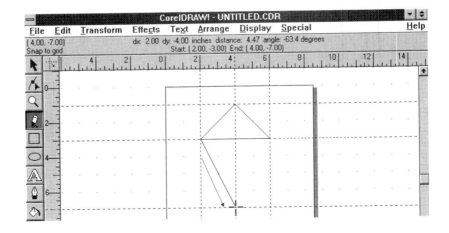

Drawing a kite: the fourth line segment
Figure 2–22.

12. Now, extend a segment upward to the lower-right corner of the original triangle, as in Figure 2–23. Click just once to finish the line and complete the basic kite shape.

13. Next, add a vertical crosspiece to the kite. Since this line must be absolutely vertical, begin by pressing and holding Ctrl and then clicking once at the top of the kite.

14. Extend this new line to the base of the kite as shown in Figure 2–24 and then click once. You are going to attach a curve to this line.

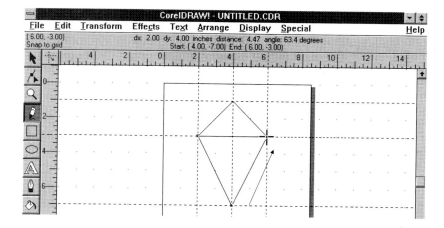

Completing the basic kite shape
Figure 2–23.

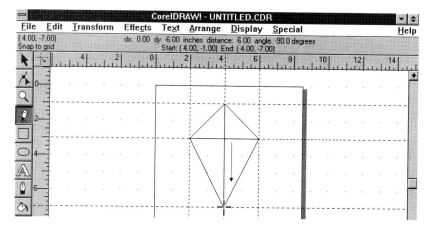

Drawing the vertical crosspiece
Figure 2–24.

15. To attach a curve to the line, press and hold the mouse button and then draw a kite tail similar to the one in Figure 2–25. Release the mouse button to complete the curve.

16. Finally, add a string to the kite. Click on the point at which the crosspieces meet and extend a line diagonally downward and to the left until you reach the margin of the printable page area. Use Figure 2–26 as a guide. Click once to complete the line.

17. Your kite should now look similar to the one in Figure 2–26. Leave the kite on your screen for the concluding section of this chapter.

Saving Your Work

As you work on your own drawings, save your work frequently during a session. If you don't save often enough, you could lost an image in the event of unexpected power or hardware failures.

In order to save a new drawing, you must establish a filename for it.

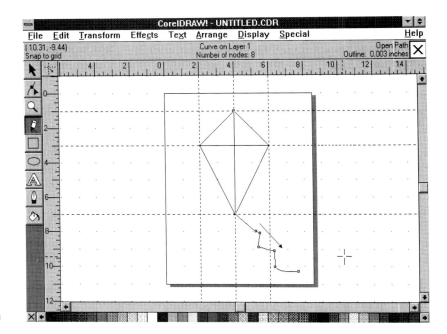

Drawing the kite "tail" (a curve)
Figure 2–25.

2

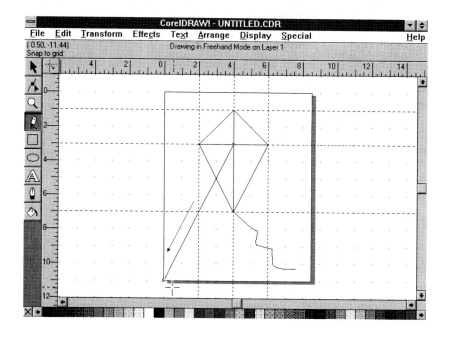

Adding a string
and completing
the kite
Figure 2-26.

To save the kite you just drew,

1. Select the Save As command from the File menu to display the
   Save Drawing dialog box in Figure 2–27. The Directories indicator

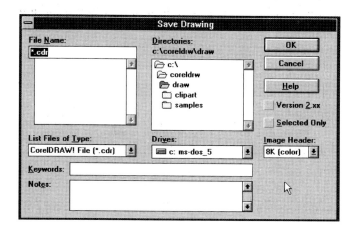

The Save
Drawing dialog
box
Figure 2–27.

should show that you are in the C:\CORELDRW\DRAW directory of your hard drive. (Path names may vary, depending on how and where you installed the software.)

2. If the Path is different from what you want or if you want to save the drawing in a different drive and/or directory, for example, C:\DRAWINGS as suggested in Appendix A, change to the correct drive and directory by double-clicking on the correct entries in the Drives and Directories list boxes. When you double-click, the selected path name will appear in the Path. If the drive or directory name you want is not visible in the Drives or Directories list boxes, position the mouse pointer over the up or down in the scroll bar, and then press and hold the mouse button until the path name becomes visible. You can then select the drive or directory name.

3. Name the drawing by clicking in the File Name text entry box, and then typing the desired name of your file. Use no more than eight characters; CorelDRAW! adds the CDR extension for you when you select the OK command button. In this case, type **KITE**.

4. Save the file by clicking on the OK command button or pressing [Enter]. CorelDRAW! adds the extension CDR to the file. You exit the Save File dialog box and return to your drawing. Notice that the title bar now contains the name of your drawing, KITE.CDR.

5. Select New from the File menu to clear the screen before continuing. Since you have just saved a picture, the Save Changes warning box doesn't appear.

The foregoing procedure applies only the first time you save a drawing. to save a drawing that has already been saved, either select the Save command from the File menu, or press [Ctrl]-[S].

Retrieving a File

To open a drawing that you have saved, use the following procedure. In this exercise, you'll open the KITE.CDR file you just saved.

1. Select Open from the File menu. The Open Drawing dialog box appears, as in Figure 2–28. Its layout is very similar to the Save As dialog box.

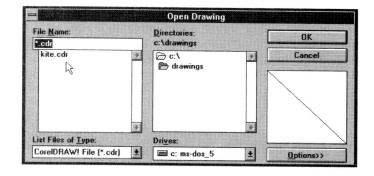

The Open
Drawing dialog
box
Figure 2-28.

2. If you saved your file in a directory other than the default directory (the DRAW directory), select the drive and/or directory name from the Directories list box. Use the scroll bar if necessary.

3. If you can't see the file KITE.CDR in the File Name list box, position the mouse pointer over the down arrow in the scroll bar and then press and hold it until the filename becomes visible.

4. Click once on filename KITE.CDR. The name appears in reverse video (white lettering on black background) and displays in the File Name text box. Also, you will see a miniature of the drawing in the display box.

5. To open the file, select the OK command or press Enter. After a moment, the file displays in the window and its name appears in the title bar.

6. Exit CorelDRAW! by pressing Ctrl-X, or by selecting Exit from the File menu.

TIP: There's a shortcut to opening a file once you are in the Open File dialog box. Instead of clicking once on the filename and then selecting Open, you can simply double-click on the filename.

That's all there is to it. You have created a complete drawing using the Pencil tool, saved it, and loaded it again. Along the way, you have learned how to do both Freehand and Bézier drawing of both lines and curves and to use the rulers, grid, guidelines, and status line to help you work.

C H A P T E R

3

DRAWING AND WORKING WITH RECTANGLES, SQUARES, ELLIPSES, AND CIRCLES

The Rectangle and Ellipse are basic shapes that underlie many complex forms created by man and nature. In this chapter you will use the Rectangle tool to create rectangles and squares and the Ellipse tool to create ellipses and circles. As you work your way through the exercises in later chapters, you will apply a host of

CorelDRAW! special effects, fills, and shaping techniques to your forms, to make them come alive.

Drawing a Rectangle

Using the Rectangle tool in the CorelDRAW! toolbox, you can initiate a rectangle from any of its four corners, as well as from the center outward. Having this degree of freedom and control over the placement of rectangles saves you time and effort when you lay out your illustrations.

Drawing from Any Corner

You can start a rectangle from any of its four corners. The corner that represents the starting point always remains fixed as you draw; the rest of the outline expands or contracts as you move the pointer diagonally. This flexibility in choosing a starting point allows you to place a rectangle more quickly and precisely within a drawing. Perform the following exercise to become familiar with how the CorelDRAW! interface reacts when you use different corners as starting points. To make your screen look like the figures in this chapter, click on the Display menu and make sure there is a check mark on Show Rulers, Show Status Line, and Edit Wireframe. If there is no check mark beside one or more of these items, click on the item to make one.

1. Load CorelDRAW! if you are not running it already.

2. Select the Rectangle tool by placing the mouse pointer over the Rectangle icon and clicking once, and then moving the mouse out of the toolbox and to the right. The mouse pointer turns into a crosshair, the Rectangle icon is selected and the status line shows "Rectangle on Layer 1."

3. Position the pointer anywhere on the printable page area, press and hold the left mouse button, and drag the mouse *downward* and to the *right* along a diagonal path, as shown in Figure 3–1. The Width and Height indications in the status bar will change as you move the pointer.

4. Experiment with different widths and heights until you achieve the shape you want. You can easily modify the shape of the

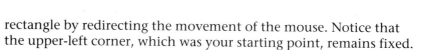

Drawing a
rectangle
Figure 3–1.

rectangle by redirecting the movement of the mouse. Notice that
the upper-left corner, which was your starting point, remains fixed.

5. When the rectangle is the size and shape you want, release the
    mouse button. This action freezes the rectangle in place, and a
    node will appear at each of the four corners. The status line
    displays the messages "Rectangle on Layer 1", and "Fill:" followed
    by a black square, as in Figure 3–2. The "Fill:" message indicates
    that the rectangle has a default interior color of black. If you do
    not have "Edit in Wireframe" selected in the Display menu, the
    rectangle you made will be black. You will learn more about fills in
    Chapter 13.

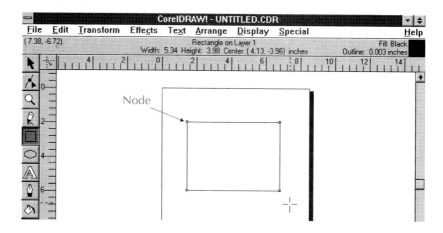

Completing a
rectangle
Figure 3–2.

6. Press and hold the mouse button at a new starting point, and then move the pointer along a diagonal path *downward* and to the *left*. Release the mouse button when the rectangle has the dimensions you want. Practice making several rectangles by starting at different corners.

7. While the last rectangle is still selected—has nodes at the corners—select Delete from the Edit menu or press (Del) to remove it.

8. Clear the whole page by choosing New from the File menu and No from the Save Changes box. Another way to clear the page is to click on Select All in the Edit Menu, then press (Del).

The type of information appearing in the status line reflects the kind of object you are drawing. When you create a line, the status line displays the x- and y-coordinates, the distance *(d)* traveled, and the angle of the line. When you create a rectangle, the status line displays the width, height, start, end, and center.

Drawing from the Center Outward

CorelDRAW! allows you to draw a rectangle from the center outward. Using this technique, you can place rectangular shapes more precisely within a graphic, without having to pay close attention to rulers or grid spacing. The width and height indicators display the exact dimensions of the rectangle as you draw. Draw a rectangle now, using the center as its starting point.

1. With the Rectangle tool selected, press and hold both (Shift) and the mouse button at the desired starting point. Keep both (Shift) and the mouse button pressed as you move the mouse. As with any rectangle, you can draw in any direction, as you see in Figure 3–3.

2. Release both (Shift) and the mouse button to complete the rectangle.

3. Press (Del) to clear the rectangle from the screen.

Drawing a Square

In CorelDRAW!, you use the same tool to produce both rectangles and perfect squares. The technique is identical, except that you bring (Ctrl) into play when creating a square.

3

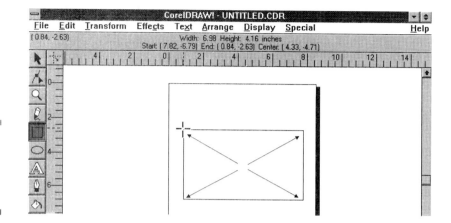

Drawing a
rectangle from
the center
outward
Figure 3–3.

Drawing from Any Corner

Follow these steps to draw a square. As with a rectangle, you can use
any corner as your starting point.

1. With the Rectangle tool selected, position the pointer at the point
   where you want to begin the square.

2. Press and hold both Ctrl and the mouse button and then draw
   diagonally in any direction. Note that the status line indicators
   show that the width and the height of the shape are equal, as in
   Figure 3–4.

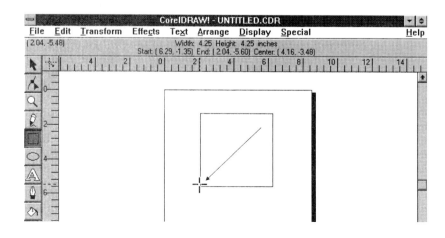

Drawing a
square
Figure 3–4.

3. To complete the square, release the mouse button first, and then release Ctrl. If you release Ctrl first, you might draw a rectangle with unequal sides rather than a square.

4. Press Del to clear the square from the screen.

Drawing from the Center Outward

To draw a square in any direction, using the center as a starting point, you must use both Ctrl and Shift as well as the mouse button.

1. With the Rectangle tool selected, position the pointer at the point where you want to begin the square.

2. Press and hold Ctrl, Shift, and the mouse button simultaneously, and draw in any direction.

3. To complete the square, release the mouse button first, and then release Ctrl and Shift. If you release Ctrl and Shift first, you might draw a rectangle with unequal sides, and the center might turn into a corner.

4. Press Del to clear the square from the screen.

Practicing with the Grid

If your work includes design-oriented applications such as technical illustration, architectural renderings, or graphic design, you may sometimes find it necessary to align geometrical shapes horizontally or vertically in fixed increments. In this section, you can practice aligning rectangles and squares while drawing; Chapter 6 will introduce you to techniques for aligning shapes *after* you have drawn them.

TIP: As you learned in the previous chapter, the grid in CorelDRAW! can either be invisible or a pattern of dots on the screen. Objects are aligned to the grid because of the Snap To feature that is similar to a magnetic attraction.

One way to align objects while drawing is to take advantage of the Grid Size and Snap To Grid commands in the Display menu. The process of aligning new objects to a grid consists of four steps:

◆ Adjusting the grid spacing

◆ Displaying the grid

◆ Displaying the rulers

◆ Enabling the Snap To Grid feature

3

1. Pull down the Display menu and select the Grid Setup command. The Grid setup dialog box in Figure 3–5 will display.

2. Adjust both the Horizontal and Vertical Grid Frequency values to 2.00 per inch. To do this, press and hold the mouse button over the lower scroll arrow until the number 2.00 appears. Alternatively, you can drag on the current value, and type **2.00**. Use Tab to go from Horizontal to Vertical. If the selected unit of measurement is something other than inches, click on the unit's drop-down list, and choose "inch."

3. Click on Show Grid and Snap To Grid, then click on OK to save these settings, and exit the dialog box.

4. Display the rulers (if they do not already appear on the screen) by selecting the Show Rulers command in the Display menu. A checkmark will appear next to the command, indicating that the rulers are now active.

5. Pull down the Display menu once more to see if the Snap To Grid feature is currently selected. If a checkmark appears next to the Snap To Grid command, it is already active, and you can align and

Adjusting Grid Frequency to 2.00 per inch

Figure 3–5.

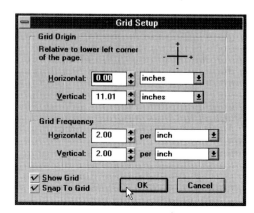

place objects automatically at the specified increment. If a checkmark does not appear, select this command to activate the feature. Once the Snap To Grid feature is on, a message appears to that effect in the lower-left corner of the status line. Also in the Display menu, the Edit Wireframe command should be checked (turned on).

6. Next, select the Rectangle tool and position the pointer at the 1-inch mark relative to both the horizontal and vertical rulers. Even if you place the pointer inexactly, the corner of the rectangle will align perfectly to the 1-inch marks when you begin to draw.

7. Press and hold the mouse button and draw a rectangle four inches wide and three inches deep.

8. Draw a second rectangle the same size as the first beginning at a point 1/2 inch to the right and 1/2 inch below the first. The extension of the mouse pointer in the rulers—a dotted line—should align exactly with the 1/2-inch marks on both rulers. The grid setting prevents you from "missing the mark."

9. Draw a third rectangle from a starting point 1/2 inch below and 1/2 inch to the right of the second. Your three rectangles should align like the ones in Figure 3–6.

10. Select New from the File menu to clear all of the rectangles from the screen. When the Save Changes message box appears, select No.

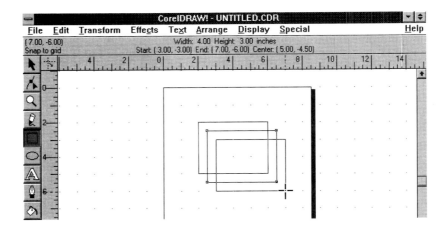

Drawing rectangles at 1/2-inch intervals
Figure 3–6.

Now that you have practiced drawing all possible types of rectangles, you are ready to build a drawing with rectangular and freehand elements.

Creating a Drawing Using Rectangles and Squares

3

In the following exercise, you will integrate all the skills you have learned so far by creating a teacup that includes rectangles, squares, and freehand drawing elements. In the process, you will also learn how to adjust the relative smoothness of curved lines you draw with the Pencil tool. The adjustment involves a feature called Freehand Tracking, which controls how closely CorelDRAW! follows the movements of your mouse pointer when you draw curves.

To prepare for this exercise, select the Grid Setup command from the Display menu and adjust both the Horizontal and Vertical Grid Frequency to 8.00 per inch. Both Show Grid and Show Rulers should still be selected, and Snap To Grid should be turned on. Refer to the steps in the preceding section if necessary. When you are ready to create the drawing, proceed through the following steps, using the numbers in Figure 3–7 as a guide. If you wish, use the rulers as an aid in laying out your work.

1. Draw a rectangle (1) to represent the body of the teacup. It should be higher than it is wide.

2. Position your pointer at the right side of this rectangle and attach a rectangular handle (2) to the body of the teacup. The handle should touch the edge of the teacup but not overlap it; the grid settings you have chosen will prevent overlapping.

3. Draw a smaller rectangle (3) inside the one you just created (2) to make the opening in the handle.

4. Now select the Pencil tool and add a straight line (4) to the base of the teacup. (Freehand mode should be selected, not Bézier. If you need to change the drawing mode, click and hold on the Pencil tool until the fly-out menu appears, then click on the left icon.) This represents the top of the saucer. Remember to press and hold [Ctrl] while drawing to ensure that the line remains perfectly

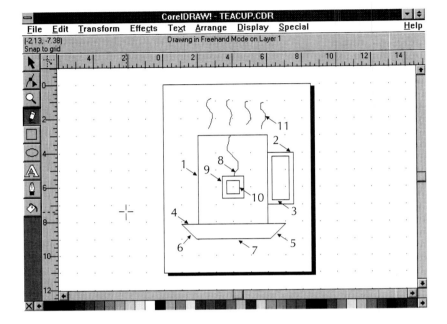

A teacup using
rectangles,
squares, and
freehand
elements
Figure 3–7.

horizontal; use the information in the status line if you need guidance.

5. Extend a diagonal line (5) and (6) down from each end of the top of the saucer. Check the status line indicators as you draw: The angle for the diagonal line to the left (6) should read -45 degrees, while the angle for the diagonal line to the right (5) should read -135 degrees. Be sure to make both lines the same length. Each line snaps to the saucer base to form a multisegment line, as you learned in Chapter 2.

6. Now add another straight line (7) to form the bottom of the saucer. Remember to constrain the line using Ctrl. The saucer base snaps to the other line segments to form a single object, a polygon.

7. With the Pencil tool still selected, press and hold the mouse button and draw a curve (8) to represent the string of a tea bag. Does your string appear excessively jagged? If it does, you can adjust the Freehand Tracking setting in the next set of steps.

8. Before adjusting the Freehand Tracking value, erase the tea bag string you have just drawn by selecting Undo from the Edit menu.

9. Select the Curves option from the Preferences command in the Special menu to display the Preferences—Curves dialog box, as shown in Figure 3–8. You used this same dialog box in Chapter 2 to adjust the AutoJoin values. The default value in the numeric entry box next to Freehand Tracking is 5 but you are going to adjust it to a higher number to facilitate smoother curves.

10. Using the scroll arrow, adjust the sensitivity level in the Freehand Tracking option to 10 pixels. This is the highest number possible and causes CorelDRAW! to smooth your curved lines as you draw. Lower numbers, on the other hand, cause the Pencil tool to track every little dip and rise as you move the mouse.

11. Select OK twice to exit the dialog boxes and save your setting.

12. Now draw the tea bag string a second time. Your curve should be somewhat smoother now, more like the one in Figure 3–7.

13. Next, attach a tag to the string: Select the Rectangle tool again, position the pointer just below the bottom of the string, press and hold Ctrl and Shift simultaneously and draw a square (9) from the center outward.

14. To add a center label to the tag, create a square (10) inside the first square. Select one of the corners as the starting point for this smaller square.

15. To add a finishing touch to your drawing, create some steam (11) by selecting the Pencil tool and drawing some curves. Since you have set Freehand Tracking to a higher number of pixels, you can create more effective "steam."

16. Finally, save your drawing. Select the Save As command from the File menu and **teacup** as shown in Figure 3–9. When you click on

3

Adjusting the Freehand Tracking value for smoother curves
Figure 3–8.

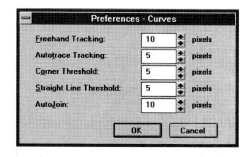

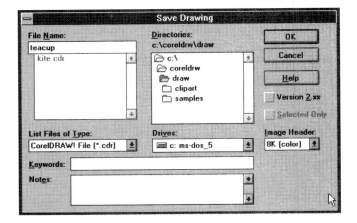

Saving the
drawing as
TEACUP.CDR
Figure 3–9.

the OK command button, CorelDRAW! adds the extension .CDR
automatically.

Drawing an Ellipse

The Ellipse tool in CorelDRAW! allows you to create both ellipses and
perfect circles. Follow the exercises in this section to create ellipses and
circles of many different shapes and sizes. In later chapters, you will
expand your skills and apply a rich variety of special effects and
shaping techniques to these basic geometrical forms.

All versions of CorelDRAW! allow you to start an ellipse from any point
on the rim. You can also draw an ellipse from the center point outward
by using the (Shift) key. This second method allows you to place ellipses
precisely within a graphic.

Using the Rim as a Starting Point

You can initiate an ellipse from any point on its rim. This flexibility in
choosing your starting point allows you to position an ellipse within a
drawing, without sacrificing precision.

Since you cannot use a corner as a starting point for ellipses and circles,
you can still use the width and height indicators as guides.

CorelDRAW! gives you an additional visual cue when you are drawing
ellipses and circles. If your starting point is on the upper half of the

rim, CorelDRAW! places the node at the uppermost point of the ellipse; if your starting point is on the lower half of the rim, CorelDRAW! places the node at the bottommost point of the ellipse. Perform the following exercises to become familiar with how the CorelDRAW! interface reacts when you choose different points on the rim as starting points for an ellipse.

3

1. Click on the Ellipse tool and position the pointer anywhere on the printable page area, press and hold the mouse button, and drag the mouse downward and to the right along a diagonal path, as shown in Figure 3–10. The indicators on the status line display the width and height of the ellipse.

2. When the ellipse is the shape you want, release the mouse button. This action completes the ellipse and freezes it in place. As in Figure 3–11, a single node appears at the uppermost point of the ellipse, and the status line changes to display the messages "Ellipse on Layer 1" and "Fill:" followed by a solid black rectangle. Press [Del] to clear the page.

3. Choose a new starting point and draw an ellipse from bottom to top. Press and hold the mouse button at a desired starting point anywhere on the bottom half of the rim and then move the pointer *upward* in a diagonal direction.

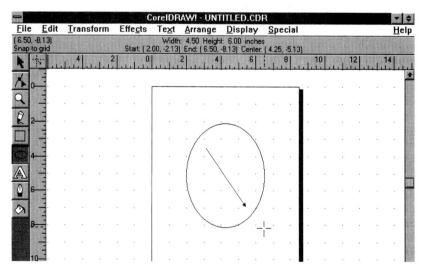

Drawing an ellipse from top to bottom
Figure 3–10.

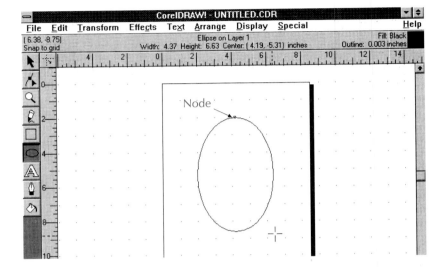

A completed
ellipse showing
the node at the
top
Figure 3–11.

4. When the ellipse has the dimensions you want, release the mouse button. Note that the node is now at the bottom of the ellipse.

5. Press (Del) to clear this ellipse from the screen.

Drawing from the Center Outward

CorelDRAW! allows you to draw an ellipse from the center outward, just as you did with rectangles and squares. This feature offers you a more interactive method of working, without sacrificing precision. The width and height indicators continue to display the exact dimensions of the ellipse as you draw. Practice drawing an ellipse using the center as a starting point.

1. With the Ellipse tool selected, press and hold both (Shift) and the mouse button at the desired starting point. Keep both (Shift) and the mouse button depressed as you move the mouse. As with any ellipse, you can draw in whichever direction you choose, as you see in Figure 3–12, in which an ellipse was drawn from its center outward.

2. Release the mouse button and then release (Shift) to complete the ellipse. Be sure to release the mouse button *before* you release (Shift)

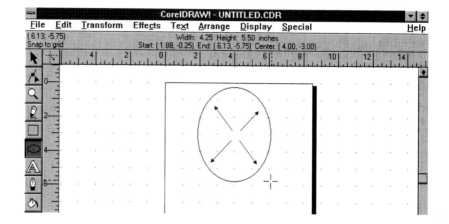

Drawing an
ellipse from the
center outward
Figure 3–12.

or the ellipse may "snap" away from the center point you have
chosen and your center point will be treated as a rim point.

3. Clear the ellipse from the screen by pressing ⌨Del.

Drawing a Circle

In CorelDRAW! you use a single tool to produce both ellipses and
perfect circles, just as you used the same tool to produce rectangles and
squares. The technique is identical; you use ⌨Ctrl to constrain an ellipse
to a circle. As with ellipses, you can choose either the rim or the center
of the circle as a starting point.

Using the Rim as a Starting Point

Perform the following exercise to create a perfect circle, starting from
the circle's rim:

1. With the Ellipse tool selected, position the pointer at a desired
   starting point.
2. Press and hold both ⌨Ctrl and the mouse button and draw
   diagonally in any direction. As you can see in Figure 3–13, the
   status line indicators show that both the width and the height of
   the shape are equal.

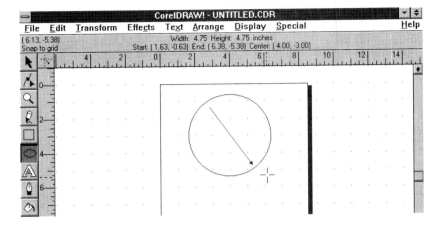

Drawing a
circle using Ctrl
Figure 3–13.

3. To complete the circle, release the mouse button and then Ctrl. Be sure to release the mouse button *before* you release Ctrl or your circle may turn into an ordinary ellipse of unequal height and width.

4. Clear the circle from the screen by pressing Del.

Because of the way CorelDRAW! works, you are actually creating an imaginary rectangle when you draw an ellipse or circle. That is why the status line indicator for a perfect circle displays width and height instead of diameter. The ellipse or circle fits inside the rectangle, as you will see more clearly when you begin to select objects in Chapter 6.

Drawing from the Center Outward

In the following brief exercise, you will draw a circle using the center as a starting point.

1. With the Ellipse tool selected, position the pointer at the point where you want to begin the circle.

2. Press and hold Ctrl, Shift, and the mouse button simultaneously and draw in any direction.

3. To complete the circle, release the mouse button and then Ctrl and Shift. If you release the keys before you release the mouse button, you may jeopardize both your circle and its central starting point.

4. Clear the circle from the screen by pressing Del.

Now that you have created some circles and ellipses using all of the available techniques, you can integrate these shapes into an original drawing. Continue with the next section to consolidate your skills.

3

Creating a Drawing Using Ellipses and Circles

The following exercise brings together all the skills you have learned so far. You will create a drawing (of a house and its environment) that will include ellipses, circles, rectangles, squares, and freehand drawing elements. The grid can assist you with some of the geometrical elements of the drawing; other elements you can draw freehand. Since this drawing will be wider than it is high, you will also learn how to adjust the page format from portrait (the default vertical format) to landscape (horizontal format). The first few steps get you into the habit of anticipating and preparing for your drawing needs before you actually begin to draw, so that you can draw quickly and without interruption. Use the numbers in Figure 3–14 as a guide in performing this exercise.

1. To prepare for the geometrical portion of the drawing, select the Grid Setup command from the Display menu and adjust both the Horizontal and Vertical Grid Frequencies to 4.00 per inch. If you need help, refer to the "Practicing with the Grid" section of this chapter.

2. Change the page setup so that your page is wider than it is long. To do this, select the Page Setup command from the File menu. When the Page Setup dialog box in Figure 3–15 appears, select the Landscape option button to set the Orientation option to Landscape. Exit by selecting the OK command button.

3. Select the Curves option from the Preferences command in the Special menu and set both the Freehand Tracking and the AutoJoin options to 10 pixels, if they are not already. As you recall from earlier in this chapter, a high Freehand Tracking setting lets you draw smoother curves and a high AutoJoin setting causes lines and curves to snap together even when their end points are a few

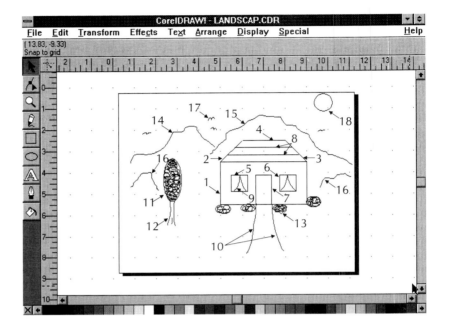

A drawing using ellipses, circles, rectangles, and freehand elements
Figure 3–14.

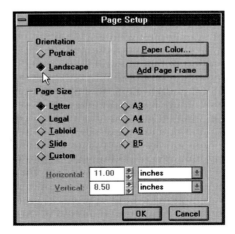

The Page Setup dialog box
Figure 3–15.

pixels apart. Click on the OK command button twice to exit both dialog boxes.

TIP: When you changed the page setup from Portrait to Landscape, the vertical ruler went back to its default of zero being in the lower-left corner. (You may remember that you moved the vertical zero to the upper-left corner in Chapter 2.) Change this again for this drawing to provide a more normal reference.

4. Move the mouse pointer to the icon at the intersection of the vertical and horizontal rulers. Click and hold the mouse button and drag the ruler cross hairs to the upper-left corner of the page as shown here:

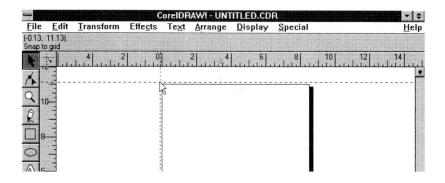

Notice the lines snap to the corner grid point. Release the mouse button and the zero point on the rulers will be opposite the upper-left corner of the page.

5. Select the Rectangle tool and position the pointer at the 5-inch mark on the horizontal ruler and the 3 1/2-inch mark on the vertical ruler. Draw a rectangle that extends from this point to the 9-inch mark on the horizontal ruler and to the 5 1/2-inch mark on the vertical ruler. This rectangle will compose the main element of the house(1).

6. Designing the roof of the house requires three steps involving constrained lines and automatic joining of lines to form a polygon. Select the Pencil tool and position your pointer at the upper-left corner of the the "house." Extend a line (2) upward and to the right at a 45-degree angle. Remember to press Ctrl while drawing to constrain this line to the correct angle automatically. End the line at the 6-inch mark on the horizontal ruler and the 2 1/2-inch mark on the vertical ruler.

7. Extend a line (3) upward and to the left at a 135-degree angle. remember to press Ctrl while drawing to constrain this line to the control angle automatically. When you reach the 8-inch mark on the horizontal ruler and the 2 1/2-inch mark on the vertical ruler, end the line with a double-click so you can continue with another line segment.

8. While continuing to hold Ctrl, extend a horizontal line (4) back to the first diagonal line (2) and single-click to end it. The two line segments should snap together and form a polygon that constitutes the "roof" of the house.

9. You will need smaller grid increments when drawing the next few objects. Select the Grid Setup command from the Display menu again and set both the Horizontal and Vertical Grid Frequencies to 8.00 per inch. Select OK to save this setting and return to your drawing.

10. Create two square windows for the house. To create the first window, select the Rectangle tool and begin a square (5) near the left side of the house, a little below the "roof." Practice drawing a square from the center outward using the Ctrl-Shift key combination. Notice the dimensions of your square just before you complete it, so that you can draw a square of the same size the next step. If you do not like the first square you draw, press Del immediately to erase it and try again.

11. Create a second square window (6) near the right side of the house. Make sure this square is the same size as the first and that it begins and ends on the same horizontal plane. The grid settings should help you place it correctly.

12. Make a rectangular door (7) for the house about halfway between the two windows. Use the rulers to help guide your movement. If

you make a mistake, press ⌦ or select Undo in the Edit menu to delete the rectangle and try again.

TIP: Change both the horizontal and vertical frequencies to 6.00 since you are trying to divide an inch into three equal parts in the next step.

3

13. To create planes of shingles for the roof, select the Pencil tool, press and hold ⌃, and draw two perfectly horizontal lines (8) across the roof.

14. Add asymmetrical curtains for the house by drawing some diagonal freehand curves (9) inside the windows. Remember to press and hold the mouse button as you draw to create curves instead of lines.

15. Draw a freehand sidewalk (10) that widens as it approaches the foreground of your picture.

16. Select the Ellipse tool and draw an elongated ellipse (11) to the left of the house. This represents the foliage of a poplar tree.

17. Select the Pencil tool and form the trunk of the poplar by adding some freehand vertical curves (12) beneath it. If you wish, you can add some small lines to the "foliage" of the poplar.

18. Select the Ellipse tool again and draw a series of "bushes" (13) immediately in front of the house. Use ellipses for the outlines of the bushes; create detail in the bushes by inserting a few ellipses and circles inside each one. Insert more ellipses to create a denser bush. (You can practice this technique on the poplar tree, too.)

19. Select the Pencil tool and create a mountain (14) behind and to the left of the house. Use curved instead of straight lines. Your mountain doesn't have to look exactly like the one in the figure.

20. Before creating the second mountain, select the Lines and Curves option from the Preferences command in the Special menu and set Freehand Tracking to 1 pixel. This will make the outlines of your subsequent freehand curves more jagged. Select OK twice to exit the dialog boxes and save the new setting.

21. Draw the second mountain (15) behind the house. Notice that the outline of this mountain looks rougher than the outline of the first mountain.

22. Continue by using freehand curves to add a little landscaping (16) beneath the mountain and, if desired, a few birds (17).

23. Select the Ellipse tool and create a sun (18) by drawing a circle from the center outward at the upper-right corner of the picture.

24. Finally, save your drawing by selecting the Save As command from the File menu. When the Save As dialog box appears, type **Landscap** and select Save. CorelDRAW! adds the .CDR extension automatically.

Congratulations! You have mastered the Rectangle and Ellipse tools and created another masterpiece with CorelDRAW!

CHAPTER

4

ADDING TEXT

CorelDRAW!'s advanced text-handling features let you turn text into a work of art. You can rotate, skew, reshape, and edit a character or a text string (a group of characters) just as you would any other object. You can perform these feats on Corel Systems fonts and on the extensive library of fonts available from other manufacturers. The more than 150 Corel Systems TrueType fonts provided with your software (over 250 Adobe Type 1 fonts on the CD-ROM version of CorelDRAW!) look similar to standard industry typefaces and will print on any printer with which CorelDRAW! is compatible. Since the Corel fonts are now in the Windows standard TrueType format (and in Adobe Type 1 format on the CD-ROM) you can use your Corel fonts with all your Windows applications—a real bonus!

In this chapter, you will learn how to insert text into a drawing and select the font, style, point size, alignment, and spacing attributes of your text. You will also learn how to enter special foreign language or symbolic characters. After you have completed the exercises in this chapter, you will be ready to tackle more advanced techniques for reshaping your text (Chapter 9, "Shaping and Editing Text") and converting other manufacturers' fonts to a format that you can use in CorelDRAW!.

Entering Text

The Text tool, the last of the four basic drawing tools in CorelDRAW!, is represented by a stylized capital letter "A." You use the text tool to insert text into your pictures, just as you use the Ellipse or Rectangle tool to insert geometrical objects. The process of inserting text into a drawing can involve up to eight steps:

1. Select the Text tool.
2. Choose between a text string and a paragraph.
3. Select an insertion point.
4. Enter text.
5. Choose the point size of your text.
6. Set the alignment for the text.
7. Select a typeface and typestyle.
8. Adjust the spacing between the letters, words, and lines of your text.

The sections that follow treat each of the preceding steps in greater detail. Since most of this chapter consists of exercises, however, the order in which you perform these steps may vary slightly from this list.

Selecting the Text Tool

You use the Text tool in CorelDRAW! to enter new text on a page. When you first load CorelDRAW!, the Pick tool is highlighted; in order to enter text, you must activate the Text tool. In the following brief exercise, you will adjust the page format, and then activate the Text tool.

1. If the printable page area is in portrait format (vertical instead of horizontal), select Page Setup from the File menu and select Land-scape format. If you did the drawing exercise at the end of Chapter 3, the printable page area is already in landscape format. This is because CorelDRAW! always "remembers" the page setup you used the last time you created a new drawing.

2. Select the Text tool by positioning the mouse pointer over the tool. Then press and momentarily hold down the mouse button. A two-icon fly-out menu appears as shown here:

The icons represent the two uses of the Text tool, text and symbol entry.

The text entry icon on the left, which is the default, allows you to enter text in either of the two modes, artistic or paragraph. The distinction between the two modes is explained in the next section. The rightmost icon, in the shape of a star, allows you to access the extensive symbols library provided by CorelDRAW! 3. Symbols and their uses are discussed later in this chapter. Select text entry mode by clicking on the leftmost icon. The mouse pointer turns into a crosshair.

Text Strings and Paragraphs

Artistic text is designed to enter shorter text strings, such as titles, captions, and notes, that can be up to 250 characters long. Paragraph text is designed for larger blocks of text, such as copy for a brochure, that can be up to 4000 characters long.

You make a distinction between text strings and paragraphs through the initial use of the Text tool. For text strings, you simply click the Text tool at the point on the page you want text to begin. For a paragraph, you drag a *bounding box* from where you want text to start to where you want text to end.

Paragraph text provides many of the attributes of word processing. Text will automatically wrap at the end of a line; text can be justified, as well as left-aligned, right-aligned, and centered; text can be cut and pasted to and from the Clipboard; you can adjust the space between paragraphs in addition to adjusting the space between characters, words, and lines; and you can create up to eight columns with a *gutter* (space between columns) you define. Also, you can import ASCII (American Standard Code for Information Interchange) text files created outside of CorelDRAW!.

Selecting an Insertion Point

The *insertion point* is the point on the printable page where you want a text string to begin. Text aligns itself relative to that point. In CorelDRAW!, you can enter text directly on the page, or you can type it in a special dialog box, where you also select its attributes. To select an insertion point and prepare for the other exercises in this chapter, follow these steps:

1. Make sure that Snap To Grid is on and set both the Horizontal and Vertical Grid Frequencies to 2 per inch. If your screen does not already display rulers and/or the grid, select Show Rulers from the Display menu and Show Grid from the Grid Setup dialog box.

2. Position the mouse pointer at the top center of the page area at 5 1/2 inches horizontal and 1 inch vertical, click once, and type **CorelDRAW!**. Select the Edit Text option from the Edit menu, or use the shortcut key combination Ctrl-T. The Artistic Text dialog box displays, as shown in Figure 4–1.

The Artistic Text Dialog Box

Using the elements of the Artistic Text dialog box, you can enter text and then customize it in five different ways. Take a moment to become

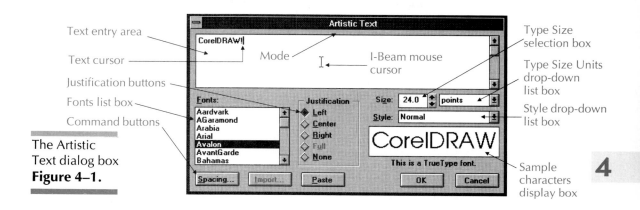

Text entry area

Text cursor

Justification buttons

Fonts list box

Command buttons

The Artistic
Text dialog box
Figure 4–1.

Type Size
selection box

Type Size Units
drop-down
list box

Style drop-down
list box

Sample
characters
display box

4

familiar with the layout of this dialog box and the way the keyboard
functions within it.

The following are the components of the Artistic Text dialog box and
their respective functions. Figure 4–1 points out the major components.
The words "Artistic Text" in the Title bar of the dialog box indicate you
are in Artistic text, or text string, mode. If you use Paragraph mode you
will instead see "Paragraph Text" in the Title bar.

Text Cursor   A flashing text pointer appears in the text entry window
when you first call up this dialog box. You can type or edit your text
string, or series of characters, in this window. A text string can include
up to 250 characters. You can include an unlimited number of text
strings in a single file.

Justification Buttons   Use the justification buttons to align your text
relative to the insertion point. The default setting for this text attribute
is Left. The dimmed Full (Left & Right) justification is for justified
paragraphs and is available only in Paragraph mode.

Fonts List Box   The Fonts list box contains the names of all the fonts
from which you can choose, including both those provided by
CorelDRAW! 3 and any you may have from other sources.

Sample Characters Display Box   When you select a font, the sample
characters display box will display in that font as much of your text as
fits in the box. This gives you a true WYSIWYG example of the font.

Additionally, CorelDRAW! 3 now adds a statement below the display box that indicates whether the font is a TrueType font supported by Windows 3.1, or a font created by another source, such as Adobe Type Manager.

Style Drop-Down List Box Once you choose a font, use the style list box to specify the style in which you want the font to appear. In CorelDRAW!, font refers to an entire character set that shares the same basic design (for example, Avalon), regardless of the size (for example, 10 points) or weight (for example, Bold or Italic). A style is narrower in scope. One style includes only a single weight (Normal, Bold, Italic, or Bold-Italic) for a particular font. Although there are four possible styles for any font, some fonts are not available in all four styles and the unavailable styles are therefore dimmed.

Type Size Selection Box Use the type size selection box to choose the size for the text you enter. The default setting for this attribute is 24 points, but you can change this value by using the scroll arrows at the right side of the dialog box (see "Selecting a Type Size" later in this chapter).

Type Size Units Drop-Down List Box Click on the arrow in this type size units box to change the unit of measuring type sizes from points (the default) to inches, millimeters, or picas and points.

Spacing Button The Spacing button gives you access to an additional dialog box where you can specify spacing between characters, words, or, if you are in Paragraph mode, paragraphs. See the "Adjusting Text Spacing" section in this chapter for detailed instructions on how to adjust spacing.

Paste Button Clicking on the Paste button transfers the contents of the Windows Clipboard to the text entry window. If the Clipboard contains more than 250 characters, the excess will be cut off and not brought into CorelDRAW!.

Import Button The dimmed Import button allows you to import a text file into CorelDRAW! if you are in Paragraph mode.

4

OK and Cancel Buttons   Press the OK button to save your attribute settings and display, on screen, the effects of these settings on your previously (or newly) entered text. To exit the Artistic Text dialog box without saving any changes, press the Cancel button.

Using the Keyboard and Mouse

You can use both the mouse and the keyboard to move between attributes and between attribute settings in the Artistic Text dialog box. If you are using a mouse to move around in the Artistic Text dialog box, you can select a text attribute in four different ways: by clicking on an option or command button, by scrolling with a scrollbar or scroll arrow, by clicking on a selection box, or by choosing from a drop-down list box. You work with option or command buttons to choose justification and spacing; with scrollbars or scroll arrows to choose fonts or to display more text in the text entry box; with a selection box to choose from different text sizes; and with drop-down list boxes to choose styles and size units.

If you prefer to use the keyboard in the Text dialog box, you can select most text attributes using Tab, Shift-Tab, and the four arrow keys on your cursor pad. When you first enter the dialog box, the text cursor appears in the text entry window. To move from the text entry box to any of the attribute settings, click on the attribute setting, or press the Alt key along with the appropriate underlined letter. Then pressing Tab moves you from one attribute to the next, while the Shift-Tab key combination moves you between attributes in the reverse order. The order in which you move between attributes depends on which version of CorelDRAW! you have. If you are using version 1.11 or later, you can access the font list box using the keyboard alone. If you have an earlier version, you must use the mouse to select a typeface.

Now you are familiar with how to get around in the Artistic Text dialog box. The differences between the Artistic Text dialog box and the Paragraph Text dialog box are discussed in the sections later in this chapter dealing with paragraph text. In the following sections you will learn how to set text attributes for yourself.

Entering Text

Text can be entered either directly on the screen or through the text entry box in the Artistic and Paragraph Text dialog boxes. In the next section, you will become acquainted with the use of the text entry box, followed by some of the unique properties of direct on-screen text entry, including the use of the Text roll-up window. The exercises on text entry and manipulation will use both methods to let you see for yourself when to use one over the other.

Entering Text in the Text Dialog Box

When you first enter the Artistic Text dialog box, the text entry box is automatically selected, as you can see by the text cursor in Figure 4–1. (On your monitor, the text cursor is flashing.) If you are not in the text entry box because of the previous exercises, click in the box now to return there. To enter a maximum of 250 text characters, simply begin typing. For this exercise, enter text in the following way:

1. Type **CorelDRAW!** at the flashing text cursor if it's not there already. Notice how "CorelDRAW!" appears in the sample character display window in the current font.
2. Press Enter to begin a new line, type **Made**, and press Enter again.
3. On the third line, type **Easy**.

Your text entry window should now look like this:

CorelDRAW!
Made
Easy

Using Keys to Move Around

The way you use your computer keys to move around in the CorelDRAW! text entry window may differ from the way you use them in a word processor. Whenever you have several lines of text in the text entry window, you can use the following keyboard commands:

✦ Press (Enter) to start a new line within the text entry window and begin entering text into it. The window will hold as many lines of text as you generate, as long as you do not exceed the 250-character limit.

✦ Press (↓), the down arrow key, to move the text cursor down one line. (This does not apply if you are already on the last line of text.)

✦ Press (Pg Dn) to move the text cursor down the last line of text. The text in the previous two lines may "jump" out of visual range, like this:

E asy|

✦ Press (↑), the up arrow key, to move the text cursor up one line. (This has no effect if you are already on the top line of text.)

✦ Press (Pg Up) to move the text cursor up to the first line of text.

✦ Press (Home) to move the cursor to the beginning of the current line.

✦ Press (End) to move the cursor to the end of the current line.

✦ Press (→), the right arrow key, to move the cursor one letter at a time to the right.

✦ Press (←), the left arrow key, to move the cursor one letter at a time to the left.

✦ Press (Backspace) to delete the character immediately preceding the text cursor.

✦ Press (Del) to delete the character immediately following the text cursor.

Using the Mouse

You can also perform some text entry operations using the mouse:

✦ Use the scroll bar at the right side of the text entry window to locate a line of text that is not currently visible.

✦ If you want to insert text at a given point, click at that point.

✦ To select one or more characters in a text string, position the text cursor at the first character you want to select and then drag the mouse across the desired characters. The characters appear highlighted, as shown here:

CorelDRAW!
Made
Easy

✦ You can delete a text string that you have selected in this way by pressing Del.

Continue to experiment with the keyboard controls and the mouse until you feel comfortable with them. Entering type directly on the screen, you will find, uses the same text editing techniques.

Entering Text Directly on the Screen

CorelDRAW! 3 now allows you to type both artistic and paragraph text on the screen, with the attributes that you choose. The mechanics of entering the text are the same as entering it in the text entry box of the Artistic Text dialog box: you establish the insertion point by clicking the mouse on the screen, and you use the same navigating and editing keys as you did in the text entry box: Home, End, Backspace, Del, and the arrow keys.

To change the attributes of the text you enter, you can use either the Artistic Text dialog box or the Text roll-up window that lets you access the more common attributes. The following exercise repeats the previous text entry, but this time on the screen:

1. Return to the screen by clicking on the OK button.

2. Choose New from the File menu and click on "No" when asked if you want to save the changes to the current file "Untitled.CDR." A blank page appears.

3. Choose Text from the menu bar and click on "Text Roll-Up..." Or, using the keyboard, press Ctrl-2. The Text roll-up window appears on your screen, as shown here:

4

The Text roll-up window lets you choose text alignment, choose the font, size, and units, and choose bold and italic styles along with super- and subscript. The dimmed Character Kerning and Frame buttons are not available with Artistic text. For any of your choices to take effect, you must choose Apply after changing the attributes.

TIP: You can use both the mouse and the Tab key to switch among the Text roll-up attributes, but the mouse works the best. Some of the attribute buttons do not allow you to easily see whether they are active.

4. Select the Text tool and place the insertion point at 5 1/2 inches horizontal and 1 inch vertical.

5. Type **CorelDRAW!**, press Enter, type **Made**, press Enter, and finally, type **Easy** and press Enter.

You should be looking at the same text entry that you did earlier in the text entry box. Select Text Edit to verify this. When you are satisfied that it's the same, return to the screen by clicking the Cancel or OK button.

As you probably noticed, the Text roll-up window is taking up some of the printable page.

6. Roll up the roll-up window by clicking on the up arrow in the upper-right corner of the roll-up window.

Now that you have the feel for both the text entry box and direct-entry ways of adding text, the following exercises will guide you through text attribute usage.

Aligning Text

The next exercise involves deciding how you want to align the text. You currently have four choices available on the Text roll-up menu: Left, Center, Right, and None. In Paragraph mode, you also have Full (both Left and Right) justification.

Left Justification

Left is the default justification setting. When you choose this setting, text will align on the page as though the insertion point were the left margin.

1. You will need to open the Text roll-up window by either clicking on the down arrow of the "rolled-up" title bar, or choosing Text Roll-Up from the Text menu. Using the mouse, select Left justification by positioning the mouse pointer over the Left icon (leftmost icon on top row) and clicking once. The Left button darkens when you select it.

2. Select Apply from the Text roll-up window. The text that you entered displays on the page in the default font, left-aligned at the 5 1/2-inch mark, as in Figure 4–2. The text string has a default fill of black like other closed objects in CorelDRAW!. The small rectangles at the base of each letter are nodes that help you edit text shape and attributes, as you will learn in Chapter 9.

Left-justified text
Figure 4–2.

NOTE: The type size in Figures 4–2 through 4–5 looks larger than what appears on your screen. The size has been increased from the default 24 points to 40 points so you can better see the text and the effects of alignment selections. You will do the same on your screen when you use the Size attribute.

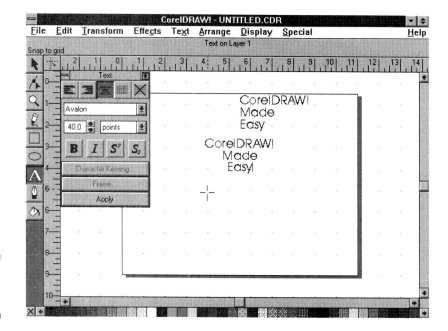

Center-justified text added
Figure 4–3.

4

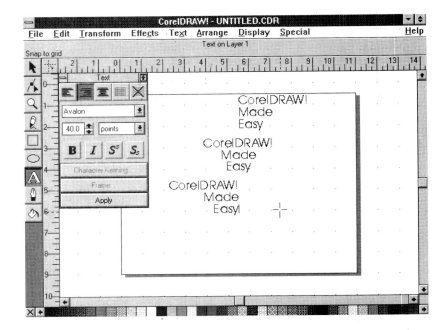

Right-aligned
text added
Figure 4–4.

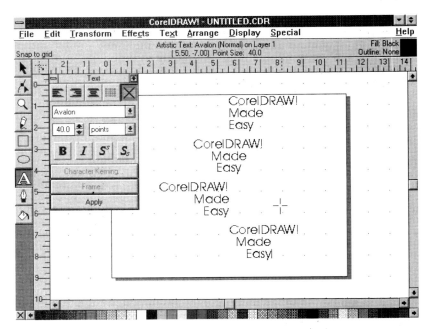

Unjustified text
added
Figure 4–5.

4

3. Leave this text on the page and select another insertion point, at the 3-inch vertical mark and the 5 1/2-inch horizontal mark, just below the first text string.

Center Justification

When you select Center justification, the insertion point becomes the midpoint of any string you type. Perform these steps to compare center alignment with left alignment:

1. Type **CorelDRAW!** on one line, **Made** on the next, and **Easy** on the third line, as you did in the last section.
2. Using the mouse, change to Center justification by positioning the mouse pointer over the Center icon (middle icon on top row) and clicking once.
3. Select Apply. The text you entered appears in the default font, center-aligned with respect to the 5 1/2-inch mark. Your page should now look like Figure 4–3.
4. Leave this text on the page. Select a third insertion point, this time at the 5-inch vertical mark and the 5 1/2-inch horizontal mark, just below the center-aligned text.

Right Alignment

When you select Right alignment, the text aligns on the page area as though the insertion point were the right margin. Perform these steps to compare right alignment with left and center alignment:

1. Type **CorelDRAW! Made Easy** on three lines as you did in the previous exercises.
2. Using the mouse, change to Right alignment by positioning the mouse pointer over the Right icon (second from left on top row) and clicking once.
3. Select Apply. The text you entered appears in the default font, right-aligned with respect to the 5 1/2-inch mark. Your page should now look like Figure 4–4. Notice the Text roll-up window remains on the screen.

4. Leave this text on the page. Select a fourth insertion point, this time at the 7-inch vertical and 5 1/2-inch horizontal mark.

No Justification

When you select None for justification, text displays on the page exactly as you enter it. This selection is useful when you want to add unusual spacing at the beginning of a line in a text string. Perform these steps to compare text with no alignment to text with Left, Center, and Right justification:

1. Type **CorelDRAW!** press ⌷Enter⌷.
2. On the second line, indent two spaces, type **Made**, and press ⌷Enter⌷ again.
3. On the third line, indent four spaces and type **Easy**.
4. Using the mouse, change the justification to None by clicking on the None icon (rightmost on the top row).
5. Select Apply. The text that you entered appears in the default font, with the spacing exactly as you typed it. Your page should now look like Figure 4–5.
6. Clear the page of text by selecting New from the File menu. Do not save the changes. Notice the Text roll-up window remains on the screen.

Selecting a Type Size

Normally, you will select alignment and font settings for a text string before you specify the type size, which is measured in *points* (72 points make up an inch). For this exercise, however, you will want to see results on the full page in a larger size than the default value of 24 points.

To change the type size from 24 to 40 points using the mouse,

1. Position the pointer over the upper scroll arrow next to the Size box in the Text roll-up and depress and hold the mouse button. As you scroll, the numerical value in the Size box increases.

2. Release the mouse button when the value in the Size box reaches 40.0.

3. Roll-up the Text roll-up window. In the next section you'll return to the text entry box.

Selecting a Type Design

So far, you have used only the Avalon typeface, which is the default typeface in CorelDRAW!. In this section, you will have the opportunity to experiment with some of the different fonts and styles supplied with your software.

4

Selecting a Font

Many books and trade magazines offer guidelines for selecting an appropriate font. A thorough discussion of the subject is beyond the scope of this book; however, when choosing the font you will use in a CorelDRAW! graphic, you should consider the tone and purpose of your work, as well as your intended audience. Look at the two fonts in Figure 4–6, for example. You probably would not choose an elaborate, flowery font such as Paradise for a graphic that you would present to a meeting of civil engineers; a font such as Frankfurt Gothic might prove a better choice.

Practice selecting fonts in the following exercise.

Comparing the "tone" of fonts
Figure 4–6.

1. Select the Text tool and then select an insertion point that is at the 1 1/2-inch mark on the horizontal ruler and the 2-inch mark on the vertical ruler.

2. Type **Paradise**. Open the Artistic Text dialog box by choosing Edit Text from the Edit menu or by pressing Ctrl-T. The dialog box appears, with the sample text box showing the word "Paradise" in the default Avalon font.

3. Select the Paradise font from the Fonts list box. You can select a typeface in one of four ways:

   A. *Click* directly on the font name if it is visible in the list box. When you do this, the font name becomes highlighted and a faint dotted outline surrounds it. If the font you want is not visible, use one of the following techniques.

   B. *Scroll continuously up or down the list* Position the mouse pointer on the up or down scroll arrow and then depress and hold the mouse button until the desired font comes into view. Click on the font name to select it.

   C. *Scroll up or down the list one line at a time* Position the mouse pointer on the up or down scroll arrow at the top or bottom of the scroll bar in the Font list box. Click repeatedly until the name of the typeface you want comes into view. Select that font name by clicking on it. This is the same as using ↑ or ↓ with the Font list box selected.

   D. *Scroll up or down the list one list box at a time* Position the mouse pointer in the right scroll bar, not on a scroll arrow, and either above or below the scroll box, and click. The list will move up or down by the height of the list box. This is the same as using Pg Up or Pg Dn with the Font list box selected.

4. Set the type size to 100 points, using either the mouse or keyboard technique described earlier in this chapter.

5. Set Justification to Left.

6. Select OK to return to the page, where you will see the Paradise text string with the selected attributes, as shown in Figure 4–7. On your screen, nodes will appear between each letter.

7. Select another insertion point at the 1 1/2-inch mark on the horizontal ruler and the 4-inch mark on the vertical ruler.

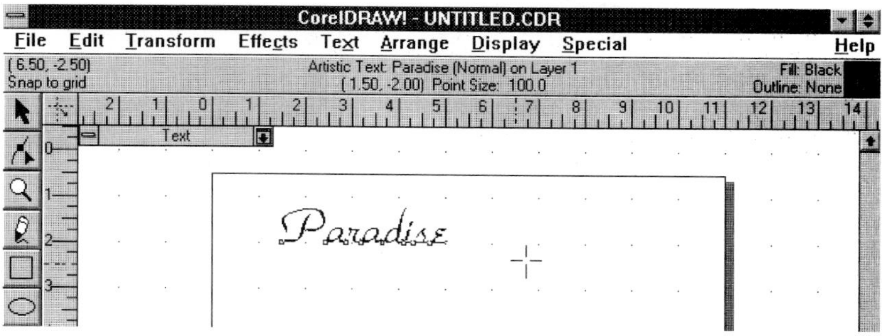

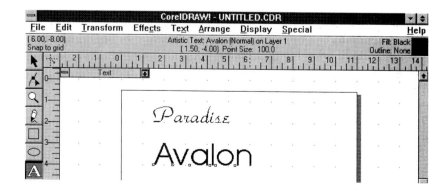

A text string
using the
Paradise font
Figure 4–7.

8. Type **Avalon** and open the Artistic Text dialog box.

9. Select the Avalon font in the Font list box.

10. Select OK to return to the page, where you will see the Avalon text string beneath the Paradise text string, as in Figure 4–8.

11. Select a third insertion point at the 1 1/2-inch mark on the horizontal ruler and the 6-inch mark on the vertical ruler.

12. Type **Aardvark** and open the Artistic Text dialog box.

13. Select the Aardvark font from the list box.

14. Select Apply to exit the Artistic Text dialog box. Your page now looks like Figure 4–9.

15. Select a fourth insertion point at the 1 1/2-inch mark on the horizontal ruler and the 8-inch mark on the vertical ruler.

16. Type **Dixieland** and open the Artistic Text dialog box.

Text strings
using the
Paradise and
Avalon fonts
Figure 4–8.

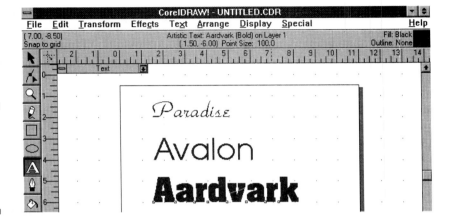

Comparing
Paradise,
Avalon, and
Aardvark
typefaces
Figure 4–9.

17. Select the Dixieland font from the list box and notice that nonalphabetic symbols, rather than letters, appear in the sample character window. This font, like the Geographic Symbols, Greek/Math Symbols, and Musical Symbols fonts, consists of symbols rather than letters.

18. Select OK to see the text on the page. Your page now resembles Figure 4–10. You will notice that even though you have entered all of the text strings at the same point size, some appear larger than others. Each font has its own characteristic width and height.

19. Clear the screen by selecting New from the File menu. Do not save any changes.

Practice trying out different fonts. When you are ready for the next section, clear the screen by selecting New from the File menu. You are ready to learn how to select one of the four available styles for a given font.

Selecting a Style

While you were experimenting with fonts in the foregoing exercise, you may have noticed that not all styles were offered for some fonts. This is because some fonts have only one or two styles available, while others have three or four.

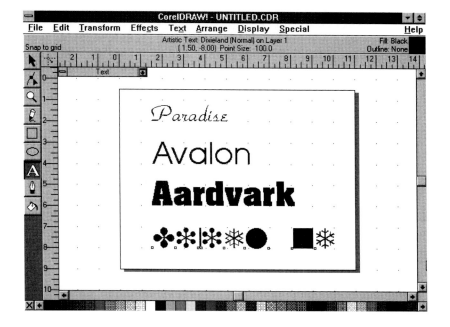

Adding a text string from a nonalphabetic (symbol) typeface **Figure 4–10.**

Perform the following exercise to practice selecting available typestyles for the CorelDRAW! fonts. This exercise uses the direct entry method and the Text roll-up window. The instructions are less descriptive since you should now have the tools to easily move through the menus.

1. Select the Text tool and then choose an insertion point that is at the 1 1/2-inch mark on the horizontal ruler and the 2-inch mark on the vertical ruler.

2. Type **Frankfurt Gothic** and highlight the words by dragging across them from the "F" in Frankfurt to the "c" in Gothic, as shown here:

> Frankfurt Gothic

3. Change the point size to 75.0 points using the Text roll-up window.

4. Select Frankfurt Gothic from the font list box.

5. Select the Italic style by clicking on the "I" (the second icon from the left on the row below the font list box). The button darkens when selected.

6. Select Apply to display the resulting text on the page, as in Figure 4–11. Leave this text on the page for now.

7. Select another insertion point at the 1 1/2-inch horizontal and 4-inch vertical ruler marks.

8. Type **Frankfurt Gothic** and highlight the text. Select the Frankfurt Gothic font, and change the point size to 75.0 points.

9. Select the Bold button on the Text roll-up window (the "B" icon at the left).

10. Select Apply to display the resulting text on the page, as in Figure 4–12.

11. Select a third insertion point at the 1 1/2-inch horizontal and the 6-inch vertical ruler marks.

12. Again, type **Frankfurt Gothic**, but this time instead of highlighting the text by dragging, you will use the Pick tool.

The Pick tool is used to select, move, or arrange objects or text.

Chapter 6, "Selecting, Moving, and Arranging Objects," provides an in-depth discussion on the use of the Pick tool, but it's necessary at this point to introduce the text-selecting properties of the tool.

Text string in Frankfurt Gothic italic
Figure 4–11.

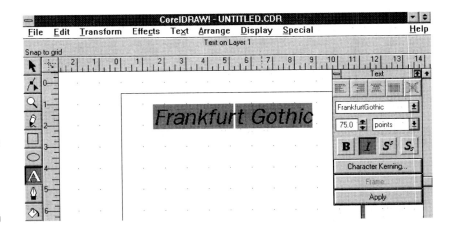

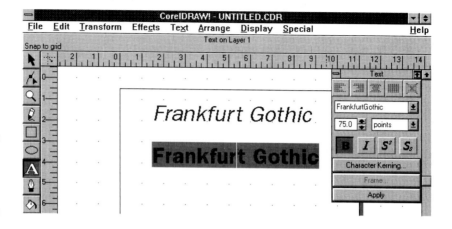

Comparing
italic and bold
typestyles
Figure 4–12.

For CorelDRAW! to change the attributes of a text string, the string must be selected. In simple cases where there is only one string, some attributes can be changed without you doing the selecting because CorelDRAW! realizes which text to change. As you increase the number of text strings, you must highlight the text by dragging; or, if CorelDRAW! does not accept the attribute change, select it with the Pick tool.

13. Click on the Pick tool, place the mouse pointer on the text string, and click once more. The words "Frankfurt Gothic" become surrounded by eight boundary markers. The full use of these boxes is discussed in Chapter 6, but for the purposes of text, they identify the text as being selected.

The Pick tool will be used again in later sections of this chapter.

CAUTION: Double-clicking on text with the Pick tool invokes the rotate and skew feature. If you accidentally do this, just click on the text again to get the selection boxes back.

14. In the Text roll-up window, change the font to Frankfurt Gothic, increase the point size to 75.0, and click on both Bold and Italic.

15. Select Apply to display the resulting text on the page. Click on a blank portion of the screen to remove the highlighting. Your screen should resemble Figure 4–13.

16. Select New from the File menu to clear the screen before continuing with another exercise.

Take a few moments to practice selecting styles for other fonts. When you have finished, continue with the next section to learn how to adjust spacing when you enter a new text string.

Adjusting Text Spacing

The Spacing command button in the lower-left corner of either the Artistic or the Paragraph Text dialog box may be easy to overlook, but it can give you enormous control over text. When you select this button, the Spacing dialog box appears, which allows you to control the spacing between characters, words, and lines of text.

In this chapter, you are working with attributes only as you enter text. However, CorelDRAW! also allows you to adjust text spacing *interactively*. This means that even after text displays on the page, you can change the spacing of one character, several characters, or an entire text string without going back to the dialog box. You will learn more about how to change spacing attributes for existing text in Chapter 9.

Comparing italic, bold, and bold italic typestyles
Figure 4–13.

4

Setting Up the Exercise

In the following exercise, you will have the opportunity to review what you have learned thus far about setting all of the attributes in the Artistic Text dialog box. If you have forgotten how to perform any of these functions, go back to the relevant section and review it.

1. Select the Text tool if it is not selected already.

2. Select an insertion point near the top of the page, aligned to the 5 1/2-inch horizontal and 2-inch vertical marks on the rulers.

3. Enter four lines of text on the screen. Type your name on the first line, your address on the second, your city, state, and zip code on the third, and your telephone number on the fourth.

4. Click on the Pick tool to highlight the four lines of text. Open the Text roll-up if it isn't already displayed on your screen.

5. Change the type size to 50.0 points.

6. Select Center alignment.

7. Select Gatineau as the font.

8. Open the Artistic Text dialog box. It should look like Figure 4–14, except that the actual text you have entered on the screen will differ from what is in the text entry box. Select the Spacing command button by clicking on it once. The Text Spacing dialog box in Figure 4–15 appears. If you had not entered text, CorelDRAW! would display an error message and not permit you to enter the Text Spacing dialog box.

Settings:
Gatineau
normal, Center
justification, 50
points
Figure 4–14.

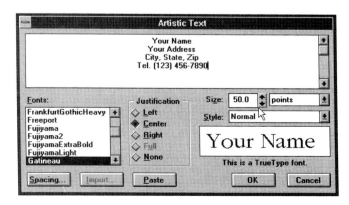

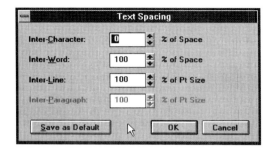

The Text
Spacing dialog
box
Figure 4–15.

The Text Spacing Dialog Box

The Text Spacing dialog box features four options for adjusting spacing: Inter-Character, Inter-Word, Inter-Line, and Inter-Paragraph. You will not change them at this point in the exercise, but take a moment to become familiar with your options.

Inter-Character   The Inter-Character option controls spacing between each pair of characters within each word of the text. The default value is 0% of space width. In other words, CorelDRAW! inserts no space at all between characters unless you change that value. This measurement is relative, rather than an absolute measurement, so that your spacing will stay constant as you scale your text or change the font. You can adjust the value of intercharacter spacing in increments of whole percentage points using the scroll arrow or you can type a value manually.

Inter-Word   The Inter-Word option controls spacing between each word of the text that you enter. The default value is 100% of space width. You can adjust the value of interword spacing in increments of whole percentage points using the scroll arrow or by typing a value manually.

Inter-Line   When your text contains more than one line, the Inter-Line option controls the amount of space between each line. In the printing industry, this type of spacing is also known as *leading*. The default value is 100% of the type size, which means that if your text size is 10 points, the total amount of space between two lines is exactly 10 points and no more. You can adjust interline spacing in increments of 1%.

Inter-Paragraph   If you are in Paragraph mode, and you have more than one paragraph, the Inter-Paragraph option controls the amount of space between each pair of paragraphs. The default value is 100% of the type size. If your text size is 10 points, the space between paragraphs will be 10 points. You can adjust the interparagraph spacing by increments of 1%.

You can adjust the values in the Text Spacing dialog box in two ways: by scrolling with the mouse or by using the keyboard.

To adjust values using the mouse only,

1. Position the mouse pointer on the up or down scroll arrow. If you want to increase the value, position it on the up arrow; if you want to decrease the value, position it on the down arrow.

2. Press and hold the mouse button until the value you want displays in the adjoining box, and then release the mouse button.

To adjust values using the keyboard,

1. Use Tab or Shift-Tab to go from item to item in the dialog box. When you reach one of the spacing number boxes, the entire number will be highlighted. This means that if you type a new number, you will completely replace the original number.

2. Type in the value you want. To go to the next setting, press Tab or Shift-Tab.

Leave the spacing options at their default settings for the current text string and select OK twice. You exit the Text Spacing dialog box, and the text that you typed in the text entry box now appears on the page. Your text string has the default settings of 100% spacing between words, no extra spacing between characters, and no extra leading between lines, as shown in Figure 4–16. If your screen still has the select boxes around your text, click on a blank area of the screen and they will disappear.

Adjusting and Comparing Text Spacing

Now that you are acquainted with the way the Text Spacing dialog box works, you will create another text string, identical to the first except

Address text
string with
default spacing
attributes
Figure 4–16.

that its spacing values differ. You can then visually compare the results of your spacing adjustments.

1. Select an insertion point at the 5 1/2-inch mark on the horizontal ruler and the 5-inch mark on the vertical ruler, just beneath the last line of text on the page.

2. Type your name, street address, city, state, and zip, and telephone number on four separate lines.

3. Click on the Pick tool and then, if necessary, on the new text to highlight it. Use the Text roll-up to set the Justification, Font, and Size attributes to what they were (Center, Gatineau, and 50 points). Click on Apply.

4. Open the Edit Text dialog box and select the Spacing command button to display the Text Spacing dialog box.

5. This time, adjust the spacing in the Inter-Character number box to 50%, Inter-Word to 200%, and Inter-Line to 130%. This means that the space between characters will equal the width of half a space, the space between words will equal two spaces and the space between lines will equal 1.3 times the height of the font itself.

6. Select OK twice to save these settings and exit to the page. The second text string now displays beneath the first. Your page resembles Figure 4–17.

7. Select New from the File menu to clear the screen. Do not save any changes.

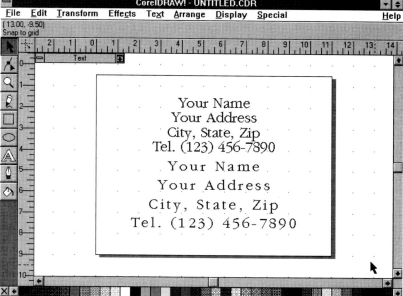

Working with Paragraphs

So far in this chapter, all of your work has been in Artistic Text mode. This is fine for titles, captions, and other pieces of text that are only a few short lines. If you are creating a brochure, a flyer, or other documents where you need large blocks of text, you should use Paragraph mode. Paragraph mode offers several features that are valuable for large blocks of text and are not available in Artistic Text mode. Among these features are:

✦ An increase in the character limit from 250 characters to 4000 characters

✦ Automatic word wrap at the end of each line

✦ Variable line length controlled by a bounding box or frame whose dimensions and attributes can be changed

✦ Full (Left and Right) justification

◆ The ability to define up to eight columns with variable intercolumn spacing

◆ The ability to paste text into the text entry window or onto the page from the Windows Clipboard

◆ The ability to import ASCII text created with a word processor

◆ Adjustable interparagraph spacing

◆ The ability to control text hyphenation

As with artistic text, paragraph text can be entered directly on the screen or you can open the Paragraph Text dialog box and use the text entry box.

Try out Paragraph mode now with these steps:

1. Select the Text tool and place the mouse pointer at 1 inch on both the horizontal and vertical rulers.

2. Press and hold the mouse button while dragging the mouse pointer to 10 inches on the horizontal ruler and 8.5 inches on the vertical ruler as shown in Figure 4–18.

The frame dimensions of the paragraph will be set, but the lines defining the perimeter disappear. Notice the pointer displays at the beginning of the frame. Though the printable page area does not show that you are in paragraph text mode, after you release the mouse button the status line will display "Text on Layer 1."

3. Release the mouse button, type at least one letter, and open the Paragraph Text dialog box by clicking on the Edit Text in the Edit menu.

TIP: If at any time you want to see the lines defining your frame, click on the Pick tool, or open and immediately close the Paragraph Text dialog box, and the lines are displayed along with the eight boundary markers.

4

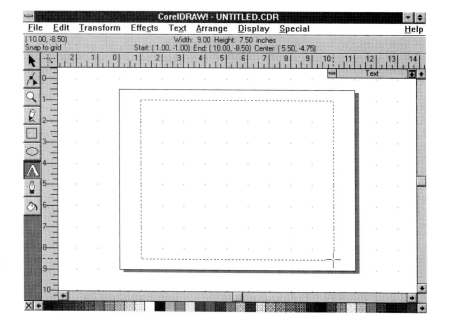

Forming the
Paragraph
mode bounding
box or frame
Figure 4–18.

As you can see in Figure 4–19, the Paragraph Text dialog box has a few
differences from the Artistic Text dialog box. The title now reads
"Paragraph Text"; the Full (left and right) justification and the Import
buttons are now turned on; and if you look at the Spacing dialog box
you will see that Inter-Paragraph spacing can now be set.

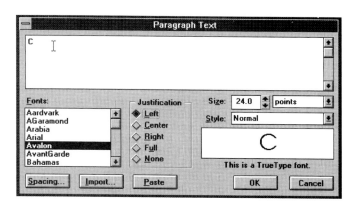

Text dialog box
in Paragraph
mode
Figure 4–19.

4. Type several paragraphs such as those shown below and your Paragraph Text dialog box should look like Figure 4–20. It doesn't matter what you type as long as you have two or more paragraphs about as long as those shown. Press Enter only at the end of the paragraphs and let CorelDRAW! automatically wrap the text at the end of each line. Put an extra line between the two paragraphs by pressing Enter a second time.

Here are two sample paragraphs you can type:

```
CorelDRAW!'s paragraph mode, first available in version
2.0 provides many features that are valuable for entering
large blocks of text. Among these features are: an increase
in the character limit from 250 to 4,000 characters,
automatic word wrap at the end of each line, a line length
that is controlled by the size of the frame, full(both left
and right) justification, text hyphenation, and the ability
to define up to eight columns.

Paragraph mode also allows you to paste text into the
Paragraph Text dialog box from the Windows Clipboard,
import ASCII text files created with a word processor,
and adjust the inter-paragraph spacing. Paragraph mode is
used in building brochures, flyers, and other documents
where large blocks of text are needed.
```

5. When you are done typing, click on Full justification, adjust the size to 24 points, select the Palm Springs typeface and the Normal style.

One of two paragraphs entered into the Text window
Figure 4–20.

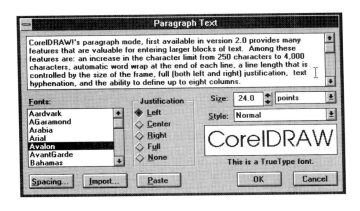

6. Click on the Spacing command button, change the inter-line spacing to 120% and the inter-paragraph spacing to 90%. Click on OK twice to return all the way out to the page.

When you return to the page, a box will form where you drew the frame and, after a moment, the text will appear. It will not be terribly readable, as shown in Figure 4–21, because of the nodes on each of the characters. By clicking on the screen you can remove the nodes. In Chapter 5, "Using Magnification and View Selection," you will see how to magnify a portion of the page to be able to read it better. (Now you can add or edit text directly on the screen.)

To preserve the typing you have done, save this file.

7. From the File menu select Save As, if necessary, change to the DRAWINGS directory, type **paratext** in the filename text box, and press ⌈Enter⌋ or click on OK.

4

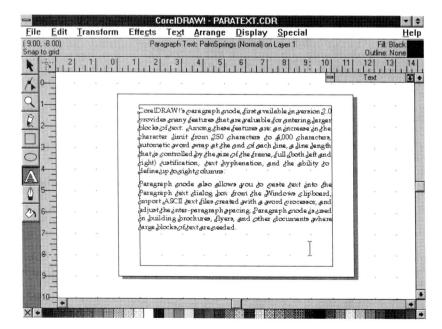

Paragraph text
as it is
displayed on
the page
Figure 4–21.

Extracting Text from CorelDRAW!

CorelDRAW!, in versions 2.0 and later, includes a feature that allows you to extract text from CorelDRAW! in a format that is usable in a word processing program. You can modify the text in the word processor and then merge the text back into CorelDRAW! automatically reattaching all of the formatting, such as font, size, and style that was originally attached to the text. (In the word processing program you will not see any of the formatting.)

In this section you will extract the text you entered, bring that text into a word processor, modify it, save it, save it again as a plain text file, and place it on the Windows Clipboard. In the next section, you will use each of these items back in CorelDRAW!.

Start by extracting the text from CorelDRAW!. The text you typed should still be on the screen with the nodes, as shown in Figure 4–21. That is, the text you want to extract should be selected.

1. From the Text menu, select Extract. The Extract dialog box will open.

2. Make sure the DRAWINGS directory is selected, type **extrpara** in the Filename text box, and click on OK. You have now written an ASCII text file containing the paragraphs you entered. In the following steps you will switch out of CorelDRAW! without closing it, open Windows Write, and edit that file. (Almost any word processor could be used in place of Windows Write.)

3. Open the Control menu in the upper-left corner and select Switch To.

4. From the Task list, double-click on Program Manager. The Program Manager window will open.

5. Open the Accessories group (if necessary) and double-click on Write. The Write word processing program will open.

6. Select Open from the File menu, In the Directories list box, locate the DRAWINGS directory, to which you extracted the EXTRPARA.TXT file. If you installed CorelDRAW! according to the instructions in Appendix A, this is C:\DRAWINGS. In the List File of Type: drop-down list box, choose Text Files (*.TXT) and then click on extrpara.txt in the File Name list box. The filename is displayed in the File Name entry box. Click on OK.

7. A dialog box will open asking, "Do you want to convert this file to Write format?" Click on No Conversion to preserve the ASCII text format. The text you entered in CorelDRAW! will appear on the Windows Write screen as shown in Figure 4–22.

The first two lines and the last two lines of text (the last line is blank) are reserved for CorelDRAW! to use in merging the text back in. It is, therefore, very important that you do not change these four lines or CorelDRAW! will not be able to merge this file. You can change all other parts of the file except the first two and last two lines.

4

8. Modify any of the text you entered. In this exercise, it doesn't matter what you modify as long as you can recognize the change when you get back to CorelDRAW!.

9. When you complete modifying the text, open the File menu and save the file under its original file name, EXTRPARA.TXT. This is the file that will be used to merge back in to your CorelDRAW! PARATEXT.CDR file.

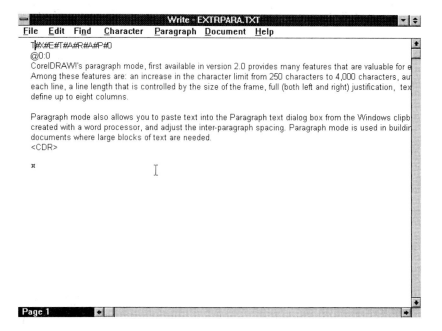

Paragraph text
in Windows
Write
Figure 4–22.

Now that you have saved the merge file, you can remove the first two and last two lines to make another text file that you can import into CorelDRAW!. Also, you will copy the remaining text to the Windows Clipboard and paste it into CorelDRAW!.

10. Delete the first two and last two lines of the file so you only have left the text you entered (select the lines by dragging over them with the mouse and press Del).

11. From the File menu, select Save As, type **test.txt**, and click on OK. This is the file you will import.

12. Select all of the text you entered and now have modified by dragging over it with the mouse, and then from the Edit menu select Copy. This places a copy of the text on the Windows Clipboard.

13. Double-click on the Control menu to close Windows Write and then open the Program Manager's Control menu and select Switch To.

14. Double-click on CorelDRAW! to switch to that program. CorelDRAW! will reappear on the screen.

Merging, Importing, and Pasting Text into CorelDRAW!

You now have four copies of the text you entered: the original file you saved in PARATEXT.CDR, the modified merge file EXTRPARA.TXT, the clean text file TEST.TXT, and finally the copy on the Windows Clipboard. Use each of the last three of these copies to see how CorelDRAW! merges, imports, and pastes text from outside CorelDRAW!.

1. From the Text menu, select Merge-Back. The Merge-Back dialog box will open.

2. Double-click on EXTRPARA.TXT in the File Name list box. After a moment you will see the revised text displayed on the page. The copy of PARATEXT.CDR in memory has now been revised with the changes you made in Windows Write. All of the formatting in the original file has been maintained. Had you had some graphic

elements in the file they would also remain unchanged. Only the words and their positions have changed.

3. Select New from the File menu to clear your screen. Save the revised file if you wish.

4. Select the Text tool and draw a paragraph bounding box from 1 inch on both the horizontal and the vertical rulers to 10 inch on the horizontal and 8.5 inch on the vertical ruler. Type any letter and open the Paragraph Text box. Note that your text settings, font, size, and style are still set. (Delete the letter you typed.)

5. Click on Import and then double-click on TEST.TXT. The revised text will be brought into the Paragraph Text dialog box as shown in Figure 4–23. The leading capital letters are the modification done in Windows Write.

6. Click on Cancel to throw away the imported text.

7. The frame that you established in step 4 returns to the screen with the same letter you typed. Open the Paragraph Text dialog box and delete the letter.

8. Click on the Paste command button. Once again the revised text will come into the Paragraph Text dialog box, this time from the Windows Clipboard.

You have now seen how you get text out of CorelDRAW! and how you can bring text back in to CorelDRAW! in three different ways. Now look at how you can use columns in CorelDRAW!.

Bottom portion
of text imported
into the
Paragraph Text
dialog box
Figure 4–23.

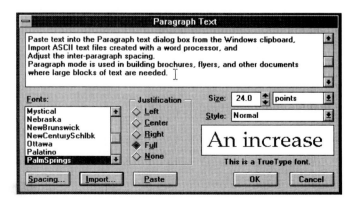

Putting Text in Columns

Many brochures, flyers, and other documents appropriate for CorelDRAW! put text into multiple columns instead of one wider column in a effort to make the text easier to read. Try it here. You should still be in the Paragraph Text dialog box with the revised paragraphs you pasted into the text entry box.

1. Click on Cancel to return to the screen. Your Paragraph frame should still be selected.

2. Select the Text menu and choose the Frame option. The Frame Attributes dialog box will open as shown in Figure 4–24.

3. Type **2** for the number of columns, press Tab to move to the Gutter Width number box, and type **.5**.

4. Click on OK to close the Frame Attributes dialog box and return to the page layout. After a moment the text will appear in a two-column format as shown in Figure 4–25.

5. Select New in the File menu to clear the page and answer No to saving the current contents.

Paragraph Attributes

The Frame Attributes dialog box shown in Figure 4–24, in addition to allowing you to create up to eight columns, has four other useful features that can enhance the appearance of your paragraph text. These

The Frame Attributes dialog box
Figure 4–24.

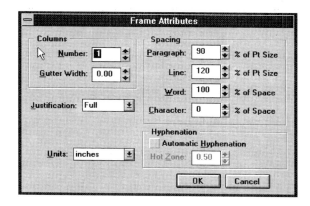

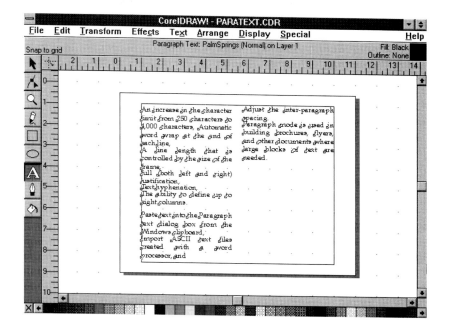

Text in a
two-column
format
Figure 4–25.

include three features that you have already seen: Justification, Units, and Spacing. The fourth is hyphenation, which is discussed in the next section.

There are two other features that CorelDRAW! 3 has added to help you create accurate text. These are a spelling checker and a thesaurus. They are discussed after hyphenation, since they are activated from the Text pull-down menu rather than from the Frame Attributes dialog box.

Hyphenation

New to CorelDRAW! 3 is the ability to turn on automatic hyphenation. When enabled by clicking on the Automatic Hyphenation check box, CorelDRAW will hyphenate words at the end of a line if three conditions occur: they begin before the left edge of the hot zone, they continue beyond the right edge of the frame, and a valid hyphenation break occurs within the zone. The hot zone extends from the right side of the Paragraph Text frame toward the left, according to the distance listed in the Hot Zone box. The unit of hot zone distance is the same as that currently entered in the Units box. If a word begins *in* the hot zone and continues beyond the frame's right edge, it will word-wrap to the beginning of the next line.

Using the Spelling Checker

CorelDRAW! 3 allows you to spell check text in either artistic or Paragraph Text mode. To use the Spelling Checker you can either highlight the text to check, which can be one word or an entire block of text, or you can type a word in the Word to Check entry box of the Spelling Checker dialog box. You open the Spelling Checker dialog box by choosing Spell Checker from the Text menu. This dialog box is shown in Figure 4–26.

NOTE: Using the Pick tool will highlight your entire text selection.

Clicking on the Check Text button starts the spell checking. If a word is found that is not among the over 116,000 words in the dictionary, it will appear in the Word not found entry box, which replaces the Word to Check entry box. You can now have CorelDRAW! offer spelling alternatives by clicking on the Suggest button. If you click on the Always suggest check box, suggestions will always be provided. If you select one of the alternatives, the word appears in the "Replace with"

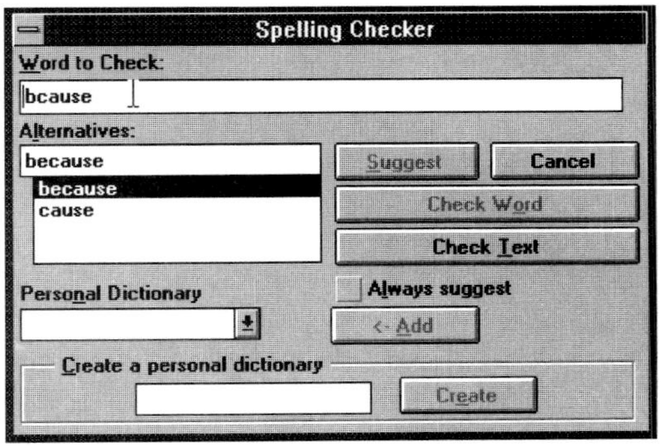

The Spelling Checker dialog box

Figure 4–26.

Spelling Checker
Word to Check:
bcause
Alternatives:
because
because
cause
Suggest   Cancel
Check Word
Check Text
Personal Dictionary
Always suggest
<- Add
Create a personal dictionary
Create

box. You can choose between replacing this particular, or all, occurrences of the word. If you don't want to replace the word with any of the suggested alternatives, you can ignore either one or all occurrences of the word. Finally, you can manually enter a word into the Replace with entry box.

The last feature offered through the Spelling Checker dialog box is the ability to create one or more dictionaries of your favorite abbreviations, acronyms, and proper names. With such a word in the Word not found entry box, create a new dictionary with these steps:

1. Type a filename like MYDICTRY in the entry box under Create a personal dictionary, next to the Create button.

2. Click on the Create button. The name you gave the dictionary appears in the Personal Dictionary drop-down list box. Once you've created one dictionary, subsequent dictionaries can be added by just typing the new name in the Create a personal directory entry box and clicking on Create.

3. Click on the Add button.

Clicking on the Cancel button closes the Spelling Checker, but does not undo any text changes you've made.

Thesaurus

CorelDRAW! 3's Thesaurus, shown in Figure 4–27, provides synonyms and definitions for selected (or manually entered) words. Simply highlight a word using the Text tool and open the Thesaurus from the text menu. Or, open the Thesaurus and enter a word in the Synonym for text entry box, then click on Lookup. In either case, CorelDRAW! offers various definitions and synonyms. If you decide to replace the word in the Synonym for text entry box, highlight the word and click on the Replace button.

Using the Symbol Library

CorelDRAW! includes a library of some 3000 symbols that are stored and retrieved like characters in a font using the Text tool. The symbols are simple, but effective, drawings that are stored as *vector images* (unlike most clip art, which is stored as *bitmapped images*). As a result,

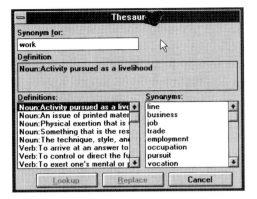

Thesaurus
dialog box
Figure 4–27.

the symbols can be enlarged, stretched, rotated, and edited like any
other CorelDRAW! objects without any loss in the quality of the image.
Also, they take very little room to store. To use the symbols, you must
have installed them on your hard disk. CorelDRAW!'s Install program
will do this for you as discussed in Appendix A, "Installing CorelDRAW!
and Associated Applications".

The symbols are organized into 50 categories like Animals, Borders,
Holidays, Space, and Weather. These categories are like fonts. You first
select a category, and then from that category you select a particular
symbol. The number of symbols in a category varies from 30 to 208,
with the average around 80. Corel includes with CorelDRAW! a catalog
of all of the symbols, giving each a number within a category. If you
know this number, once you have selected a category you can enter the
number and get the symbol. Also, as you will see in a moment, you can
select a symbol from a display box that shows ten symbols at a time,
once you have decided on a category.

Try this feature now by selecting several symbols.

1. Click on the Text tool, momentarily hold down the mouse button,
   and select the Symbol icon from the fly-out menu.
2. Click the mouse pointer at 2 on both the horizontal and vertical
   rulers.

The Symbols dialog box opens as shown in Figure 4–28.

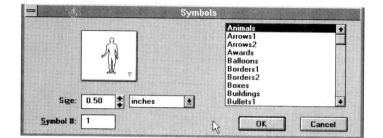

Symbols dialog box

Figure 4–28.

4

3. Click on several categories in the list box in the upper-right corner.

For example, click Computers. The first symbol of the category displays in the sample window.

4. Click on the sample window and a small window of 16 symbols appears on the screen. Use the scroll bar to see additional symbols.

Use steps 3 and 4 to look at a number of symbols. Notice on the left above the Symbol # box there is a number box where you can specify the initial size of a symbol when it is placed on the page. In future chapters you will see how you can also size symbols that have already been placed on the page.

5. Change the size to 1 inch and then click on OK to place the symbol on the page.
6. With the Symbol tool still active, move the mouse pointer to 4 on the horizontal ruler and 2 on the vertical ruler, click, choose another symbol, and click on OK to put that symbol on the page.
7. Move the mouse pointer to first 6 and then 8 on the horizontal ruler, and repeat step 6. When you are done, you should have a string of symbols like Figure 4–29.

The Symbol Library provides a good source of quick art that can be used for many purposes.

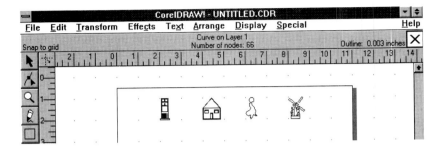

Sampling of
symbols on the
page
Figure 4–29.

Entering Special Characters

CorelDRAW! includes five different proprietary character sets beyond
the standard alphabet and characters that appear on your computer
keyboard. You enter special characters in the text entry window of the
Text dialog box, and can adjust alignment, type size, and spacing for
these special characters, just as you can for alphabetic characters. The
five character sets are Corel, Dixieland, Greek/Math, Musical, and
Geographic.

✦ The Corel character set includes all keyboard characters, foreign
language characters, currency symbols, and copyright and other
popular commercial symbols. This character set applies to most of
the 150 fonts you have available in CorelDRAW! 3 (250 fonts are
available on the CD-ROM).

✦ The character set in the Dixieland font includes decorative and
directional symbols and callouts.

✦ The character set in the Greek/Math font includes a variety of
scientific and mathematical symbols.

✦ The character set in the Musical font contains common musical
notes and notations.

✦ The character set in the Geographic font includes geographical,
military, and industrial symbols.

A complete listing of the contents of each character set appears on the
Character Reference Chart provided with your software. Also, the
Dixieland, Musical, Geographic, and Common Bullets character sets are

available as symbols in the Symbol Library. Each of the fonts is a category in the list box and each of the characters is a symbol.

No matter which of the five character sets you are using, characters above ASCII 126 are not accessible by pressing a single key on your keyboard. To type one of these special characters, depress and hold [Alt] and then type the appropriate number on your numeric keypad. Be sure to include the "0" that precedes each number. For example, to type the character "u" in the Corel character set, type **0129**.

4

CAUTION: The text you see in the text window of either the Artistic or Paragraph dialog box uses the standard Windows character set. If you are using a different character set, you must look at either the type display box in the dialog box or on your drawing to see the true character set.

Always refer to your CorelDRAW! Character Reference Chart when you are entering special characters.

CHAPTER

5

USING MAGNIFICATION AND VIEW SELECTION

Until now, you've done your work in CorelDRAW! using full-screen view, the default view when you load CorelDRAW! or open a file. But it has obvious limitations if you need to edit images or do fine detail work. The Magnification tool can customize the viewing area of your screen any way you wish. As you become familiar with this tool, you will experience greater drawing convenience and ease in editing.

The Magnification Tool

The Magnification tool, the third tool in the CorelDRAW! toolbox, resembles a small magnifying glass. Unlike the Pencil, Rectangle, Ellipse, and Text tools, the Magnification tool is not a drawing tool. It could be called a view adjustment tool, because it allows you to zoom in or out of the viewing area in a variety of different ways. Because the Magnification tool gives you complete control over the content of the viewing area, it helps enhance every object you draw and increases the usefulness of every tool in the CorelDRAW! toolbox.

The Magnification tool is five tools in one. When you select this tool, the fly-out menu shown in Figure 5–1 appears, giving you five options for adjusting your viewing area.

Zoom-In   The Zoom-In tool allows you to zoom in on any area of a drawing that you select.

Zoom-Out   The Zoom-Out tool either zooms out of your current image by a factor of two or, if your screen currently shows a zoom-in view, returns you to the previous view.

Actual Size   Selecting the Actual Size icon lets you see your drawing in the actual size it will be printed.

Fit-In-Window   Selecting the fit-in-window icon fits all of the current graphic, everything you have placed on the page, into your viewing window.

Show Page   The Show Page icon returns you to the default full-page view of your graphic.

The five viewing options for the Magnification tool
Figure 5–1.

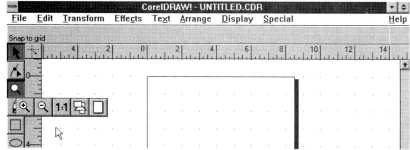

In order to have something to magnify, switch to your aircraft clip art directory by using the Open option in the File menu. Then open the file, F111_S.CDR that was provided with CorelDRAW!. If you installed CorelDRAW! using the default directories discussed in Appendix A, you can use the path you see here:

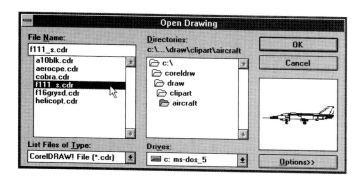

If this file is not available to you, open the landscape drawing you made in Chapter 3. When you have a picture on your screen, perform these steps.

1. Select the Magnification tool by positioning the mouse cursor over the Magnification tool icon in the toolbox and clicking once. The menu containing the five viewing options flies out below and to the right of the Magnification tool.

2. Select an icon from the fly-out menu using either the mouse or your keyboard. To select an icon using the mouse, simply click on it or drag the mouse cursor until you highlight the tool and then click. To select an icon using the keyboard, you must use individual function keys for each of the Magnification tools (the Actual Size tool is not available through the keyboard). The function keys and the Magnification tools they activate are:

✦ F2 Zoom-In

✦ F3 Zoom-Out

✦ F4 fit-in-window

✦ Shift-F4 Show Page

All of the five Magnification tools except the Zoom-In tool perform their functions automatically when you select them. The following sections discuss each Magnification tool and present hands-on exercises that allow you to practice using these tools.

The Zoom-In Tool

The Zoom-In tool icon looks like the main Magnification tool icon, except that it is smaller and contains a plus sign. The Zoom-In tool is the most versatile of the five Magnification tools, because it lets you define precisely how much of your picture you want to view at once. It is therefore invaluable for drawing fine details or editing small areas of a picture.

Defining the Viewing Area

Unlike the other Magnification tools in the fly-out menu, the Zoom-In Tool does not perform its function automatically. You have to define the zoom-in area in a series of four general steps. Try this yourself now on the aircraft:

1. Select the Zoom-In tool by first activating the Magnification tool and then selecting the Zoom-In tool icon from the fly-out menu or press F2 . The pointer changes to an image of a magnifying glass containing a plus sign.

2. Position the cursor at any corner of the area you want to magnify; usually it is most convenient to start at the upper-left corner.

3. Press and hold the mouse button at that corner and then drag the mouse diagonally towards the opposite corner of the area on which you want to zoom in. A dotted rectangle (the *marquee*) will follow your cursor and "lasso" the zoom-in area, as in the example in Figure 5–2.

4. When you have surrounded the area on which you want to zoom in, release the mouse button. The screen redraws as in Figure 5–3, and the viewing window now contains a close-up view of only the objects you selected.

You can zoom in on successively finer areas of the screen using the Zoom-In tool. You must re-select the Zoom-In tool each time you wish

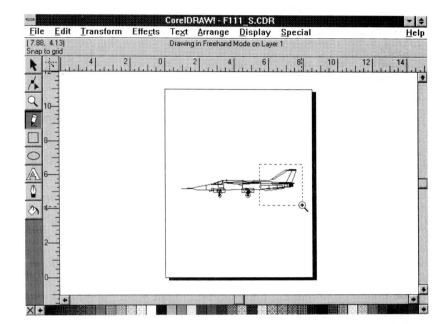

Selecting an area with the marquee
Figure 5–2.

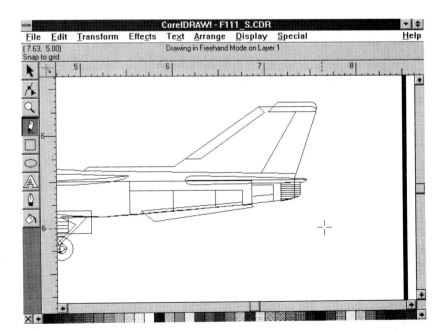

A close-up view of the selected area
Figure 5–3.

to magnify further, however, for as soon as you have redrawn the screen, CorelDRAW! automatically returns to the Pick tool. Simply select the Zoom-In tool again and select another area, as in Figure 5–4. The number of times you can zoom in depends on the type of monitor and display adapter you use. Try zooming in on progressively smaller areas; eventually, you reach a point where you are unable to zoom in any further. When this occurs, you have reached the maximum magnification possible for your monitor and display adapter. At that point, 1 pixel on the screen represents approximately 1/1000 of an inch. You must use another Magnification tool first before you can use the Zoom-In tool again.

TIP: You can set the right mouse button to zoom in, by a factor of two, on any point you select. Do this by choosing Preferences in the Special menu, then click on Mouse. A Mouse dialog box will appear and you can select one of the five options. Click on 2X zoom and on OK, then OK again in the Preferences dialog box. After setting the mouse button, a single click of the right button will zoom in, while a double-click will zoom out. The area where you click will be at the center of the new screen.

Zooming In and Editing TEACUP.CDR

The following exercise lets you practice using the Zoom-In tool on the teacup illustration you created in Chapter 3, "Drawing and Working with Rectangles, Squares, Ellipses and Circles." You will edit this illustration by entering text inside a tiny area of the drawing, a function you couldn't perform without using the Magnification tool. This exercise also allows you to practice the text entry skills you learned in Chapter 4, "Adding Text."

1. Select Show Rulers from the Display menu if the rulers do not already appear on the screen.

2. Make sure that a checkmark appears in front of the Snap To Grid command in the Display menu. If a checkmark does not appear, select this command.

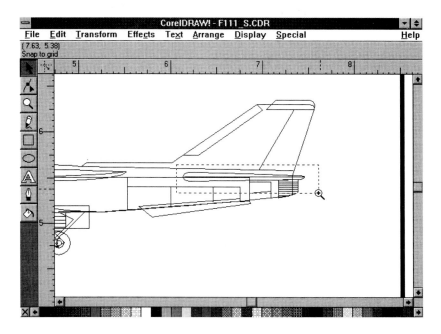

Zooming in a
second time
Figure 5–4.

3. Select Grid Setup from the Display menu and set both Horizontal and Vertical Grid Frequency to 16 per inch and make sure both Show Grid and Snap to Grid are checked.

TIP: A new feature of CorelDRAW! 3 is the ability to go to the Grid Setup dialog box by double-clicking on the ruler crosshair icon.

4. Select Open from the File menu, select the file TEACUP.CDR, and click on the Open button.

5. Select the Magnification tool, and then select the Zoom-In tool from the fly-out menu. The cursor changes into a replica of the Zoom-In tool as soon as you move into the drawing window.

6. Zoom in on the tag for the teabag: Position the cursor at the top left corner of the tag, press the mouse button, and drag the mouse diagonally downward until you have surrounded the tea tag, as in Figure 5–5.

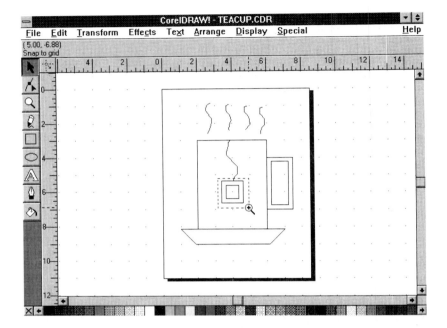

7. Release the mouse button. The screen redraws and displays only the tea tag and its immediate environment. Notice that in magnified view, the scale of the ruler changes from 1/4 inch to 1/16 inch.

8. Select the Text tool. The mouse cursor turns into a crosshair.

9. Position the cursor near the top center of the inner tea tag square and align it with a horizontal ruler marker.

10. Click once to select this point as the insertion point and type a *"J"* as in Figure 5–6.

11. The *J* you just typed should still be selected. Choose Edit Text from the Edit menu and the Artistic Text dialog box will appear, as you can see in Figure 5–7. Then select Bangkok Normal, 10.0 points, and Center justification. Place the insertion point beyond the *J* in the text entry window, and type the remainder of the text, ASMINE TEA, in all capital letters on two lines.

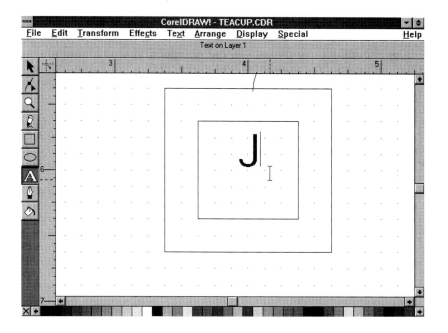

Placing text at
insertion point
Figure 5–6.

12. Now click on the Spacing button and the Text Spacing dialog box
    will appear. Make Inter-Character spacing 40%, Inter-Word 100%,
    and Inter-Line 200%, as shown here:

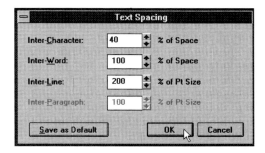

13. Select OK twice to return to the magnified display window. The text
    you typed now appears within the tea tag label, as in Figure 5–8.

14. Finally, select the Save As command from the File menu. When
    the Save As dialog box appears, type **teacup2** in the File Name
    text entry box, and then select OK.

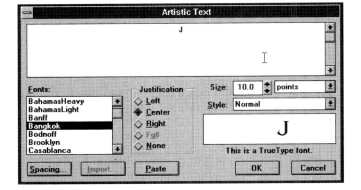

Text attributes
for JASMINE
TEA
Figure 5–7.

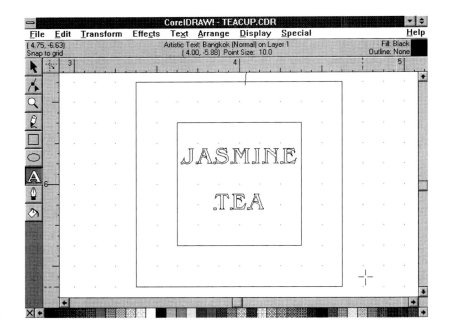

Entering text in
close-up view
Figure 5–8.

The Zoom-Out Tool

The Zoom-Out tool looks like the main Magnification tool, except that
it is a little smaller and contains a minus sign. As soon as you select this
tool, it defines the zoom-out area for you automatically in one of two
ways:

✦ If you are currently in an Actual Size, Fit In Window, or Show Page viewing magnification, selecting the Zoom-Out tool causes your current viewing area to zoom out by a factor of two.

✦ If you are currently in a Zoom-In viewing magnification, selecting the Zoom-Out tool causes you to return to the previously selected view. You can therefore use the Zoom-Out tool to back out of successive zoom-ins one step at a time.

The maximum zoom-out you can achieve is a full view of the page at 50% of the original size.

To use the Zoom-Out tool, select the Magnification tool, and click on the Zoom-Out tool icon or press F3. The cursor does not change shape when you select this tool, but the screen redraws according to the preceding rules.

In the following simple exercise, you will practice using both the Zoom-In and Zoom-Out tools while editing the LANDSCAP.CDR file that you created in Chapter 3. Remember the few extra circles and ellipses you drew inside the bushes of that picture? Now that you can see the bushes up close, you can add even more detail. Turn Snap To Grid off before you begin.

1. Select Open from the File menu and open the file called LANDSCAP.CDR that you created in Chapter 3. The image first appears in full-page view.

2. Select the Magnification tool and then click on the Zoom-Out tool icon to select the Zoom-Out tool. You can still see the full page, but it now appears at half size, as in Figure 5–9.

3. Select the Zoom-Out tool again. This time, you zoom out only a little further. You cannot zoom out further than this.

4. Select the Zoom-In tool and then lasso the house and bushes. The screen redraws to include just these objects.

5. Select the Zoom-In tool again and magnify the bushes only.

6. Select the Zoom-In tool once more and lasso a single bush.

7. Select the Ellipse tool and add detail to the bush by inserting small ellipses and circles, as shown in Figure 5–10.

5

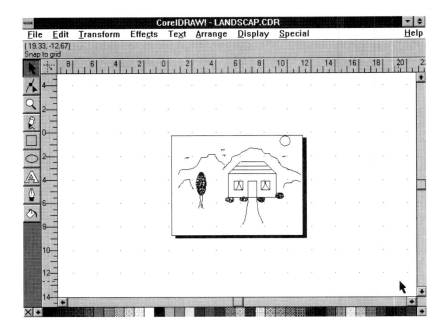

Zooming out to
a 50% page
view
Figure 5–9.

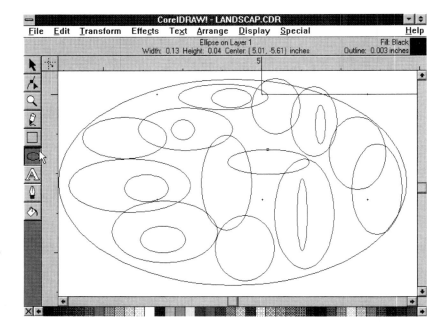

Adding detail to
a magnified
view
Figure 5–10.

8. Now, select the Zoom-Out tool. The screen displays the view you magnified in step 5 but the bush you worked on has more detail.

9. Select the Zoom-Out tool again. This time, the screen displays the view you selected in step 4.

10. Select the Zoom-Out tool a third time. This time, the screen displays the full page at 50% of its size, as in step 2. The bush you edited probably looks denser than the others because of the detail you have added.

11. Select the Save As command from the File menu. When the Save As dialog box appears, type **LANDSCA2** in the File Name text entry box, and then select OK or press ⌐Enter⌐.

12. Select New from the File menu to clear the screen.

You have seen how the Zoom-In and Zoom-Out tools work well together when you are interested in editing a picture in minute detail. In the next section, you will learn how to achieve the kind of view that is useful when you want to print your image.

5

Viewing at Actual Size

When you want to see approximately how large your image will look when printed, use the Actual Size tool in the Magnification fly-out menu. At a 1:1 viewing magnification, 1 inch on your screen corresponds to about 1 inch on the printed page. The amount of the page you see at this magnification may vary, depending on the way Microsoft Windows works with your monitor.

To achieve actual-size viewing magnification, select the Magnification tool and click on the **1:1** icon. You can practice using this tool on the TEACUP2.CDR image that you edited earlier in this chapter.

1. Open the file TEACUP2.CDR using the Open command from the File menu. Unless you have a full-page, 19-inch, or 24-inch monitor, the full-page view of the image is too small to allow you to read the text you entered earlier in this chapter.

2. Select the Actual Size tool. The screen redraws to display an area of your image similar to Figure 5–11. The actual area may vary because of the variety of monitors and display adapters available.

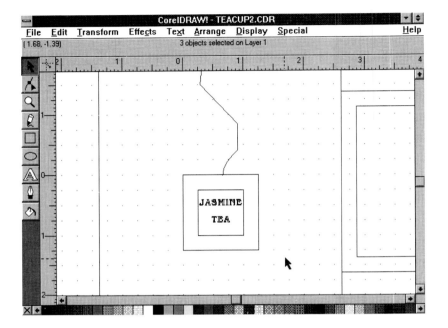

Viewing an
image at actual
size
Figure 5–11.

At this viewing magnification, your text still appears small but it is legible.

3. Select the Zoom-In tool and lasso the tea tag with the marquee. The screen redraws to display only this portion of the image.

4. Select the Zoom-Out tool. Since you were in a 1:1 view previously, you zoom out by a factor of two.

5. Clear the screen by selecting New from the File menu.

The next section shows you how to fit an entire image within the viewing window. This is a different type of magnification than the 1:1 ratio.

Fitting a Graphic in a Window

When the pictures you draw extend all the way to the edge of the page, they already fit within the viewing window. The Fit-In-Window tool is not of much use to you in such cases. When some blank space exists, however, you can use the Fit-In-Window tool to view everything you have drawn, but no more. This can be especially useful for small designs, such as logos.

To select the Fit-In-Window tool, first select the Magnification tool, then click on the fit-in-window or press ⌐F4⌐. The screen redraws to fill the entire viewing area with the graphic image. Practice using this tool on one of the sample CorelDRAW! files in the following exercise.

1. Open the file APELICAN.CDR from the clip art directory. Note that there is some blank or "white" space at both the bottom and top of the page, as in Figure 5–12.

2. Select the fit-in-window view by selecting the Magnification tool and clicking on the fit-in-window icon. Now you see only the pelican, as shown in Figure 5–13.

5

Viewing an Entire Page

The full-page view is the default view when you load CorelDRAW! or open a picture. It is easy to return to this view from any other view you

Image with unused blank space at top and bottom
Figure 5–12.

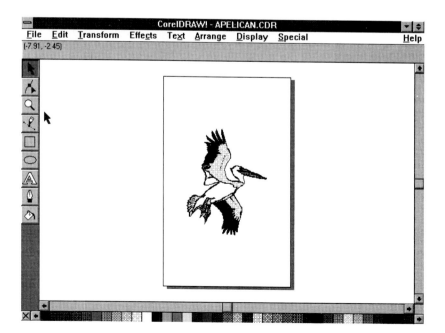

Fitting the
image within
the viewing area
Figure 5–13.

have selected. Simply select the Magnification tool and click on the Show Page icon or press Shift - F4 .

You have mastered all of the view selection tools but there is still another method, called panning, that you can use to control your viewing area.

Viewing Outside the Current Area

Use the Zoom-In tool to select a small portion of the pelican. That portion will fill the viewing area, and even though you see only the selected part, the whole drawing has been expanded.

Regardless of which view you are in, you can always move beyond your current viewing area to see what lies beyond it. This operation is called panningmoving the image around on the screen so you can see different parts of it. The horizontal and vertical scroll bars at the bottom and right sides of your screen are the tools you use to pan a picture. The callouts in Figure 5–14 point out the three different parts of the scroll bars you can use for panning.

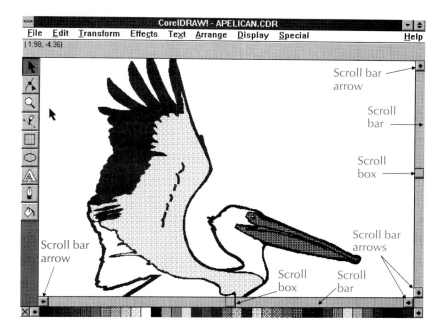

The parts of the
scroll bar
Figure 5–14.

✦ To pan in small increments, click on a scroll bar arrow. The size of the increment varies, depending on your monitor and display adapter combination. If you click on the right horizontal scroll arrow, the image in the viewing window appears to move to the left. If you click on the left horizontal arrow, the image appears to move to the right. This is an excellent method to use when you need to edit an image in fine detail.

✦ To pan in large increments, click on either side of the scroll box, located in the middle of the horizontal and vertical scroll bars. Once again, the image appears to move in the opposite direction from where you clicked. This method has only limited usefulness for editing, because the movement of the screen is rather jumpy and unpredictable.

✦ To control the exact distance that you pan, position the cursor over the scroll box and drag it across the scroll bar in the direction that you want to pan. Release the mouse button when you reach the desired area.

Now that you are familiar with all of the magnification tools and with the scroll bars, you have complete control over the portion of your picture that you display at any one time. In Chapter 7, you will put this new skill to work to help you select, arrange, and move objects and text.

CHAPTER

6

SELECTING, MOVING, AND ARRANGING OBJECTS

In order to change the appearance or position of any object or text string, you must first select it. Once you have selected an object, you can move and rearrange it, stretch, scale, rotate or skew it, give it a custom outline, or fill it with a color or pattern. Learning how to select an object is therefore an important prerequisite to mastering most of the skills in CorelDRAW!. Though you were introduced to the basics of text selection in Chapter 4, this chapter shows you the full capabilities of object and text selection.

You use the Pick tool, the first tool in the CorelDRAW! toolbox, to select objects and text. When you first load CorelDRAW!, the Pick tool is automatically active and remains active until you choose a different tool. If you are already working with one of the other tools, you can activate the Pick tool by clicking on the Pick tool icon in the toolbox.

TIP: Pressing the (Spacebar) once is more efficient. This is a time-saving shortcut that allows you to switch back and forth between tools quickly. To reactivate the tool you were working with before you selected the Pick tool, press the (Spacebar) again. Use this shortcut often when you want to draw objects, immediately move, rearrange, or transform them, and then continue drawing.

The Pick tool performs more than one function; it has both a select mode and a transformation mode. The select mode includes all those functions—selecting, moving, and arranging—that do not require you to change the size or structure of the object. The transformation mode allows you to stretch, scale, rotate, skew, or reflect objects. This chapter covers the functions of the select mode; Chapter 7, "Transforming Objects," will acquaint you with the use of the Pick tool in the transformation mode.

Selecting and Deselecting Objects

You can select objects only when the Pick tool is active. This tool is always active when you first open a picture, when you begin a new picture, and immediately after you save your work. To activate the Pick tool when you're using the Shaping tool or one of the drawing tools, you either press the (Spacebar) or click on the Pick tool icon once.

Once the Pick tool is active, you can select one or more objects by clicking on their outlines, by using (Shift) with the mouse, or by lassoing the objects. The technique you choose depends on the number of objects you are selecting, the placement of the objects within the graphic, and whether it's more convenient to select objects with the mouse or with the keyboard shortcuts.

The CorelDRAW! screen gives you three visual cues to let you know that an object is selected. First, a *highlighting box* consisting of eight small rectangles, called *boundary markers*, surrounds the object. These markers allow you to stretch and scale the object, as you'll learn in Chapter 7. Second, one or more tiny hollow nodes appear on the outline of the object or group of objects. The number of nodes displayed depends on the type and number of objects selected. The nodes are the means by which you can change an object's shape, as you'll learn in Chapters 8 and 9. Finally, the status line tells you the type of object you have selected (rectangle, ellipse, curve, and so on) or the number of objects you have selected if you have selected more than one.

Single Objects

Any time you activate the Pick tool while working on a graphic, it automatically selects the last object you created. If you want to select a different object, simply click once anywhere on the object's *outline*. Clicking on the inside of a rectangle or ellipse, or on an open space inside a letter, has no effect. Also, you must click on a point unique to that object; it cannot share that point with the outline of any other object. Only when an object is the same type and size as another object on top of it does it have no unique selection point available. For information on how to select superimposed objects without unique selection points, see the "Cycling Through Objects" section of this chapter.

6

To *deselect* an object or text string so that the tools or menu commands you use no longer affect it, click in any open area on the page. Alternatively, you can select a different object and thereby automatically deselect the previously selected object.

In the following exercise, you will practice selecting and deselecting single objects in the LANDSCA2.CDR file that you edited in Chapter 5. You will use the (Spacebar) to select objects that you have just drawn and the mouse to select other objects.

1. Make sure that the Show Status Line and Edit Wireframe commands in the Display menu are turned on, and that the Show Rulers and Snap to Grid commands are turned off. Also, turn off Show Grid in the Grid Setup dialog box.

2. Open the LANDSCA2.CDR file. Note that when the picture displays on the screen, the Pick tool is already active.

3. Select the Magnification tool and then select the Zoom-In tool from the fly-out menu and lasso the lower-right quarter of the picture. The screen redraws an area of the image similar to that in Figure 6–1.

4. Select the Pencil tool and use the mouse to draw a large pond in the lower-right corner of the picture. Be sure to connect the starting point to the finish point, so that the curve representing the pond becomes a closed path that you can fill later. Notice that as soon as you finish drawing this object, nodes appear along the path of the curve, as in Figure 6–2.

5. As soon as the pond appears, press the (Spacebar) to activate the Pick tool. Since the pond is the last object you drew, CorelDRAW! automatically selects it. A highlighting box surrounds the pond and the status line indicates "Curve on Layer 1" as in Figure 6–2.

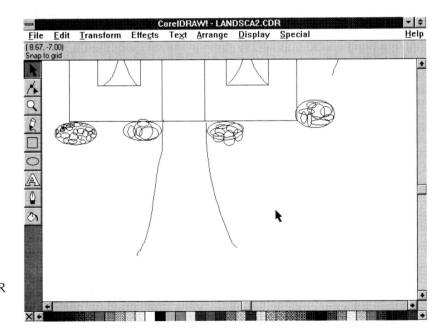

Magnifying the lower-right quarter of the file LANDSCA2.CDR
Figure 6–1.

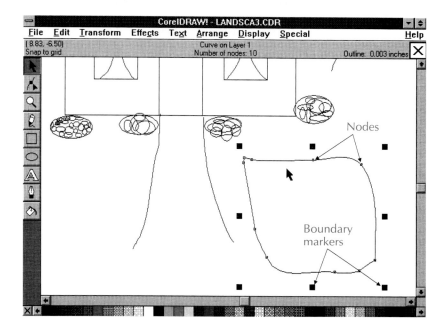

Using the
[Spacebar] to
select the last
object drawn
Figure 6–2.

6

6. Click on the outlines of the curve object again. As Figure 6–3 shows, black two-way arrows replace the boundary markers of the highlighting box. Your second click has enabled the rotate and skew functions of the Pick tool. Click on the object's outlines again to toggle back to the select mode.

7. Now, zoom out of your magnified view using the Zoom-Out tool in the Magnification tool fly-out menu. Practice selecting objects that you drew in previous sessions. For example, click on one of the curves that form the branches of the poplar tree. Each time you select a new object, the previously selected object becomes deselected; the highlighting box disappears from the previously selected object and surrounds the new one instead. The name of the currently selected object type always appears in the status line. If you select any objects within other objects (the detail inside one of the bushes, for example), you may notice that the highlighting box is sometimes much larger than the object itself. If several objects of the same type are crowded closely together, it may be difficult to tell which one you have selected. Use the Zoom-In tool

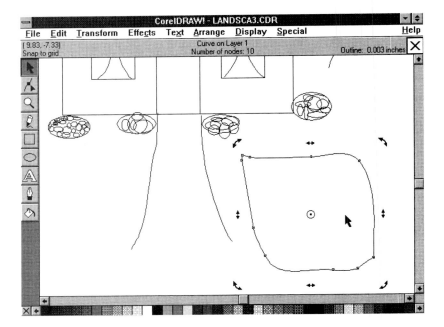

Enabling the
transformation
mode of the
Pick tool
Figure 6–3.

to magnify a small portion of a crowded area before you attempt to
select single objects.

8. When you have practiced enough to feel comfortable with
   selecting objects, select Save As from the File menu and type
   landsca3.cdr to save the file.

9. Select New from the File menu to clear the screen.

Multiple Objects

It's often more convenient to perform an operation on several objects
simultaneously than to perform the same operation on a series of single
objects individually. Assume, for example, that you want to move the
tree in the LANDSCA3.CDR file to another location within the picture.
Since the tree consists of several separate objects, moving each
component object individually would be tedious and might even lead
to inaccurate placement.

CorelDRAW! gives you three alternative solutions to this type of problem. The first solution, simply *selecting* the objects, is appropriate when you want to keep multiple objects together only temporarily, without merging them into a single entity. For example, you might want to fill a certain number of objects in a picture with the same color or pattern or move them all by the same distance. You can select multiple objects by using the mouse and [Shift] key, by drawing a marquee around them, or by using the Select All command in the Edit menu. Your choice of technique depends on both the number of objects you want to select and their location within the graphic.

If the multiple objects are components of a larger whole and should remain together at all times, you might choose to *group* them, as you will learn to do later in this chapter. CorelDRAW! will still remember that grouped objects have separate identities. If the multiple objects belong together and contain many curves, you can choose to *combine* them into a single object. Combining objects, unlike grouping them, reduces the amount of memory they require and also allows you to reshape the entire resulting object.

You will learn more about the uses of grouping and combining multiple objects in the "Arranging Objects" portion of this chapter. The following group of sections lets you practice common methods of selecting multiple objects.

Selecting with the Shift Key

When you want to select a few objects at a time, you can conveniently select them one after another using the mouse and [Shift] together. The [Shift] key method is especially useful when the objects you want to select are not next to one another within the graphic. Practice selecting multiple objects using this method:

1. Select the first object by clicking on its outline.
2. Depress and hold [Shift] and select the next object.
3. Continue selecting objects in this way, holding down [Shift] continuously.
4. When you have selected all desired objects, release [Shift].

To deselect one or more of the objects you have selected in this way, hold down [Shift] and click again on that object's outline. This action

6

affects only that object; other objects in the group remain selected. To deselect all of the selected objects simultaneously, click on any free space.

Each time you select another object using [Shift], the highlighting box expands to surround all the objects you have selected so far. Objects that you did not select also may fall within the boundaries of the highlighting box, making it difficult for you to see just which objects you have selected. The following exercise shows how you can use the status line information and the preview window as aids in selecting multiple objects with [Shift].

1. Open the TEACUP2.CDR file that you edited in Chapter 5.

2. Use the Maximize button to enlarge the size of the working area. Magnify the area that extends from the upper-left corner of the picture to the bottom of the tag on the teabag.

3. Click on the leftmost wisp of "steam" above the teacup to select it. A highlighting box surrounds the object, and the status line indicates that you have selected a curve.

4. Depress and hold [Shift] and click anywhere on the outlines of the text "JASMINE TEA." The message in the status line changes to "2 objects selected on Layer 1," but the highlighting box shown in Figure 6–4 seems to surround many more objects. It is difficult to tell whether you have selected the text string or one of the rectangles on the tea tag surrounding it. To find out, you need help from the preview window.

5. Press [Shift]-[F9] to display the preview window. Do not be concerned at this point that all of the objects in your drawing seem to blend into a solid black mass. You will learn how to edit the outlines and colors of individual objects in Chapters 11, 12, and 13.

6. From the Display menu, choose Preview Selected Only to turn it on, and then click on Show Preview. These two commands cause only the currently selected objects to appear in a full-screen preview window. As Figure 6–5 shows, you can now be certain that you selected the correct objects.

Selecting
nonadjacent
objects using
Shift
Figure 6–4.

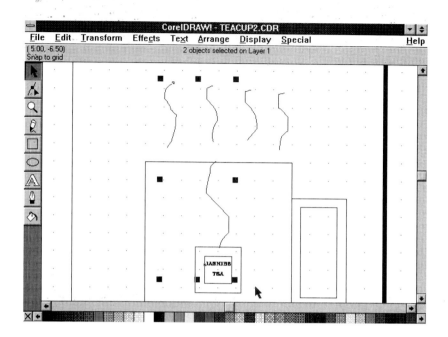

Using Preview
Selected Only
to confirm
object selection
Figure 6–5.

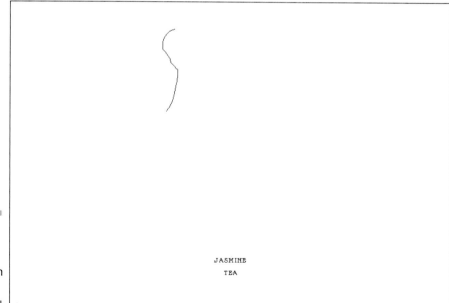

TIP: If you cannot see the "steam" when it is selected, click on the Outline tool 🖉 and again on the first or second line width in the first row of the fly-out menu. This action ensures that selected lines and curves have a visible outline.

7. If you accidentally selected one of the tea-tag rectangles instead of the text string, press F9 to return to the drawing, and deselect the incorrect object by holding Shift while clicking again on that object. When the highlighting box no longer surrounds that object, continue to hold down Shift and select the text string instead.

8. Still holding down Shift, select the rightmost wisp of "steam" and add it to the group of selected objects. The status line now displays the message "3 objects selected on Layer 1," and the preview window displays all three objects. Again, if you can't see the steam when it is selected, click on the Outline tool and click again on the first or second line width in the fly-out menu.

9. Click on the Preview Selected Only command in the Display menu again to turn off this feature, and then select New from the File menu to clear the screen.

Selecting with the Marquee

If you need to select a large number of objects at once, using the mouse and Shift can be tedious. A quick shortcut is to draw a marquee around all of the desired objects with the Pick tool. Perform the following exercise to practice using a marquee:

1. Position the mouse pointer just above and to the left of the first object you want to select. (You can begin from any corner of the group of objects, but the upper-left corner is usually most convenient.)

2. Depress the mouse button and drag the mouse diagonally in the direction of the other objects you want to select. A dotted rectangle (the marquee) follows the cursor. Make sure that every object you want to select falls completely within this rectangle, or CorelDRAW! will not select it.

3. When you have enclosed the last object you want to select within the marquee, release the mouse button. The highlighting box appears, encompassing all of the objects within the selected area.

If you want to exclude some of the objects that fall within the selected area, you can deselect them using (Shift). Lasso the entire group of objects first, depress and hold (Shift), and click on a particular object's outline to deselect that object. You can also use the status line and preview window as "quality control" aids to guide you in selecting exactly the objects you want.

Perform the following exercise to gain skill at selecting objects quickly with the marquee. Use magnification, status line information, and the preview window to make the selection process more efficient. Use (Shift) to fine-tune your selection and add or subtract objects to or from the group you selected with the marquee.

6

1. Open the file LANDSCA3.CDR. Note that the poplar tree you drew in an earlier lesson contains several objects: the ellipse that forms the main body of the foliage, a few curves that form the foliage, and curves that make up the trunk. Since all of these objects are adjacent to one another, the tree is a perfect example of the types of multiple objects you can select easily with the marquee.

2. Select the Magnification tool and then select the Zoom-In tool from the fly-out menu. Zoom in to display the left half of the picture. As soon as you have magnified this area, the Pick tool becomes highlighted again.

3. Position the mouse pointer above and to the left of the poplar tree. Drag the mouse downward and to the right until the marquee surrounds all of the component objects of the tree completely and release the mouse button. The highlighting box appears and the status line indicates the number of objects you have selected, as in Figure 6–6.

4. Depress and hold (Shift) and then click once anywhere on the outline of the ellipse that makes up the main body of the foliage. CorelDRAW! deselects it and the status line shows there is one less selected object.

5. Click on any white space to deselect all of the objects, and then select New from the File menu to clear the screen.

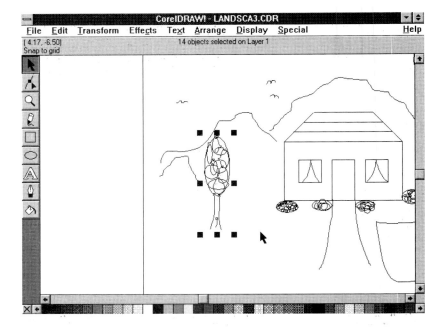

Selecting all
component
objects of the
tree
Figure 6–6.

Selecting All Objects in a Graphic

If you want to perform an operation on all the objects in the graphic, you can select them by drawing a marquee. A quicker way to select all objects is simply to invoke the Select All command in the Edit menu. Using this command, you can be sure that you haven't left out any objects.

You now know several methods for selecting single and multiple objects. Most of the time, selecting objects is a straightforward process in CorelDRAW!. But what if your graphic contains many small objects or you want to select an object that may have several other layers of objects on top of it? The next section makes that process easy for you.

Cycling Through Objects

The object selection techniques you have learned so far in this chapter are adequate for most applications. However, when working with complex drawings containing many objects or superimposed objects,

you may find it more convenient to cycle through the objects using
[Tab]. The following exercise summarizes this technique:

1. Select an object near or on top of the object you want to select.
2. Press [Tab]. CorelDRAW! deselects the first object and selects the
   next object in the drawing. The "next" object is the one that was
   drawn just prior to the currently selected object. Each time you
   press [Tab], CorelDRAW! cycles backward to another object. If you
   press [Tab] often enough, you eventually select the first object again,
   and the cycle begins once more.

The following sections show you two different situations in which you
might choose to cycle through objects in a drawing. The first section
provides an example of objects that have other objects superimposed
on them. The second section demonstrates how to locate and select
small objects in a complex drawing.

6

Cycling Through Superimposed Objects

You may recall that in order to select an object in CorelDRAW!, you
must click on a unique point on its outline, a point not shared by any
other object. This limitation does not apply to most superimposed
objects, because you can usually see separate outlines. The only
exception is when two or more objects are the same size and shape and
overlay one another exactly.

Why might you choose to create two identical overlapping objects? You
could achieve interesting design effects by varying the color and
thickness of their respective outlines and fills, as shown in the example
in Figure 6–7. The window shows that what appears to be a single
rectangle in the editing window is actually two separate rectangles,
each with its own outline color, outline thickness, and fill color. In
Chapters 11, 12, and 13, you will learn more about outlines and fill
colors. For now, you need only know that to select the object in the
background, you can select one object and then press [Tab]. The Fill box
on the right end of the Status Line confirms which rectangle is selected,
although this is not shown in Figure 6–7, which we're referring to.

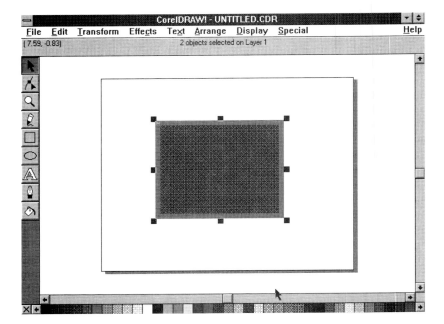

An example of
objects exactly
superimposed
Figure 6–7.

Cycling Through Many Objects

There is another, more common use for Tab when selecting objects in
CorelDRAW!. Clip art, technical illustrations, and other complex
drawings often contain many small objects close together. Even in
magnified view, trying to select one or more of these with the mouse
can be difficult at best. To ease the process, you can select one object,
and then press Tab repeatedly until the fine little detail you are looking
for is selected. CorelDRAW! cycles backward through the objects,
selecting them in the reverse order to which you drew them. To cycle
forward through the objects in a drawing, press Shift-Tab. Perform the
following brief exercise to gain a clearer understanding of how the Tab
key method of selection works.

1. Open the file SNOWBARN.CDR, which should be in your
    SAMPLES directory.

NOTE: You can view the SNOWBARN.CDR drawing in full color or wireframe mode by turning the Display menu option Edit Wireframe off or on, respectively. The full color mode will take much longer to appear on your screen due to the color memory requirements.

2. Choose the Select All command from the Edit menu. The status line shows you that there are 171 separate objects that have not been grouped or combined.

3. Click on any white space to deselect all the objects, and then select the barn as shown in Figure 6–8. Notice the status line says "53 objects selected on Layer 1" (your count might differ slightly depending on where you lassoed the barn), so you have actually selected a group of objects, not a single object. You'll learn more about this later in this chapter under "Grouping and Ungrouping Objects."

6

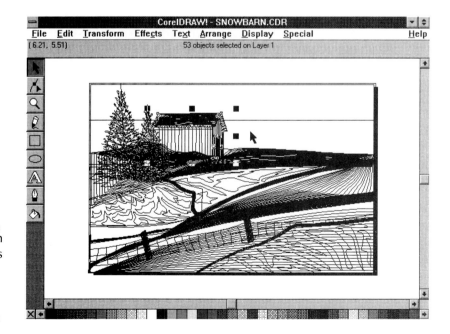

Cycling through multiple objects in a complex drawing
Figure 6–8.

4. Press [Tab] several times. CorelDRAW! cycles through the other objects on the drawing each time you press [Tab].

5. Press [Shift]-[Tab] several times. Now CorelDRAW! selects objects in the opposite order.

6. If you have the patience to cycle through all 171 objects, keep pressing [Tab] or [Shift]-[Tab] until CorelDRAW! selects the barn again.

7. Select New from the File menu to clear the screen before you proceed.

Now you are familiar with all of the available techniques for selecting any number of objects. In the next portion of this chapter, you will begin moving selected objects to other areas within the illustration.

Moving Objects

Once you have selected an object, you can move it by positioning the cursor over any point on its *outline* (not on the highlighting box) and then dragging the mouse along with the object to the desired location. The status line provides you with precise, real-time information about the distance you are traveling, the *x* and *y* components of that distance, and the angle of movement. You can achieve precision worthy of the most demanding technical illustrations if you choose to work with the status line and grid.

Factors such as the number of objects you want to move, whether you want to constrain movement to a 90-degree angle, and whether you want to make a copy of the object determine your choice of technique. The following sections provide examples and exercises that show how to move objects in specific situations.

Moving a Single Object

The appearance of an object undergoes several changes during the process of moving it. Try the following simple exercise to become familiar with those changes.

1. If you have done the exercises earlier in this chapter, your drawing page is in landscape orientation. Change this by choosing Portrait in the Page Setup dialog box reached from the File menu.

2. Select the Ellipse tool and draw an ellipse in the upper area of the page.

3. Activate the Pick tool and select the ellipse. (Recall that you can simply press the (Spacebar) to select the last object you have drawn.) The highlighting box surrounds the ellipse.

4. Move the mouse to any point on the outline of the ellipse, press and hold the mouse button, and begin dragging the mouse downward and to the right. The screen does not change immediately, because CorelDRAW! has a built-in, 3-pixel safety zone; you must drag the mouse at least 3 pixels away from the starting point before the object begins to "move." As soon as you pass the 3-pixel safety zone, the mouse pointer changes to a four-way arrow, and a dotted replica of the highlighting box follows the cursor, as shown in Figure 6–9. This dotted box represents the object while you are moving it; as you can see in the figure, the object itself seems to remain in its original position.

6

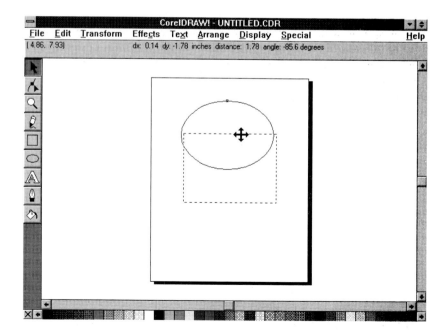

Dragging the dotted move box to move an object
Figure 6–9.

5. When you have dragged the dotted box to the lower edge of the page, release the mouse button. The ellipse disappears from its original position and reappears in the new location.

6. Press ⌈Del⌋ to clear the screen before proceeding.

These are the basic steps involved in moving an object, but CorelDRAW! offers you additional refinements as well. The next three sections provide details on moving multiple objects, constraining an object to move at a 90-degree angle, and retaining a copy of an object while moving it.

Moving Multiple Objects

The technique for moving multiple, selected objects differs very little from the way you move single objects. When more than one object is selected, you simply press and hold the mouse button on the outline of *any one* of the objects within the selected group. The entire group moves together as you drag the mouse. Complete the following exercise to practice moving multiple objects in the LANDSCA3.CDR file.

1. Open the file LANDSCA3.CDR. The Pick tool is automatically activated when you open a new picture.

2. Draw a marquee and lasso the entire poplar tree in the front foreground of the picture to select it. The status line displays the number of selected objects. If you are not sure whether you have selected all of the objects that make up the tree, get confirmation by turning on the preview window and selecting Preview Selected Only from the Display menu.

3. Position the mouse pointer over any of the outlines in the tree, and then drag the mouse until the dotted move box reaches the extreme right of the picture, as shown in Figure 6–10.

4. Release the mouse button. The tree disappears from its original location and reappears in the new location. The tree is now in part of the pond, so you will move the pond next.

5. Select the pond and move it to the left side of the picture where the poplar tree formerly stood.

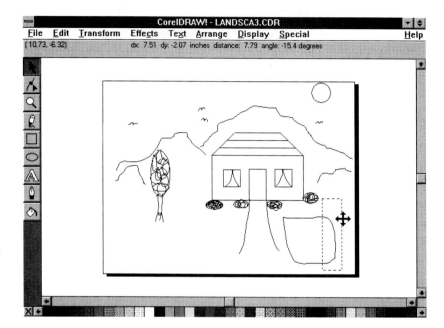

Moving
multiple objects
to a new
location
Figure 6–10.

6

6. Select the Zoom-In tool from the Magnification tool fly-out menu
   and magnify the area around the leftmost bush in front of the
   house. Your viewing area should look similar to Figure 6–11.

7. With the Pick tool, select (lasso) the entire bush, including the
   detail you drew inside it, and then move the bush a little to the left
   of the house.

8. Zoom out to full-page view. Your picture should now resemble
   Figure 6–12.

9. Save this altered picture as LANDSCA4.CDR and leave it on the
   screen.

Moving at a 90-Degree Angle

The techniques you have learned so far in this chapter apply to moving
objects in any direction. But what if the nature of your drawing requires
that you move objects straight up or down or directly to the right or
left? You could, of course, use the coordinates information in the status
line to reposition the object precisely. But CorelDRAW! also offers you a

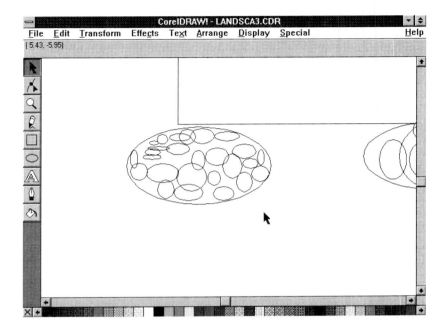

Magnifying the
area around the
leftmost bush
Figure 6–11.

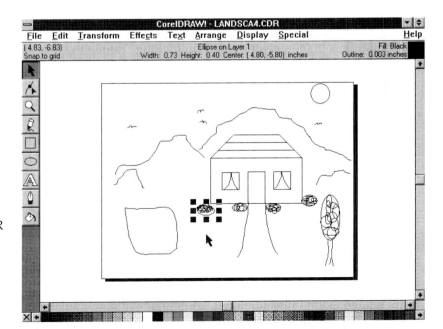

LANDSCA3.CDR
after moving
the
multiple-object
bush
Figure 6–12.

more intuitive method of moving objects at an exact 90-degree angle using Ctrl. This is a convenient method for obtaining precision without slowing your drawing pace. Perform the following exercise to practice constraining the movement of objects vertically or horizontally.

1. With the LANDSCA4.CDR file still displayed, select one of the birds at the top of the picture.

2. Press and hold Ctrl and then drag the bird to the right. Even if you don't have a steady hand, the bird remains at exactly the same horizontal level of the picture. The information on the status line verifies the steadiness of your movement: both the *dy* indicator and the angle indicator remain at zero, as in the following illustration:

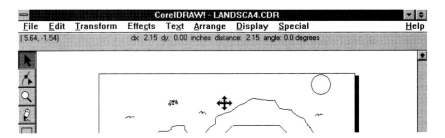

Release the mouse button first and then release Ctrl to reposition the bird at the new location. If you release Ctrl first, the selected object is no longer constrained and can move up or down relative to the starting point.

3. Press and hold Ctrl and the mouse button a second time. This time drag the bird to the left of its current location. Again, the bird remains at the same horizontal level and the *dy* indicator remains at zero. This time the angle indicator displays 180 degrees:

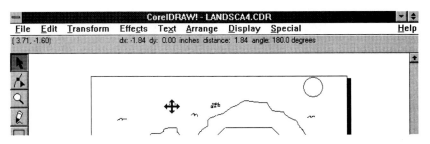

6

Release the mouse button and Ctrl when you reach a satisfactory location.

4. Press and hold Ctrl and the mouse button again and drag the bird directly downward. This time, the *dx* indicator remains at zero, and the angle indicator displays –90 degrees:

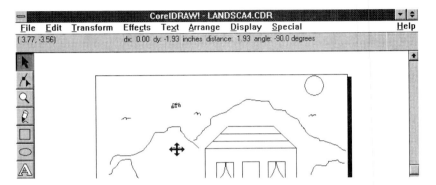

Release the mouse button and then Ctrl to reposition the bird at the new vertical location. If you accidentally release Ctrl first, the selected object is not constrained, and you can move it both horizontally and vertically relative to the original location.

5. Continue to depress both Ctrl and the mouse button and drag the bird directly upward. The *dx* indicator remains at zero, but the angle indicator reads 90 degrees:

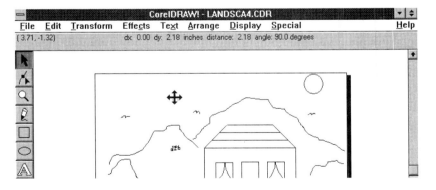

6. Continue practicing this technique with other objects in the picture.

Moving Objects with the Keyboard (Nudge)

As you moved objects in the preceding exercises, you probably found that it was difficult to move an object in very small increments with any precision—most people repeatedly overshoot the mark.

CorelDRAW!, version 2.0 and on, has a feature called *Nudge* which allows you to use the arrow keys on your keyboard to move the selected object(s) by as little as 0.01 inch. The amount by which you move an object each time you press an arrow key and the unit of measure are determined in the Preferences dialog box reached from the Special menu. The default increment is 0.10 inch. Also, since you only have arrow keys pointing in 90-degree increments, nudging is always constrained to 90-degree increments.

1. If you don't have a currently selected object, reselect one of the birds and practice nudging it.
2. Open the Preferences dialog box from the Special menu and verify that the Nudge increment is set to 0.10 inch.
3. Press ➡ three times and then press ⬇ three times. The bird you selected should move to the right and down by 0.3 inch in each direction.

Practice this on your own for several minutes. Nudging can be very useful.

When you are finished, select New from the File menu but do not save any changes.

Copying an Object While Moving It

You may recall that while you are moving an object, it seems to remain in place and you appear to be moving only a dotted rectangular substitute. CorelDRAW! lets you take this feature a step further; you can make an identical copy of the object as you move it. The copy remains at the initial location while you move the original to a new location. This handy technique has interesting design possibilities, as you can discover for yourself by performing the next exercise.

6

1. Select the Grid Setup command in the Display menu, set both the Horizontal and Vertical Grid Frequencies to 2.0 per inch, set the Vertical Origin to 8.5 inches, and turn on Show Grid and Snap to Grid. Click OK. Then, from the Display menu, turn on the Show Rulers option and turn off Edit Wireframe. Since you just finished working on a picture in Landscape (horizontal) mode, the blank page area is also in this mode. (If you worked on something else in the meantime, change to Landscape mode now, using the Page Setup command in the File menu.)

2. Select the Text tool and then select an insertion point at the 1-inch mark on both the horizontal and vertical rulers. Type the word **Arrow** in upper- and lowercase. Select the word with the Pick tool, open the Text roll-up, and set the text attributes to Bangkok Normal and 100 points. Click on Apply, and close the Text roll-up.

3. Press and hold the mouse button over the outline of any letter and begin to drag downward and to the right. Since you have set grid spacing in large units, the dotted move box travels and snaps in visibly discrete increments.

4. Continue holding down the mouse button. When the upper-left corner of the dotted move box snaps to a point half an inch below and to the right of the starting point (about midway down and across the letter "A"), press and release the ⊞ key in the numeric keypad or click the right mouse button in version 2.01 and on. At the right of the status line, the message "Leave Original" appears, as in Figure 6–13. The ⊞ key in CorelDRAW! is also called the Leave Original key.

5. Release the mouse button. An exact copy of the object appears at the starting point and the original appears at the new location.

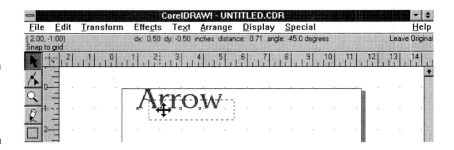

Copying an object while moving it
Figure 6–13.

6. Make four more copies of the text string in the same way, using the ⊕ key or right mouse button and moving the text object in 1/2-inch increments downward and to the right. You should now have a total of six identical text strings.

7. Change the direction in which you move the text object. Make five additional copies as you move the text object downward and to the left in 1/2-inch increments. When you are finished, 11 identical text strings form an arrowhead shape. Your screen should look like Figure 6–14.

8. Select Save As from the File menu, and save this picture under the name ARROW1.CDR.

Using the preceding exercise as an example, you can probably think up additional design ideas for copying single or multiple objects as you move them. Go on to the later sections of this chapter to discover ways of changing the relative order of objects within a drawing.

6

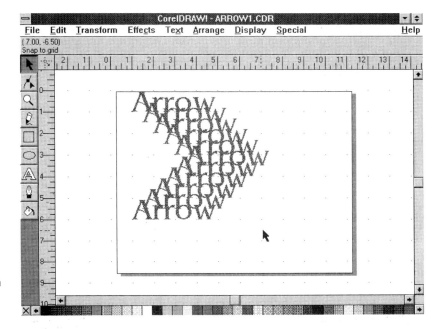

A preview of the arrow design
Figure 6–14.

Arranging Objects

In CorelDRAW!, you can change the order of superimposed objects, group and combine separate objects, and align objects relative to one another. All of these techniques are ways of arranging objects on the page. The Arrange menu contains all of the commands you will use in this chapter, plus a few others (such as Fit Text To Path) that are discussed in Chapter 17, "Combining CorelDRAW! Features." The next four sections demonstrate the most common methods of arranging selected objects.

Reordering Superimposed Objects

When you draw a series of objects, CorelDRAW! always places the object you drew *last* on top of all of the other objects. If you could look at the ARROW1.CDR file in 3D, for example, you would see that the first text string you created is beneath all of the others you subsequently copied.

You can change the order of objects at any time by applying one of five commands in the Arrange menu—To Front, To Back, Forward One, Back One, and Reverse Order—to a selected object or group of objects. The To Front, To Back, Forward One, and Back One commands rearrange the selected objects *relative* to the other objects on the page, but they do not rearrange objects within a selected group. The Reverse Order command, on the other hand, rearranges the objects *within* a selected group, but it does not alter the relationship between the selected objects and the other objects in the picture. Practice working with these commands now, using the clip art file POW_.CDR that came with your software.

1. Select the Open command from the File menu and open the file POW_.CDR in your CELEBRAT clip art directory.

2. Choose the Select All option from the Edit menu. When the drawing is selected, you'll see it's a group of 18 objects.

3. Choose the Ungroup command in the Arrange menu to allow rearrangement of the individual objects.

4. Select ("lasso") the letters "POW!." Be sure to include all of the letters and the exclamation point but not the star shape. You have selected everything you want if you have selected 17 objects.

5. Press F2 to select the Zoom-In tool, click to magnify just the center, "POW!," portion of the image.

6. Pull down the Arrange menu and select the To Back command. The entire group of selected objects disappears behind the background objects, as shown in Figure 6–15. When you apply this command to a group of objects, however, the relative order of the objects *within* the group does not change.

7. With the same group of objects still selected, select the To Front command in the Arrange menu. Now the objects reappear in their original order, in front of the background objects.

8. Leave these objects selected and select the Back One command from the Arrange menu. This command moves the selected objects back behind the first layer beneath them. Since there is only one object behind the 17 that make up the word, this has the same effect as To Back.

9. Select the Forward One command to return the objects to their original order on the screen. Leave this drawing on the screen for the next exercise.

6

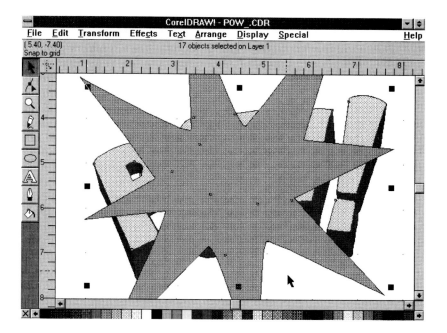

Using the To Back command on selected objects

Figure 6–15.

Grouping and Ungrouping Objects

Selecting multiple objects with the marquee or Shift key is fine if you want to apply certain commands or operations to them on a one-time basis only. However, most drawings contain subsets of objects that belong together, such as the elements of a logo on a business card. If you want the same set of objects to form a single entity at all times, consider *grouping* them instead of merely selecting them.

To group multiple objects, you first select them and then apply the Group command in the Arrange menu. Thereafter, the group responds to any operation collectively. You can move, align, color, and outline them together, without individually selecting each component of the group. However, CorelDRAW! still "knows" that the component objects have separate identities. As a result, you cannot apply the Reverse Order command to a group or reshape the group using the Shaping tool. You can also create groups within groups, and then use the Ungroup command to break them down into their component objects again.

In the last exercise, all objects in the POW_.CDR file were selected and then ungrouped. Continue working with the POW_.CDR file to become familiar with the basics of grouping and ungrouping objects.

1. The group made up of the word "POW!" should still be selected. The status line should display the message "17 objects selected on Layer 1," as shown in Figure 6–16.

2. Select the Group command in the Arrange menu. The status line message changes immediately from "17 objects selected on Layer 1" to "Group of 17 objects on Layer 1."

3. Open the Arrange menu and notice that Reverse Order is dim—it isn't available, since the selected objects have been grouped. Select Ungroup, and then select the Reverse Order command from the Arrange menu. The 17 objects that used to form the group are now reversed in order—what was on the top is now on the bottom relative to the other 16 items in the group. The only change is *within* the group.

4. Select the Reverse Order command again from the Arrange menu. The original order returns.

5. Select the Group command from the Arrange menu. The message in the status line changes back to "Group of 17 items on Layer 1."

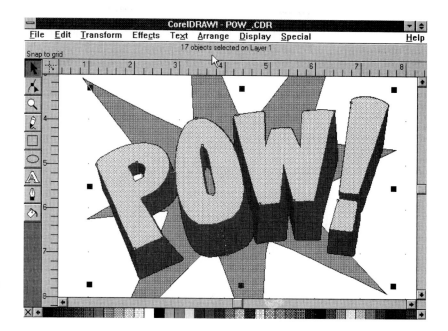

Grouping
multiple objects
Figure 6–16.

6. Press `F3` to Zoom-Out and return to a normal screen.

7. Press and hold the mouse button at any point along the outline of any of the letters in "POW!" and drag the mouse with the selected objects to the bottom of the screen. The entire group moves together and relocates when you release the mouse button as shown in Figure 6–17.

8. Practice moving the group around, ungrouping, forming new groups, rearranging the layers, and moving various objects in relation to one another.

Before and after grouping objects and text strings, look at the menus to see how grouping affects which commands you can and cannot select.

9. When you are done, select New from the File menu to clear the screen before proceeding. Do not save any changes to this picture.

Moving the
entire
foreground
group
Figure 6–17.

Combining and Breaking Objects Apart

The Arrange menu contains two sets of commands that seem almost identical in content, but are actually two different operations: Group/Ungroup and Combine/Break Apart. Combining objects differs from grouping them in several complex respects that are beyond the scope of the current chapter; you will gain more experience with the Combine command in Chapter 17. In general, however, you use Combine in the following situations:

✦ When you want multiple objects to become a single object *that you can reshape* with the Shaping tool

✦ When the objects contain many nodes and curves and you want to reduce the total amount of memory they consume

✦ When you want to create special effects such as transparent masks, behind which you can place other objects.

In these situations, simply grouping objects would not yield the desired results.

Later chapters contain several examples of creative uses for the Combine command. There is one interesting use of Combine, however, that you can practice in this chapter. Recall that when you first activated the preview window in this chapter, you couldn't distinguish the component objects of the TEACUP2.CDR file because they all contained a default fill of black. If you combine objects with other objects contained within them, however, the net result is a reverse video effect that makes alternating objects transparent and creates contrast. For a clearer understanding of how this works, try the following exercise.

1. Open the TEACUP2.CDR file. The window displays a solid black mass because you haven't yet applied different fill colors or outlines to separate objects, as shown in Figure 6–18.

2. Press Shift-F9 to go to Wireframe and select both the larger rectangle that forms the outline of the handle and the inner rectangle. Use either the marquee or the Shift key method. When you are done, the status line should say "2 objects selected on Layer 1."

6

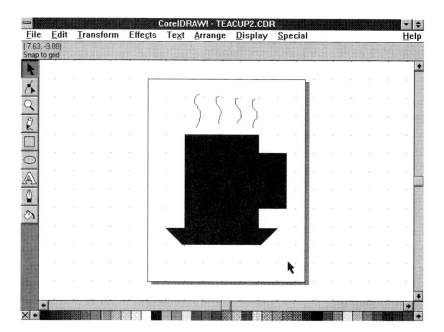

Magnifying the handle of the teacup
Figure 6–18.

3. Select the Combine command from the Arrange menu. Press
    [Shift]-[F9] again to turn off Wireframe and the inside of the inner
    rectangle becomes transparent, as shown in Figure 6–19. This
    "special effect" comes about because the Combine command
    causes all overlapping areas in a graphic to appear transparent.
    Notice that the status line now refers to the combined object as a
    single curve object.

4. Because of the hollow areas you created when you selected the
    Combine command, you can now distinguish the handle from the
    rest of the cup.

5. Save this file under the new name TEACUP3.CDR.

6. Select the newly combined handle if it is not still selected, and
    then select the Break Apart command from the Arrange menu. All
    objects revert to their previous state and become black again.

7. Clear the screen using the New command in the File menu. Do not
    save any changes.

Using the
Combine
command to
create a hollow
inner region
Figure 6–19.

Aligning Objects

Earlier in this chapter, you saw how you can move objects precisely using the (Ctrl) key as a substitute for the grid. The Align command in the Arrange menu offers you another quick and easy method for aligning selected objects without having to spend all of your drawing time measuring. To align objects, you simply select the objects, click on the Align command, and then adjust the horizontal and vertical alignment settings in the Align dialog box.

You could try to memorize the abstract effects of all 15 possible settings, but experiencing those settings for yourself might be more meaningful. In the following exercise, you will create the surface of a billiard table complete with six pockets, combine all the elements of the table into one object, and then add a billiard ball and apply various alignment settings to the ball and the table.

6

1. Start with the page in Landscape orientation with the rulers and grid displayed, the Snap To Grid turned on, and both the horizontal and vertical grids set to 16 per inch. Select the Rectangle tool and draw a rectangle 9 inches wide and 4 inches deep. This rectangle represents the surface of the billiard table.

2. Magnify the area of the page that contains the rectangle, select the Pencil tool, and draw six billiard "pockets," as shown in Figure 6–20. You can draw the pockets either as curved or multisegment lines, as you wish.

TIP: If you want to draw the billiard pockets as curves, set Freehand tracking in the Preferences Curves dialog box to 10 pixels and then magnify each area as you draw a pocket in it. The smaller the area in which you are drawing, the smoother your curves become. Zoom out when you have finished drawing the fine details.

3. Activate the Pick tool and draw a marquee around the billiard table to select both the table and the pockets and then apply the Combine command in the Arrange menu. This combines the pockets and the table surface into a single object to prevent accidental realignment of the pockets later on in this exercise.

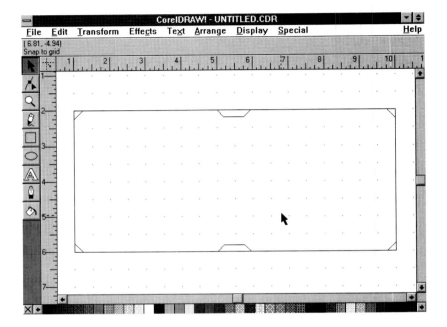

A billiard
"table" with six
"pockets"
Figure 6–20.

4. Select the Ellipse tool, press and hold (Ctrl), and draw a perfectly
    circular "ball" in the center of the table.

5. Press the (Spacebar) to switch to the Pick tool and select the ball, next
    press (Shift) and select the table, and then select the Align command
    in the Arrange menu. The Align dialog box in Figure 6–21 appears.
    The dialog box contains two areas of option buttons; the settings
    in the upper-right area of the dialog box pertain to the relative
    horizontal alignment of the selected objects, while the settings in
    the left part of the dialog box pertain to their relative *vertical*
    alignment. You can set horizontal and vertical alignment
    independently of each other or mix them, for a total of 15 possible
    settings. When multiple objects are selected and you choose the
    Horizontal Left, Horizontal Right, Vertical Top, or Vertical Bottom
    alignment option, CorelDRAW! repositions all but one of the
    objects. The object *last selected* remains in place. All other objects
    are moved to carry out the desired alignment. When you select
    Horizontal Center or Vertical Center alignment, however,

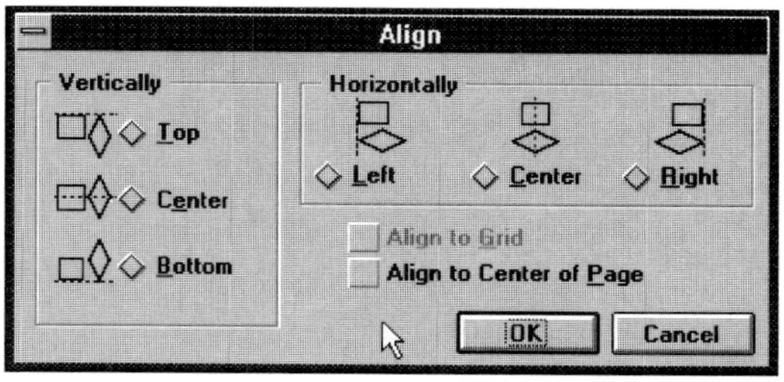

The Align
dialog box
Figure 6–21.

CorelDRAW! repositions all of the selected objects, unless one of
them is already in the desired location.

6. Select Horizontal Left and then click on the OK command button.
The billiard ball reappears in position (1) in Figure 6-22, aligned to
the left edge of the table.

If your screen does not look like Figure 6-22 you can see only half
of your table, your table moved, and the ball stayed stationary
then you selected your table first and the ball last. The last object

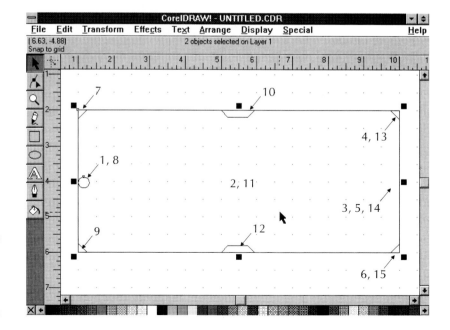

Results of Align
dialog box
settings
Figure 6–22.

selected stays stationary and previously selected items are moved the first time you do an alignment.

7. Select the Align command repeatedly and choose each of the numbered settings in the following list, one at a time. As you select each setting, check the location of the billiard ball against the corresponding callout numbers in Figure 6–22. Six of the following settings will cause your ball to "go" into one of the billiard table pockets.

    (1) Horizontal Left
    (2) Horizontal Center
    (3) Horizontal Right
    (4) Vertical Top
    (5) Vertical Center
    (6) Vertical Bottom
    (7) Horizontal Left-Vertical Top
    (8) Horizontal Left-Vertical Center
    (9) Horizontal Left-Vertical Bottom
    (10) Horizontal Center-Vertical Top
    (11) Horizontal Center-Vertical Center
    (12) Horizontal Center-Vertical Bottom
    (13) Horizontal Right-Vertical Top
    (14) Horizontal Right-Vertical Center
    (15) Horizontal Right-Vertical Bottom

If you do the above alignments without reselecting the ball and the table, you will notice that the first time you do the alignment to the horizontal left, the ball moved as you would expect. The second alignment, the table moved, the third time, the ball moved again and so on, switching back and forth between objects. If you want the table to remain stationary, you must reselect first the ball and then the table before each pair of alignments.

The Align dialog box has two additional options, Align to Grid and Align to Center of Page. When used, you want to set either of these options before setting the horizontal and/or vertical alignments. Try both of these options now.

1. Open the Align dialog box and click on Align to Center of Page. Notice that the Center Horizontal and Center Vertical alignment have also been selected as a default. Click on OK. The ball returns

to the center of the table and both objects are positioned in the center of the page as they were when you started this exercise.

2. Again select Align to Center of Page from the Align dialog box. Then click on Left Horizontal and Top Vertical and click on OK. The ball moves to the upper-left corner of the table and the upper-left corner of the table moves to the center of the page as shown in Figure 6–23.

In Align to Center of Page, the objects first position themselves in accordance with the Horizontal and Vertical alignment instructions, and then the common point of alignment is positioned in the center of the page.

1. Click on anything other than the ball or the table to deselect them both, then click on the table to select only it.

2. In the Grid Setup dialog box reached from the Display menu, set both the Horizontal and Vertical Grid Frequencies to 2.

6

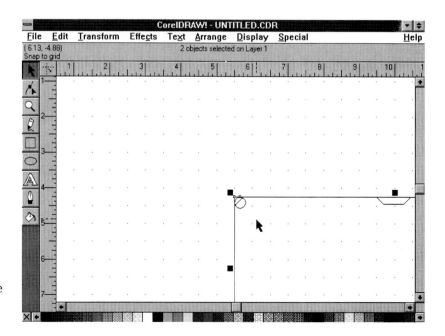

Upper-left corner aligned to center of page
Figure 6–23.

3. Using the arrow keys, nudge the table so that it is away from grid lines in both directions.

4. Select Align to Grid in the Align dialog box, click on Left Horizontal and Top Vertical, and click on OK. The table will move to the nearest grid point that is up and to the left of the table's original position.

The Align to Grid command does not position objects in relation to each other but rather it individually aligns objects (all that are selected) in relation to the nearest grid point in the direction specified by the horizontal and vertical alignment commands.

Experiment on your own, perhaps with other objects in drawings you have already created. Other objects may align in a slightly different way, depending on the order in which you select alignment settings.

When you are through practicing using the align feature, clear the screen using the New command in the File menu. Do not save any changes.

Layers

CorelDRAW! 3 has the ability to design your drawing in different layers. Just as you can stack transparencies on an overhead projector, you can design your drawing in distinct layers so that you can hide certain objects, prevent certain objects from being changed, and control the printing of the drawing by layer. This last feature is important in more complex drawings where printing time becomes a factor.

You probably noticed in the examples throughout this book that the Status Line displays the current object followed by the words "on Layer 1." This is the layer assigned to all new drawings. You can have as many layers as you want, but new objects are placed only on the active layer.

Layering is controlled by the Layers roll-up window, the first option on the Arrange menu. When opened through the Arrange menu (or by pressing Ctrl-1) the Layers roll-up appears.

The three layers which appear in the Layers roll-up are CorelDRAW!'s defaults: Layer 1, Guides, and Grid. (The third layer, Grid, is active only if "Show Grid" is selected first.) The highlighted Layer 1 is the active layer and all new objects and text will be on it. A layer becomes active when you select and highlight its name in the Layers roll-up window.

The Guides layer contains any guidelines that you may choose. These are the same guidelines available from the Display menu, and drawings made on other layers will snap to them. You can also draw on the Guides layer, by making it the active layer. The Grid layer is similiar to the Guides layer, except you cannot make it the active layer. Subsequently, it is a locked layer on which nothing can be drawn. The Grid layer is simply a series of points that can help you draw accurately in other layers.

Layer Features

Clicking on the right pointing arrow below the Layers roll-up window's title bar opens up a fly-out menu which allows you to create a new layer, or to edit, delete, copy, or move existing layers. Additionally, you can change the stacking order of your layers, or use multi-layering to select any object on any layer.

6

Creating or Editing a Layer

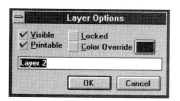

When either New or Edit is selected, the Layer Options dialog box opens. This dialog box contains four check boxes. It allows you to choose whether to make a layer visible, printable, or locked. You can also set the Color Override, which determines whether you see your object as a color outline or a black solid on the screen. (The default is a black solid.) You can change the color of the outline by clicking on the color button. Also, there is a text box that displays the name of the current layer. You can rename the layer anything you want, using up to 32 characters. This dialog box can also be displayed by double-clicking on any layer's name in the Layers roll-up window's scroll box.

NOTE: If you double-click on the Guides or Grid layer's name in the Layers roll-up window, the Layers Options dialog box will open with an added Setup button. Depending on which layer is selected, the Guidelines Setup or Grid Setup dialog box will open when Setup is selected.

Deleting a Layer

To delete a layer, simply click on the layer name in the Layers roll-up window and then click on the right pointing arrow. Choose Delete and the layer and all of its objects are deleted. When you delete a layer, the layer below it on the list becomes the active layer.

Moving or Copying Objects or Text From One Layer to Another

The procedures are the same for moving and copying objects and text from one layer to another. First, you must select the object you want to move or copy. You can tell which layer it is on by the displayed message on the status line. Next, from the Layers roll-up window, click on the right pointing arrow and choose either Move To or Copy To. A "To?" arrow appears. Finally, click the "To?" arrow on the new layer in the Layers roll-up window where you want the object located.

Multi-layering

Generally, in order to select an object, it must be on the active layer. By choosing the Multilayer option from the Layers roll-up window menu, you can select and edit any object regardless of the layer on which it resides. There are two things to note about multi-layering: First, locking a layer overrides the multilayer option's access to objects on that layer. Second, in order to perform the moving and copying features, MultiLayer must be active.

Changing the Layer Stacking Order

The order in which the layers are listed in the Layers roll-up window is the same order in which the layers are stacked in your drawing; the top being first and the bottom last. To change the existing order, drag the layer name you want to move from its present location in the scroll box, and place it on top of the name of the layer you want it to overlay in your drawing. When you release the mouse button, the list will be rearranged—as will the order of the layers in your drawing.

By now, you have had an opportunity to practice all of the functions of the Pick tool that do not require you to change the size or structure of selected objects. In Chapter 7, "Transforming Objects," you will explore the transformation mode of the Pick tool, and learn to stretch, scale, rotate, skew, and mirror a selected object or group of objects.

6

C H A P T E R

7 TRANSFORMING OBJECTS

In Chapter 6, you learned how to use the Pick tool to select, move, and arrange objects. In this chapter, you will use the Pick tool to transform the size or shape of selected objects.

When you transform an object with the Pick tool, you do not alter its fundamental shape; a rectangle continues to have four corners and an ellipse remains an oval. (This is not the case when you reshape an object using the Shaping tool, which you will learn about in Chapters 8 and 9.) The five basic transformation techniques you will learn in this chapter enable you to stretch, scale, mirror, rotate, and skew an object in any direction. You will also learn how to retain a copy of the original object, repeat transformations automatically, and return an object to its original format even if you have transformed it several times.

The exercises in this chapter introduce not only the basic skills that make up the art of transformation, but also the alternative ways you can practice them. CorelDRAW! lets you customize the way you work when transforming objects. If you like to work interactively, you can carry out these functions using the mouse and keyboard alone. For a little extra guidance, you can look to the status line and rulers. And, if you have to render a technical illustration that requires absolute precision, you can specify transformations using the commands and dialog boxes in the Transform menu.

Throughout most of this chapter, you will practice each skill using a sample text string that you create in the following section. However, the stretch, scale, rotate, and skew functions of CorelDRAW! work exactly the same way with multiple selected objects as with single ones. In later exercises, you can practice combining transformation operations with other skills you have learned in previous chapters.

Stretching and Mirroring an Object

As you discovered in Chapter 6, a rectangular highlighting box, made up of eight black boundary markers, surrounds an object when you select it. These boundary markers, shown in Figure 7–1, have special functions in CorelDRAW!; you use them to stretch and scale objects. When you *stretch* an object, you change its *aspect ratio* (the proportion of its width to its height), because you lengthen or shorten it in one direction only. When you *scale* an object, you change the object's length and width at the same time, so the aspect ratio remains the same. To stretch an object, you must drag one of the four *middle* boundary markers, as shown in Figure 7–1. To scale an object, you drag one of the four boundary markers in the *corners* of the highlighting box.

This section covers all of the available techniques for stretching objects. You have the additional option of creating a mirror image or making a copy of the original object as you stretch it. The exercises in this section

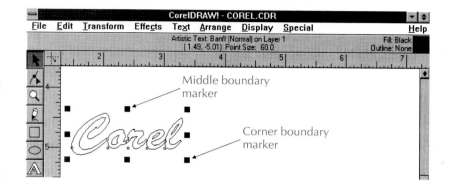

introduce you to both the interactive and menu-assisted methods for
stretching, mirroring, and copying objects.

If you prefer to work interactively, bypassing menu commands and
dialog boxes, you can stretch a selected object using the mouse and
keyboard alone. You do not sacrifice precision when you work this way,
for the status line assists you in setting precise values as you stretch an
object. Practice stretching a text string interactively in the following
sections.

Stretching Horizontally

You can stretch an object in either a horizontal or vertical direction. In
the following exercise, you will create a text string and stretch it toward
the right.

1. Make sure your page is in portrait format before you begin. If it is
   not, choose the Page Setup command from the File menu and
   select the Portrait and letter option buttons.

2. Make certain the Edit Wireframe command in the Display menu is
   still selected with a check mark, and turn on Show Rulers. Also
   from the Display menu, select Grid Setup. In the Grid Setup dialog
   box, turn off the Show Grid and Snap to Grid options, set the
   vertical grid origin to 11 inches, then click OK.

3. Select Text Roll-Up from the Text menu, or press Ctrl-2. Set the
   font to Banff, 60 points, click on the Left justify button, then click

on Apply. You can close the roll-up or click the roll-up button and leave only the title bar on the screen.

4. Select the Text tool, then select an insertion point at the 1.5-inch mark on the horizontal ruler and the 5-inch mark on the vertical ruler. When the insertion point appears, type the text string, **Corel**.

5. Select the Magnification tool and choose 1:1 from the fly-out menu.

6. Select the Save As command from the File menu and type **corel.cdr**.

7. Press the ⌷Spacebar⌷ to activate the Pick tool. A highlighting box surrounds the text string immediately, since it was the last object you drew. Your screen should resemble Figure 7–1.

8. Position the pointer directly over the center right boundary marker of the highlighting box. The mouse pointer changes to a crosshair like the one in Figure 7–2.

9. Depress and hold the mouse and drag the boundary marker to the right. The original object seems to stay in the same place, but a dotted rectangular box follows the pointer, which turns into a two-way horizontal arrow as shown in Figure 7–3. As you drag, the status line displays the message: "x scale:" followed by a numeric value and a percent sign. This value tells you by how much you are stretching the selected object in increments of 1/10 of a percentage point.

Preparing to stretch a selected object horizontally **Figure 7–2.**

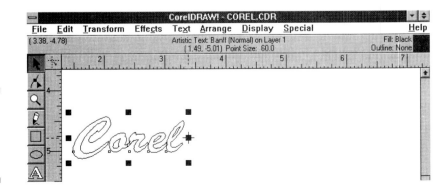

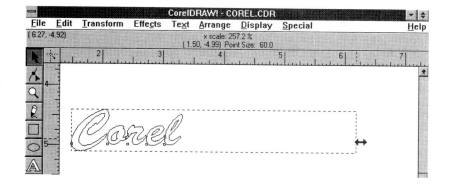

Stretching an object horizontally to the right
Figure 7–3.

10. After you have stretched the object to the desired size, release the mouse button. Corel redraws a horizontally stretched version of the original object, like the one in Figure 7–4.

11. Select the Undo command from the Edit menu to return the text string to its original size. The original text string remains selected for the next exercise.

7

To stretch a selected object to the left instead of to the right, drag the middle boundary marker at the *left* side of the highlighting box. Practice stretching the text string from the left side if you wish, but select Undo after you are finished so that the original text string remains on the screen.

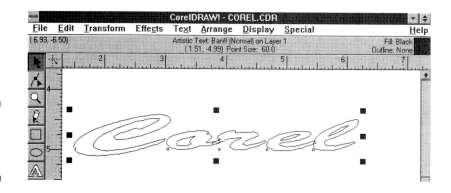

A text object stretched horizontally
Figure 7–4.

NOTE: When the mouse pointer is allowed to cross a window
border, the object will continue to transform until the pointer is
moved back inside the window. This is called Auto-Panning. If you
don't like Auto-Panning, you can turn it off in the Preferences dialog
box reached through the Special menu.

Stretching Vertically

You can also stretch an object in a vertical direction. The mouse pointer
and status line information change to reflect the direction of your
stretch.

1. Select the "Corel" text string if it is not selected already.

2. Position the mouse pointer directly over the top middle boundary
   marker of the highlighting box. The mouse pointer changes to a
   crosshair.

3. Depress and hold the mouse and drag the boundary marker
   upward. The original object seems to stay in the same place, but a
   dotted rectangular box follows the pointer, which turns into a
   two-way vertical arrow, as shown in Figure 7–5. As you drag, the
   status line displays the message: "y scale:" followed by a numeric
   value and a percent sign. This value tells you by precisely how
   much you are stretching the selected object in increments of 0.1%.

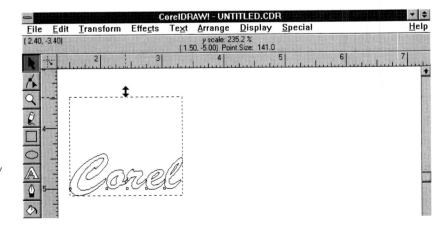

Stretching an
object vertically
and upward
Figure 7–5.

4. After you have stretched the object to the desired size, release the mouse button. CorelDRAW! redraws a vertically stretched version of the original object.

5. Select the Undo command from the Edit menu to return the text string to its original size.

If you wish, practice stretching the text string downward in a vertical direction. When you are finished, undo your changes to the original object and then proceed with the next exercise.

Stretching in Increments of 100%

In previous chapters, you saw how to use Ctrl to constrain your drawing or move operations to fixed increments or angles. The same holds true when you are stretching a selected object. To stretch an object in fixed increments of 100%, press and hold Ctrl as you drag the boundary marker in the desired direction. The status line keeps track of the increments in which you are stretching the object. As always, remember to release the mouse button *before* you release Ctrl, or the object may not stretch in exact increments. In the following exercise, you will triple the width of the original object using Ctrl.

7

1. Select the text string if it is not selected already.

2. Press and hold Ctrl and then drag the right middle boundary marker to the right. Notice that the dotted rectangular outline does not follow the two-way arrow pointer continuously; instead, it "snaps" outward only when you have doubled the width of the object.

3. When the status line displays the message, "x scale: 300.0%" as shown in Figure 7–6, release the mouse button first and then Ctrl. The text string redisplays at triple its original width.

4. Select the Undo command from the Edit menu to revert to the original unstretched object.

Retaining a Copy of the Original Object

A useful design technique is to make a copy of the original object as you stretch it, so that both the original and the stretched objects appear on the screen. To retain a copy of the original object, just press the +

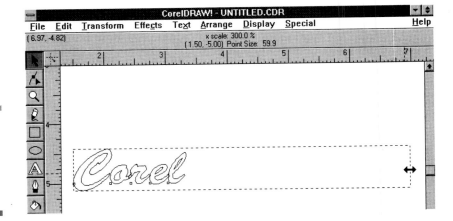

A horizontal stretch constrained to 300% original size
Figure 7–6.

key or click the right mouse button once as soon as you begin the stretching, when the outline box appears.

NOTE: Pressing the right mouse button while dragging to leave the original, does not conflict with the function you assign to the right mouse button in the Preferences dialog box.

You can also retain a copy of the original object when using Ctrl. Try this technique now:

1. Select the text string "Corel" if it is not already selected. Position the mouse pointer over the bottom middle boundary marker and begin to drag this marker downward.

2. As soon as the dotted outline box appears, press the ⊕ key on your numeric keypad or press the right mouse button once. The message "Leave Original" appears at the right side of the status line.

3. Press and hold Ctrl and continue to drag the bottom middle boundary marker downward until the status line reads "y scale: 200.0%."

4. Release the mouse button and then Ctrl. The screen displays both the original and stretched object, as in Figure 7–7.

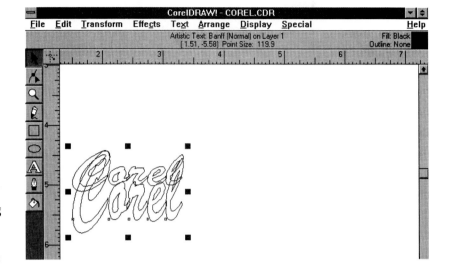

5. Undo your changes to the original text string before continuing.

If the stretched object does not appear in the correct proportions, you either failed to press and hold Ctrl, or you released Ctrl before releasing the mouse button. Keep practicing until you feel comfortable with the technique, but remember to undo your changes. In the next exercise, you will create mirror images of both the original and stretched text strings.

Creating a Mirror Image

Using the middle boundary markers on the highlighting box, you can create a horizontal or vertical mirror image of an object. You have several choices of technique, depending on your needs. If, for example, you choose to retain a copy of the original object, you need to use the + key or click the right mouse button. If you choose to make the size of the mirror image an exact multiple of the original, you need to use Ctrl. You can just as easily decide not to copy the original object, or make the mirrored object a custom size. In every case, however, you will drag the *opposite* center boundary marker until it "flips" in the direction in which you want the mirror image to appear.

The following exercise assumes that you want to create a perfect horizontal mirror image of an object, like the one in Figure 7–8. In this figure, the original object is retained but neither the original nor the mirrored object is stretched. At the end of the exercise are suggestions for obtaining other results.

1. Select the text string "Corel" if it isn't selected already.
2. Position the mouse pointer over the left middle boundary marker and begin to drag this marker to the right.
3. As soon as the dotted outline box appears, press the ⊕ key on your numeric keypad or click the right mouse button once. The message "Leave Original" appears at the right side of the status line.
4. Press and hold Ctrl and continue to drag the marker to the right. The Ctrl key ensures that the size of the mirrored object will be an exact multiple of the original, in this case the identical size (100%).
5. When the dotted outline box "snaps" beside the original object and the status line reads "x scale: –100.0%," as in Figure 7–9, release the mouse button and then Ctrl. CorelDRAW! redraws the screen showing both the original and the mirrored object, as in Figure 7–8. The mirrored object is selected. If your text strings look different, select Undo and try the exercise again.
6. Press Alt-Backspace for Undo and to return the text string to its original unmirrored state.

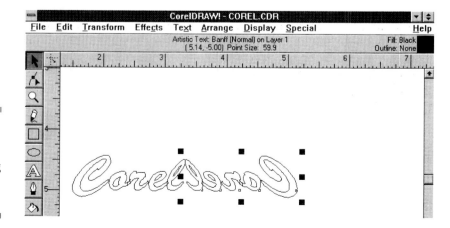

Retaining a copy of the original object while mirroring it
Figure 7–8.

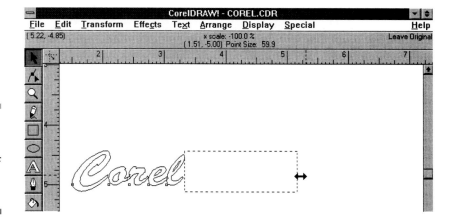

Creating a
perfect
horizontal
mirror image of
an object
Figure 7–9.

You can vary this exercise to achieve different results. For example, to create a vertical mirror image that appears beneath the object, drag the upper middle boundary marker downward. To make the mirror image double or triple the size of the original, keep stretching the mirror object using Ctrl. To make the mirror image a custom size, just drag the boundary marker *without* using Ctrl. If you want to create a mirror image only, without retaining the original object, do not use the ⊕ key or the right mouse button.

If you want to create a mirror image appearing at a diagonal to the original object, you first need to be familiar with how to scale an object. See the section, "Scaling an Object", later in this chapter for instructions.

The Stretch & Mirror Command

If you find the use of the mouse and the keyboard controls inconvenient, you can perform all of the possible stretch operations using the Stretch & Mirror command in the Transform menu. The dialog box that opens when you select this command allows you to choose the direction of the stretch, specify the exact amount of stretching, retain a copy of the original object, and create horizontal or vertical mirror images.

7

Stretching an Object

Take another look at the COREL.CDR file that you created in the first part of this chapter. Then try the following exercise to become familiar with the Stretch & Mirror command.

1. Select the "Corel" text string and then click on the Stretch & Mirror command from the Transform menu. The dialog box shown in Figure 7–10 appears. The controls in the center of the dialog box let you specify the direction and amount of stretch in increments of 1%. The controls at the right allow you to mirror the object horizontally or vertically. The Leave Original checkbox determines whether you make a copy of the original object as you stretch or mirror it.

2. Set the numeric value next to Stretch Vertically to 175%, using either the scroll arrow or the keyboard, and then select OK. The text string has increased in height. Notice, however, that when you stretch an object using the Stretch & Mirror dialog box instead of the mouse, the stretched object is centered on the same position as the original. If you want it to appear in another location, click on the object's outline and drag it to the desired location.

3. Select the Clear Transformations command from the Transform menu to return the object to its original size. (You can also use Undo.)

4. Select the Stretch & Mirror command again, set the Stretch Horizontally value to 175%, and then select OK. This time, the text string increases in width.

The Stretch & Mirror dialog box

Figure 7–10.

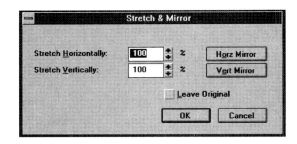

5. Clear the current transformation by selecting the Clear Transformations command in the Transform menu. Then select Stretch & Mirror again. This time, you will constrain the stretch of the image to an exact multiple of the original, as you did using Ctrl and the mouse button.

6. Set the Stretch Vertically value to 300% and then click on the Leave Original checkbox to retain a copy of the original object.

7. Select OK to exit the dialog box. CorelDRAW! redisplays the original object against a vertically stretched image three times the size of the original. Notice that when you use the Stretch & Mirror dialog box for these operations, the stretched object is superimposed on the original and both objects share a common center point as shown in Figure 7–11. If you want the stretched object to appear above, below, or to the side of the original, you must drag its outline to the desired location.

8. To erase the transformed copy of the object so that only the unaltered original remains, select the Undo command from the Edit menu.

7

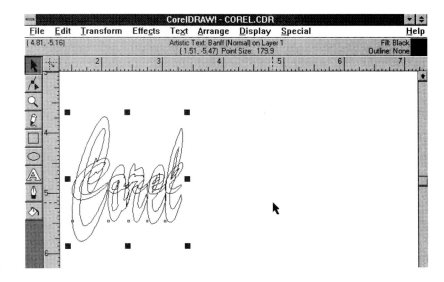

300% vertical transformation sharing same center with original
Figure 7–11.

CAUTION: If you desire to erase the copy of the original object after a transformation that leaves the original in place, use the Undo command rather than the Clear Transformations command. If you use the Clear Transformations command, the transformed object on the top layer is not erased, but instead becomes an exact copy of the original. The transformation is cleared, but not the object itself. As a result, what looks like one object on the screen is actually two, superimposed, objects.

Mirroring an Object

The following exercise shows you how to create a vertical or horizontal mirror image using the Stretch & Mirror command instead of the mouse and keyboard. Once you create a mirror image, you can choose whether or not to retain a copy of the original object. You should continue working in actual size viewing magnification for this exercise.

1. With the text string in the COREL.CDR file selected, select the Stretch & Mirror command from the Transform menu.

2. Click on the Vert Mirror command button in the Stretch & Mirror dialog box. Notice that the value next to Stretch Vertically becomes a negative number automatically. Leave this value at −100%.

3. If a checkmark appears in the Leave Original checkbox, click on the checkbox again to remove it. Then select OK to exit the dialog box. A vertical mirror image of the object replaces the original, as shown in Figure 7–12.

4. Select Clear Transformations to return the object to its original state.

5. Select the Stretch & Mirror command again, but this time click on the Horz Mirror command button. Notice that the Stretch Horizontally value becomes a negative number automatically.

6. Select OK to exit the dialog box. A horizontal mirror image of the original text appears.

7. Select Clear Transformations to return the image to its original state.

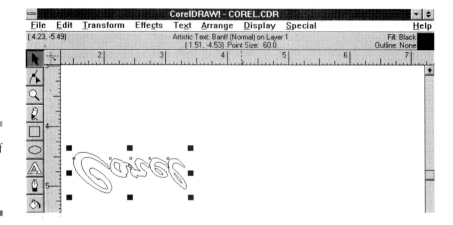

A vertical
mirror image of
the original
object
Figure 7–12.

You can customize the settings in the dialog box to achieve different
results. If you want to merge a copy of the original object with the
mirrored version, for example, just click on the Leave Original
checkbox. If you want to make the mirror image larger or smaller than
the original, set the Stretch Horizontally value accordingly. Remember
that this value must always be a negative number if it is to result in a
mirror image.

Keep in mind, too, that when you use the Stretch & Mirror dialog box
instead of the mouse to create a mirror image, the mirror image
occupies the same position as the original. If you want the mirrored
object to appear above, below, or to the side of the original, you must
drag its outline to the desired location.

Scaling an Object

As you have just seen, stretching an object involves changing its size in
one direction (horizontal or vertical) only. When you *scale* an object,
you change its size horizontally and vertically at the same time, thereby
maintaining the same proportions and aspect ratio. You can scale an
object interactively using the keyboard and mouse, or you can scale an
object using the Stretch & Mirror dialog box instead. If you prefer to
work more spontaneously, without menus and dialog boxes, you can
scale an object using the mouse and keyboard controls. Recall that
when you stretch an object, you drag it by one of the *middle* boundary

markers. Scaling an object is similar, except that you drag one of the *corner* boundary markers instead.

To practice scaling objects interactively, try this exercise:

1. Open the COREL.CDR file if it is not open already and select the "Corel" text string.

2. Position the mouse pointer directly over one of the corner boundary markers. You can scale from any corner but, for the sake of this exercise, use the lower-right corner marker. The pointer changes to a crosshair, just as when you prepared to stretch an object.

3. Drag the lower-right boundary marker diagonally downward. As you drag, the pointer changes to a four-way arrow, similar to the move arrow except that it is rotated diagonally, as in Figure 7–13. The original object appears to stay in the same place, but a dotted outline box follows the scaling pointer. The scaling pointer increases or decreases in size, depending on the direction in which you drag the marker. Figure 7–13 shows an object increasing in scale from the lower-right corner marker. Note that the status line displays the message "scale:" followed by a percentage value. This

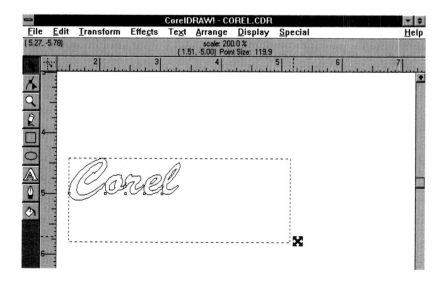

Dragging the scaling cursor to scale an object
Figure 7–13.

value tells you precisely how much larger or smaller you are making the object.

4. When the dotted outline box is the size you want the text string to be, release the mouse button. The selected object reappears in a scaled version.

5. Select Clear Transformations in the Transform menu or Undo in the Edit menu to return the object to its original size.

Scaling in Increments of 100%

To scale an object in increments of 100% of its size, all you need to do is press and hold Ctrl while scaling the object. Just as when you stretched objects using Ctrl, the dotted outline box does not move smoothly but instead "snaps" at each 100% increment. Likewise, the message in the status line changes only when you reach the next 100% increment. Remember to release the mouse button *before* you release Ctrl, or the increments will not be exact.

Keep in mind, too, that an object scaled to 200% of its original size takes up four times the area of the original object, not twice as much, because you are increasing both the height and width of the object by a factor of two.

Retaining a Copy While Scaling

To retain a copy of the object in its original location as you scale it, just press and release the + key on the numeric keypad or click the right mouse button as soon as you begin to scale the object. The status line displays the message, "Leave Original," just as when you leave a copy while stretching an object.

Creating a Diagonal Mirror Image

Using the corner boundary markers on the highlighting box, you can create a mirror image that appears at a *diagonal* to the original object. You have several choices of technique, depending on your needs. If you choose to retain a copy of the original object, you need to use the right mouse button or the + key. If you choose to make the size of the mirror image an exact multiple of the original, you need to use Ctrl. You can just as easily decide not to copy the original object or to make the mirrored object a custom size. In every case, however, you drag the *opposite* corner boundary marker until it "flips" in the direction in which you want the mirror image to appear.

The following exercise assumes that you are going to create a perfect diagonal mirror image of an object like the one in Figure 7–14. In this figure, the original object remains, but neither the original nor the mirrored object is scaled beyond the original size. At the end of the exercise you will find suggestions for obtaining other results.

1. Select the text string "Corel," if it is not selected already.

2. Position the pointer over the boundary marker in the upper-left corner of the highlighting box and begin to drag the marker downward and to the right.

3. As soon as the dotted outline box appears, click the right mouse button or press the ⊕ key on your numeric keypad once to leave a copy of the original object. The message "Leave Original" appears at the right side of the status line, as shown in Figure 7–14.

4. Press and hold Ctrl and continue dragging the boundary marker until the dotted outline box "snaps" at a diagonal to the original object and the status line reads "scale: –100.0%." (The Ctrl key ensures that the size of the mirrored object will be an exact multiple of the original, in this case 100%.)

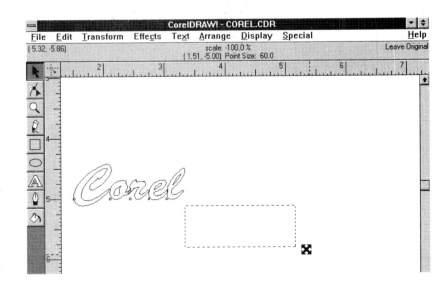

Creating a diagonal mirror image of an object while scaling
Figure 7–14.

5. Release the mouse button and then Ctrl. CorelDRAW! redraws the screen showing both the original and the mirrored object. The mirrored object is selected. If your text strings do not match this figure, try the exercise again.

6. Select Undo from the Edit menu or press Alt-Backspace to return the object to its original unmirrored state.

You can vary this exercise to achieve different results. For example, to place the mirror image at the upper-right corner of the original object, drag from the lower-left corner marker upward. To make the mirror image double or triple the size of the original, keep stretching the mirror object using Ctrl. To make the mirror image a custom size, just drag the opposite boundary marker without using Ctrl. If you want to create a mirror image only, without retaining the original object, do not use the right mouse button or the + key.

Scaling with the Stretch & Mirror Command

If you find the use of the mouse and keyboard controls inconvenient, you can perform all of the scaling operations precisely, using the Stretch & Mirror command in the Transform menu. You can specify the amount of scaling desired, retain a copy of the original object, and create mirror images that appear at a diagonal to the original. Work through the following exercise to become familiar with using the Stretch & Mirror command to scale an object.

1. With the COREL.CDR file open and in an actual size viewing magnification, select the "Corel" text string, and then select the Stretch & Mirror command from the Transform menu.

2. To scale an object, you need to set both the Stretch Horizontally and the Stretch Vertically values to the same number. Set both of these values to 150%, using either the scroll arrow or the keyboard.

3. Make certain that a checkmark does not appear in the Leave Original checkbox, and then select OK. The text string has increased in both height and width. Notice, however, that a scaled object created with the Stretch & Mirror command appears in the same location as the original and has the same center point. If you want the scaled object to appear elsewhere, move it to the desired location.

4. Select the Clear Transformations command from the Transform menu to return the object to its original size.

Retaining a Copy While Using Stretch & Mirror

It is easy to make a copy of the original object from the Stretch & Mirror dialog box. Simply place a checkmark in the Leave Original checkbox before you exit the dialog box.

1. Select the text string "Corel" and then select the Stretch & Mirror command. This time, you will constrain the stretch of the image to an exact multiple of the original, as you did using ⟨Ctrl⟩ and the mouse. You will also leave a copy of the original object in its original location.

2. Set the Stretch Vertically and Stretch Horizontally values to 200% and then click on the Leave Original checkbox to retain a copy of the original object.

3. Select OK to exit the dialog box. CorelDRAW! redisplays the original object along with a scaled text string four times the size of the original. Again, notice that when you copy and scale an object using the Stretch & Mirror dialog box, the scaled object is superimposed on the original and the two objects share a common center point. If you want the stretched object to appear elsewhere, you must move it by dragging its outline.

4. To erase the transformed copy of the object so that only the unaltered original remains, select the Undo command from the Edit menu. If you have moved the copy of the original, select it and press ⟨Del⟩ to clear it.

Stretching and Scaling from the Center

In the previous exercises of stretching and scaling using the mouse, the object was modified in one dimension (stretching) or two dimensions (scaling) from a fixed opposite side or sides. In other words, when you dragged the right side of the object to the right, the left side remained fixed and was in the same position as was the right side of the modified object. Similarly, when you dragged the lower-right corner down and to the right, the top and left sides remained fixed and had the same horizontal and vertical position as the modified object.

When you used the Stretch & Mirror dialog box and modified an object in one or two dimensions, the opposite sides moved proportionally. That is, with the dialog box, the object was being modified from a fixed center point instead of a fixed side or sides. When you changed the horizontal and vertical percentages, all four sides changed, leaving the same center point as the original object.

You can also stretch and scale an object from the center point by pressing (Shift) while dragging with the mouse. This is the same as drawing an ellipse or rectangle from the center by pressing (Shift) while dragging with the ellipse or rectangle tool.

Recall how you stretched and scaled with the mouse originally and see how this changes when you press (Shift):

1. The COREL.CDR text object should be selected on your page in an actual size view.

2. As you did in an earlier exercise, drag the middle boundary marker on the right side to the right several inches. Notice how the left side remains fixed. Release the mouse button and press (Alt)-(Backspace) to undo the modification with the Undo command.

3. Press and hold (Shift) while dragging the right middle boundary marker to the right an inch or so. Notice how the left side now moves a proportionate amount—the left and right sides are moving outward in equal amounts. Release the mouse button and press (Alt)-(Backspace) to undo the modification.

4. Again, as you did before, drag the lower-right corner boundary marker down and to the right several inches. Notice how the left and top sides remain fixed. Release the mouse button and press (Alt)-(Backspace) to undo the modification.

5. Press and hold (Shift) while dragging the lower-right corner boundary marker down and to the right an inch or so. Notice how the top and left sides are now moving proportionately with the right and bottom sides. Release the mouse button and press (Alt)-(Backspace) to undo the modification.

The ability to stretch or scale an object from the center allows you to more easily fill a regular enclosing space.

7

Rotating an Object

When you click on an object once using the Pick tool, you can move, arrange, stretch, or scale it. In addition, the Pick tool can *rotate* and *skew* an object. Rotating involves turning an object in a clockwise or counterclockwise direction, at an angle that you define. When you skew an object, on the other hand, you slant it toward the right, left, top, or bottom in order to create distortion or three-dimensional effects.

As with stretching and scaling, you can rotate an object interactively, using the mouse and keyboard, or you can use the Rotate & Skew command in the Transform menu. If you feel more comfortable working with dialog boxes than with the mouse and keyboard, you can select the Rotate & Skew command after clicking on an object only once. To rotate an object interactively, however, you must either click on a selected object a second time, or double-click on an object that you have not yet selected.

Practice entering the interactive rotate/skew mode now, using the text string in the COREL.CDR file.

1. With the COREL.CDR file open and displayed at the Actual Size viewing magnification, click once on the outline of the text string. The normal highlighting box with its eight black boundary markers appears.

2. Click on the outline of the text string a second time. CorelDRAW! replaces the eight boundary markers with eight two-way arrows, as shown in Figure 7–15. You can drag any one of the corner arrows to rotate the object but, for the sake of this exercise, you will work with the upper-right corner arrow.

3. Position the mouse pointer over the two-way arrow in the upper-right corner of the rotate/skew highlighting box. When the pointer becomes a crosshair, press and hold the mouse button and drag the mouse in a counterclockwise direction. As soon as you begin to drag, the mouse pointer changes to an arc with arrows at either end. A dotted outline box representing the text string begins to rotate in a counterclockwise direction, as in Figure 7–16. Notice that the status line displays the angle of rotation as a positive number.

4. Continue to drag the corner highlighting arrow in a counterclockwise direction until you have rotated the object more

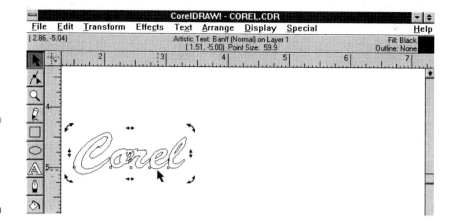

A selected
object in
rotate/skew
mode
Figure 7–15.

than 180 degrees. At that point, the status line begins to display a
negative number for the angle of rotation, and the number begins
to decrease from 180. Use the number on the status line to inform
yourself how far you have rotated a selected object.

5. Continue rotating the text object until the number becomes
   positive again. Release the mouse button when the status line
   indicates an angle of about 17 degrees. CorelDRAW! redisplays the
   object at the selected angle of rotation.

6. Select the Clear Transformations command from the Transform
   menu to return the object to its original angle.

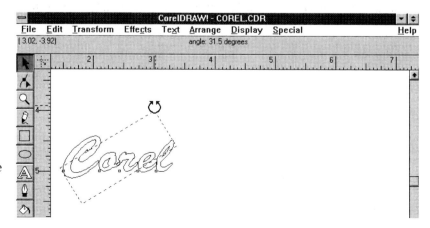

Rotating an
object in a
counterclockwise
direction
Figure 7–16.

7. The text object should again appear selected, with its normal boundary markers. Click on its outline to redisplay the curved-arrow boundary markers. Drag the highlighting arrow in the upper-right corner again, but in a clockwise direction. The angle indicator on the status line displays a negative number until you rotate the text string more than 180 degrees. At that point, the number becomes positive and begins to decrease from 180 degrees downward.

8. Release the mouse button to redisplay the object at the new angle of rotation.

9. Select the Clear Transformations command from the Transform menu to return the object to its original angle.

NOTE: You may sometimes rotate an object several times in succession. The angle of rotation displayed in the status line, however, refers to the amount of the current rotation, not to the cumulative angle.

Continue with the next section to find out how you can constrain rotation of an object to increments of 15-degree angles.

Rotating in Increments of 15 Degrees

As in almost every drawing or editing function of CorelDRAW!, you can use Ctrl to constrain movement in the rotation of objects. Simply press and hold Ctrl while dragging a corner arrow of the rotate/skew highlighting box, and the object rotates and "snaps" to successive 15-degree angles. The status line keeps track of the angle of rotation. As always, remember to release the mouse button before you release Ctrl, or you will not constrain the angle of rotation. You will use the constrain feature in the following exercise.

1. Double-click on the text string if it is not selected already or click once on its outline if it is selected. The two-way arrows appear to show that you are in the rotate/skew mode.

2. Position the pointer over the upper-right corner highlighting arrow until the pointer turns into a crosshair. Press and hold the Ctrl key and the mouse button and drag the highlighting arrow in

the desired direction. Notice that the dotted rectangular box does not follow the rotation pointer continuously; instead, it "snaps" each time you reach an angle that is a multiple of 15 degrees.

3. When you reach the desired angle, release the mouse button first, and then release Ctrl. The object redisplays at the new angle of rotation.

4. Select Clear Transformations from the Transform menu to return the object to its original angle.

Retaining a Copy While Rotating

If you like to experiment with design, you may find it useful to make a copy of the original object as you rotate it. Figure 7–17 illustrates one design effect you can achieve easily. This text pinwheel, suitable for desktop publishing applications, was created by rotating a text string in increments of 30 degrees and copying the original each time.

You can also retain a copy of the original object using Ctrl, but this operation requires a bit more coordination. Try this technique now:

7

1. With the COREL.CDR file open and in an actual size viewing magnification, click on the text string "Corel" if it is already selected, or double-click if it is not selected. The rotate/skew

A text pinwheel created by repeatedly rotating and retaining a copy of a text string
Figure 7–17.

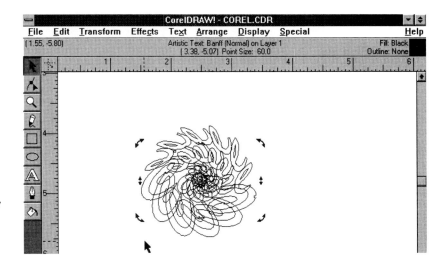

highlighting arrows appear. Use the window scroll arrows to move the text object to the center of the screen. This does not change the orientation of your drawing on the page.

2. Position the mouse pointer over the upper-right highlighting arrow marker and begin to drag this marker upward. As soon as the dotted outline box appears, click the right mouse button or press the ⊕ key on your numeric keypad once to leave a copy of the original.

3. Press and hold Ctrl and continue dragging the arrow marker upward until the status line reads "angle: 30 degrees."

4. Release the mouse button and then the Ctrl key. The screen displays both the original and the rotated object, as shown in Figure 7–18.

5. Continue copying and rotating the text strings four more times at the same angle to create the design shown in Figure 7–17. Then undo your changes to the original text string before going further. Use Undo or press Del to erase the last rotation, then select the remaining objects one at a time and press Del for each object. It may sometimes be easier to use Open in the File menu and again open the original object file.

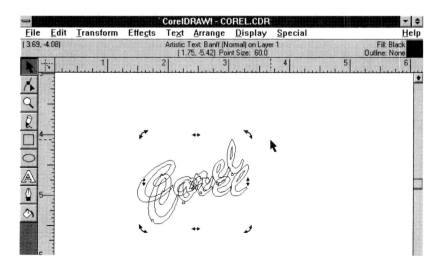

Retaining a copy of the original object while rotating
Figure 7–18.

Changing an Object's Rotation

Look at an object on your screen when it is in rotate/skew mode. In the center of the object is a small dot surrounded by a circle. This graphic aid appears every time you activate the rotate/skew mode and represents the center of rotation of an object. The object turns on this axis as you rotate it. The center of rotation does not have to be the center of the object, however. If you want the object to rotate on a different axis, you can alter the center of rotation freely by dragging the center of rotation symbol to the desired location using the mouse. In the following exercise, you will create a simple text design that involves changing the center of a text string's rotation.

1. Select the text string if it is not selected already and move it to the center of the display. Click on its outlines again to access the rotate/skew mode.

2. When the rotate/skew highlighting box appears, position the mouse pointer over the center of rotation symbol until it becomes a cross. Drag the rotation symbol to the upper-right corner of the rotate/skew highlighting box, as shown in Figure 7–19. Then release the mouse button.

3. Position the mouse pointer over any one of the corner highlighting arrows and begin dragging the arrow in a clockwise

7

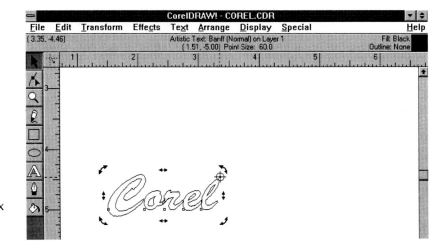

Relocating an object's center of rotation to a corner of the highlighting box
Figure 7–19.

direction. As soon as the dotted outline box appears, click the right mouse button or press the ⊞ key on your numeric keypad once to leave a copy of the original. Notice that because you have changed the center of rotation, the text string turns on its end rather than on its center point.

4. Press and hold Ctrl and continue dragging the marker until the status line shows that you have rotated the text string by –90 degrees.

5. Release the mouse button first, and then Ctrl. Both the original object and the rotated object display at 90-degree angles to one another.

6. Repeat this process two more times, until you have a text design similar to the one in Figure 7–20. To make all the text strings behave as though they were one object, click on the Select All command in the Edit menu, group the text strings, and then reposition the group to the center of the display.

7. Save this figure as 4CORNERS.CDR.

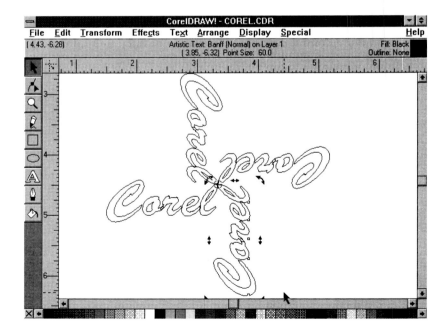

A text design created by rotating and copying an object with an altered center of rotation

Figure 7–20.

8. Clear the screen by selecting New from the File menu.

Your new center of rotation does not have to be a highlighting arrow; you can relocate the center anywhere within the highlighting box. But a corner or boundary of the selected object often proves to be a convenient "handle" when you are performing rotations.

Rotating with the Rotate & Skew Command

If you find the use of the keyboard controls inconvenient, you can perform all of the preceding rotation operations with precision using the Rotate & Skew command in the Transform menu. You can select this command regardless of whether the normal highlighting box or the rotate/skew highlighting box is visible around a selected object. Perform the following brief exercise to familiarize yourself with the workings of the Rotate & Skew dialog box.

1. Open the COREL.CDR file and set the viewing magnification to 1:1. Click once on the text string to select it.

2. Select the Rotate & Skew command from the Transform menu. The Rotate & Skew dialog box appears as in Figure 7–21.

3. Enter a number in the numeric entry box next to "Rotation Angle:". You can enter a number either by scrolling in increments of 5 degrees or by clicking on the numeric entry box and typing in a number in increments of 1/10 of a degree. Note that as soon as you enter a number in this box, the Skew Horizontally and Skew

7

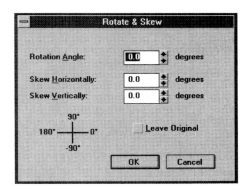

The Rotate & Skew dialog box

Figure 7–21.

Vertically entry boxes become unavailable for selection. You cannot skew and rotate an object at the same time.

4. If desired, click on the Leave Original checkbox to make a copy of the original object as you rotate it.

5. Select OK to exit the dialog box and see the results of your settings. When you are finished, select Undo to return the original object to its former angle. Leave this image on the screen for the next exercise.

That's all there is to rotating an object at the angle and axis of your choice. You can leave a copy of the original object while rotating it, just as when you copy an object that you are stretching or scaling. In the next section, you will practice skewing an object to achieve interesting distortion effects.

Skewing an Object

When you *skew* an object, you slant and distort it a horizontal or vertical angle, thus warping its appearance. This technique can be useful for creating three-dimensional or surrealistic effects. As with the other techniques you have learned in this chapter, you can skew an object either interactively or by using the controls in the Rotate & Skew dialog box.

1. With the COREL.CDR file open and in an actual size viewing magnification, select the "Corel" text string. Then click a second time anywhere on its outline to enter rotate/skew mode.

2. To begin skewing the object horizontally, position the mouse pointer directly over the upper-middle highlighting arrow and drag it to the right. The mouse pointer changes to two half arrows pointing in opposite directions, and a dotted outline box slants to the right, the direction you are moving your mouse, as shown in Figure 7–22. The status line keeps track of the current angle of horizontal skew.

3. When you reach the desired skewing angle, release the mouse button. CorelDRAW! redisplays the object as you have skewed it, as shown in Figure 7–23.

4. Select Clear Transformations from the Transform menu to return the object to its original unskewed state.

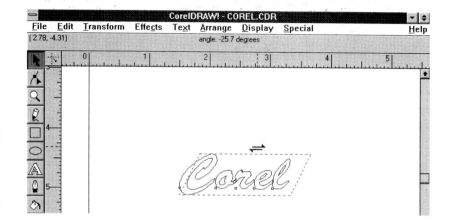

Skewing an
object to the
right
Figure 7–22.

5. Practice different angles of horizontal skewing. You can skew an object up to 75 degrees to the right or left. If you drag one of the middle highlighting arrows along the left or right *side* of the highlighting box, you can skew the object in a vertical direction.

6. When you feel comfortable with basic skewing operations, select Clear Transformations from the Transform menu. Leave the text string on the screen for the next exercise.

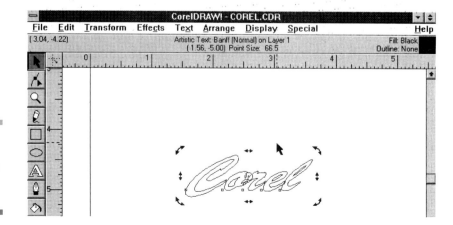

An object
skewed
horizontally to
the right
Figure 7–23.

Skewing in Increments of 15 Degrees

Once again, you can use Ctrl to introduce an extra measure of precision to the interactive transformation of objects. When skewing an object, pressing and holding Ctrl forces the object to skew in increments of 15 degrees. Try using this constraint feature now.

1. Select the text string "Corel" and enter the rotate/skew mode.

2. Position the mouse pointer over the upper-middle highlighting arrow, press and hold Ctrl, and begin dragging the mouse to the right or left as desired. The mouse pointer changes to the skew pointer, and the dotted outline box "snaps" in the desired direction in increments of 15 degrees.

3. When you reach the desired angle, release the mouse button first, and then release Ctrl. If you release Ctrl first, you might not constrain the skewing operation to a 15-degree increment.

4. Select Clear Transformations from the Transform menu to return the skewed object to its original state. Leave the text string on the screen.

Retaining a Copy While Skewing

For an interesting design effect, you can skew an object and then make a copy of the original. As you will see in the following exercise, you can then position the skewed object behind the original to make it seem like a shadow.

1. Select the "Corel" text string and enter rotate/skew mode.

2. Position the mouse pointer over the upper-middle highlighting arrow and begin dragging the arrow to the right. As soon as the dotted outline box appears, press the + key on your numeric keypad or click the right mouse button to leave a copy of the original.

3. Press and hold Ctrl and continue dragging the marker until the status line shows a –60-degree skewing angle.

4. Release the mouse button first and then release Ctrl. The skewed object, which is selected automatically, appears on top of the copy of the original, as in Figure 7–24.

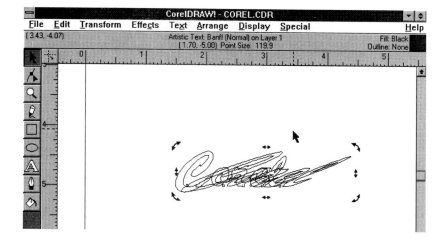

5. Select the To Back command from the Arrange menu to position the skewed object behind the unskewed original.

6. You can manipulate the skewed object like any other object. Click once on its outline to toggle back to select mode, and then scale it to a smaller size by dragging the upper-right corner boundary marker of the highlighting box.

7. Adjust the viewing magnification to fit-in-window and activate the preview window to obtain a WYSIWYG display of the original object and its skewed "shadow." Go to the preview screen by clicking on Show Preview in the Display menu, or by pressing F9 . Your preview should look roughly similar to Figure 7–25. When you learn about filling objects in Chapter 13, "Defining Fill Color," you can refine the appearance of skewed background images to

Preview of a
"shadow"
created by
skewing and
resizing an
object
Figure 7–25.

create a clearer "shadow" than this one. To turn the preview screen off, press F9. This is a toggle key and turns Preview on or off.

8. To remove the transformed copy of the object so that only the unaltered original remains, select the Clear command from the Transform menu.

TIP: CorelDRAW! has included the option of setting the right mouse button to toggle between the editing window and Full screen Preview. If you want to do this, select the Mouse option from Preferences in the Special menu and select Full screen Preview.

Skewing with the Rotate & Skew Command

If you find the use of keyboard controls inconvenient, you can perform all of the possible skewing operations using the Rotate & Skew command in the Transform menu. You can select this command regardless of whether the normal highlighting box or the rotate/skew highlighting box is visible around a selected object. Perform the following brief exercise to familiarize yourself with using the Rotate & Skew command to skew an object.

1. Open the COREL.CDR file and set the viewing magnification to 1:1. Click once on the text string to select it.

2. Select the Rotate & Skew command from the Transform menu. The Rotate & Skew dialog box appears.

3. First, skew the text object horizontally. Enter a number in the numeric entry box next to "Skew Horizontally:". You can enter a number either by scrolling in increments of 5 degrees or by clicking on the numeric entry box and typing in a number in increments of 1/10 of a degree. Only values between –75 and 75 degrees are valid. You will recall that a positive number results in skewing to the left, while a negative number results in skewing to the right.

4. If desired, click on the Leave Original checkbox to make a copy of the original object as you rotate it.

5. Select OK to exit the dialog box and see the results of your settings. When you are finished, select Undo to return the original object to its former angle (and erase the copy, if you have made one).

6. Select the Rotate & Skew command from the Transform menu once more. This time, enter a number in the numeric entry box next to "Skew Vertically:". You can adjust this value in the same way that you adjusted the "Skew Horizontally:" value in step 3.

7. Select OK to exit the dialog box and see the results of your settings. When you are finished, select Clear Transformations from the Transform menu to return the original object to its former angle.

In the final section of this chapter, you will have the opportunity to combine additional transformation techniques and apply your most recently performed operation to other objects in a drawing.

 ## Repeating a Transformation

CorelDRAW! stores the most recently performed transformation in memory until you quit the current session. You can save design and drawing time by automatically repeating your most recent stretch, scale, rotate, or skew operation on a different object or set of objects. Just remember that the second object, the one on which you wish to repeat the transformation, must exist on the screen *before* you perform the transformation the first time. If you perform a transformation and then create another object and try to repeat that transformation on it, nothing happens. Perform the following brief exercise to see how this feature can work for you.

 7

1. With the COREL.CDR file open and in actual size viewing magnification, select the Ellipse tool and draw a long, narrow ellipse well to the right of the "Corel" text string.

2. Press the (Spacebar) to activate the Pick tool. Select the "Corel" text string and then start to drag the lower-right boundary marker downward and to the right. Leave a copy of the original by using the (+) key or by clicking the right mouse button, as described earlier in this chapter. Then use the (Ctrl) key to help you scale the text string to 200%.

3. Select the ellipse that you drew next to the text string.

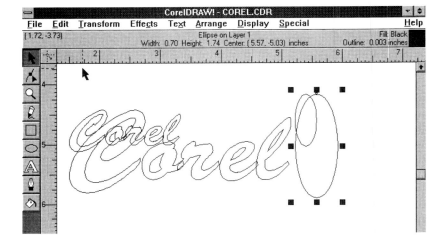

Repeating a
transformation
on a different
object
Figure 7–26.

4. Select the Repeat command from the Edit menu or press the shortcut keyboard combination Ctrl. CorelDRAW! scales the ellipse to 200%, leaving a copy of the original, as shown in Figure 7–26. If the objects extend beyond your viewing window, adjust viewing magnification to fit-in-window.

5. Select New from the File menu to clear the screen. Do not save any changes to your work.

You have seen how stretching, scaling, rotating, and skewing objects can lead to creative ideas for advanced designs. Continue practicing some of the techniques you have learned and see what original ideas you can come up with on your own. Chapters 16 and 17, "Creating Special Effects" and "Combining CorelDRAW! Features," will expand on these and other techniques and provide additional stimulation for your imagination.

CHAPTER

8

SHAPING LINES, CURVES, RECTANGLES, AND ELLIPSES

The power to reshape any object to the limits of the imagination is at the very heart of CorelDRAW!. Using the Shaping tool, you can change any type of object into an image that can showcase your creativity.

The Shaping tool, ⬚, the second tool in the CorelDRAW! toolbox, allows you to change the underlying shape of an object. Although the Pick tool, in transformation mode, allows

233

you to resize, rotate, or skew an object, it leaves the fundamental shape of the object intact. When you edit an object with the Shaping tool, however, it becomes something quite different from what you originally drew.

You can apply the Shaping tool to all object types: lines and curves, rectangles and squares, ellipses and circles, text, and pixel-based (bitmapped) graphics. Shaping functions for text and bitmapped graphics, however, is part of a broader range of editing functions that apply specifically to those object types. You will find information specifically about shaping text in Chapter 9, "Shaping and Editing Text," and about shaping curves to fit traced bitmaps in Chapter 18, "Tracing Bitmapped Images." This chapter covers techniques for shaping lines, curves, rectangles, and ellipses.

About the Shaping Tool

The Shaping tool performs several different functions, depending on the kind of object to which you apply it. You take advantage of the most powerful capabilities of the Shaping tool when you use it to edit curves, but it has specific effects on other object types as well.

When you are working with lines and curves, the Shaping tool is at its most versatile. You can manipulate single curve points (nodes) interactively, move single or multiple curve segments, control the angle of movement, and add or delete curve points in order to exercise greater control over the degree of curvature. You can break apart or join segments of a curve and change one type of node into another. You can even convert curves to straight lines and back again.

When you apply the Shaping tool to rectangles and squares, you can round the corners of a rectangle and turn rotated, stretched, or skewed rectangles into near-ellipses and circles. When you apply the Shaping tool to ellipses and circles, you can create pie-shaped wedges or arcs. If these shaping options for rectangles and ellipses seem limited, you will be pleased to learn that you can convert any object in CorelDRAW! to curves—and then proceed to apply the most advanced shaping techniques to it.

Selecting with the Shaping Tool

You must select an object with the Shaping tool before you can edit it. CorelDRAW! allows you to select only one object with the Shaping tool at a time. Although the Shaping tool affects each type of object in a different way, the basic steps involved in editing are similar with all object types. To select an object for editing,

1. Activate the Shaping tool by clicking on it. The pointer turns into a thick arrowhead as soon as you move it away from the toolbox and toward the page area.

2. If the object you want to work with is already selected, its nodes enlarge in size automatically as soon as you select the Shaping tool, and the highlighting box around the object disappears. The number of nodes varies, depending on the object type and (in the case of curves) the way your hand moved when you drew it. If the object you want to work with is not selected, click on any point of the object's outline with the arrowhead pointer. Enlarged nodes appear on the object, while the status line shows the object type and information about the nodes on the object. If the selected object has multiple nodes, the first node appears larger than the others, as in the example in Figure 8–1. The first node is the one closest to where you started drawing the object. Often this is the farthest to the left on lines and curves, the one at the top left corner in rectangles, and at the topmost point on ellipses.

3. Refer to the chapter that covers your object type for more help on how to edit the shape of that object.

8

Selecting an object with the Shaping tool
Figure 8–1.

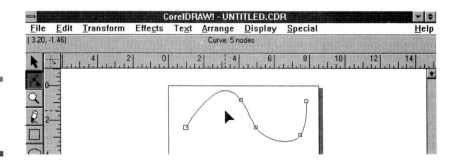

If multiple objects are selected when you activate the Shaping tool, CorelDRAW! automatically deselects all of them, and you must select a single object to edit with the Shaping tool. If you try to apply the Shaping tool to grouped objects, the outlines of the objects become dotted and your mouse actions have no effect. The only time you can edit more than one object simultaneously is when you *combine* the objects prior to selecting the Shaping tool. You will see examples of editing combined objects in the "Shaping Lines and Curves" section of this chapter.

To deselect an object that you are editing with the Shaping tool, either click on the outline of a different object, or select another tool from the CorelDRAW! toolbox.

The following sections show you how to use the Shaping tool to edit specific types of objects. These sections follow the order of the drawing tools in the CorelDRAW! toolbox: lines and curves, rectangles, and ellipses.

Shaping Lines and Curves

The Shaping tool is at its most powerful when you use it to edit a curve. Ways in which you can reshape a curve include moving, adding, or deleting nodes, changing node shape, breaking nodes apart or joining them together, and manipulating the control points that define the shape of a curve segment.

You may recall that every object in CorelDRAW! has nodes, which appear when you first draw an object and become enlarged when you select it with the Shaping tool. Nodes on a curve (shown in Figure 8–1) are the points through which a curve passes, and each node is associated with the curve segment that immediately precedes it. The *control points* that appear when you select a single node with the Shaping tool (see Figure 8–5) determine the curvature of the node and of the curve segments on either side of it. You can use the Shaping tool to manipulate both nodes and curves.

Your options for shaping straight lines with the Shaping tool are much more limited than for curves; lines have no angles of curvature and, therefore, no control points that you can manipulate. When you edit a line segment with the Shaping tool, you can only move the nodes or stretch or diminish the length of the line segment. In the course of creating and editing a complex curve object, however, you often need to fuse curve and line segments, change curves into lines, or turn lines into curves. The Shaping tool allows you to do all of these things, and so a discussion of shaping both kinds of freehand objects belongs together.

Selecting a Line or Curve

You must select a line or a curve with the Shaping tool before you can begin to manipulate its nodes. The status line provides you with information about the number of nodes in the object.

In the following exercise, you will draw a straight line and a freehand curve and then select each object in turn. Turn off the Snap To Grid option before you begin this exercise.

1. Activate your Magnification tool, turn on your rulers if they're not already and zoom in on the upper half of your page. Then, select the Pencil tool and draw a straight horizontal line across the top half of the screen, as shown in Figure 8–2.

2. Below the line, draw a Freehand curve in a horizontal "S" shape. Small nodes appear on the curves.

3. Select the Shaping tool. The pointer turns into an arrowhead, and the S-curve is automatically selected, because it was the last object you drew. The nodes of the S-curve increase in size, and the status line displays the number of the nodes in the curve, as shown in Figure 8–2. The number of nodes in your curve may differ from the number in the figure. Notice that the node farthest to the left is probably larger in size than the others, because it is where you started drawing the curve.

4. To deselect the S-curve and select the line, simply click on any point of the line with the Shaping tool. Only two nodes appear on the line, one at each end. Again, the node farthest to the left is probably larger. The status line displays the message, "Curve: 2 nodes," as shown in Figure 8–3. (As far as the Shaping tool is concerned, every line has the potential of becoming a curve.)

5. Clear the screen before continuing by selecting New from the File menu. Do not save your work.

8

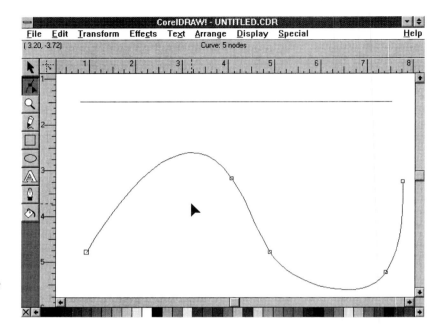

Displaying the
number of
nodes in a curve
Figure 8–2.

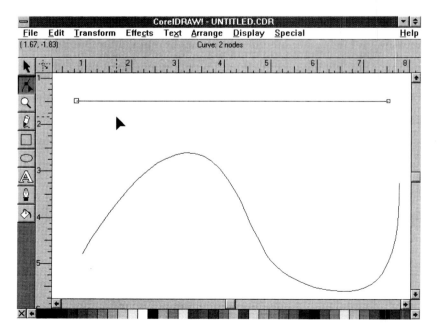

Displaying the
number of
nodes in a line
Figure 8–3.

Your next step in shaping a selected line or curve is to select one or more of its nodes. Continue with the next section to explore the choices open to you.

Selecting Nodes of a Line or Curve

Although you can shape only one curve or line at a time, you can select and shape either single or multiple nodes. The shaping options available to you depend on whether you select one node or several. You can reshape a single curve node interactively in one of two ways: by dragging the node itself or by dragging the control points that appear when you select the node. Moving a node stretches and resizes the associated curve segment(s) but does not allow you to change the angle of curvature. Dragging the control points, on the other hand, allows you to change both the angle of curvature at the node and the shape of the associated curve segment(s). When you select multiple nodes, you can move only the nodes, not their control points; as a result, you reshape all of the selected segments in the same way.

In general, you should select single nodes when you need to fine-tune a curve, and multiple nodes when you need to move or reshape several segments in the same way without changing their angle of curvature.

The exercises in the following sections guide you through the available techniques for selecting nodes in preparation for moving or editing them. Along the way, you will become familiar with the different types of nodes that CorelDRAW! generates and how they indicate the shape of a particular curve.

 TIP: Nodes of a straight line segment are always cusp nodes and contain no control points. They become important only when you begin adding or deleting nodes or changing a line into a curve. You will concentrate on working with curves in the next few sections.

When you click on a single curve node, the status line provides information about the type of node you have selected. There are three

8

node types: cusp, smooth, and symmetrical. Each type of node indicates what will happen when you drag the control points to reshape a curve. In the following exercise, you will practice selecting and deselecting single nodes.

1. Using the Pencil tool, at Actual Size (1:1) magnification and with Edit Wireframe turned on, draw a curve object that looks roughly like Figure 8–4. The object should have sharp curves, gentle curves, and some in between. Don't worry if it doesn't look exactly like Figure 8–4.

2. Select the Shaping tool and click anywhere on the outline of the curve object. The status line indicates that this curve object contains 18 nodes (yours may be different).

3. Click on the node farthest to the left on the selected curve object. The node becomes a black-filled square, and two control points, tiny black rectangles connected to the node by dotted lines, pop out, as shown in Figure 8–5. (You will also see a control point extending from nodes on either side of the selected node.) The

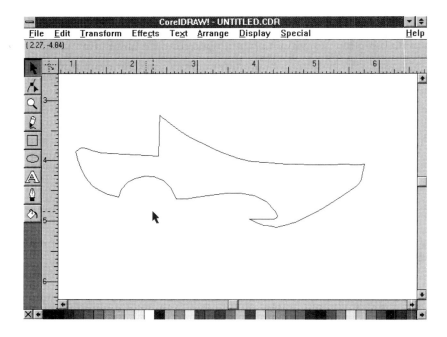

Magnifying the curve object
Figure 8–4.

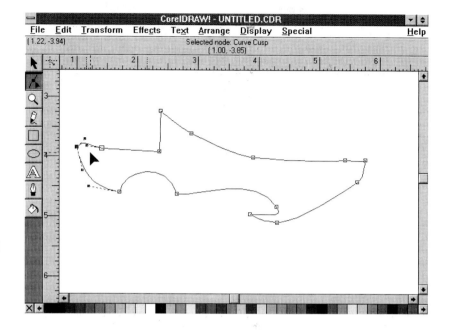

Selecting a
single node and
displaying
control points
Figure 8–5.

message "Selected node: Curve Cusp" appears on the status line.
"Cusp" refers to the node type, which you will learn about shortly.

4. Click on each node in turn to select it and deselect the previous
   node. Each time you select a node, control points pop out, and the
   status line tells you what type of node you have selected. Notice
   that some of the nodes are cusp nodes, while others are smooth.

5. Leave this object on the screen for the next exercise.

CorelDRAW! generates three different kinds of nodes when you draw
lines and curves: cusp nodes, smooth nodes, and symmetrical nodes.
These names describe both the curvature at the node and, in the case of
curve objects, the way you can shape the node. Straight lines contain
only cusp nodes, while curves can contain all three node types.

Cusp Nodes   Cusp nodes occur at the end point of a line or curve or
at a sharp change of direction in a curve. When you edit the control
points of a cusp node, you can alter the curvature of the segment that
precedes the node without affecting the segment that follows it.

Smooth Nodes   Smooth nodes occur at smooth changes of direction in a curve. When you edit a smooth node, you alter the shape and direction of both the segment preceding and the segment following the node. The curvature of the two segments does not change in identical degrees, however.

Symmetrical Nodes   Symmetrical nodes occur where the segments preceding and following the node curve in identical ways. (Symmetrical nodes occur less frequently than other node types in freehand drawing but you can change any node type to symmetrical using the Node Edit menu, which you will learn about shortly.) When you edit a symmetrical node, you alter the shape and direction of the curve segments before and after the node in identical ways.

You can always change the node type by using the pop-up Node Edit menu, as you will see shortly. But you can also control whether the majority of nodes you generate during the freehand drawing process are smooth or cusped. To generate mostly cusped nodes (and create more jagged curves), select the Curves option from the Preferences command in the Special menu, and set the Corner Threshold option in the Preferences—Curves dialog box to 3 pixels or lower. To generate mostly smooth nodes and create smoother curves, set the Corner Threshold option to 8 pixels or higher.

You will become familiar with techniques for moving control points in a moment. First, finish the next section to learn how to select more than one node at a time.

Selecting and Deselecting Multiple Nodes

You select multiple nodes with the Shaping tool in the same way that you select multiple objects with the Pick tool, using either Shift or the marquee technique. When multiple nodes are selected, you are unable to move control points to shape your object. You can only move the nodes and reshape their associated curve segments in a more limited way. Review the selection techniques in the following brief exercise.

1. Select the node that the mouse pointer is aimed at in Figure 8–6. While pressing and holding Shift, select two additional nodes to the left of the first node. As in Figure 8–6, the nodes turn dark but

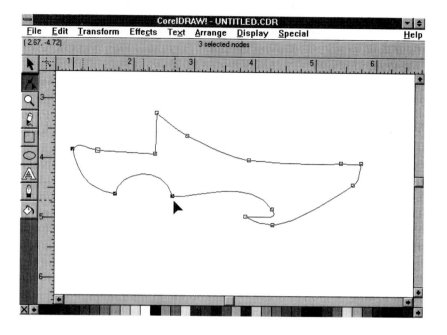

Curve with
multiple nodes
selected
Figure 8–6.

display no control points, and the status line changes to show the total number of nodes you have selected.

2. Deselect the original node farthest to the right of the selected group by pressing and holding (Shift) and then clicking on the node with the Shaping tool. The other nodes remain selected.

3. Deselect all of the selected nodes by clicking on any white space. The curve object itself remains selected for further work with the Shaping tool, however.

4. Select the three nodes at the left side of the object by drawing a marquee around them, as shown in Figure 8–7. The selected nodes turn dark after you release the mouse button, and the status line tells you how many nodes you have selected.

5. Deselect one node at a time using (Shift) and the mouse button, or deselect all of the nodes by clicking on any other node or on any white space.

6. When you have finished, clear the screen by selecting New from the File menu. Do not save the changes you have made.

8

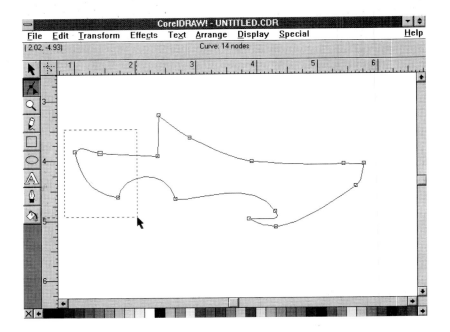

Selecting
multiple nodes
with the
marquee
Figure 8–7.

Now that you are familiar with how to select nodes, you are ready to
begin editing a curve object. You can edit a curve by moving nodes and
control points interactively or by selecting options in a pop-up Node
Edit menu. The next portion of the chapter discusses the first of these
methods.

Moving Nodes and Control Points

You can reshape a curve interactively in one of two ways: by moving
one or more nodes or by manipulating the control points of a single
node. You can move any number of nodes, but in order to work with
control points, you can select only one node at a time.

You move nodes when your aim is to stretch, shrink, or move the curve
segments on either side of a node. The angle of curvature at selected
nodes doesn't change as you move them, because the control points
move along with the nodes. The end result of moving nodes is a limited
reshaping of the selected area of the curve object.

In general, your best strategy when reshaping curves is to move the nodes first. If just repositioning the nodes does not yield satisfactory results, you can fine-tune the shape of a curve by manipulating the control points of one or more nodes. When you drag control points to reshape a curve, you affect both the angle of curvature at the node and the shape of the curve segment on one or both sides of the node. The effects of this kind of reshaping are much more dramatic. The way you move control points is determined by the type of node you select.

Try the exercises in each of the following sections to practice moving single or multiple nodes, manipulating control points, and constraining node movement to 90-degree increments.

Moving a Single Node

To move a single node, you simply select the curve and then select and drag the node in the desired direction. In the following exercise, you will draw a waveform curve, select a node, and move the node to reshape the curve.

1. To prepare for the exercise, make sure that the Snap To Grid and Show Rulers options are turned off. Check to see that all the settings in the Curves option of the Preferences command are at 5 pixels. (This will result in curves with a fairly even distribution of cusp and smooth nodes.) Set viewing magnification to an Actual Size (1:1) ratio.

2. Select the Pencil tool and draw a waveform curve similar to the one in Figure 8–8. Don't be concerned if your curve is shaped a little differently.

3. Select the Shaping tool and then select a node near the crest of one of the curves. Elongate this curve by dragging the node (not the control points) upward and to the right, as shown in Figure 8–9. As you begin to move the node, the status line provides information about dx- and dy-coordinates, the distance you have traveled, and the angle of movement relative to the starting point. Release the mouse button when you are satisfied with the stretch of your curve.

4. Select Undo from the Edit menu to return the curve to its original shape. Leave this curve on the screen for now. You can use it to move multiple nodes in the next exercise.

8

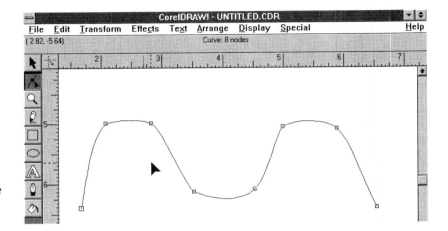

Drawing a
waveform curve
Figure 8–8.

Moving Multiple Nodes

There are many cases in which you might choose to move multiple
nodes instead of a single node at a time. You might move multiple
adjacent nodes, for example, if you need to reposition an entire section
of a curve at one time. Or you might select nonadjacent nodes and
move them all in the same direction for special design effects.
Whatever the case, all you need to do is select the nodes and drag them.

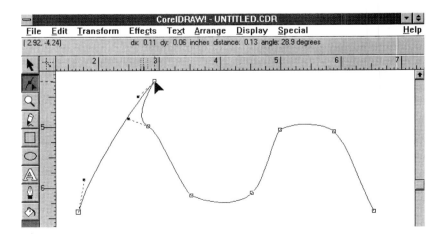

Moving a single
selected node
Figure 8–9.

1. Using the mouse button and (Shift), select one node near the beginning of your waveform curve and one near the end. Again, do not be concerned if the nodes in your curve are in different positions from the nodes in the figure. The process of freehand drawing is so complex that two people rarely produce the same results.

2. Drag one of the nodes downward and to the right. Even though the two selected nodes are separated by several others, they move at the same angle and over the same distance, as shown in Figure 8–10.

3. Release the mouse button when you are finished. Select Undo from the Edit menu to return the curve object to its former shape.

If you prefer to draft even the most "creative-looking" freehand curves with precision, you may wish to exercise greater control over the angle at which you move nodes. The next section will show you how to move nodes with precision.

Constraining Node Movement to 90-Degree Angles

You have the option of moving nodes and their associated curve segments in increments of 90 degrees relative to your starting point.

8

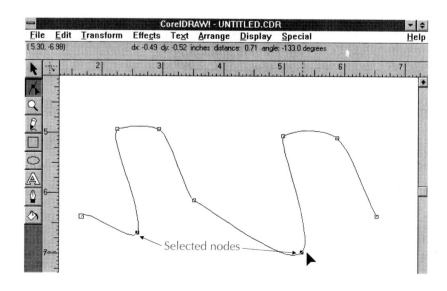

Moving
multiple
selected nodes
Figure 8–10.

You use the now-familiar ⌈Ctrl⌉ key to achieve this kind of precise movement.

1. Select the same two nodes you worked with in the preceding section, press and hold ⌈Ctrl⌉, and drag one of the nodes to the left. At first the two nodes do not seem to move at all; then, they "snap" at a 90-degree angle from their starting point. The status line on your screen reflects this precise angle of movement, as in Figure 8–11.

2. Release the mouse button when you reach the desired angle. Select New from the File menu to clear the curve from the screen. Do not save your changes.

What if you have moved one or more nodes every which way but you are still not satisfied with the shape of the curve segments on either side of the node? In the next section you will fine-tune your curves by manipulating the control points of a node.

Moving Control Points

By moving one or both control points of a node, you can control the shape of a curve segment more exactly than if you move just the node itself. The effect of moving control points varies, depending on the type

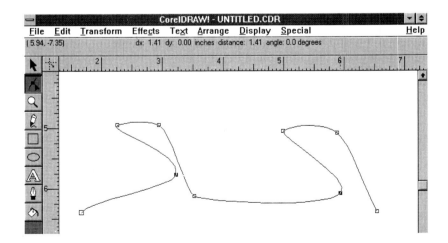

Moving multiple nodes by increments of 90 degrees
Figure 8–11.

of node—cusp, smooth, and symmetrical. Figure 8–12 (a through d) illustrates this difference.

The control points of cusp nodes are not in a straight-line relationship to one another. This means that you can move one control point and change the shape of one curve segment at a time, without affecting the other associated segment. The control points of smooth nodes, on the other hand, *are* in a straight line relative to one another. If you move one control point of a smooth node, you affect the curvature of both

a.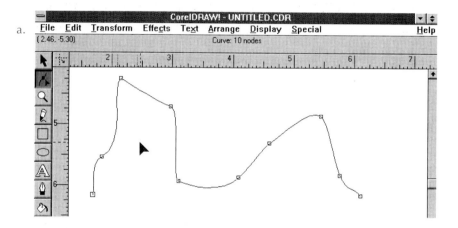

b.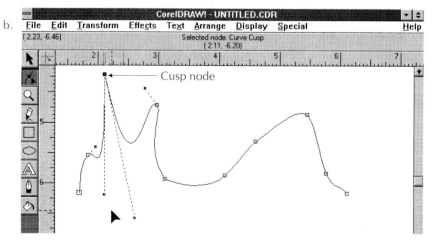

Moving control points of a cusp, smooth, and symmetrical node

Figure 8–12.

8

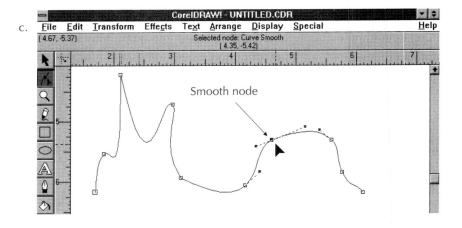

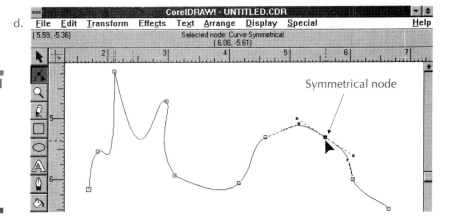

Moving control points of a cusp, smooth, and symmetrical node *(continued)*
Figure 8–12.

line segments at once, though not to the same degree. Finally, the control points of a symmetrical node are at an equal distance from the node. When you move one control point of a symmetrical node, the curvature of both associated curve segments changes in exactly the same way. Your waveform curve may not have a symmetrical node, because due to the steadiness of hand required, symmetrical nodes rarely occur naturally in freehand drawing. You can practice moving the control points of smooth and cusp nodes, however, by following the steps in the next exercise.

1. Select the Pencil tool and draw a curve similar in shape to the one in Figure 8–12a. Don't be concerned if your curve has a slightly different shape. You should draw part of the curve with a steady hand and part using more jagged movements. This will result in an even distribution of node types.

2. Select individual nodes on your waveform curve until you find a cusp node. You will know what type of node you have selected by referring to the status line. Do not use one of the end nodes, however; end nodes have only one control point, because only one curve segment is associated with them. If you can't find a cusp node, redraw the curve to be more jagged, and then try again. For your reference, Figure 8–12a shows the waveform curve with no nodes selected and no control points moved.

3. Drag one of the cusp node's control points outward as far as you can without extending it beyond the viewing window. The farther you drag the control point outward from the node, the more angular the curvature of the associated segment becomes. Note also that the curve segment associated with the other control point does not change.

4. Drag the other control point in any direction you choose. The angle of the second curve segment associated with the node changes, independently of the first one. If you have extended both control points independently, you will see a sharp change in curve direction at the node, as in Figure 8–12b.

5. When you have played with this technique to your satisfaction, find and select a smooth node. Note that the two control points of this node lie along a straight line.

6. Drag one of the control points of the smooth node outward, and notice that the curvature of *both* of the segments associated with the node changes. As shown in the example in Figure 8–12c, however, the two segments do not change in exactly the same way. (The curvature of your curve segments may differ from those in the example, depending on how you drew the curve.)

7. If your waveform curve contains a symmetrical node, select it and move the control points. If you do not have a symmetrical node, observe the curvature changes in Figure 8–12d when the control points of a symmetrical node are moved. The curvature of these segments changes by an identical angle.

8

8. When you have played with control points to your satisfaction, activate the Pick tool and press [Del] to delete the waveform curve from the screen.

Now you have a working knowledge of all the possible interactive techniques for moving and editing curves. It may sometimes happen, however, that even these techniques are not enough to shape your curve just as you want it. What if you are working with a cusp node and just can't make it smooth enough? Or what if you need an additional node at a certain point to enable you to fit a curve to an exact shape? For these and other node-editing tasks, you can call up the Node Edit menu. Using this menu to edit curves is the subject of the remaining sections on shaping lines and curves.

Editing Nodes

Selecting a curve object and moving nodes and control points are interactive operations that you can perform without invoking a special command or menu. There are times, however, when you need to *edit* the nodes themselves: to change their shape, or to add nodes, delete nodes, join nodes together, or break them apart. Editing nodes requires that you use a special Node Edit menu that pops up when you double-click on a node or on the curve segment that immediately precedes it.

Working with the Node Edit Menu

To call up the Node Edit menu, you double-click on the node you wish to edit. Alternatively, you can double-click on the curve or line segment that immediately precedes the node. As the example in Figure 8–13 shows, double-clicking on a node or curve segment causes that segment to thicken temporarily. The Node Edit menu appears exactly at the selected node. If multiple nodes are selected, their associated curve segments thicken.

The commands in the Node Edit menu allow you to add or delete selected nodes, join two nodes or break them apart, convert lines to curves and curves to lines, change the node type or align sets of nodes on two separate subpaths. Not all commands are available to you for every node, however. Some commands appear in gray and are

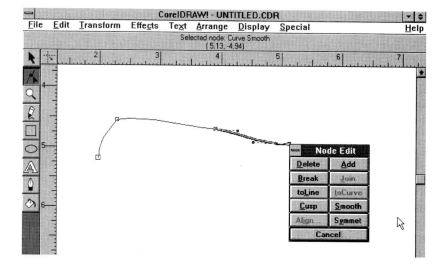

Invoking the
Node Edit menu
Figure 8–13.

unavailable, depending on the number and type of node(s) you have
selected. See the section pertaining to the relevant Node Edit command
for more information about why particular commands are not available
at certain times. To select commands that are available, click once on
the command name.

8

TIP: The underlined letter in the command names of the Node Edit
menu allow you to select a command by typing the underlined
letter.

If the Node Edit menu conceals an area of a curve that you want to
view, just click on the title and drag the entire menu out of the way.
Figure 8–14 shows the Node Edit menu from Figure 8–13 moved down
and to the left of its original location.

Except for the Align command, as soon as you select any command
from the Node Edit menu, the menu disappears, and CorelDRAW!
immediately applies the command to the selected node(s). If you

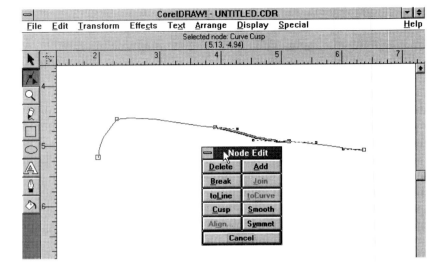

The Node Edit
menu moved
away from the
selected node(s)
Figure 8–14.

accidentally invoke the Node Edit menu at any time, select Cancel to
remove it from the display.

Try the exercises in each of the following sections to become familiar
with using the commands in the Node Edit menu.

Adding a Single Node

If you have moved nodes and manipulated control points to the best of
your ability but still cannot achieve the exact shape you want, consider
adding one or more nodes where the curvature seems most inadequate.
You can add a single node or multiple nodes, depending on how many
nodes are selected.

If the node you have selected is the first node of a line or curve, you
cannot add a node to it. In CorelDRAW!, a first node can never have a
node or segment preceding it.

The following exercise furnishes the necessary steps to add a single
node between two existing nodes. Set the viewing magnification to
Actual Size (1:1). Make sure that the Snap To Grid and Show Rulers
commands are turned off for this and all of the other exercises in the
"Editing Nodes" portion of this chapter.

1. Select the Pencil tool and draw a waveform curve similar to the one shown in Figure 8–15a. Activate the Shaping tool to select the curve for editing. Your curve may contain a different number of nodes from the one in Figure 8–15a.

2. Double-click with the Shaping tool on either the node or the curve segment immediately in front of the point at which you want to add a node. The Node Edit menu appears, with its left side on the selected node, as shown in Figure 8–15b.

3. Select the Add command from the Node Edit menu. A new node appears on the curve or line segment preceding the selected node, as shown in Figure 8–15c. If you first deselect all of the selected nodes by clicking on any white space, you can move this added node or manipulate its control points just like any other node.

4. Leave the current curve on your screen for use in the next exercise.

If you add a node to a straight line segment instead of to a curve, then move the new node, you effectively add a new line segment.

Adding Multiple Nodes

Perform the following brief exercise to add several nodes to a curve at one time. The technique is the same as when you add a single node, except that multiple nodes must be selected.

8

1. You should have a waveform curve on your screen in Actual Size magnification, and the Shaping tool should be selected as you left it in the last exercise.

2. Select two or more nodes using either [Shift] or the marquee method. You will add nodes in front of each of these selected nodes. All of the squares that mark the selected nodes blacken.

3. Using the Shaping tool, double-click on any of the selected nodes or segments. The Node Edit menu appears at the node on which you double-clicked, as in Figure 8–16a.

4. Click on the Add command of the Node Edit menu. A new node appears in front of each of the selected nodes, as shown in Figure 8–16b. If you deselect all of the currently selected nodes, and then select the added nodes, you can move any or all of them. If you select the new nodes individually, you can manipulate their control points to suit your drawing needs.

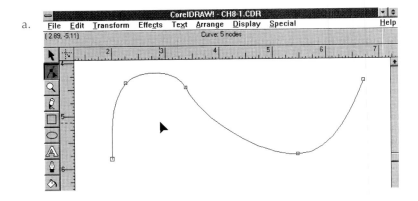

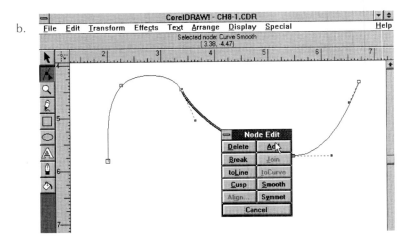

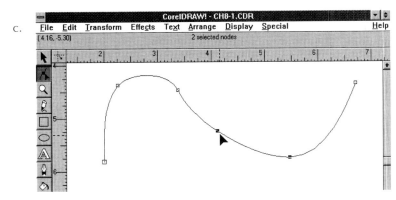

Adding a single
node
Figure 8–15.

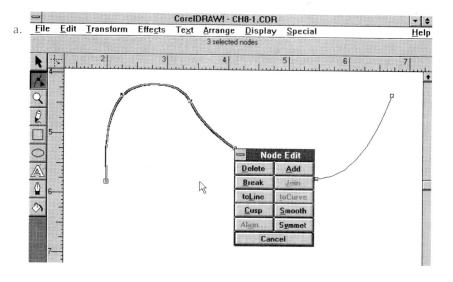

a.

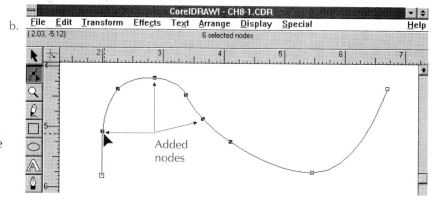

b.

Adding multiple
nodes
Figure 8–16.

5. Again, leave the current curve on your screen for use in the next exercise.

The counterpart to adding nodes is deleting them. Continue with the next sections to practice deleting one or more nodes from a curve.

Deleting a Single Node

When you draw freehand curves, it is often difficult to control mouse movement completely. Changing the Freehand Tracking, Corner Threshold, and AutoJoin settings in the Preferences—Curves dialog box may help, but erratic movements while you execute a curve still can produce occasional extraneous nodes. You can smooth out an uneven curve quickly and easily by deleting single or multiple extraneous nodes.

CAUTION: Always delete nodes with caution. Deleting a node at random, without checking to see if other nodes are nearby, can radically alter the shape of a curve in ways that are not always predictable.

Perform the following exercise to delete a single node from a curve.

1. You should still have a waveform curve on your screen in Actual Size magnification, and the Shaping tool should be selected as you left it in the last exercise.

2. Using the Shaping tool, double-click on either the node or segment that you want to delete. The Node Edit menu appears, as in Figure 8–17a.

3. Select the Delete command from the Node Edit menu. CorelDRAW! deletes the node that you selected and redraws the curve without it, as in Figure 8–17b. The shape of your redrawn curve could be quite different from your original one; just how different it is depends on the location of the node you selected for deletion.

4. Keep the curve on your screen for the next exercise.

Keep in mind that if you delete one of the end nodes of a curve, you delete the associated curve segment as well. If you try to delete either node of a straight line, you delete the entire line in the process.

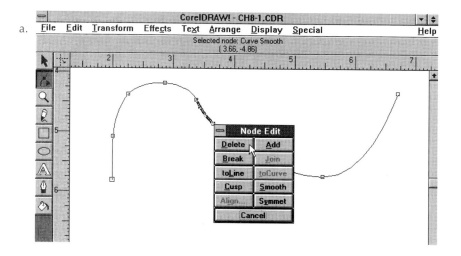

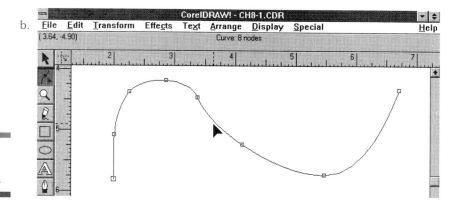

Deleting a
single node
Figure 8–17.

8

TIP: As a shortcut to deleting a node, you can select a node and press Del instead of invoking the Node Edit menu.

Deleting Multiple Nodes

You can delete multiple nodes as well as single nodes from a curve, as long as all of the nodes you want to delete are selected. To delete multiple nodes,

1. With the previous curve still on screen, select the nodes you want to delete, using either ⟨Shift⟩ or the marquee method; Figure 8–18a

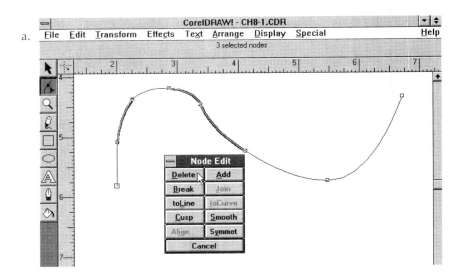

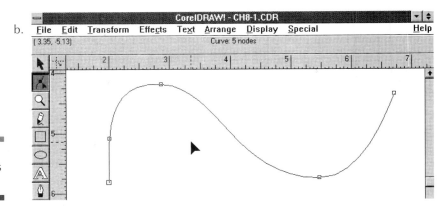

Deleting
multiple nodes
Figure 8–18.

shows three nodes selected—they have a thicker line segment behind them. Keep in mind that if you try to delete an end node, you will delete the associated curve segment along with it.

2. Double-click with the Shaping tool on one of the nodes or curve segments in the selected group. The Node Edit menu appears, as in Figure 8–18a. (The menu has been moved in the figure.)

3. Select the Delete command in the Node Edit menu. CorelDRAW! immediately deletes the selected nodes from the screen and redraws the curve without them, as in Figure 8–18b. The shape of the curve can change subtly or dramatically between node positions; the extent of the change depends on the original positions of the selected nodes.

4. Keep the curve for the next example.

You have learned to add and delete nodes when you need to reshape a curve more than the existing nodes allow. Sometimes, though, you may want your curve to flatten to the extent that you need to replace a curve segment with a straight line segment. You accomplish this by converting one or more curve segments to straight lines.

8

Converting a Single Curve Segment to a Straight Line Segment

CorelDRAW! allows you to convert curve segments to line segments. Before you convert a curve to a line, you need to be able to identify whether a selected segment is a curve or a straight line. Some important guidelines to follow are

✦ A curve segment has two control points; a straight line segment has none.

✦ When you select the segment or its node, the status line indicates whether the segment is a line or curve.

✦ The shape of the *selected* node identifies the type of segment that precedes it. A black fill in the selected node signifies a curve segment, while a hollow selected node signifies a straight line segment.

Perform the following exercise to gain experience in converting a single curve segment into a straight line segment.

1. Again, use the curve from the previous example. If your curve has only a couple of nodes left, add a node using the steps you recently learned, so that there is a curve segment that is a good candidate for a straight line.

2. Using the Shaping tool, double-click on a segment or node of a curve that you want to convert to a straight line. The Node Edit menu appears, as in Figure 8–19a.

3. Now, select the toLine command in the Node Edit menu. The two control points related to the selected curve disappear and the curve segment becomes a straight line segment, as shown in Figure 8–19b. You can reposition, stretch, or shorten this line segment by using the Shaping tool to drag the nodes at either end.

Converting Multiple Curve Segments to Straight Line Segments

Continue with the next exercise to practice converting multiple curve segments to straight lines.

If you want a curve object in your drawing to be more angular, you can change its appearance by selecting multiple nodes or curve segments and converting them to straight lines. To convert multiple curve segments to straight line segments,

1. Press Alt -Backspace to undo making the curve segment a line and, if necessary, add a node, so that there are at least two curve segments that are good candidates for straight lines.

2. Select the curve segments or nodes you want to convert to straight lines, using either Shift or the marquee technique.

3. Using the Shaping tool, double-click on any one of the selected nodes or curve segments. The Node Edit menu appears, as shown in Figure 8–20a.

4. Select the toLine command in the Node Edit menu. The selected curve segments convert to straight lines and all associated control points are eliminated (straight lines do not include control points). The object becomes much more angular, as in Figure 8–20b. You

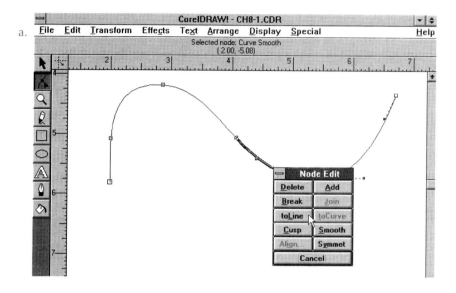

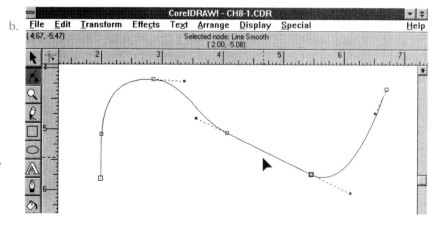

Converting a curve segment to a straight line segment
Figure 8–19.

can now reposition, stretch, or shrink any or all of the line segments by dragging the node(s).

If your object consists of angular line segments but you want to give it much smoother contours, you can convert line segments to curves. The next section shows you how.

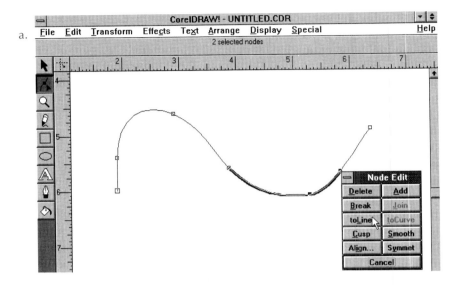

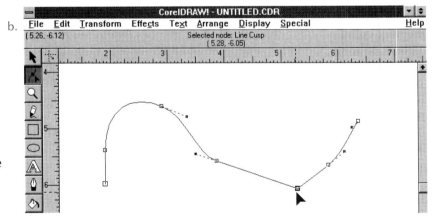

Converting
multiple curve
segments to line
segments
Figure 8–20.

Converting Single and Multiple Straight Line Segments to Curve Segments

With CorelDRAW! you can convert straight line segments to curve segments through the Node Edit menu. Before you convert a line segment to a curve segment, you need to identify whether a selected segment is a straight line or a curve. If you are uncertain about identifying segments, review the guidelines in the last section before you proceed.

Try the following exercise to practice converting a single line segment into a curve segment.

1. Using the Shaping tool, double-click on one of the straight line segments you just created, or on the *second* node of a straight line. The Node Edit menu appears, as in Figure 8–21a. (If you select the

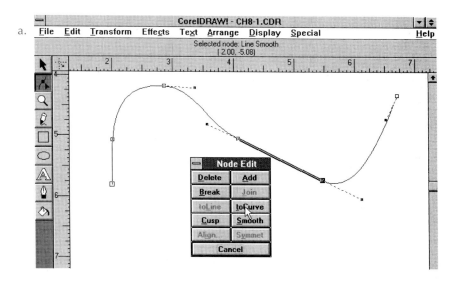

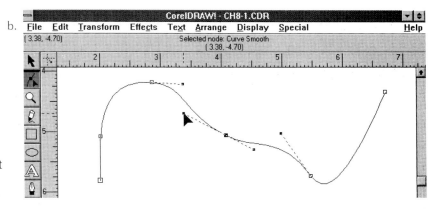

Converting a
line segment to
a curve segment
Figure 8–21.

8

first node of the line segment, you will not be able to convert it to a curve.)

2. Now, select the toCurve command in the Node Edit menu. CorelDRAW! turns the selected straight line segment into a curve, causing two control points to appear on the line segment. Drag these control points up, as shown in Figure 8–21b.

You can turn several straight line segments into curve segments at the same time, as long as they are part of the same object. You simply select the several segments and choose the toCurve command in the Node Edit menu. The selected straight line segments convert to curve lines. On the surface, the segments do not appear to have changed. However, if you deselect all nodes and then select any one of the converted nodes, two control points appear. You can reshape the peaks and valleys like any other curve.

3. Experiment with converting several segments to curves, and prove to yourself that you really are working with curves now.

You have experimented with adding and deleting nodes, and with changing lines to curves and curves to lines. Another group of commands in the Node Edit menu allows you to change the type of single or multiple nodes. These commands are Cusp, Smooth, and Symmetrical and are the subject of the next several sections.

Cusping Single or Multiple Nodes

When you work with a cusp node, you can move either of its control points independently of the other. This makes it possible to independently control the curvature of both of the curve segments that meet at the node, without affecting the other segment. Cusp nodes are especially desirable when you want to render an abrupt change in direction at a node.

The following exercise shows you how to turn a single smooth or symmetrical node into a cusped node.

1. Using the Shaping tool, double-click on the node you want to cusp. Select any node except an end node; CorelDRAW! designates all end nodes as cusp nodes.

2. When the Node Edit menu appears as in Figure 8–22a, select the Cusp command. The appearance of the curve will not change. However, if you manipulate the control points of this node as shown in Figure 8–22b, you will find that you can move one control point without affecting the curve segment on the other side of the node.

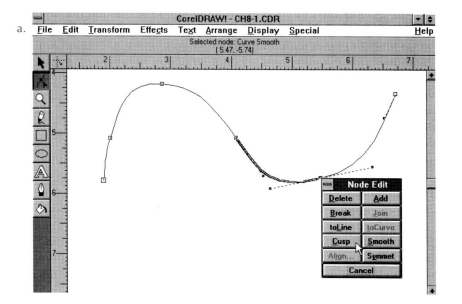

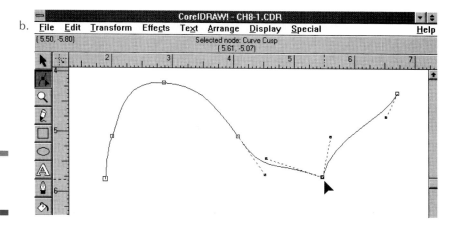

Cusping a
single node
Figure 8–22.

8

When you want a curve object to have a relatively jagged appearance but you do not want to turn your curves into straight lines, the next best solution is to change multiple smooth or symmetrical nodes into cusp nodes. You can then shape the cusp nodes to create a more angular appearance for the affected portions of the object.

3. Save your drawing, using File Save As. You can call it anything you like, for example, **CH8-22**. You will use it again in a later exercise.

4. Select New from the File menu to clear the screen.

In the next section, you will become familiar with changing cusped or symmetrical nodes into smooth nodes.

Smoothing Single or Multiple Nodes

In the previous section, you saw that cusp nodes are desirable when you want to create a rougher, more jagged appearance for an object. When you want to make an object's curves smoother, however, you seek out the cusped nodes and turn them into smooth ones.

A smooth node can be defined as a node whose control points always lie along a straight line. A special case exists when a smooth node is located between a straight line and a curve segment, as in Figure 8–23a. In such a case, only the side of the node toward the curve segment contains a control point, and you can only move that control point along an imaginary line that follows the extension of the straight line. This restriction maintains the smoothness at the node.

In the next exercise, you will convert a single cusp node that lies at the juncture between a straight line and curve segment into a smooth node.

1. Set viewing magnification to Actual Size (1:1), select the Pencil tool, and then draw a straight line connected to a curve segment, as shown in Figure 8–23a. Remember to double-click at the end of the line segment to attach it to the curve segment automatically.

2. Activate the Shaping tool. Your curve object may not include the same number of nodes as the one in this figure, but that is not important for the purpose of this exercise.

3. Using the Shaping tool, double-click on the cusp or symmetrical node that you want changed to a smooth node. When the Node Edit menu appears (Figure 8–23b), select the Smooth command.

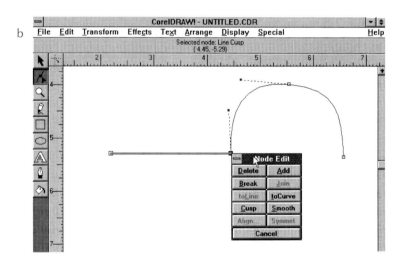

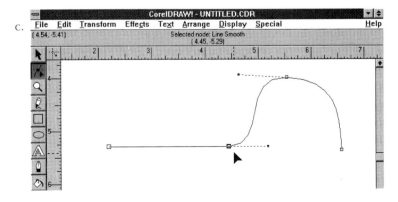

Smoothing a
single cusp node
Figure 8–23.

The curve passing through the selected node is smoothed, like the one in Figure 8–23c, and will remain smooth when you move either the node itself or its control points. The straight line segment does not change, of course.

4. Select New from the File menu to clear the screen.

To smooth multiple nodes, you simply select multiple nodes and then repeat the steps for smoothing a single node.

Go on to the next section to learn how you can turn smooth or cusp nodes into symmetrical nodes and how this affects the drawing process.

Making Single or Multiple Nodes Symmetrical

Symmetrical nodes share the same characteristics as smooth nodes, except that the control points on a symmetrical node are equidistant from the node. This means that the curvature is the same on both sides of the symmetrical node. As with the smooth nodes, when you move one of the control points, the other control point moves. In effect, symmetry causes the two control points to move as one.

Another important point to remember is that you cannot make a node symmetrical if it connects to a straight line segment. The node must lie between two curve segments in order to qualify for a symmetrical edit.

Perform the following brief exercise to convert a single cusp node to a symmetrical node, using the drawing with a cusp node that you saved earlier.

1. Open the cusp node drawing you saved in the earlier exercise. If its filename (possibly CH8-22.CDR) appears in the lower part of the File menu, you can open it by clicking on the name.

2. Set viewing magnification to 1:1, activate the Shaping tool, and select the curve.

3. Find a cusp node that you want to make symmetrical and then double-click on it. The Node Edit menu appears, as in Figure 8–24a.

4. Click on the Symmet command. The selected node is now converted to a symmetrical node and CorelDRAW! redraws the curve so that it passes through the node symmetrically, as in Figure 8–24b.

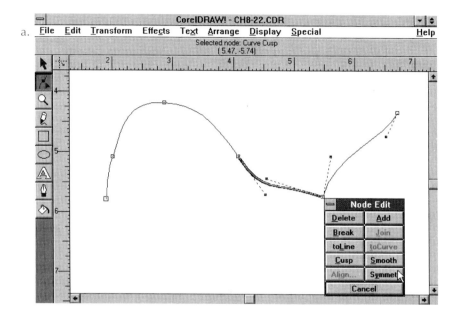

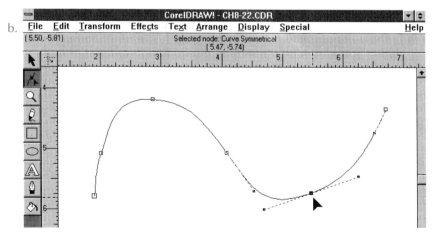

Making a cusp
node
symmetrical
Figure 8–24.

5. Move the control points of this node until you have a satisfactory
   understanding of how symmetrical nodes work.

Making multiple nodes symmetrical is just as easy as making single nodes symmetrical. The only difference is that you select more than one node at a time, using either [Shift] or the marquee method.

In the next sections, you will find out how to master the art of breaking nodes apart and joining them together—and why you might choose to do so.

Breaking Curves at Single or Multiple Nodes

Breaking a node involves splitting a curve at a selected node, so that two nodes appear where before there was one. Although you can move the separate sections of a broken node as though they were separate curves, CorelDRAW! does not regard them as separate. These split segments actually constitute different *subpaths* of the same curve. Breaking a node into separate subpaths gives the impression of spontaneous freehand drawing, yet it allows you to keep separate "drawing strokes" together as one object. Breaking curves at the nodes is also a useful "trick" when you need to delete a portion of a curve and leave the rest of the curve intact.

Keep in mind that you cannot break a curve at an end node, because there is no segment on the other side of the end point with which to form a separate subpath.

When you break a node, it becomes two unconnected end nodes. You are then free to move either end node and the entire subpath to which it is connected. The two subpaths remain part of the same object, however, as you can see when you select either subpath with the Pick tool. In the following exercise, you will use the curve from the last exercise, break it at a single node, and then observe how CorelDRAW! handles the two resulting subpaths.

1. With the Shaping tool, select a node on the side of the curve and double-click on it to pop up the Node Edit menu, as in Figure 8–25a.

2. Select Break from the Node Edit menu. The single node splits into two nodes. Since they are close together, however, the change is not visible until you begin to move the new end nodes.

3. Move the left end point away from the subpath to the right as shown in Figure 8–25b, and then deselect both nodes. The object

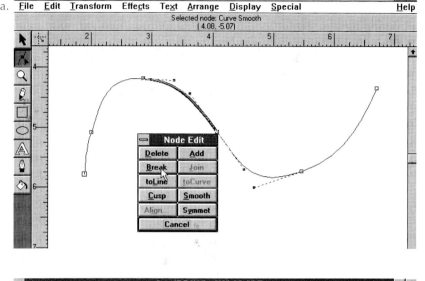

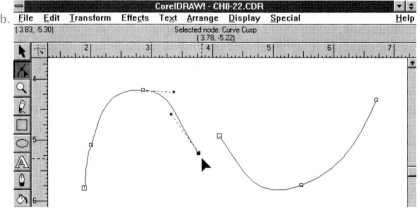

Breaking a
curve at a
single node
Figure 8–25.

    itself remains selected for editing, and the status line informs you
that the curve now has two subpaths.

4. Press the spacebar to activate the Pick tool. Notice that the Pick
tool treats these two subpaths as a single curve object, even though
they look like separate curves. There may be times when you want
to make subpaths into truly separate objects, so that you can

manipulate and edit them independently. As the next step shows, CorelDRAW! provides a means for you to turn the subpaths into independent curves.

5. To separate the two subpaths into two truly distinct objects, leave the Pick tool active and then select the Break Apart command from the Arrange menu. This command is available only when multiple subpaths of a single curve object are selected.

6. Select New from the File menu to clear the screen.

In this brief exercise, you have seen some applications for breaking a curve at a node. For example, you can create two separate objects from a single object, or create separate subpaths that move together as a single object.

CAUTION: If you break a closed curve object at a node, you will not be able to fill the object with a color or pattern.

When you break a curve at multiple nodes, the result is multiple subpaths, which still remain part of the same object.

The reverse of breaking curves apart is joining them together. In the next section, you will find out when you can and cannot join nodes together, as well as some reasons why you might want to do so.

Joining Nodes

By now, you have probably noticed that the Join command is rarely available for selection when you invoke the pop-up Node Edit menu. You can join nodes only under very specific conditions.

✦ You can join only two nodes at a time, so only two nodes can be selected.

✦ The two nodes must be either end nodes of the same object or end nodes of separate subpaths of the same object.

✦ You cannot join an end node of an open curve to a closed object such as an ellipse or a rectangle.

When might you want to join two nodes, then? The two chief occasions are when you want to close an open path, or when you want to make a single continuous curve from the two separate paths.

Joining Nodes to Close an Open Path   An open path, as you will recall from your previous freehand drawing experience in CorelDRAW!, is a curve object whose end points do not meet and which therefore cannot be filled with a color or pattern. To prevent open paths, you can set the AutoJoin option in the Preferences dialog box to a higher number and make it easier for end nodes to snap together as you draw. There are still times, however, when you might choose to join end points after drawing an open curve. In such cases, you use the Join command in the pop-up Node Edit menu. The following exercise presents a situation in which you could use the Join command to make a drawing process easier.

1. Set magnification to Actual Size (1:1). Select the Pencil tool and draw a more or less oval curve, but do not finish the curve at a point close to where you started it. See Figure 8–26a for an example.

2. Activate the Shaping tool to select this curve object, and then select both of the end nodes using the marquee or Shift key technique.

3. Double-click on either of the selected end nodes to call up the Node Edit menu, as shown in Figure 8–26b.

4. Select the Join command in the Node Edit menu. CorelDRAW! redraws the curve as a closed path, like the one in Figure 8–26c. You can then fill this path with a color or pattern, as you will learn in Chapter 13.

5. Select New from the File menu to clear the screen before going further.

It is easy to close an open path with the Shaping tool. Joining nodes from separate curves, however, is a bit trickier. Read on to learn how to combine the curves so that you can join the nodes.

Joining Nodes on Separate Subpaths to Form a Continuous Curve (Combined Objects)   You can also join two end nodes if they are on two subpaths of the same curve. The two subpaths then become a

8

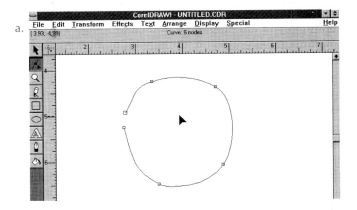

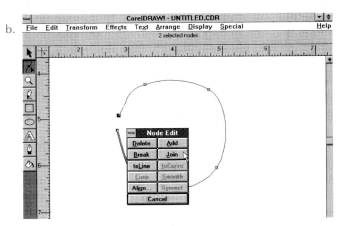

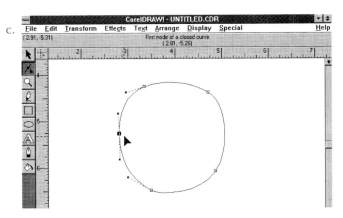

Joining nodes to
close an open
path
Figure 8–26.

single, continuous curve segment. A special case exists when you have two separate curve objects (not two subpaths of the same curve) and want to make them into a single curve. Knowing that you cannot join nodes from two separate objects, what do you do? Your best option is to combine the curves using the Pick tool, and the Combine command in the Arrange menu. Even though the curves continue to look like separate objects, from the standpoint of CorelDRAW! they become two subpaths of a single curve. You can then join their end nodes to unite the subpaths.

1. Select Actual Size magnification, and with the Pencil tool draw four separate curve segments as shown in Figure 8–27a.

2. With the Pick tool, draw a marquee around all four curve segments to simultaneously select them.

3. From the Arrange menu, select Combine to make a single, broken curve out of the four segments. The result of this is shown in Figure 8–27b.

4. With the Shaping tool, select the curve. Then select one of the three pairs of end points to be joined, double-click on the smaller of the two end points to get the Node menu, and select Join. Repeat this for the two remaining pairs. The result is a single continuous curve, as shown in Figure 8–27c.

8

TIP: The only trick to this is to first combine the curve segments with the Pick tool and the Arrange menu before trying to join the segments with the Shape tool.

5. Select New from the File menu, but do not save the changes you have made.

Going through this process is a good way to familiarize yourself with all the steps involved in both joining and breaking nodes apart. Perhaps you have some new ideas for using the Join command for some of your own original drawings.

a.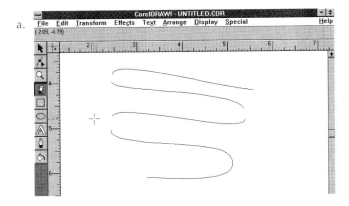

b.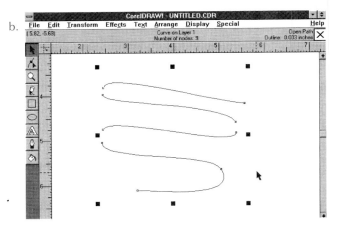

c.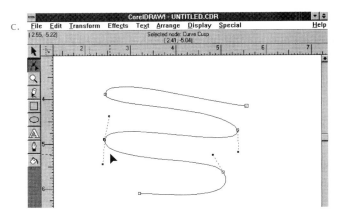

Joining nodes to form a continuous curve

Figure 8–27.

Aligning Nodes

If you want two objects to share a common edge, like two pieces in a puzzle, the Align command in the Node menu can accomplish it for you. The two objects must first be combined with the Arrange menu, and you must add or delete nodes until there are the same number of nodes in each object in roughly the same location. Once you have completed aligning the two objects, you can break them apart.

Objects can be aligned vertically or horizontally and they can literally share a common border through the alignment of their control points. If you want to superimpose one object on the other, you would align them both horizontally and vertically and align their control points. The latter is the default.

The following exercise will allow you to experiment with the Align command in the Node menu.

1. At Actual Size (1:1) magnification and with the Pencil tool, draw two curve objects similar to those shown in Figure 8–28a (Edit Wireframe should be turned on).

2. With the Pick tool, draw a marquee, around both objects to select them. Then, from the Arrange menu, select Combine.

3. With the Shaping tool, add or delete nodes until the two objects have the same number of nodes in roughly the same position as shown in Figure 8–28b.

4. For each pair of nodes you want to align, perform these steps with the Shaping tool in the order given:

   a. Select the node to be *realigned* (moved).

   b. Press Shift and select the node to *align* to (move to).

   c. Double-click on one of the nodes to open the Node menu.

   d. Select Align. The Node Align dialog box will open as shown here:

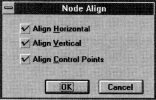

8

a.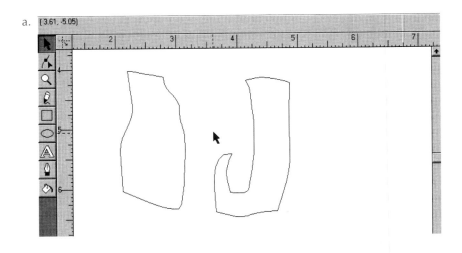

b.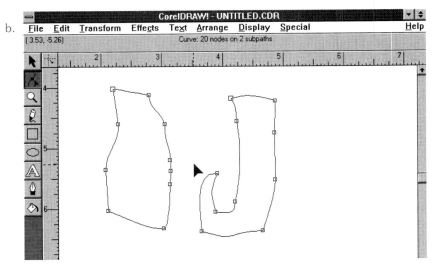

Aligning the
nodes of two
curve objects
Figure 8–28.

e. Click on OK to accept the default choice of all three options,
which will superimpose the nodes and align the control points.

When you have aligned all of the node pairs you want to align, you
should have a single curve segment shared by both objects whose shape
is the same as the object to which you aligned, as shown in Figure
8–28c.

c.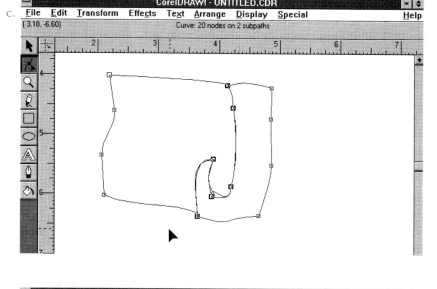

d.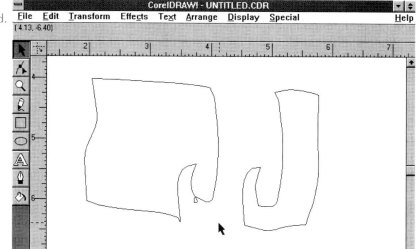

Aligning the
nodes of two
curve objects
(continued)
Figure 8–28.

5. With the Pick tool, select the combined object and choose Break
    Apart from the Arrange menu.

6. Still with the Pick tool, click on white space to deselect the combined object and then select and drag one of the original objects until you can see the two individual objects again. Now the two objects, though, have a common, although mirror-image, shape on one side as shown in Figure 8–28d.

Edit Cancellation

If you invoke the Node Edit menu by accident or change your mind about editing a node once the Node Edit menu has appeared, simply select the Cancel command. The Node Edit menu disappears from the screen but the selected node or nodes remain selected for further work.

This concludes your exploration of the techniques for shaping lines and curves. In the remaining sections of this chapter, you will have a hands-on opportunity to explore techniques for shaping rectangular and elliptical objects.

Shaping Rectangles and Squares

The Shaping tool has a specific function when you apply it to rectangles and squares in CorelDRAW!. It rounds the corners of a rectangle, thus creating a shape separate from a rectangle or square. The status line keeps track of the radius of the rounded corner as you drag. You can control the degree of rounding either interactively or by using the grid to ensure exactness.

For interesting distortions, you can stretch, rotate, or skew the rectangle or square before rounding its corners.

Rounding the Corners of a Rectangle

Complete the following exercise to practice rounding rectangles and squares using the Shaping tool. You will begin by rounding corners interactively; later, you will use the grid to perform the same work.

1. For the beginning of this exercise, make sure that the Snap To Grid and Show Rulers commands are inactive, that Edit Wireframe is turned on, and that you are working in Actual Size viewing magnification. Then select the Rectangle tool and draw a rectangle of unequal length and width.

2. Activate the Shaping tool and select a node at one of the corners of the rectangle. As shown in Figure 8–29a, the status line indicates that the corner radius of this rectangle is 0.00 inches. The corner radius helps you measure the degree to which you have rounded the corners of a rectangle or square with the Shaping tool.

3. Position the Shaping pointer at this node and begin to drag the corner slowly toward the nearest other corner. As shown in Figure 8–29b, each corner node separates into two separate nodes, with each node moving farther away from the original corner as you drag. The status line also informs you just how much of a corner radius you are creating. The further you drag the nodes from the corners, the rounder the corners become and the more the corner radius increases.

4. Continue dragging the mouse until you reach the logical limit of rounding: when the nodes from adjacent corners meet at the sides of the rectangle. At this point, your rounded rectangle has become almost an ellipse, similar to the rectangle shown in Figure 8–29c.

5. Begin dragging the selected node from the middle of the line back to the former corner. As you do so, the corner radius diminishes. You can return the rectangle to its original shape by dragging the nodes all the way back to the corner.

6. Delete the rectangle from the screen, then draw a square and repeat steps 2 through 5. Notice that when you begin with a square and then round the corners to the logical limit, the square becomes a nearly perfect circle rather than an ellipse, as in Figure 8–30.

7. Press Del to clear the screen of the square turned circle.

8

Although the status line information helps you round corners precisely, you can gain even greater precision using the grid and rulers. The next exercise guides you through the process of rounding corners of a rectangle or square with the help of these aids.

1. Open the Grid Setup dialog box, set the grid frequency to 4 per inch, turn on Show Grid and Snap To Grid, and click OK. Turn on Show Rulers.

2. Draw a rectangle 2 inches wide by 1.25 inches deep. Activate the Shaping tool and select one of the corner nodes of the rectangle.

a.
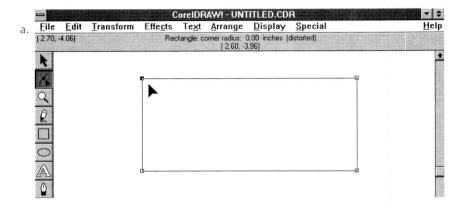

b.
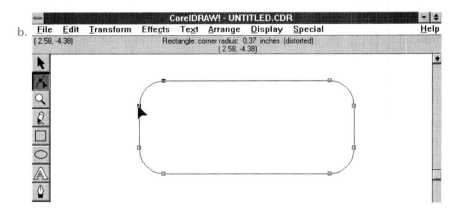

c.
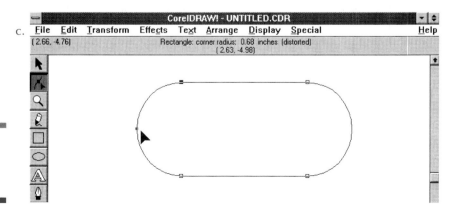

Rounding the
corners of a
rectangle
Figure 8–29.

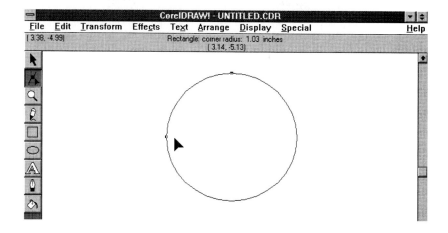

Rounding the
corners of a
square
Figure 8–30.

3. Drag this corner node away from the corner to round the rectangle. This time, the corner radius changes in precise increments of 0.25 inches because of the grid setting.

4. Draw a square and round its corners. The radius of the square also changes in increments of 0.25 inches.

5. When you have finished experimenting with the rectangle and the square, select New from the File menu to clear the screen.

8

In the next section, you will see what can happen when you stretch, rotate, or skew a rectangle or square before attempting to round its corners.

Stretched, Rotated, or Skewed Rectangles and Squares

When you transform a rectangle or square by stretching, rotating, or skewing it with the Pick tool and then round its corners, the value of the corner radius may be distorted. The corner radius indicator on the status line is followed by the word "distorted" in parentheses. As Figure 8–31 shows, the final shape of such a rounded rectangle may also be distorted; in extreme cases it can resemble a skewed flying saucer or rotated ellipse. Figure 8–32 shows a skewed square whose corners have been rounded.

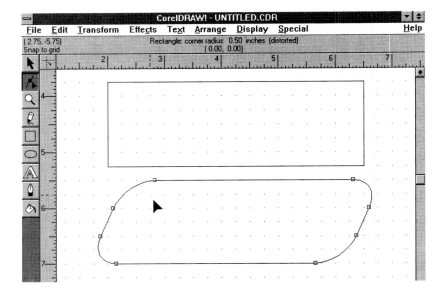

Rounding the
corners of a
skewed
rectangle
Figure 8–31.

Practice this technique on your own and then go on to the final section
on shaping rectangles. In this next section, you will find out how to
turn a rectangle into a curve so that you can shape it in an infinite
number of ways.

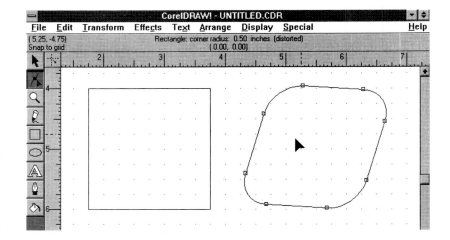

Rounding the
corners of a
skewed square
Figure 8–32.

Converting a Rectangle to a Curve Object

If the shaping options for rectangles or squares seem limited to you, don't worry. You can convert any rectangle or square into a curve object and, from that point onward, you can turn a formerly four-cornered object into anything at all. The technique is simple, as you will see in the following brief exercise.

1. Set magnification to Actual Size (1:1) and turn off the ruler, Show Grid, and Snap To Grid, but leave Edit Wireframe turned on, in preparation for this exercise.

2. Select the Rectangle tool if it is not selected already and then draw a rectangle of any size or shape.

3. Activate the Pick tool, select the rectangle, and select the Convert To Curves command from the Arrange menu. The status line message changes from "Rectangle on Layer 1" to "Curve on Layer 1." Note that the new four-cornered "curve" still has the same number of nodes as when it was a rectangle.

4. Activate the Shaping tool and then select and drag one of the nodes in any direction. As the example in Figure 8–33 shows, dragging the node no longer forces the associated line/curve segment to move parallel to the other line segments.

5. Continue warping the shape of this rectangle-turned-curve in a variety of ways. For example, you could add nodes, convert line segments to curves, create symmetrical nodes, or even turn the former rectangle into a candy cane or other hybrid object.

8

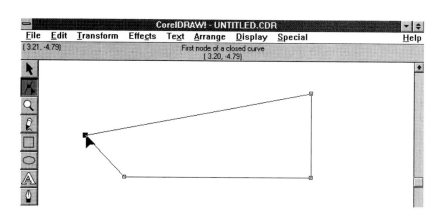

Editing a rectangle that has been converted to curves

Figure 8–33.

6. Press ⌈Del⌋ to clear the screen before going further.

Now that you have mastered the art of shaping rectangles and squares, you are ready to apply the Shaping tool to ellipses and circles for some quite different effects.

Shaping Ellipses and Circles

When you shape ellipses or circles with the Shaping tool, you can create either an open arc or a pie wedge. You can even shift back and forth between these two shapes as you draw, depending on whether the tip of the shaping pointer lies inside or outside the ellipse or circle. You also have the option of constraining the angle of an arc or pie wedge to 15-degree increments.

Creating an Open Arc

To turn an ellipse or circle into an arc, you position the tip of the shaping pointer just *outside* of the rim at the node and then drag the node in the desired direction. Make certain that the tip of the pointer remains outside the rim of the ellipse as you drag, or you will create a wedge instead of an arc. The status line provides information about the angle of the arc as you draw. Practice creating arcs from both ellipses and circles in the following exercise.

1. Turn off the Snap To Grid command if it is active and set the viewing magnification to Actual Size.
2. Select the Ellipse tool and draw a perfect circle.
3. Activate the Shaping tool to select the circle automatically.
4. Position the tip of the Shaping tool exactly at the node but just outside the rim of the circle, and then drag the node downward slowly in a clockwise direction. As Figure 8–34 shows, the single node separates into two nodes, with the second node following your pointer as you drag. If the circle seems to be turning into a pie wedge instead of an arc, the tip of your mouse pointer is inside the rim of the circle. Move it outside of the rim and try again.

Note that the status line provides information about the angle position of the first and second nodes and about the total angle of the arc. This

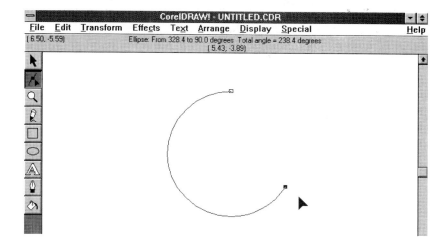

Creating an arc
from a circle
Figure 8–34.

information is based on a 360-degree wheel, with 0 degrees at 12
o'clock, 90 degrees at 9 o'clock, 180 degrees at 6 o'clock, and 270
degrees at 3 o'clock.

5. Continue to drag the shaping pointer, but now press and hold the
   Ctrl key as well. The angle of the arc snaps in increments of 15
   degrees. Release the mouse button when your arc has the angle
   you want.

6. Select the Ellipse tool and again draw a perfect circle. Then repeat
   steps 4 and 5, completing this arc at an approximate 105-degree
   angle. If you use an ellipse instead of a circle, the "total angle"
   information on the status line is followed by the message
   "distorted" in parentheses. This message occurs because
   CorelDRAW! bases its calculation of an arc on a perfect circle
   rather than on an ellipse with different height and width. The
   angle assignments for arcs created from an ellipse are therefore
   approximate.

7. Press the spacebar to activate the Pick tool and select the newly
   created arc. Notice that the highlighting box, like the one in Figure
   8–35, is much larger than the arc itself; in fact, it seems to
   surround the now invisible but complete original ellipse. The
   purpose of this large highlighting box is to make it easy for you to
   align an arc or wedge concentrically, using the Align command in

8

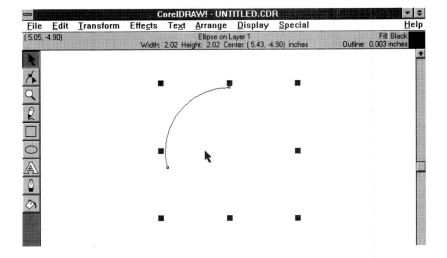

Selecting an arc
for alignment
purposes
Figure 8–35.

the Arrange menu. The disadvantage of this large highlighting box is that when you are selecting objects with the marquee, you must make certain that your marquee surrounds the entire highlighting box.

8. Select New from the File menu to clear the screen before going further.

Creating a wedge shape from an ellipse is just as easy as creating an arc, as you will see in the next section.

Creating a Pie Wedge

The only difference between creating an arc and creating a pie wedge is that in the latter case, you position the tip of the shaping pointer *inside* the ellipse or circle as you drag. Perform the following exercise to see the difference for yourself.

1. Set magnification to Actual Size, and then select the Ellipse tool and draw a circle. Activate the Shaping tool to select it for editing.

2. Position the tip of the shaping pointer inside the circle exactly at the node, and then begin dragging the node downward in a clockwise direction. The two nodes separate as before, but this time

the circle turns into a shape like a pie missing a piece, suitable for pie charts and wedges, as shown in Figure 8–36.

3. Press and hold ⌈Ctrl⌉ and continue dragging the mouse. The angle of the wedge shape now moves in fixed increments of 15 degrees. Release the mouse button when you have obtained the desired angle.

4. Just as you did with the arc, press the spacebar to activate the Pick tool and select the wedge. Notice the oversized highlighting box once more. Make sure to surround this highlighting box completely whenever you attempt to select a wedge with a narrow total angle.

5. Press ⌈Del⌉ to clear the screen.

That's all there is to creating arcs and wedges from ellipses and circles. If these shaping techniques are not flexible enough for you, you can always convert the arc or wedge to a curve object, as you will see in the next section.

Converting Ellipses and Circles to Curve Objects

8

If the shaping options for ellipses and circles seem limited to you, don't worry. You can convert any ellipse, circle, arc, or wedge into a curve

Creating a pie wedge from a circle
Figure 8–36.

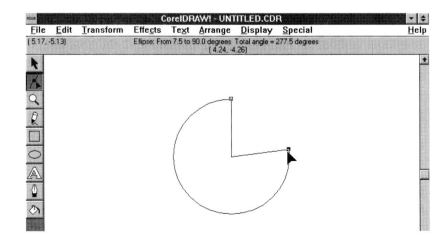

object and, from that point onward, you can add and delete nodes, drag nodes and control points, or change node types. In the following exercise, you will create a wedge from a circle, convert the wedge to curves, and then reshape the new curve object into the body of a baby carriage.

1. Select the Ellipse tool and draw an ellipse that is wider than it is high, starting from the upper-left area of the rim and moving downward as you drag.

2. Activate the Shaping tool and position the arrowhead pointer over the node of the circle. Drag the node downward, keeping the tip of the shaping pointer inside the rim, and create a wedge with a total angle of about 240 degrees, as shown in Figure 8–37.

3. Press the spacebar to activate the Pick tool and select the wedge, and then select the Convert To Curves command from the Arrange menu. Notice that because of the shape of the wedge, the new curve object has five nodes, whereas the ellipse had only one node.

4. Reactivate the Shaping tool and drag the node furthest to the right upward and outward, as shown in Figure 8–38. Since the segment next to this one is a straight line, the selected node has only one control point. Moving this node upward and outward has the effect of stretching the straight line.

A wedge created from an ellipse, with a total angle of 240 degrees
Figure 8–37.

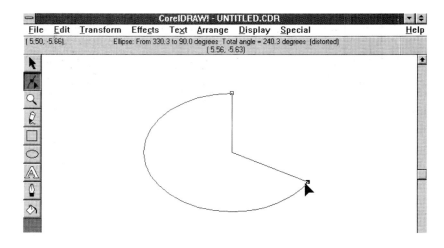

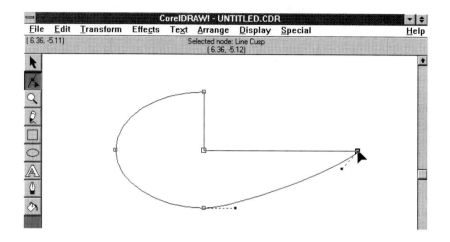

Dragging a
node to form
the top of a
carriage
Figure 8–38.

5. The curvature of the segment associated with the node you just
   moved is not adequate to round out the bottom of the "carriage."
   To remedy this, double-click on the curve segment and select Add
   from the Node Edit menu. A new node appears between the
   selected node and the one below and to the left of it, as shown in
   Figure 8–39. It's a smooth node because of the existing curvature,
   and because the object originated as an ellipse.

8

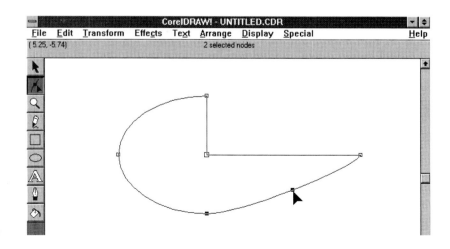

Adding a node
to obtain better
curve control
Figure 8–39.

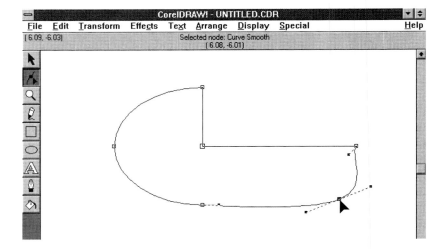

Rounding out
the bottom of
the carriage
Figure 8–40.

6. Select and drag this newly added smooth node downward and to the right, until it forms a nicely rounded bottom to the "carriage" body, as shown in Figure 8–40.

Perhaps the example in the preceding exercise will stimulate your imagination to create any number of complex objects from the basic objects available to you through the drawing tools. The Shaping tool makes it all possible!

C H A P T E R

SHAPING AND EDITING TEXT

Text can be an important design element, whether you specialize in original art, graphic or industrial design, technical illustration, or desktop publishing. Every choice you make concerning font, style, spacing, alignment, type size, and placement can affect how your intended audience receives your work. You should have the option of editing text attributes at any time, not only when you first enter text on a page.

With CorelDRAW!, you do have that option. Using the

Pick tool and the Shaping tool, you can edit existing text in ways that enhance both its typographic and pictorial value. You already edited text as a graphic element in Chapters 6 and 7 by using the Pick tool to rotate, stretch, scale, skew, and reflect text strings. In this chapter, you will concentrate on editing the *typographical* text attributes (such as font and type size) of individual characters, groups of characters, and complete text strings. You will also learn to customize your text picture even further by converting a text string to a set of curves and then reshaping each curve. The Pick and Shaping tools share these editing functions between them.

Editing Attributes for a Text String

Remember the two ways you selected attributes when you first entered a text string—the Text dialog boxes and the Text roll-up window? You can also use each of these methods to change text attributes that already exist. Do this by clicking in the text string with the Pick tool and then selecting either Edit Text from the Edit menu, or Text Roll-up from the Text menu. The changes you make will apply to every character in the text string. To change attributes for selected characters within a text string, you need to use the Shaping tool as described in the section entitled "Selecting and Editing with the Shaping Tool."

In the following exercise, you will create a short text string that you will use in many different exercises throughout this chapter. Then, you will select the text string and change some of its attributes using the Edit Text command from the Edit menu.

1. Set your viewing magnification to Actual Size. Turn the Show Rulers, Show Grid, and Snap To Grid commands off for this portion of the chapter. Also, ensure you are in full color mode, not wireframe.

2. Pick the Text tool and then select an insertion point midway down the left edge of your viewing window. Type the following text string on three separate lines:

   Doing
   what comes
   naturally

3. Open the Artistic Text dialog box and use the default text attributes Avalon Normal, 24.0 points, and Left Justification. Adjust your dialog box if it shows other settings.

4. Select OK to exit the dialog box and return to the text on the page. It will still be selected.

5. Open the Text roll-up.

6. Change the text attributes to Cupertino Italic, 65.0 points, and Center Justification; then select Apply. Because you have changed the alignment, some of the text may not appear within viewing range. If this is the case, drag its outlines until it fits within the viewing window, as shown in Figure 9–1.

7. Deselect the text string and save your work as the file named DOINWHAT.CDR. Leave the text on the screen for the next exercise.

You can change attributes for a text string as often as desired. However, as long as you use the Pick tool to select text, any attribute changes you make will affect the entire text string. If your work requires highly stylized text designs, where attributes must be decided on a character-by-character basis, you need to use the Shaping tool.

9

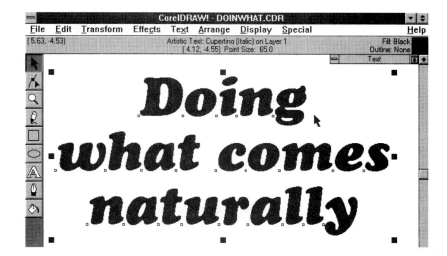

Changing font, style, justification, and type size
Figure 9–1.

Selecting and Editing with the Shaping Tool

When the Shaping tool is active, you can select any number of characters within a text string and edit their typographical attributes. Depending on how you prefer to work, you can edit attributes either interactively, or use the Artistic Text dialog box, the Text roll-up, or the Character command in the Text menu. Some of these attributes, specifically, font, style, and type size, overlap within the two dialog boxes and the roll-up. Others, including horizontal and vertical shift and character angle, are adjustable only through the Character Attributes dialog box. Or, you can move letters and adjust spacing and kerning interactively, without using menu commands, roll-ups, or dialog boxes. If all these adjustments fail to give your text the desired look, you can gain more editing control by converting text to curves and then manipulating its nodes and control points.

Before you can edit text attributes on a character-by-character basis, you must first use the Shaping tool to select the text string in which the characters are located. This is similar to selecting a curve object as a prerequisite to selecting one or more of its nodes. After you select a text string, you can select a specific character, multiple adjacent or nonadjacent characters, or all characters in the text string. Practice selecting different combinations of characters in the following exercise.

1. Open the DOINWHAT.CDR text file that you created in the last exercise, if it is not open already. If the Pick tool is active, make sure that the text string is not selected; it should not be surrounded by a highlighting box.

2. Activate the Shaping tool and click once on the outline of any character in the text string. A square node appears at the base of each letter in the text string, and vertical and horizontal arrow symbols appear at the lower-left and lower-right corners of the text string, respectively:

You will become acquainted with the meaning of these symbols in a moment. For now, it is enough to recognize that this change in the text string's appearance indicates that you have selected it for editing with the Shaping tool. The status line showns that you have selected all 23 characters.

3. Select a single character in the text string, the letter "n" in "naturally." Do this by clicking *once* on the node of this character. The status line now contains the message "1 character(s) selected," and the node at the bottom left of the letter turns black, like this:

naturally

4. Deselect the letter "n" by clicking anywhere outside the text string. Notice that the string itself remains selected, however.

5. Select the initial letter of each word. Click once on the node for the "D" in "Doing." Then press and hold the [Shift] key and click on the node for the initial letter of each of the other words. Check the status line to keep track of the number of characters you select.

6. To deselect these characters, either click on any white space, or press and hold [Shift] and click on each selected character node one by one.

7. Select the entire word "Doing" by lassoing its nodes with a marquee:

Your marquee does not have to surround the characters completely, as long as it surrounds the nodes. All the nodes of this word become highlighted after you release the mouse button.

9

8. Deselect these characters, and then draw a marquee that surrounds all of the text string. All of the characters are now selected for editing.

9. Deselect all of the characters by clicking on any white space. Leave the text on the screen, with the text string selected for editing with the Shaping tool, but with no individual characters selected.

You may be wondering, "Why should I bother to select all the characters with the Shaping tool, when I could activate the Pick tool and change attributes for the entire text string?" You can control *some* attributes that way, but the Character Attributes dialog box offers you even more options for altering the appearance of text. Read on to find out how those additional attributes can enhance the design of text in CorelDRAW!.

The Character Attributes Dialog Box

When you use the Character Attributes dialog box, you can control other characteristics of selected characters besides font, style, and point size. You can tilt characters at any angle, shift them up, down, or sideways, or make them into small subscripts and superscripts. Practically the only thing you can't do is change the characters themselves. In this section, you will learn how to access this dialog box and work with each of the controls in it. As you work thorugh the exercises, you will learn about useful applications for each type of attribute. By the end of the section, you will altered the design of the DOINWHAT.CDR text string substantially.

You can access the Character Attributes dialog box either by double-clicking on a selected character node, or through the Text menu. Any attributes that you alter in this dialog box apply only to the characters you have selected. Make sure, then, that you have selected all of the characters you want to edit before accessing the Character Attributes dialog box.

1. With the Shaping tool active, select the node in front of the letter "n" in "naturally."

2. Access the Character Attributes dialog box in the way that is most convenient for your working habits. If you prefer to use menu commands, select the Characters Attributes option from the Text

menu. If you like using the mouse best, double-click on any of the selected nodes. The Character Attributes dialog box shown in Figure 9–2 appears.

Take a moment to become familiar with the options available to you in this dialog box and with the significance of each attribute.

Reviewing the Dialog Box

The options in the Character Attributes box in Figure 9–2 allow you to control seven different type of text attributes: font, style, type size and its unit of measure, horizontal shift, vertical shift, character angle, and text Placement (superscript and subscript). You are familiar with the first three attributes, but the concepts behind horizontal and vertical shifts, charcter angle, superscript, and subscript may be new to you. If so, browse through this section to find out more about these attributes.

Horizontal Shift   The Horizontal Shift option controls the distance, in % of point size, by which selected characters shift to the right or left of their original location. This unit is variable, depending on the font of the selected characters.

Vertical Shift   The Vertical Shift option controls the distance by which selected characters shift above or below their starting location (baseline). CorelDRAW! expresses this distance as a percentage of the point size of the selected characters. This distance is therefore variable, too.

9

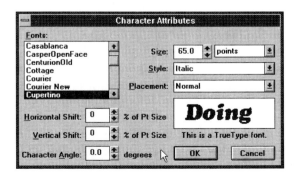

The Character
Attributes
dialog box
Figure 9–2.

Character Angle   The Character Angle option allows you to tile the selected characters in any direction and at any angle. You can turn characters upside down, sideways, or anywhere in between.

Superscript and Subscript   The Superscript and Subscript options, available from the Placement drop-down list box, let you place selected characters above or below the rest of the text, respectively. Superscript text bottom-aligns with the imaginary line at the top of surrounding text (example: the "2" in $E=mc^2$). Subscript text top-aligns with the baseline or surrounding text, for example, the "2" in H_2O. The term baseline refers to the imaginary straight line to which text is normally anchored and with which it aligns.

TIP: The values that display in the Character Attributes dialog box depend on how you invoke the dialog box. If you access this dialog box by double-clicking on a character, you will see the settings assigned to that character, even if you have selected other characters at the same time. If you call up the dialog box by selecting the Character Attributes command, the values displayed correspond to the first character in the selected group.

You can move between options in the Character Attributes dialog box either by using the mouse, or by pressing the Tab or Shift-Tab and the cursor keys. Of course, using the mouse is much simpler!

In the next five sections, you will have the opportunity to redesign text imaginatively, using all of the options in the Character Attributes dialog box.

Editing Font and Style

In the following exercise, you will assign a different font and/or style to each letter in the word "naturally." You selected the first letter of the word before entering the dialog box, so you will alter the letter "n" first of all.

1. Select the Aardvark font in the Font list box and then select OK. Your text string redisplays on the screen, but now the letter "n" looks quite different from the surrounding letters.

2. Double-click on the character node of the "n" once more. When the dialog box appears this time, it shows the current font of the *selected* character of characters. (See the tip in the previous section.) Select Cancel to exit the dialog box.

3. Select each of the other letters in the word "naturally" in turn. Assign fonts and styles to them in the following order: Paradise Normal, Frankfurt Gothic Bold Italic, Cupertino Normal, Renfrew-Normal, Switzerland Italic, Unicorn Normal, USA Black Italic, Banff Normal. When you are finished, the word "naturally" displays an interesting patchwork of fonts:

4. Save the changes you have made by pressing ⌈Ctrl⌋-⌈S⌋, and leave your work on the screen for the next exercise.

Go on to the next section to apply different point sizes to the letters whose fonts and styles you have already altered.

Editing Type Size

When you changed fonts for each letter in the word "naturally," you left the type sizes unaltered, yet the letters do not appear to be the same size. You have probably guessed by now that different fonts have different heights and widths and the point size is only one way to measure text size.

In the following exercise, you will make the letters in this word closer to one another in actual size.

1. Using the Shaping tool again, double-click on the character node of the first letter "a" in "naturally." When the Character Attributes dialog box appears, change the point size for this letter to 140.0 and then select OK. Even though you have more than doubled its point size, this letter only now approximates the height of its neighbors. Point size is measured from the baseline of one line to

the baseline above it and is not necessarily a measure of the actual type. (You may need to scroll your screen downward to see the word "naturally.")

2. In the same way, select the first letter "I" and change its type size to 75.0 points.

3. Finally, select the letter "y" and change its point size to 90.0. Now, all of the letters seem more uniform in height and size:

4. Save your work by pressing Ctrl-S, leaving the text string on screen.

To edit the work "naturally" so that it conveys a sense of a more natural state, you can shift some of the characters up or down relative to the baseline and move others sideways. In the next exercise, you will practice moving individual characters.

Horizontal and Vertical Shift

When you shift selected characters horizontally, you move them to the right or left of their starting position, causing them to overlap with other characters on the same line. You can use this technique to convey a sense of being rushed or crowded, or simply to adjust spacing between letters precisely. When you shift characters vertically, they fall above or below the baseline, which can create a feeling of spontaneity or excitement.

In the next exercise, you will shift some of the characters in the word "naturally" to enhance the sense of spontaneity and a natural look in the text.

1. Activate the Shaping tool and then double-click on the character node for the letter "n" in the word "naturally" to enter the

Character Attributes dialog box. Set Horizontal Shift to -25% of the point size and then select OK. Because you set the value to a negative number, the letter shifts to the left of its original position.

2. Select the character node for the next letter "a" and set Vertical Shift to 20% of point size. When you select OK, the position of the letter shifts above the baseline.

3. Select the following letters in turn and change the shift settings for each as follows. Change "r" to Vertical Shift -25%, the second "l" to Vertical Shift 10%, and the "y" to Horizontal Shift 25% and Vertical Shift 25%. Notice that a negative value for Vertical Shift causes the selected character, "r," to reposition itself below the baseline. The resulting text should now look like this:

4. Save your changes and leave this text on the screen.

So far, you have edited attributes for one letter at a time. In the next section, you will select a group of characters and practice positioning them as superscripts and subscripts.

9

Creating Superscripts and Subscripts

Perform the following exercise to simulate a superscript and subscript.

1. With the Shaping tool select the character nodes of all of the letters in the word "come" except the letter "c." Double-click on the node in front of "o" to access the Character Attributes dialog box.

2. Click on the Placement down arrow, click on Superscript option button and then select OK. The selected letters have become small and appear as a superscript to the letter "c," like this:

c^{omes} . . .

3. Select the Undo command in the Edit menu to return the selected characters to their original position.

4. Select the same characters again and return to the Character Attributes dialog box by double-clicking on the "o" node. This time, click on the Subscript option button. When you select OK, the letters display as a subscript to the letter "c."

5. Press Alt - Backspace to return the selected characters to their original position.

In the next section, you will complete the last exercise pertinent to the Character Attributes dialog box. You will practice tilting the characters in the word "naturally" to different angles.

Editing Character Angle

You can tilt selected characters at any angle using the Character Angle setting in the Character Attributes dialog box. Values between 0 and 180 degrees indicate that you are tilting the characters above an imaginary horizon, in a counterclockwise direction. Values between 0 and -180 degrees indicate that you are tilting the characters below an imaginary horizon, in a clockwise direction. At a 180-degree angle, the characters are upside down Practice adjusting character angle in the following exercise.

1. With the Shaping tool active, select the character nodes of the letter "n," the letter "u," and the letter "y" in the word "naturally." Double-click on one of these nodes to access the Character Attributes dialog box. Set Character Angle to -15 degrees and then select OK. The selected characters now appear tilted toward the right.

2. Deselect these three letters and select the letter "t," the second letter "a," and the second letter "l." Double-click on one of these nodes to access the Character Attributes dialog box. Set Character Angle to 15 degrees and then select OK. These characters appear tilted toward the left. The word "naturally" now seems to fly off in all directions:

3. Save your changes and then select New from the File menu to clear the screen.

This concludes the tutorial on the use of the settings in the Character Attributes dialog box. No doubt you have come up with a few creative ideas of your own while practicing on the exercises in the preceding sections. When you are ready to proceed, continue through the next portion of this chapter, where you will learn some convenient ways to kern text and adjust spacing interactively.

Kerning Text Interactively

Kerning, simply defined, is the art of adjusting the space between individual pairs of letters for greater readability. There are many possible letter pair combinations in the 26 letters of the English alphabet, but most font manufacturers provide automatic kerning for only a few hundred commonly used pairs. Occasionally you will see too much or too little space between adjacent letters. You can kern these letter pairs by moving one of the letters subtly to the right or left.

Using kerning as a design element can enhance the power of your message. For instance, you will draw more attention to your text when you kern letters to create special effects, such as expanded letter spacing in selected words of a magazine or newspaper headline.

The exercises in this session offer more extreme examples of kerning than you are likely to find in most text, but they will help you become familiar with the concept of kerning. Follow the steps in each exercise to learn how to kern single or multiple characters. Integrated within the

exercises is information on using constraint and alignment techniques
to kern more easily and precisely.

Kerning Single Characters

The following exercise lets you practice adjusting spacing between any
two text characters. As you work through the steps, you will learn how
to ensure that characters align properly with the surrounding text after
you move them. Before starting the exercise, adjust viewing
magnification to actual size. Turn on Snap To Grid, Show Rulers, Show
Status Line, and Show Grid, and set both the Horizontal and Vertical
Grid Frequency to 8 per inch. Retain these settings for both exercises on
kerning.

1. Select the Text tool and then select a text insertion point at the
   1 1/2-inch mark on the horizontal ruler and the 4 1/2-inch mark
   on the vertical ruler.

2. Type the word **Kerning** in upper- and lowercase letters. Leave a
   space after the "K" and another after the "e." Press Enter to begin a
   new line and type the word **Text** on this line. Leave one space
   after the letter "T," one space after the "e," and two spaces after
   the letter "x."

3. Select the Pick tool, open the Text roll-up, and set the justification
   to None, the type size to 80.0 points, the font to Bodnoff, and click
   on Apply.

4. After the text string appears on the screen as in Figure 9–3, select
   the Shaping tool. Since the text string was the last object you
   created, the Shaping tool selects it automatically. A node appears
   next to each character in the text string; vertical and horizontal
   spacing control handles appear at each end of the last line of the
   text string.

5. You will need to bring the letter "e" in "Kerning" much closer to
   the "K" and the letters "rning" closer to the "e." To adjust the
   spacing between "K" and "e" so that the text will appear more
   uniform, press and hold the left mouse button on the node in
   front of the letter "e." When you begin to move the mouse, the
   pointer turns into a fourheaded arrow. Use the status line's "dx"
   indicator to help you drag the letter 0.41 inches to the left, as
   shown in Figure 9–4. A dotted outline of the letter follows the

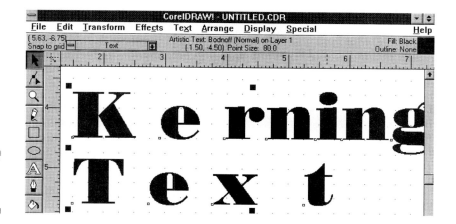

Text in need of
kerning
Figure 9–3.

pointer as you drag. When you release the mouse button, the letter
itself appears in this location.

6. If the "e" is not aligned with the rest of the text, snap this letter
   back to its original position by selecting the Straighten Text
   command in the Text menu, and then repeat step 5. This
   command erases any previous kerning information, so use it only
   when you want to return text to its original location. Alternatively,
   you can select the Align To Baseline command, also in the Text
   menu. When you accidentally position a character to align above
   or below the baseline, this command forces the character to align
   with the baseline again. Unlike the Straighten Text command, the

9

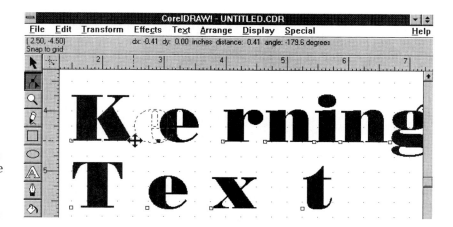

Kerning a single
letter
Figure 9–4.

Align To Baseline command does not erase any previous kerning information.

7. Save your kerned text as KERN1.CDR and leave it on the screen for the next exercise.

TIP: If you require a high degree of precision in the placement of kerned text, zoom in on the character(s) you want to move. Alternatively, you can press and hold Ctrl while moving the characters, thereby constraining the text to align with the nearest baseline. Be sure to release the mouse button before you release Ctrl to make certain of proper alignment.

Kerning Multiple Characters

In this section, you will learn how to move and kern multiple characters within a text string simultaneously. In practice, your most common use for this feature will be to move the remaining characters of a word closer to another letter that you have already kerned. However, you can select and reposition any group of characters, including nonadjacent characters, to another location in the same way.

1. With the KERN1.CDR file displayed in an Actual Size viewing magnification, select the Shaping tool and draw a marquee around the letters "rning."

2. Click on the node for the letter "r" and then drag the mouse 0.71 inches to the left. Refer to the status line for assistance. All the letters in the selected group follow, as shown in Figure 9–5. If the selected characters do not line up with the adjoining text when you release the mouse button, review step 6 in the previous exercise. You may want to use the Align To Baseline and Straighten Text commands. Deselect the letters "rning" when you have them in the desired location.

3. Use Shift to select the "e" and the second "t" in "Text." Click on the node in front of the letter "e" and drag .37 inches to the left as shown in Figure 9–6a. Both selected letters should move together across the screen without disturbing the "x." After you release the mouse button the letters "e" and "t" will appear as shown in Figure 9–6b.

Kerning
multiple
adjacent letters
Figure 9–5.

4. As you can see, the letters "x" and "t" still are not close enough to the "e." Experiment by moving these two letters on your screen until the text string appears normal.

5. Save your changes to the file by pressing Ctrl-S. Then select New from the File menu to clear the screen.

Kerning is not the only text attribute that can adjust interactively with the Shaping tool. In the next section, you will learn how to adjust spacing between characters, words, and lines for an entire selected text string.

Adjusting Spacing Interactively

There are two ways to edit inter-character, inter-word, and inter-line spacing of existing text in CorelDRAW!. The first way, as you will recall, is to select the text string with the Pick tool and then invoke the Artistic Text dialog box using either Ctrl-T or the Edit Text command in the Edit menu. Using this method, you can click on the Spacing command button in the Artistic Text dialog box and set spacing in the sub-dialog box provided. You enjoy the advantage of precision but experience the disadvantage of going through a series of additional steps.

If you prefer to work more spontaneously, CorelDRAW! offers you an interactive method of spacing as well. This method involves selecting

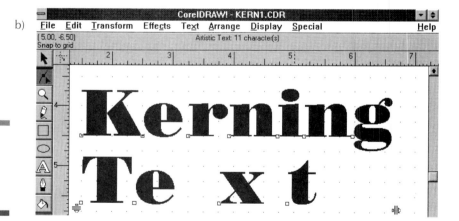

Kerning
multiple
nonadjacent
letters
Figure 9–6.

the text string with the Shaping tool and then dragging one of the two stylized arrows that appear at the text string's lower boundary. Keep in mind, however, that you adjust spacing for *all* of the characters in the text string when you use this technique. To adjust spacing between two individual characters, see the "Kerning Single Characters" section of this chapter.

To alter inter-character spacing interactively, you drag the horizontal arrow at the lower-right boundary of the text string. To alter inter-word spacing, you drag the same arrow while holding down Ctrl. And to alter inter-line spacing, you drag the vertical arrow at the lower-left boundary of the text string.

The next three sections provide a short tutorial on altering each of the three types of spacing interactively.

Adjusting Inter-character Spacing

In the following exercise, you will create a text string and adjust the inter-character spacing, observing the changes in the CorelDRAW! interface as you work.

1. Set viewing magnification to Actual Size, then activate the Text tool and select an insertion point near the upper-left corner of your viewing window.

2. Type **Running out of** on the first line of the text entry window and **space** on the second. Click on the Pick tool, open the Text roll-up, and set text attributes to Fujiyama Normal, Left Justification, and 75.0 points, and then select Apply. The text displays in your viewing window. If the text string is not completely visible on the display, select the text string and move it to the location shown in Figure 9–7.

Displaying the
spacing
adjustment
arrows
Figure 9–7.

9

3. Activate the Shaping tool. Each character node increases in size, and stylized vertical and horizontal arrows appear at the lower-left and lower-right boundaries of the text object, just as in Figure 9–7.

4. Position the Shaping pointer directly over the horizontal arrow at the lower-right boundary of the text object, until the pointer turns into a crosshair. Then, drag this arrow to the right. Notice that, just as in the example in Figure 9–8, the characters do not seem to move immediately; instead, you see a dotted outline following the two-way arrow pointer. As you drag, the status line displays the message "Inter-Character," followed by information about the horizontal distance by which you are increasing the size of the text boundary.

5. When the right boundary of the text string (represented by the dotted outline) reaches the desired point, release the mouse button. The text repositions itself to align with that boundary, and the space between each character increases proportionally, as shown in Figure 9–9.

6. If you would like to know the exact inter-character spacing measurement you have obtained, select the text string with the Pick tool and access the Artistic Text and Spacing dialog boxes. This is a good way to check for precision.

Adjusting
inter-character
spacing
Figure 9–8.

Increasing
inter-character
spacing
Figure 9–9.

7. Select the Undo command from the Edit menu to return the text to its former position. Then re-select the Shaping tool and *decrease* the space between characters by dragging the horizontal arrow to the left instead of the right. If you decrease the space drastically, letters may even overlap each other, like this:

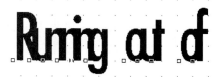

8. Select Undo once more to return the characters to their original positions. Leave this text on the screen for now.

This method is useful when you want to fit text into a defined space within a drawing, without changing the point size or other attributes. Go on to the next section to practice changing inter-word spacing independently of the spacing between characters.

Adjusting Inter-word Spacing

Suppose that you don't need to change the spacing between letters but your design calls for increased or decreased spacing between words. To adjust inter-word spacing interactively, you drag the same horizontal arrow that you used for inter-character spacing. The difference is that you also hold down Ctrl at the same time. Try the following exercise, using the text string you created in the previous section.

1. With the Shaping tool active and the text string selected, position the pointer over the horizontal arrow until the pointer turns into a crosshair. Then press and hold Ctrl and drag the two-way arrow pointer to the right. The status line displays the message "InterWord," followed by the horizontal distance by which you are stretching the text boundary.

2. When the outline that you are dragging has the desired width, release the mouse button first, and then Ctrl. (If you release Ctrl first, you will adjust the inter-character rather than the inter-word spacing.) The text redisplays with increased space between each word, as shown in Figure 9–10.

3. Select the Undo command in the Edit menu to return the text to its original inter-word spacing.

Increasing
inter-word
spacing
Figure 9–10.

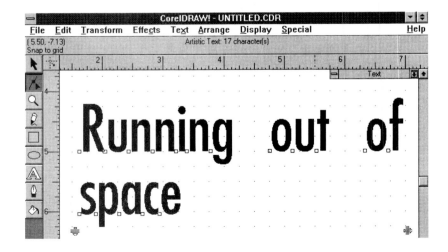

4. Try decreasing the amount of inter-word spacing by dragging the horizontal arrow to the left instead of the right. When you are finished experimenting, select the Undo command once more. Leave this text on the screen for the next exercise.

You can change the spacing between lines of a text string, as well as between words or characters. The next section gives you hands-on practice in editing inter-line spacing.

Adjusting Inter-line Spacing

To edit inter-line spacing with the Shaping tool, you drag the vertical arrow located at the lower left of the text boundary. Try increasing and decreasing the space between lines now, using the same text string you have been working with for the past two sections. Note that if your text string contains only one line, dragging the vertical arrow has no effect.

1. With the Shaping tool active and the text string selected, position the mouse pointer directly over the vertical arrow that appears at the lower-left text boundary and drag this arrow downward. The mouse pointer turns into a two-way vertical arrow. Simultaneously, the status line displays the message "Inter-Line," followed by the vertical distance measurement, which tells you how much you have increased the size of the text boundary.

2. When you have increased the boundary by the desired size, release the mouse button. The text repositions itself to fit the new boundary; as in Figure 9–11, only the spacing between lines changes, not the length or size of the text itself.

3. To see the precise amount of inter-line spacing that you have added, press the (Spacebar) or activate the Pick tool and then select the Edit Text command in the Edit menu. Then, click on the Spacing command button to see the Spacing dialog box. When you are finished, select Undo from the Edit menu to return the text string to its former inter-line spacing.

4. Reduce the inter-line spacing of the text string by dragging the vertical arrow upward instead of downward. When you are finished, select Undo to return the text to its former spacing.

9

Increasing
inter-line
spacing
Figure 9–11.

5. Select New from the File menu and click on No when asked if you want to save current changes, to clear the screen before beginning the next section.

By now, you have explored all of the possible text attributes that you can change using the Pick and Shaping tools. If you need to give your text an even more customized look, however, you have the option of converting text to a curve object and then editing its nodes. This is the topic of the next and final section of this chapter.

Reshaping Characters

Graphics designers and desktop publishers often need stylized text characters that give their messages extra flair, but that just don't exist in standard fonts. CorelDRAW! can help you create such "text pictures" easily. All you have to do is select text attributes that approximate the effect you want to achieve, and then convert the text string to curves. You can then reshape the text using the Pick and Shaping tools.

The following exercise contains a simple step-by-step example of how to create stylized text pictures. Carry out the steps and give your own imagination a boost!

1. To prepare for this exercise, turn off Show Rulers, Snap To Grid, and Show Grid, and set the viewing magnification to actual size.

2. Activate the Text tool and select an insertion point about midway down the left edge of your viewing area.

3. Type **Snake** in upper- and lowercase letters and open the Artistic Text dialog box. Test each of the fonts in the Fonts list box against the sample display character. The capital "S" of the Gatineau font bears a fairly strong resemblance to a snake, so set text attributes to Gatineau Bold Italic, 150.0 points, and Left Justification. Select OK to exit the Artistic Text dialog box and display your text on the page, as shown in Figure 9–12.

4. Activate the Shaping tool and double-click on the node for the letter "S" to open the Character Attributes dialog box.

5. Your aim is to increase the size of the letter "S" and make it a *drop cap*—a first capital letter that falls below the baseline of the remaining text. To achieve this aim, set the type size for the letter "S" to 250.0 points and set Vertical Shift to -25% of type size. Select OK to make these changes take effect. Your text should now look like Figure 9–13.

6. Activate the Pick tool (or press the [Spacebar]) to select the entire text string, and then click on the Convert To Curves option in the Arrange menu. The text redisplays with many little nodes,

9

"Snake" text: Gatineau Bold Italic, 150.0 points
Figure 9–12.

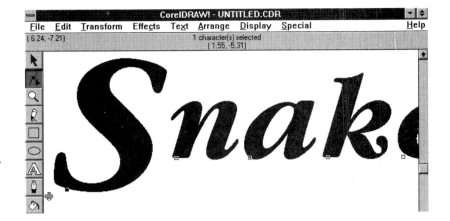

Increasing the size of the letter "S"
Figure 9–13.

indicating that it has become a curve object. If you activate the Shaping tool again, the status line displays the message, "Curve: 213 nodes on 8 subpaths." This message indicates that CorelDRAW! now considers this text string to be one object with eight combined segments.

7. Activate the Pick tool again and select the Break Apart command in the Arrange menu. Each letter is now a separate object.

NOTE: The space inside the "a," "k," and "e," fill in because the letters are formed by two objects which you just broke apart. When the two objects are combined, their common area becomes transparent, causing the space. Remember the teacup handle example under "Combining and Breaking Objects Apart" in Chapter 6. If you want the spaces to reappear, select the characters with the Pick tool and choose Combine from the Arrange menu.

8. Deselect all of the letters and then click on the letter "S" with the Pick tool. Stretch the letter vertically by dragging the middle boundary markers on the upper and lower sides of the highlighting box. Your goal is to elongate the letter, thereby enhancing the "snake-like" appearance. You may need to Scroll your screen to see all of the "S."

"S" converted
to curves and
reshaped with
the Shaping tool
Figure 9–14.

9. Now, activate the Shaping tool and manipulate the nodes of the "S" so that you achieve the general look of Figure 9–14. Make some areas of the "snake" narrower and other broader. You will want to reshape and move the snake's head, too. Make the "tail" of the snake narrower, as well.

10. You can try to match the results in Figure 9–14 exactly or develop your own creative enhancements utilizing all of the skills you have learned at this point in the book. When you are satisfied with the appearance of the snake, save the image under the filename SNAKE.CDR.

11. Select New from the File menu to clear the screen.

As you can see, the possibilities for creating custom characters for text are virtually endless. If you find yourself fired up with new ideas for your own projects, experiment until you design a word picture that best enhances your message.

9

CHAPTER

10

CUTTING, COPYING, PASTING, AND OBJECT LINKING AND EMBEDDING (OLE)

So far you have learned how to select, move, rearrange, transform, and reshape objects within a single graphic. An equally important part of the editing process involves the transfer of image information within a graphic, between pictures, or between *CorelDRAW! and other Windows applications. The editing functions that allow* you to transfer image data include copying, cutting, and pasting objects and pictures, deleting or duplicating objects, and copying object attributes. You access these operations using the Cut, Copy, Paste, Delete, Duplicate, and Copy Style From commands in the Edit menu.

These editing functions have many uses that will save you time and design effort. You don't have to start from scratch each time you need to duplicate an object or its style attribute. You can simply transfer image information, using the editing commands. You perform some of the transfer operations within a single picture; others allow you to transfer information between CorelDRAW! files, and even between CorelDRAW! and other Windows applications.

CorelDRAW! allows you to transfer objects to and from the Windows clipboard. This means that you can copy or cut objects between different image files in CorelDRAW!, or from CorelDRAW! to a file in another Windows application. Conversely, you can copy or cut objects from files in other Windows applications and paste them to the page of your choice in CorelDRAW!.

This chapter covers the use of the Windows clipboard, both within CorelDRAW! and between CorelDRAW! and other Windows applications. It introduces you to some additional object and style copying functions in CorelDRAW! that complement the use of the Windows clipboard. You'll find out how to duplicate objects within a drawing and how to copy attributes from one object to another. You'll review the difference between cutting objects from a file and deleting them permanently. Finally you will work with Object Linking and Embedding, usually referred to by the acronym OLE (pronounced O'lay). OLE provides new ways to utilize objects from different applications.

About the Windows Clipboard

If you haven't used Windows applications before, you may be wondering how the clipboard works. Think of the Windows clipboard as a temporary storage bin that can contain only one item at a time. When you select an object and then click on the Copy or Cut command in the Edit menu, you send a copy of the object from the clipboard to place it in your drawing at the desired location. The copy you sent to the clipboard remains there until you overwrite it by copying or cutting another object, or until you exit Windows and end a session.

Windows creates its own file format, called a *metafile*, out of the information that you send to the clipboard. This standard metafile format allows you to share information between different applications that run under Windows. A metafile can be larger or smaller than the object you send to the clipboard, depending on the complexity of the information you are trying to transfer. As a rule of thumb, the more complex an object is in terms of its attributes, the more memory it requires when you send it to the clipboard.

Theoretically, all Windows applications should be able to trade information through the clipboard. In practice, however, some types of information in objects or files transfer better than others. When you have completed the basic exercises on copying, cutting, and pasting objects within CorelDRAW!, turn to the section entitled "Between Applications." There you will find tips for trouble-free transfer operations through the clipboard.

Copy, Cut, Duplicate, or Delete

In order to duplicate or delete one or more objects, or copy or cut them to the clipboard, you must first select the objects with the Pick tool. The Edit menu commands and their keyboard shortcuts are unavailable to you unless one or more objects are already selected.

You can select a single object, multiple objects, or all objects in a graphic for any of the Edit menu operations discussed in this chapter. To select a single object for one of the transfer operation, just click on its outline once. To select multiple objects for a transfer operation, use [Shift] or the marquee method you first learned in Chapter 6. (You might also want to group the objects after you select them in order to avoid separating them from each other accidentally.) To select all of the objects in a graphic, click on the Select All command in the Edit menu.

10

Copying and Pasting Objects

The Copy and Paste commands in the Edit menu enable you to copy CorelDRAW! objects and paste them to the same file, to another file in CorelDRAW!, or to another Windows application. When you *copy* an object to the clipboard, the original object remains in position on the page. When you *paste* the object, Windows makes another copy from the copy in the clipboard. The copy in the clipboard remains there until you overwrite it by copying or cutting another object or group of objects, or until you exit Windows.

To practice copying objects to the clipboard and pasting them to the same or different pictures, you will use a file that you created in Chapter 8.

Copying and Pasting Objects Within a Picture

When you copy an object to the clipboard and then paste it to the same picture, the copy overlays the original object exactly. The copy is selected as soon as it appears on the page, however, so you can move it safely without displacing the original object.

A more convenient way to copy an object within the same picture is to use the Duplicate command. When you invoke this command, CorelDRAW! automatically offsets the copy of the object from the original and the copy at the same time. See the "Duplicating Objects" section of this chapter for more details.

1. Open the ARROW1.CDR file and group all of the text strings in the picture, using the Select All command in the Edit menu and then the Group command in the Arrange menu.

2. To copy the grouped objects to the clipboard, either select the Copy command from the Edit menu as shown in Figure 10–1, or press Ctrl-Ins. The pointer turns into an hourglass until CorelDRAW! finishes copying the selected object to the clipboard.

3. Select Paste from the Edit menu or press Shift-Ins. The screen redraws, with the pasted object selected. You will not notice anything different because the pasted object appears exactly on top of the original.

4. To move the pasted object away from the original, press and hold the mouse button directly over any outline of the selected object and drag it as desired. You can now scale, rotate, stretch, skew, or otherwise edit the pasted object.

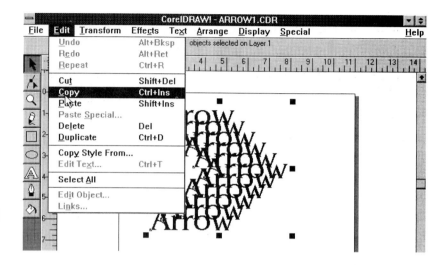

Selecting the
Copy command
Figure 10–1.

5. Select New from the File menu to clear the screen before
    continuing. Do not save any changes to the ARROW1.CDR
    document.

In the previous exercise, you copied a group of objects to the same
picture. In the next section, you will copy an object to a different
picture and use it as a design enhancement there.

Copying and Pasting Between Pictures

In the following exercise you will copy the text string from the
DOINWHAT.CDR file and paste it to the KITE.CDR file.

1. Open the DOINWHAT.CDR file and select the text string.

2. Select Copy from the Edit menu or press [Ctrl]-[Ins] to copy the text to
    the clipboard. The pointer may temporarily turn into an hourglass
    until CorelDRAW! finishes copying the text string. This lets you
    know it's busy.

3. Open the KITE.CDR file and drag all of the guidelines off the
    screen. Make sure Edit Wireframe is checked (turned on) in the
    Display menu.

10

4. From the Edit menu, choose Select All; then from the Arrange menu, select Group. The status line should contain "Group of 4 objects."

5. Position the pointer at any of the four corner boundary markers of the group. Then drag the marker diagonally inward to scale down the kite to approximately 50% of its original size.

6. Drag the kite so it is approximately centered horizontally (and leaves about one-third of the vertical white space at the top). See Figure 10–2.

7. Select Paste from the Edit menu or press Shift-Ins. The text string will come into the center of the page.

8. Drag the text to the top of the page to complete the image (to be produced here) as shown in Figure 10–3.

9. Select Save As from the File menu, type **kite2**, and select Save.

As you can see from the preceding exercise, you don't have to start from scratch to design an attractive picture. You can copy and paste

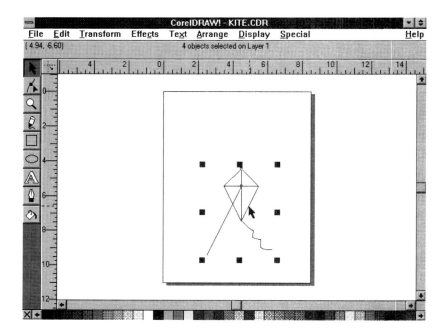

Kite positioned to receive pasted text
Figure 10–2.

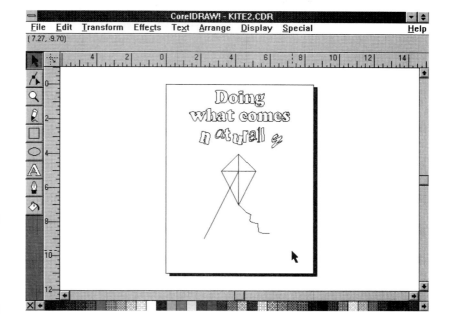

Copying and
pasting an
object to an
existing image
Figure 10–3.

existing objects and images to an illustration in progress, saving
yourself work without sacrificing quality or originality. In the next
sections, you will experiment with the Cut and Paste menu commands
and see how their operation differs from that of Copy and Paste.

Cutting and Pasting Objects

When you select an object and then invoke the Cut command in the
Edit menu, the object disappears and goes to the clipboard. When you
then select the Paste command, Windows places a copy of the cut
object on the page.

The original object that you cut remains in the clipboard until you
overwrite it by cutting or copying another object, or until you end a
Windows session.

To begin practicing cutting and pasting objects, you will use the
LANDSCAP.CDR file you created in Chapter 4.

10

Cutting and Pasting Within a Picture

There are two ways to remove an unwanted object from a picture in CorelDRAW!. You can either cut it to the clipboard using the Cut command, or delete it from the program memory entirely by using the Delete command. Use the Cut command unless you are absolutely certain that you will never need the object again. If you delete an object using the Delete command, CorelDRAW! doesn't store a copy anywhere; unless you immediately select the Undo command, you won't be able to recover the object.

CorelDRAW! always pastes a cut or copied object as the top layer of the picture. Therefore, when you cut and paste objects within an image that contains several layers of objects, remember to restore the original object arrangement using the commands in the Arrange menu.

1. Open the LANDSCAP.CDR file that you created in Chapter 4.

2. With the Pick tool, draw a marquee around the tree and its trunk to select it (make sure your marquee is large enough to completely enclose the boundary markers for the top of the tree).

3. From the Arrange menu, select Group.

4. Select Cut from the Edit menu or press Shift-Del. The tree disappears from the drawing as shown in Figure 10–4.

5. Select Paste from the Edit menu and the tree comes back onto the drawing in the same place it was originally.

   If the tree was not on the top layer of the drawing, it will be after pasting. In the case, it is not *exactly* where it was originally.

6. Select a bird and then choose Delete from the Edit menu or press Del.

   Once an object has been cleared or deleted from a drawing you can use Undo to restore it. If you do so, select Undo prior to doing anything else; otherwise the object is gone. Undo only remembers the last action.

7. Press Shift-Ins or select Paste again. Another tree comes onto the drawing, not the bird—the bird is not on the clipboard; the tree still is. There will be a second tree because the second tree came in on top of the original tree. Drag the second tree off to one side to see the other tree. Press Del to get rid of the second tree.

The tree cut from LANDSCAP.CDR
Figure 10–4.

Go immediately on to the next section of this chapter because you will need to use the contents of the clipboard (the tree) in the next section, where you will cut and paste objects between different pictures in CorelDRAW!.

Cutting and Pasting Between Pictures

Earlier in this chapter, you created a poster by combining the kite you drew in Chapter 2 with some text you created in Chapter 9. In the following exercise, you will add two copies of the tree you cut from the LANDSCAP.CDR drawing and the word "CorelDRAW!" you will cut from a drawing that you will create.

1. From the File menu, select Open. Answer No to saving changes to the LANDSCAP.CDR file and select KITE2.CDR as the file to open.

2. Press `Shift`-`Ins` to paste the tree from the clipboard onto the kite poster. When the tree comes onto the drawing, drag it down about a quarter of an inch.

10

3. Again select Paste and drag the second tree to the right side of the poster and then approximately align it with the first tree. See Figure 10–5.

4. Save the file as KITE3.CDR and then select new from the File menu. From the Display menu, click on Show Rulers to turn them off and on Edit Wireframe to change to full color mode.

5. Select the Text tool and place the insertion point near the center of the page. Choose Text roll-up from the Text menu, then select the font, Times New Roman 60 point Italic. Select the Center-justification button and click on Apply.

6. Using all capital letters, type **CORELDRAW!**, then press F4 to go to Fit-in-window magnification (the second icon from the right in the fly-out menu).

7. Select the Shaping tool, then select all the characters in "DRAW!". From the Text roll-up, select the font Freeport 80 point, and then click on Apply. Close the Text roll-up.

Trees pasted onto the kite poster
Figure 10–5.

Your text should look similar to Figure 10–6. Select Save As from the File menu and name the drawing CDLOGO.CDR.

8. With the Pick tool, select the word "CorelDRAW!," and select Cut from the Edit menu.

9. Select Open from the File menu, answer No if asked whether you want to save the current file, and again select KITE3.CDR.

10. Select Edit/Paste. The word "CorelDRAW!" appears in the middle of the drawing.

11. Drag "CorelDRAW!" to the bottom of the poster. Then by dragging on one of the corner boundary markers, scale it to fit in the space available as shown in Figure 10–7.

12. Save the completed poster as KITE4.CDR and select New to clear your workspace.

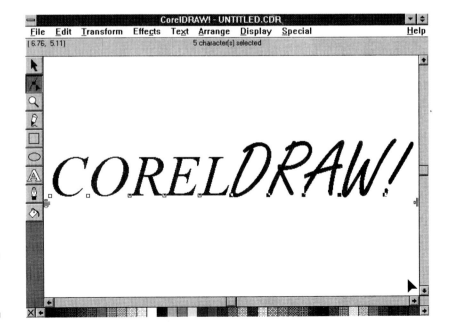

Text Object,
CORELDRAW!
Figure 10–6.

10

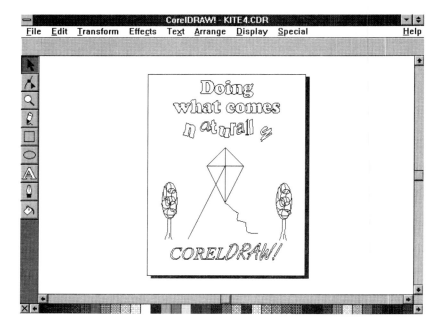

Completed
poster with four
pasted objects
Figure 10–7.

Working with Different Applications

The number of software packages running under Microsoft Windows is
increasing almost daily. These programs include such diverse
applications as word processors, desktop publishing and presentation
software, database managers and forms generators, and, of course, paint
and illustration software. If your other favorite Windows applications
also support the Windows clipboard, you should be able to transfer
data back and forth between them and CorelDRAW!

Features and techniques differ with every application; however, as a
result, not all visual information transfers equally well between
programs. There are too many Windows applications to catalog what
happens to each file type as it transfers to or from CorelDRAW! through
the clipboard. However, the following sections should give you an idea
of how the clipboard handles graphic information that you transfer
between CorelDRAW! and some of the most popular software.

Clipboard Memory Limits

There is a slight chance that at some point you may get an error message that says "CorelDRAW! clipboard format too large to put on clipboard." Should this happen, you can break the object into smaller groups of objects, and then transfer them in several passes. You can also save the object as a new drawing, then use the Import command to move it.

In most cases when you get the "CorelDRAW! clipboard format..." message, CorelDRAW! will actually have copied the selected objects to the clipboard in spite of the message. Check the Paste command in the Edit menu; if it is now available for selection, the objects have been successfully copied. If this command is not available, CorelDRAW! could not copy the selected object.

In general, you'll have the best chance of success when copying, cutting, and pasting CorelDRAW! objects that don't take advantage of too many advanced features at one time. An image that includes text, custom calligraphic outlines, PostScript fills, or fountain fills, for example, will be more difficult to transfer to the clipboard than an apparently complex geometrical image that contains none of these features.

Transferring Objects to Other Applications

When you copy or cut a CorelDRAW! object to the clipboard, you are transferring not only the shape of an object, but also its attributes. Attributes include outline, outline fill, object fill, and text characteristics. Some attributes do not transfer well in their original form, owing in some cases to the diversity of Windows applications and in others to the complexity of CorelDRAW! features.

10

Most problems with transferring CorelDRAW! objects into the clipboard have to do with objects taking too much memory. The following tips should help you avoid clipboard memory or Windows metafile compatibility problems.

Fountain fills and PostScript fills (both discussed in Chapter 13) are extremely memory intensive from the standpoint of the Windows clipboard, and they may go through unpredictable changes when transferred to another program. For example, the following anomaly has been observed when transferring objects containing fountain and PostScript fills:

✦ Objects with PostScript fills may be represented by blank or gray space when they are pasted into some applications. Even the outline disappears.

When an object with PostScript fill is transferred through the clipboard, you often get the outline and then either no fill, or the little "PS"s that you see on the CorelDRAW! screen. The PostScript fill itself is not transferred in any instance.

Text sent from CorelDRAW! files to the clipboard can be sensitive also. The greater the number of letters and/or attributes in a text string, the more likely that some information will not transfer properly. The specific program to which you want to send the text may further influence the transfer of information. As a general rule text comes in as a graphic object rather than as editable text.

On the positive side, a number of applications such as PageMaker can import CorelDRAW!-produced lines, curves, fills, fountain fills, and text, with all of their attributes, from the clipboard without a problem.

Transferring Objects from Other Applications

When you transfer objects from your other favorite Windows applications to CorelDRAW!, you may not always receive exactly what you sent to the clipboard. Sometimes this limitation depends on what the Windows clipboard can interpret; at other times, the apparent discrepancy is specific to the interaction between the other program and CorelDRAW!.

The clipboard, for example, has difficulty transferring special text kerning or text rotation information, pattern or flood fills, pixel-by-pixel manipulations, and combined pen colors from other Windows applications to CorelDRAW!.

Text that you import into CorelDRAW! from another Windows application comes in with the default text attributes. If you know the font, style, alignment, and other attributes you want, set these before importing the text. You can import a maximum of 4000 text characters at a time.

Some features do not transfer well into CorelDRAW!. Bitmaps, for example, often don't transfer well. Text sent from other graphics applications (as opposed to word processors) often arrives in CorelDRAW! as curves. A fill or fountain fill from another program may transfer into CorelDRAW! as solid, or as an outline and separate fill object. Circles and ellipses may come in as connected line segments, while curves may become straight line segments. As CorelDRAW!, Microsoft Windows, and other Windows applications are constantly being upgraded, however, you can expect compatibility to improve. In the remaining sections of the chapter, you will learn about special commands in the CorelDRAW! Edit menu that make it easy for you to copy objects or their attributes within a CorelDRAW! file.

Object Linking and Embedding

Object Linking and Embedding (OLE) is similar to copying and pasting. With OLE, though, the source object is from an application other than the one you bring it into, and a connection is maintained to the source document, so that any editing in the source document will automatically appear in the destination document. Most importantly, with OLE you can double-click on an object in the destination application, and the source application will open and allow you to edit the object. With a normal copy and paste operation you would not be able to edit the pasted object; you would have to delete the object, go to the source to change it, and then copy it back in. There are two forms of OLE: object linking and object embedding. They are the same, except that in embedding, a copy is made of the source document and changes made to the copy do not affect the original.

10

Linking

When an object is linked to its source, the object is not actually copied, but rather a dynamic link is formed. When you double-click on the destination object, the link causes the source application and source object to open and the changes are made there. When you return to the destination application, the changes will appear. To demonstrate linking, follow these steps:

1. Switch to the Program Manager and start CorelPhoto-Paint!.

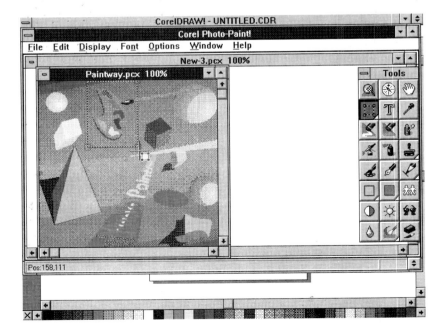

2. Open the file, PAINTWAY.PCX in your SAMPLES directory. Save this file to another name to prevent changes to the original; use the name, LINKOBJ.PCX.

3. Using the Box Selection tool, select some part of the picture, as shown in Figure 10–8.

4. Select Copy from the Edit menu, then close CorelPhoto-Paint!. Reactivate the CorelDRAW! window.

5. Select Paste Special from the Edit menu to establish the object link. The source object is now on the page. You can size and move the object, but to change its actual contents you must use the source application.

6. Double-click anywhere on the object and CorelPhoto-Paint! restarts, with the object ready to be edited. When you have finished making changes, close CorelPhoto-Paint! by double-clicking on its Control Menu box. The changes will appear on the CorelDRAW! screen.

Source
Application
Document
Figure 10–8.

Embedding

Embedding is similar to linking, except that embedding makes a copy of the source object, and once the copy is pasted in the destination document there is no connection between the copy and the source object. As in linking, you can double-click on the destination object and the source application will open. The difference is that you will be editing the destination copy and not the source object. To see object embedding in action, follow these steps.

1. Clear the screen by choosing New from the File menu and answering No to the question about saving the file. Then, from the CorelDRAW! screen, choose Insert Object from the File menu. The Insert Object dialog box appears, as you see here.

2. Select the type of object you want to bring in (CorelPhoto-Paint! Picture), and click on Insert. CorelPhoto-Paint! will open with a blank screen. Once more open PAINTWAY.PCX.

3. Select an object in the picture and copy it to the clipboard. Close the application. After returning to CorelDRAW!, use the Edit menu's normal Paste command to place the object on the page.

4. Double-click on this embedded object to open the source application. After making changes, go to the File menu and select Update CorelDRAW!. This item would not be present in the File menu if the objects have been linked instead of embedded.

If you now go back to CorelPhoto-Paint! and open the original object, it will not have the changes you just made. Had you linked this object rather than embedded it, the changes would have been transferred.

10

Duplicating Objects

As you saw earlier in the chapter, you can use the Copy and Paste commands in the Edit menu to make a copy of an object within a picture. This process can be somewhat time-consuming if you use it frequently, because you need two separate menu commands or keyboard combinations to perform one action. A more convenient way of achieving the same end is to use the Duplicate command in the Edit menu or its keyboard shortcut, Ctrl-D.

The Duplicate command causes a copy of the selected object or objects to appear at a specified *offset* from the original. In other words, the duplicate copy does not appear directly on top of the original, but at a horizontal and vertical distance from it, which you specify. This makes it easier to move the duplicate to a new location.

You can also use the Duplicate command alone or with the Combine command in the Arrange menu to achieve unusual logo or graphic designs, or special effects. In the next exercise, you will create and duplicate three different series of rectangles, each with a different specified offset. Then you will combine them to create the design shown in Figure 10–13.

1. Starting with a blank page, change the page format to Landscape using the Page Setup command from the File menu. Also, make sure that Show Rulers and Edit Wireframe modes are turned on (as indicated by a check mark next to each option in the Display menu).

2. Select the Preferences command from the Special menu. Check the Place Duplicate settings at the top of the Preferences dialog box. The numeric entry and units boxes should each show the default value setting of 0.25 inches, as shown in Figure 10–9.

   If the values are correct, select OK and exit the dialog box. If you see a different setting, change it to 0.25 inches.

3. Select the Rectangle tool and draw a rectangle about halfway down the left edge of the page. The rectangle should be wider than it is long.

4. Press Ctrl-D or select the Duplicate command from the Edit menu. An exact copy of the rectangle appears 0.25 inches to the right and above the original. Press Ctrl-D repeatedly until you have created 14 copies of the rectangle, as in Figure 10–10.

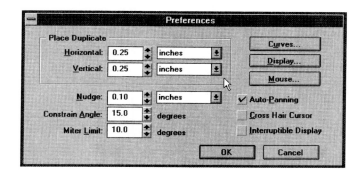

Place Duplicate
settings
Figure 10–9.

5. Change the Place Duplicate setting in the Preferences dialog box to 0.05 inches in both the Horizontal and Vertical numeric entry boxes.

6. With the Rectangle tool still selected, draw another rectangle to the right of the first series. Then, press Ctrl-D twenty (20) times in succession. This time, the duplicates appear at much shorter intervals, as shown in Figure 10–11, giving a smoother appearance to the transitions between the series of duplicated objects.

7. Refer to the Place Duplicate setting in the Preferences dialog box one more time, and change both values to –0.10 inches. The negative numbers indicate that the duplicates will appear below and to the left of the original object.

10

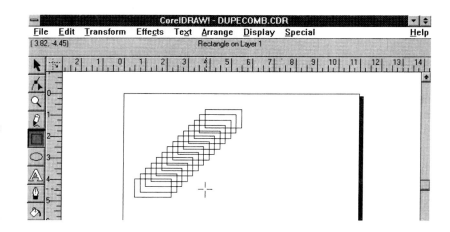

Creating and
duplicating the
first set of
rectangles
Figure 10–10.

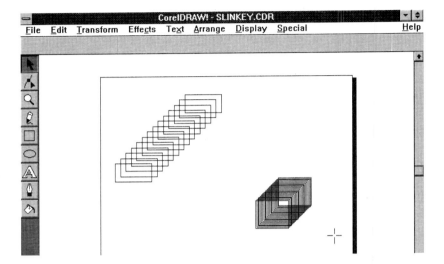

A second set of duplicate rectangle with smaller offset values
Figure 10–11.

8. Draw a third rectangle between the first and second series of rectangles and then press Ctrl-D twenty (20) times in succession. This time, the duplicates appear to the left of, and below, the original object, as shown in Figure 10–12.

9. Now set the right mouse button so you can toggle between the Edit screen and the Full Screen Preview. Do this by selecting Mouse in the Special|Preferences dialog box, then click on Full screen preview, and finally click the OK buttons in both dialog boxes. With the Pick tool, select each of the series of objects in turn, and apply the Combine command from the Arrange menu to combine the series. You will recall from Chapter 6 that using the Combine command causes alternating objects in a group to become transparent.

10. When you have combined all three series of objects, click the right mouse button to toggle to Full Screen Preview. As you can see from Figure 10–13, the various offsets lead to different special effects when you combine each group of rectangles.

11. Save this file as DUPECOMB.CDR and then select New to clear the screen.

The preceding exercise shows you only one potential use for the Duplicate command. You can probably think of many others that will

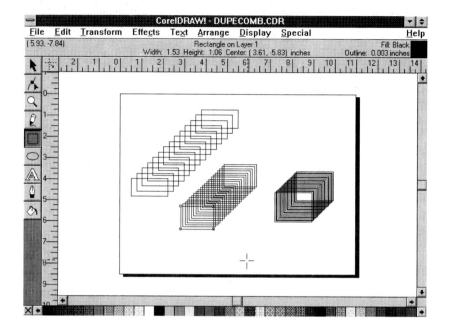

Creating and
duplicating a
third set of
rectangles
Figure 10–12.

spark your creativity and enhance your design abilities, especially since
you can apply this command to multiple or grouped objects as well as
single objects. In the next section, you will see an example of another
interesting CorelDRAW! copying technique—one that transfers
attributes rather than the objects themselves.

Copying an Object's Style

10

Suppose that you have spent a lot of time designing an object, giving it
a custom calligraphic outline, special fills, or a unique combination of
text attributes. You would like to give the same set of attributes to
another object, but you don't want to waste time setting up all those
attributes from scratch. CorelDRAW! allows you to save time and
enhance the design of your image by using the Copy Style From
command in the Edit menu. You will practice using this command in
the following exercise.

1. Select the Page Setup command in the File menu and change the
   page format to Portrait. Then go to the Display menu and turn off
   both Show Rulers and Edit Wireframe.

Special effects
created with the
Duplicate and
Combine
commands
(with full screen
preview)
Figure 10–13.

2. Adjust magnification to actual size (1:1), then activate the Text
    tool, select an insertion point near the top left of the screen, and
    type **Corel**. Activate the Pick tool, selecting the text object, then
    from the Edit menu choose Edit Text. Set text attributes to
    Aardvark bold, 100.0 points, and justification None. Click on the
    Spacing command button, change inter-character spacing to 40%,
    and then select OK twice.

3. Click on any white space to deselect the word Corel. Open the
    Text roll-up and set attributes to Avalon Italics, 50 points and left
    justification. Click on Apply. Select a second insertion point a little
    below the first one. This time type **DRAW!**. When this string
    appears, your screen should look similar to Figure 10–14.

4. Close the Text roll-up and activate the Pick tool. The second text
    string is automatically selected. Click on the Copy Style From
    command in the Edit menu. The Copy Style dialog box shown in
    Figure 10–15 appears. This dialog box contains four
    options—Outline Pen, Outline Color, Fill, and Text
    Attributes—each with its own checkbox. You can choose to copy
    any or all of these attributes to the selected object. If you use the
    Shaping tool instead of the Pick tool to select your text, Text
    Attributes will be grayed-out and unavailable. Since you haven't
    worked with the Outline or Fill tools yet, just click on the Text
    Attributes checkbox to place a checkmark in it. Notice that a
    message at the bottom of the dialog box instructs you to select the
    object from which you want to copy the attributes.

Preparing to copy text attributes from one text string to another
Figure 10–14.

5. Click on the OK command button to exit to the page. The pointer turns into a thick arrow containing the word "From?". This reminds you to click on the object from which you want to copy attributes.

6. Select the "Corel" text string by clicking anywhere on its outlines with the tip of the arrow. The "DRAW!" text string immediately changes to reflect the same attributes as the "Corel" text string, as shown in Figure 10–16. If you miss the outline when you click, a dialog box comes up giving you the chance to try again.

10

The Copy Style dialog box
Figure 10–15.

Selected object
with attributes
copied from
adjoining object
Figure 10–16.

7. Select New from the File menu to clear the screen. Do not save these changes.

You will have opportunities to use this dialog box again in Chapters 11 through 15. In the final section of this chapter, you will review techniques for deleting objects in CorelDRAW!.

Deleting Objects

As mentioned previously, you can delete objects from a CorelDRAW! drawing in one of two ways: by cutting them to the clipboard (Shift)-(Del) or by selecting the Delete command from the Edit menu (keyboard shortcut: (Del)). It is generally advisable to cut an object to the clipboard if you might want to paste it back to the same or to a different drawing later. Use the Delete command or its keyboard shortcut only if you are certain that you will not need the removed object later, because CorelDRAW! doesn't save a deleted object anywhere in memory.

To delete a single object, select the object, and then apply the Delete command. You can also choose to delete multiple objects or all objects in the picture, using any of the multiple selection techniques you learned in earlier chapters.

You have experimented in this chapter with the available techniques for copying, cutting, and pasting objects and attributes within or between CorelDRAW! files, and between CorelDRAW! and other applications. In the next three chapters, you will learn about outline width, outline fill, and object fill—important attributes that you can assign to any new or existing object.

CHAPTER

11

DEFINING THE OUTLINE PEN

In CorelDRAW!, all objects have outline pen, outline color, and object fill attributes. In addition, text has its own set of attributes, as you learned in Chapter 9. All of the objects you created and edited until now had standard black fills and fixed-width black outlines. In this chapter, however, you will start to modify outline attributes, using the CorelDRAW! Outline tool ▣.

The Outline tool is actually two tools in one. In order to create an outline for any object, you need to define the *outline pen* and the *outline color* in two separate steps. Think of the Outline tool as a calligraphic pen having an almost infinite number of replaceable nibs. The outline pen, which you will explore in this chapter, represents the shape of the nib and emulates the possible ways you can slant your hand while drawing. And the outline color, which you will learn about in Chapter 12, "Defining Outline Color," represents the ink and textures that flow from the pen.

When defining an outline pen for any object, you can vary the width, line type, corner shape, line end styles, and nib shape of the pen. You can also control the placement of the outline relative to the object's fill color. Only CorelDRAW! allows you so great a degree of control over the shape and appearance of your drawings. With your first try, you can create ornate calligraphic effects and simulate a hand-sketched look electronically.

Defining Outline Pen Attributes

The method you use to define outline pen attributes depends on whether you are creating new objects with the current default settings, editing attributes for existing objects, or altering default outline settings. The following checklist summarizes the order of steps involved.

◆ To create an object with the current default outline pen attributes, you select the appropriate drawing tool and draw the object. You can then select the Outline tool to view the current default outline attributes (optional).

◆ To edit outline pen attributes for an existing object (including grouped or combined objects), you activate the Pick tool, select the object, and then click on the Outline tool.

◆ To begin setting new outline pen default attributes, you click on the Outline tool and then on the desired icon.

Once you have selected the Outline tool, you can choose between defining a custom outline pen or selecting a preset outline width. In the remaining sections of this chapter, you will practice customizing outline pen attributes and selecting preset outline pen widths for both planned and existing objects.

Customizing the Outline Pen

You have complete control over the attributes of the outline pen in CorelDRAW! thanks to a dialog box that appears when you click on the outline pen icon in the Outline tool fly-out menu. By altering the settings in this dialog box, you can vary the outline's placement and width, change the shape of corners and line end styles, design custom nibs, and create an array of calligraphic effects.

The way you access this dialog box varies, depending on whether you are creating objects with default attributes, editing attributes for existing objects, or altering default attributes. Alternatively, you can use the Pen roll-up. As with other roll-up windows you used in previous chapters, the Pen roll-up allows you to quickly see the results of your attribute changes without opening the dialog box. In the following exercises, you will create an object with default outline pen attributes and become familiar with the settings in the Outline Pen dialog box and the Pen roll-up. Then, you will edit outline pen attributes for existing objects in the sample files that came packaged with your software. Finally, you will set up new default outline pen attributes that will apply to objects you draw later.

If you simply want to specify outline width, without creating a custom outline pen, turn to the section "Selecting a Preset Outline Pen Width." There, you will find out how to alter the width of the outline pen quickly, without accessing a dialog box or the roll-up.

Creating Objects with Default Attributes

When you create a new object, CorelDRAW! applies the current default settings to it automatically. You can leave those settings as they are or edit them. When you edit outline pen settings for a newly created object, however, your changes apply only to the object. Other objects that you create continue to have the default outline pen attributes until you set new defaults.

11

In the exercise that follows, you will create a text string, select the Outline tool fly-out menu and access the Outline Pen dialog box, and observe the default outline pen attributes that are standard with CorelDRAW!.

1. Make sure that the Show Rulers, Show Grid, and Snap To Grid commands are turned off, select the Magnification tool and set magnification to Actual Size (1:1).

2. Activate the Text tool and select an insertion point near the upper-left edge of the page. Type **outline pen** and then open the Artistic Text dialog box. Set text attributes to Gatineau Normal, 90.0 points, and Left Justification. Set inter-character spacing to 10%, and then select OK twice.

3. Assuming that Edit Wireframe is off (if it isn't make it so), the interior of the text string is black or whatever the default fill color is. For the purposes of this exercise, you want to remove the fill color to clearly view your outline. To do this, click on the X at the left end of the on-screen color palette.

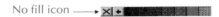

4. Use the Pick tool to size and move the text string so that it looks similar to Figure 11–1.

   The text string redisplays with just the outline. The center is hollow, as shown in Figure 11–1. (If your text seems to have vanished completely, you will find a solution in the next step.)

5. Click on the Outline tool. A fly-out menu appears.

Outline text
with fill
removed
Figure 11–1.

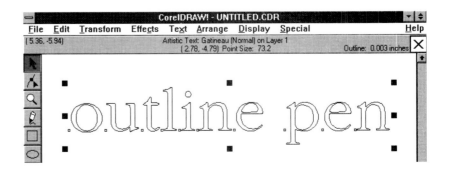

The Outline tool fly-out menu contains two rows of options. The top row consists of controls for the outline pen, which you will use throughout this chapter. The second row of the fly-out menu, which you will work with in Chapter 12, contains controls for the outline fill color. (If the text string has disappeared from your screen, click on the solid black icon in the second row of this fly-out menu to make it reappear.)

6. For the moment, ignore all but the first (leftmost) icon in the top row of the fly-out menu. The seven icons after the first one allow you to open the Pen roll-up window and quickly specify fixed outline widths. You will practice working with outline widths in the "Selecting a Preset Outline Pen Width" section of this chapter. For now, click on the first icon in the top row, the *Custom Outline Pen* icon. It looks just like the Outline tool icon, but it has the more specialized function of allowing you to specify all the possible attributes of the outline pen. The Outline Pen dialog box displays, as in Figure 11–2. Leave this dialog box on the screen for now.

The Outline Pen dialog box contains controls for nine outline pen attributes. The default settings on your screen should match the settings in Figure 11–2, unless you or another user has altered them since installing the software. If your dialog box shows different settings, adjust them to match the ones in the figure. Then, take a moment to become familiar with the attributes and how they function.

11

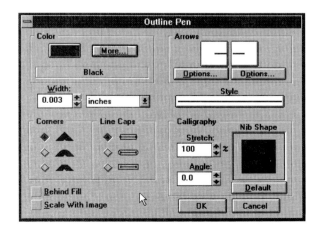

The Outline
Pen dialog box
Figure 11–2.

Color   At the top of the dialog box is a display box that shows you the current fill color. Additionally, it allows you to open a color palette, identical to the normal on-screen palette except for the arrangement of the color choices. Next to the color display box is the More button, which opens the Outline Color dialog box, giving you access to the full range of outline coloring. In the next chapter, "Defining Outline Color", you will learn how these features are used.

Line Style   Under the color area are two boxes that show the current line width and its units of measure. To their right, there is a third box that shows the current line style. Clicking on this Style display box opens a fly-out display box that allows you to choose from a number of dotted and dashed line styles, as you can see here:

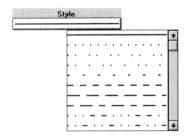

To choose a line style, use the scroll bar to display the style you want, and click on that line style. You'll be returned to the Outline Pen dialog box, and the line style you choose will now be in the display box. The solid line shown in Figure 11–2 is the default line style.

Arrows   Above the Style display box is a pair of boxes that allow you to select or construct a line ending to go on either end of a line. These line endings are displayed in a fly-out that you can open by clicking on either the left (line-beginning) or right (line-ending) Arrows display box. Figure 11–3 shows the left Arrows box selected. To select a line ending, scroll through the boxes of line endings until you see the one you want. Click on the line ending you want and it will appear in its respective small Arrows display box. The beginning of a line (normally the left end) or the end of a line (normally the right end) can be found by clicking on the line with the Shaping tool and seeing which end has the larger node; the one that does is the beginning. Clicking on the Options button for either the line-beginning or line-ending arrow

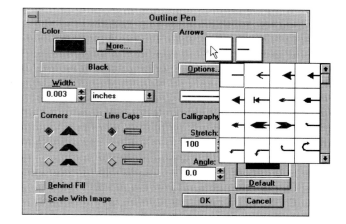

Arrowhead
Selection
display box
Figure 11–3.

opens a four-option menu, which is identical for each. Choosing None
removes a line ending you previously selected. You can reverse the
beginning and ending arrows by choosing Swap. If you want to remove
a line ending from the fly-out box of line endings, select it and click on
Delete From List. After you have selected a head or tail shape, the Edit
option will be enabled. Clicking on it opens the Arrowhead Editor
dialog box shown here:

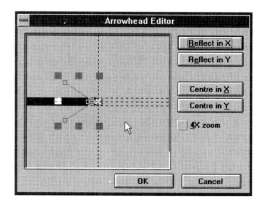

The Arrowhead Editor displays an enlarged arrowhead and allows you
to move, scale, and stretch the arrowhead by dragging on it or one of
its boundary markers; you can center the arrowhead relative to the X in
the middle of the editor by selecting Center in X to center horizontally

11

with Reflect in X or vertically with Reflect in Y. Also, you can magnify the arrowhead image by clicking on 4X zoom.

Behind Fill   The Behind Fill checkbox lets you specify whether the outline of an object should appear in front of or behind the object's fill. The default setting is in front of the fill (empty checkbox), but if you create objects with thick outlines, you will want to activate Behind Fill. This is especially advisable with text, where thick outlines appearing in front of the fill can obliterate empty spaces and cause text to appear smudged, like this:

When you place an outline behind the fill, only half of it is visible. The outline therefore appears to be only half as thick as specified.

Scale With Image   When the Scale With Image checkbox contains an X, the width and angle of the outline change proportionally as you resize, rotate, or skew the object. CorelDRAW! automatically updates the width and angle settings in the Outline Pen dialog box when Scale With Image is active. When the Scale With Image setting is *not* active, the width and angle of an object's outline do not change, no matter how you stretch, scale, rotate, or skew the object. This can lead to some interesting but unintended changes in appearance when you define a calligraphic pen nib for the object, as you will see in the "Scaling the Outline with the Image" section of this chapter.

Corners   The Corners options pertain to objects that tend to have sharp corners: lines, open and closed curve objects, rectangles, and some angular fonts. The three option buttons in this area of the dialog box allow you to choose just how CorelDRAW! shapes those corners. The first (default) option shows a sharp or *miter* corner, where the outer edges of two joining line or curve segments extend until they meet. By altering the Miter Limit setting in the Preferences dialog box, you can control the angle below which CorelDRAW! flattens or bevels the edge of a sharp curve. When you choose the second option button, CorelDRAW! *rounds* the corners where two lines or curve segments meet. When you choose the third or *bevel* corner option button, corners of joining curve or line segments are flattened. The results of the Corners settings are usually subtle, unless you magnify an object or combine Corners settings with Pen Shape attributes for calligraphic effects.

Line Caps   The Line Caps options apply to lines and open curves, but not to closed path objects such as rectangles, closed curves, or ellipses. These settings determine the end styles of lines and curves. The first or default option is a *butt* line end style, where the line ends exactly at the end point. The second option gives you *rounded* line end points. When you choose either the second or the third (*square* line end type), the line extends beyond the end point for a distance equal to half of the line thickness. When you select any of the line end caps, that style applies to both end points of the line or curve. If you have selected dashed lines as your line type for an object, each dash takes on the shape of the line end style you choose.

Calligraphy   The remaining two outline pen attributes—stretch and angle—help you define a custom pen shape, analogous to the *nib* or point of a calligraphic fountain pen. With default values of 100% stretch and 0 degree angle, the pen shape is square, resulting in a plain outline. On their own, these settings will not create calligraphic effects. When you alter them in combination, however, they allow you to outline objects with varying thick and thin strokes at the angle of your choice. You can set the shape of the nib by changing the values in the Stretch and Angle numeric list boxes, or interactively. Using the interactive method, you click and drag the mouse pointer inside the Nib Shape display box, where it changes to a cross. The Stretch and Angle settings are automatically adjusted as you distort the Nib Shape. You can restore the default square nib by selecting the Default command button below the Nib Shape box. The Corners settings work with the Calligraphy settings to define the appearance of calligraphic strokes, as you will learn in "A Pen Shape for Calligraphic Effects" section of this chapter.

Now that you are familiar with the functions of the attributes in the Outline Pen dialog box, exit the dialog box by selecting Cancel. Clear the screen by selecting New from the File menu before going further.

11

A Custom Outline Pen for New Objects

Different artists have different styles, and you may prefer to create most of your objects with outline pen style that differ from the standard settings. If so, perform the exercise in this section to learn how to customize outline pen defaults. Objects that you create after changing the default attributes will then conform to the appearance that characterizes your working style.

Creating objects with new outline pen defaults is a three-stage process. First, you access the "New Object" Outline Pen dialog box. Then you change the outline pen attributes. Finally, you create new objects, which automatically adhere to the new default attributes. The dialog box that you use to edit default settings is identical to the Outline Pen dialog box, except for its title and the way you access it.

1. Start with a blank page. (If you are in an existing drawing and want to change default settings, make sure that no object is selected.) Then select the Outline tool and click on the Custom Outline Pen icon. Since no object is selected, the message box in Figure 11–4 appears.

2. Select OK to access the Outline Pen for New Object dialog box and have the defaults apply to all new objects. The contents of this dialog box are identical to the contents of the normal Outline Pen dialog box. Only the title is different, to remind you that you are changing default attributes for the outline pen.

Outline Pen for
New Object
dialog box
Figure 11–4.

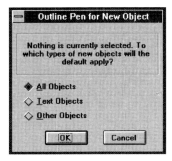

3. For now don't change the defaults. As you go through this chapter you will exercise each of the options in this dialog box and become familiar with their effects and what your likes and dislikes are. When you are done with the chapter, you can come back here and set the defaults to what is right for you.

4. Select Cancel to close the dialog box without change and return to the work area.

It's that easy to alter default settings for the outline pen. As with almost every other CorelDRAW! feature, customization is the key word. CorelDRAW! encourages you to create images according to your unique working habits and style.

On the other hand, if you are involved in technical illustration or your normal CorelDRAW! tasks are relatively uncomplicated, you may seldom require calligraphy or other special options in the Outline Pen and Outline Pen for New Object dialog boxes. The next section shows you how to change the outline pen width quickly and interactively, without the use of a dialog box.

Selecting a Preset Outline Pen Width

If Width is the outline pen attribute you change most frequently, CorelDRAW! offers shortcuts that save you time and keeps you out of the Outline Pen dialog box. The first row of the fly-out menu that appears when you select the Outline tool, as shown in Figure 11–5, contains five preset outline widths from which you can choose.

You can choose one of these options for a currently selected object, or you can set a fixed line width as a new default. When you choose a preset outline width for a selected object, you apply that width to the selected object only. When you click on one of these options without having first selected an object, however, CorelDRAW! assumes that you want to set the option as a new default width and the message box shown in Figure 11–4 pops up. OK to set the selected line width as a new default for objects that you draw in the future, If you meant to select an existing object first, click on the Cancel command button instead.

11

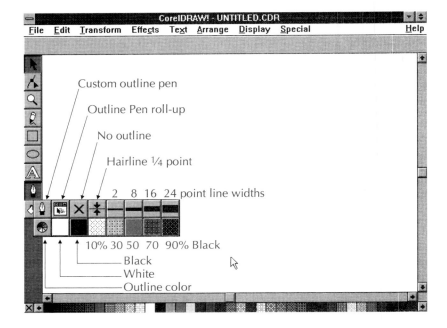

The first option, next to the Custom Outline Pen icon on the left (see Figure 11–5), is the Pen roll-up, as shown here:

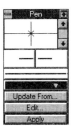

The top option in the Pen roll-up allows you to adjust the outline thickness. The default width that should appear is a hairline, shown by a thin line 1/4 point wide, met by two arrows. By clicking on the downward-pointing scroll arrow, you can place an X through the box, signifying no outline. By clicking on the upward-pointing arrow you can increase the line width in one-point increments, starting with the hairline, and then a line one point wide.

The next icon in the Outline Pen fly-out is an X; as in the Pen roll-up window, you can click on this option when you want a selected object to have no outline at all.

The next option, similar to that in the Pen roll-up, represents a hairline or a line 1/4 point wide. The screen, however, does not display a true WYSIWYG representation of an outline this thin.

As Figure 11–5 shows, the remaining four options in the fly-out menu represent fixed outline widths from 2 points to 24 points. Think of these options as "package deals," in which each width selection includes an angle of 0 degrees and a stretch value of 100% in the Outline Pen dialog box.

If you have altered any of the other default outline pen settings using the Outline Pen for New Object dialog box, they are still effective when you select a preset outline pen width. For example, if you previously had selected the Behind Fill or Scale With Image options as defaults, your outlines will exhibit these attributes even when you select a preset outline width. Since the Angle and Stretch settings are standardized for preset widths, however, you cannot achieve calligraphic effects.

Editing Outline Pen Attributes of Existing Objects

To define outline pen attributes for an existing (not newly created) object, you must select the object before you access the Outline tool fly-out menu. If you try to access the Outline Pen dialog box without having selected an object, CorelDRAW! assumes that you want to set new defaults for the outline pen, and any changes you make in the Outline Pen dialog box will not affect existing objects.

When you define outline pen attributes for an existing object that is selected, you are in effect *editing* its current outline style. The changes you make apply to that object only and have no effect on the default settings for objects you create later.

If you use the (Shift) method to select multiple objects in order to change their outline pen attributes, the Outline Pen dialog box displays the settings for the last object that you selected in the group. If you use the marquee method to select the objects, the dialog box displays the settings for the last object that you drew. Any changes you make will

11

apply to all of the selected objects, however, so be very careful about changing outline pen attributes for more than one object at a time.

Each of the following sections concentrates on the effects of editing a specific attribute or related set of attributes in the Outline Pen dialog box. You will work with sample files that best demonstrate how changes to an attribute can alter the overall design and mood of a picture.

Adjusting Line Width

The line width you assign to an object's outline pen helps define the balance and weight of that object within a picture. In the following exercise, you will alter the line width for several elements in the clip art drawing named TECHTIPS.CDR and observe how your changes affect it.

1. Open the file TECHTIPS.CDR in the SIGN clip art directory.

2. Select the words "TECH TIPS" using the Pick tool (select only the text, not the flags), and drag the words toward the bottom of the printable page.

3. Magnify the area around the words "TECH TIPS." Your screen should now display an area similar to Figure 11–6.

4. Open the Text roll-up and scale the text string to approximately 60 points and center it on the screen.

5. Select the Outline tool and click on the line width after the hairline, a 2-point line. Now, the words "TECH TIPS" should look like this:

6. Select the Outline tool a third time and click on the third line width from the right, an 8-point line. "TECH TIPS" should now look like this:

DOESALL.CDR
text as it starts
out
Figure 11–6.

7. Select the Outline tool again, and open the Outline Pen dialog box. Notice that outline width is at 0.111 inches, which is equivalent to 8 points (a point is 1/72 of an inch or 0.0389 inches), as shown in Figure 11–7. Remember that the default line width is 0.014 inches, which is one point.

As you can see, the variation in line width makes a big difference in how an object looks, and you can vary the line width either by selecting one of the established options on the fly-out menu, or by entering an exact width in the Outline Pen dialog box.

Leave the dialog box open and the TECHTIPS.CDR drawing on your screen for further use. The next section explores the design possibilities of placing outlines of objects behind or in front of their fills.

Adjusting Placement of Outline and Fill

The Behind Fill setting in the Outline Pen dialog box determines whether the outline of a selected object is placed behind or in front of the object's fill. This attribute is most important when you are working

11

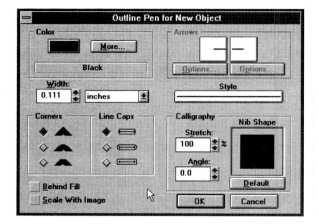

Outline Pen
dialog box with
a 8-point line
width
Figure 11–7.

with text. Thick outlines appearing in front of the fill can clog up the
open spaces in letters, making the letters appear unclear as you saw in
the 8-point example in the last exercise. In the following exercise, you
will adjust outline placement for the letters in the TECHTIPS file that
currently is open.

1. In the open Outline Pen dialog box, notice that the Behind Fill
   option is not selected.

2. Click on the Behind Fill check box to select it and then select OK
   to exit the dialog box. The word reappears with a much thinner
   outline as shown here:

Actually the outline is just as thick as before, but half of it is hidden
behind the fill. You can see this if you watch the screen redraw (unless
you have a super-fast computer).

You have seen how the Behind Fill option affects the appearance of
objects and can be especially useful with text. In the next section, you
will observe how the Scale Width Image setting impacts the appearance
of resized or transformed objects.

Scaling the Outline with the Image

A wide outline, such as the 8-point width you applied in the last exercise, may be appropriate for large letters, say 75 points and above. When you scale that large type down to, say, 15 points, the wide border doesn't look good at all, as you can see.

The CorelDRAW! Outline Pen dialog box has an option to scale an outline's attributes with the image. If you select Scale Width Image by clicking on the check box, an outline's attributes will be appropriately scaled as you change the image. The default, though, is to not scale the attributes, and you are likely to get something that looks like the last illustration.

1. With the TECHTIPS.CDR file still on the screen with an 8-point outline placed behind the fill, use the Text roll-up to scale the image to about one-quarter its former size. You should get an image on your screen that looks like that shown in the last illustration.

2. Press Alt-Backspace to return the text to its original size.

3. Select the Outline tool, open the Outline Pen dialog box, click on the Scale With Image check box, and click on OK.

4. Again, scale the text image to about one-quarter its original size. You now get a much more usable image:

5. Clear the image from the screen by selecting New from the File menu and not saving the changes.

11

Setting Sharp (Miter), Rounded, or Beveled Outline Corners

The effect of changing corner attributes of the outline pen is so subtle that it is almost unnoticeable—unless the selected object has a thick outline as well as sharp corners. A thick outline enables you to see the shape of the object change as you cycle through the Corners options. Perform the following exercise to practice altering Corners settings for the letter E.

1. Select the Text tool, and click anywhere on the page and type the capital letter E.
2. Select the letter "E" with the Pick tool, and select Avalon bold, 154 points using the Text roll-up.
3. Move the letter "E" to the center of the printable page, magnify the character until it fills the window, select the Outline tool and click on the 16-point line width (the second from the right). Next click on the X to the left of the on-screen color palette, to turn off the fill.

When you have completed the above steps your screen should look like Figure 11–8. On the screen you see the outline of the letter "E" with 12 corners on which to test the three corner styles. The default, the sharp or miter corner, is currently displayed and is shown in Figure 11–9a.

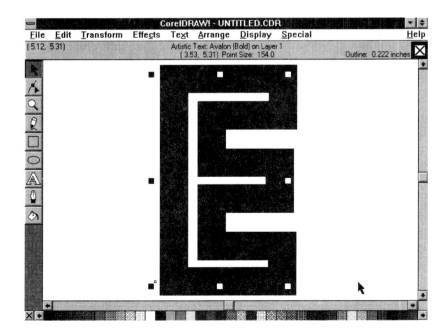

The letter "E" set up to test the types of corners
Figure 11–8.

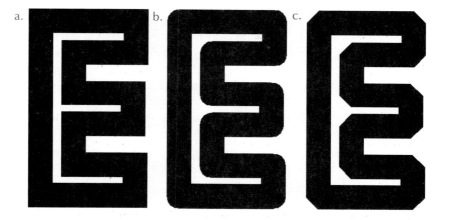

The letter "E" with (a) sharp or miter, (b) rounded, and (c) beveled corners
Figure 11–9.

4. Select the Outline tool, open the Outline Pen dialog box, click on the rounded corner option button, and click on OK. You should see a distinct change in the corners as shown in Figure 11–9b.

5. Again open the Outline Pen dialog box, select the beveled corner option, and click on OK. Again the corners change as shown in Figure 11–9c.

6. Select New from the File menu to clear the screen. Do not save your changes.

In creating your own drawing, you will find the effects of the Corners options most dramatic when you assign thick outlines to objects that contain at least some cusp nodes. In the next section, you will explore when and how changes to the line end styles can alter an object's appearance.

Selecting Line End Caps

Line end options (*end caps*) apply only to straight lines and open-ended curves. It is difficult to see the difference between line end types unless you create very thick lines or magnify the line a lot—you'll do both here.

1. From the Display menu select Snap To Guidelines and Show Rulers. Set the vertical grid origin to 11 inches.

2. Drag vertical guidelines from the ruler on the left to 2 and 4 inches.

11

3. Magnify the area from 1 horizontal and 2 vertical to 5 horizontal and 4 vertical.

4. With the Pencil tool, draw two straight, vertical lines down the guidelines from 2.0 inches to 4.0 inches. These should be hairline width. If they don't appear to be hairline width, select both lines and then select hairline width icon from the Outline tool fly-out menu. Deselect these lines by clicking on the Pick tool any place in the work area except on one of the lines.

5. Select the Outline tool and click on the far-right line width, which is 24 points or .333 inches. Click on OK to apply this width to all new objects.

6. Draw three straight, horizontal lines from 2 to 4 inches on the horizontal ruler at 2.50, 3, and 3.50 inches on the vertical ruler. Your screen should look like Figure 11–10.

   The default line end cap, the *butt* end, is shown in Figure 11–10. The lines end exactly at the termination of the line and are squared off.

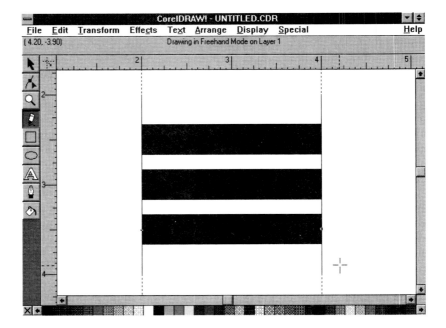

Lines prepared for testing line end caps
Figure 11–10.

7. Select the middle horizontal line, open the Outline Pen dialog box, select the middle or rounded line end cap, and click on OK. The line ends on the middle line are now rounded and project beyond the termination of the line by one-half of the line width as shown here:

8. Select the bottom horizontal line, open the Outline Pen dialog box, select the bottom or square line end cap, and click on OK. The line ends on the bottom line are now square and project beyond the termination of the line by one-half of the line width. Figure 11–11 compares the three line end caps.

9. Clear the screen by selecting New from the File menu.

If an image contains many open-ended curves, selecting rounded line end caps can soften the image, even if the lines are thin. Conversely, you can select butt or square line end styles to give an object a more rough-hewn, sharp appearance.

Using Different Line Styles

So far in this book, all the lines you have drawn, including the lines in the characters you have typed, have been solid lines. CorelDRAW! 3 provides a list box full of line styles and, if that is not enough, you can edit a file named CORELDRAW.DOT and add more.

11

Butt, rounded, and square line end caps

Figure 11–11.

In the following exercise you'll try out various line styles, look at them in various widths, and apply the different line end caps to them.

1. Select Outline tool, click on the Outline Pen icon, and click on OK to apply the default line width you will set to all objects.
2. When the Outline Pen for New Object dialog box opens, change the line width to 0.014 inches (1 point) and click on OK.

You are starting with a 1-point line because a hairline (1/4-point) is too small for demonstrating the different types of lines. The dots in a dotted line are the same height as the line is wide. Therefore, a dotted hairline has dots that are .003 inches high—three thousandths of an inch! These will print on most laser and PostScript printers, but many other printers cannot print them, and the screen does not display them correctly without magnification.

3. Select Actual Size magnification and, with the Pencil tool, draw four straight horizontal lines, each about 3 1/2 inches long, at 4, 4 1/2, 5, and 5 1/2 inches on the vertical ruler.
4. Click on the Text tool, type **Corel** on the left side of the page at about 6 1/2 inches on the vertical ruler, select it with the Pick tool, and use the Text roll-up to select Bodnoff normal, 60 points, and then click on Apply.
5. While the text is still selected, click on the X at the end of the on-screen palette to turn off the fill. Your screen should look like Figure 11–12.
6. With the Pick tool, click on the second horizontal line, open the Pen roll-up and click on the third button from the top. A dashed and dotted line styles list box will open as shown here:

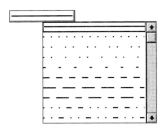

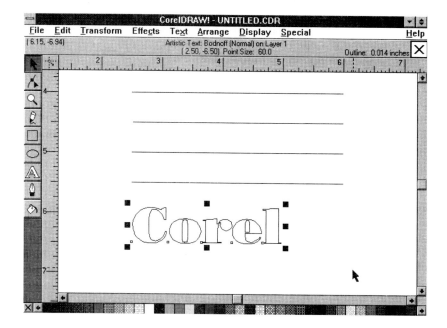

Lines and text
prepared for
testing line
styles
Figure 11–12.

7. Select the second line type from the top. The list box closes and a normal dotted line appears in the Pen roll-up's line styles field. Click on Apply.

8. Select the third horizontal line and then, from the dashed and dotted line styles list box, select the second dashed line (the seventh line type). Click on Apply.

9. Select the fourth horizontal line and, from the dashed and dotted line styles list box, select the dash, double-dot line (the tenth line type). Again, click on Apply.

10. Select the text and, from the dashed and dotted line styles list box, select the first dotted line and click on Apply. Your screen should now look like Figure 11–13.

    Next, quickly look at how dotted and dashed lines look at various line widths and with various line end caps.

11. With the Pick tool, draw a marquee around the four lines (not the text).

12. From the Outline tool fly-out menu, select various line widths: first 2-point (fourth line width from the right) and then 8-point (third

11

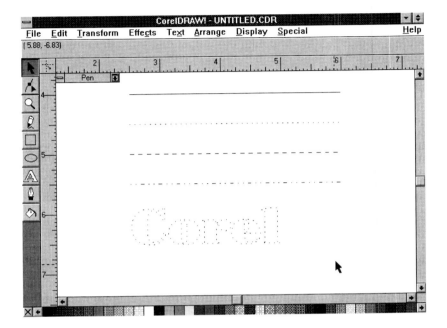

line width from the right). Figure 11–14 compares the effects of 1-, 2-, and 8-point line widths on dotted and dashed lines.

13. Select the second and third horizontal lines, and then from the Outline Pen dialog box, select first the rounded line caps and then the square line caps to see the effect on dotted and dashed lines, as shown in Figure 11–15. Note that the end caps are placed on both ends of each dotted or dashed segment.

14. Select File New and No to clear the work area.

If you want to add additional dotted and/or dashed lines, leave CorelDRAW!, bring up an ASCII text editor such as Windows Notepad, and edit the file CORELDRAW.DOT that is in the directory in which CorelDRAW! was installed. Instructions on adding line types are in the beginning of the file.

There is much variety in the styles, widths, and ends you can use with lines. In the next section you will see how you can further enhance a line with many different arrowheads and tail feathers.

a. ————————————————————

b. ————————————————————

. . . .

. . . .

– – – – – – – – – – – – – – – – – – –

– – – – – – – – – – – – – – – –

. –. –. –. –. –. –. –. –. –. –. –. –

. . – . . – . . – . . – . . – . . –

Effect of
(a) 1-point,
(b) 2-point,
(c) 8-point line
widths on
dotted and
dashed lines
Figure 11–14.

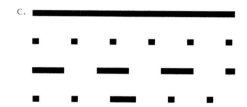

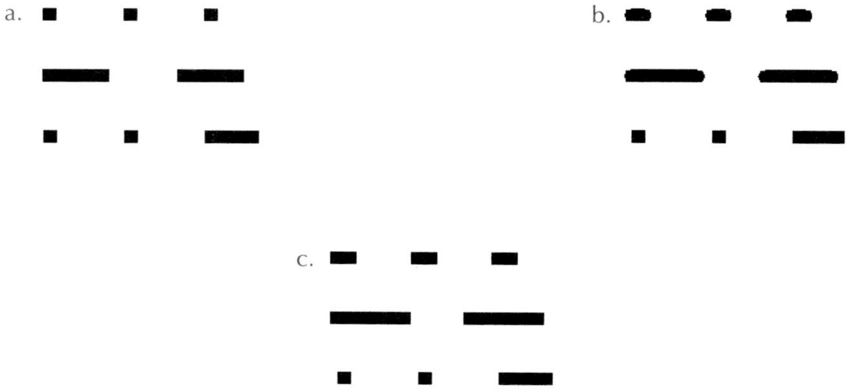

c.

(a) Butt,
(b) rounded,
and (c) square
end caps on
dotted and
dashed lines
Figure 11–15.

a.

b.

c.

11

Adding and Editing Arrowheads

In the section, "Selecting Line End Caps," you saw one technique for ending lines. Additionally, there are a number of arrowhead and tail feather options that you can place on the end of a line. You can also customize an existing arrowhead with the Arrowhead Editor, and add new arrowheads to the arrowhead display boxes. In this exercise you will add some arrowheads and then customize one using both the Outline Pen dialog box and the Pen roll-up window.

1. Select the Outline tool, click on the fourth line width from the right (2-point), and click on OK to apply this to all new objects.

2. Draw three horizontal lines about 2 inches long at 2, 4, and 6 inches on the vertical ruler. Be sure to draw the lines from left to right so the left end is the beginning of the line. Set the magnification to actual size. Use the scrollbars to center the three lines on your screen.

3. With the Shaping tool, click on the first line and notice that the left end of the line has the larger node as shown here:

4. Change to the Pick tool. The first line should automatically be selected.

5. From the Outline Pen dialog box, click on the Arrows line-ending (right) display box. An arrowhead selection display box will open.

6. To put an arrowhead on the right end of this line, click on the second arrowhead from the right on the top row.

7. To add some tail feathers on the left end of the line, click on the Arrows line-beginning (left) display box, scroll the set of arrowhead display boxes by pressing the down scroll arrow three times, and then click on the last set of tail feathers on the bottom row, as shown in Figure 11–16.

8. Click on OK to return to your drawing, and click on a blank area of the screen. Your arrow should look like this:

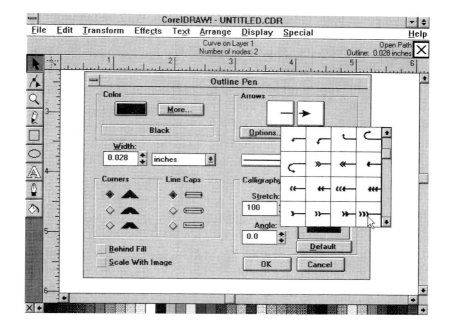

Arrowhead
display box
Figure 11–16.

9. In a similar manner, use the Pen roll-up to place line endings of your choice on the second and third lines. Open the Pen roll-up from the Outline Pen icon if it's not already on your screen. The second field down contains line-beginning (left) and line-ending display boxes identical to those in the Outline Pen dialog box. Click on a box and make your selection, repeat this for the other end, and then click on Apply. One possible set of choices is shown in Figure 11–17.

10. With the Pick tool, draw a marquee around the three lines and set the line width, first, to 4 points (open the Outline Pen dialog box, change the line width to 0.056 inches, and click on OK. You can use the Pen roll-up window's Edit button to open the Outline Pen dialog box, saving you mouse movements and keystrokes), and then to 8 points (you can use the third icon from the right on the Outline tool fly-out menu). Figure 11–18 shows the three variations of line width, with the line endings. Notice how the size of the line endings changes with the size of the line.

11. Select New from the File menu (and don't save the changes) to clear the work area.

11

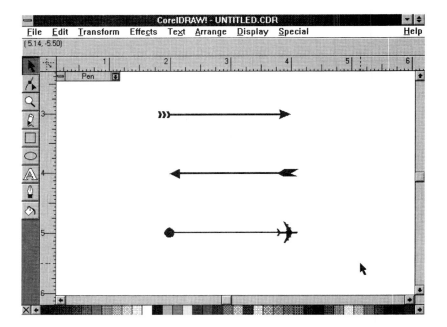

One possible
set of line
endings
Figure 11–17.

Next, use the Arrowhead Editor to modify an existing arrowhead.

CAUTION: If you close the Arrowhead Editor after modifying an arrowhead, you will have permanently modified the arrowhead you were working on. You can again modify the arrowhead to try and re-create the original, but you may not get it exactly the way it was.

TIP: To prevent permanently modifying your arrowhead file, leave CorelDRAW!, go to the directory in which CorelDRAW! is installed, and make a copy of the file that contains the arrowheads— CORELDRW.END. Call the new file CORELDRW.EN1. Then you can modify arrowheads as you wish and when you are done, leave CorelDRAW! once again, and copy CORELDRW.EN1 back to CORELDRW.END to restore the original arrowheads.

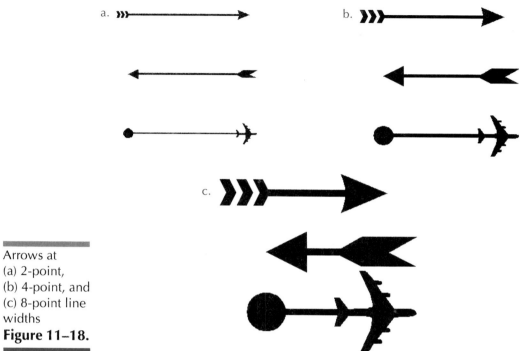

Arrows at
(a) 2-point,
(b) 4-point, and
(c) 8-point line
widths
Figure 11–18.

12. At Actual Size magnification, draw a horizontal line in the middle of the page.

13. Using the Pen roll-up, click on Edit to open the Outline Pen dialog box. Change to a 4-point (0.056 inches) line width.

14. Select the Arrows line-ending (right) box, click on the second arrowhead from the right on the top row. Click on the Options button and choose the Edit option.

15. By clicking and dragging one the eight boundary markers, modify the arrowhead. Stretch out both the left and right ends and then reduce the height. In the latter operation it is likely that the arrowhead will get off center vertically. Use the Center in Y command button to correct this. Try Reflect in X to see the effect of this, and use it to return the arrowhead to its original

11

orientation. When you are done, your dialog box should look like Figure 11–19.

CAUTION: If you click on OK and close the Arrowhead Editor, you will permanently modify this arrowhead in the Arrows display box. You can come back and move everything back to its original position (see the illustration under "Arrows" in the early part of this chapter to see how this should look). But unless you want to do that, choose Cancel to exit the Arrowhead Editor.

16. If, on the other hand, you don't mind permanently modifying the second arrowhead, click on OK to close the Editor and return to the Outline Pen dialog box, click on the second arrowhead again to select your modifications, and click on OK to return to your drawing. Your arrow should look like this:

17. Select File New and No to clear the work area.

The Arrowhead Editor is used to stretch, scale, and position an existing arrowhead in relation to the line it will be applied to. If you want to create a new arrowhead, do so in CorelDRAW! like you would any other

Arrow Head Editor with modified arrowhead
Figure 11–19.

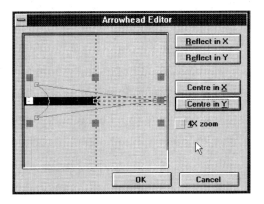

object (if you build an arrowhead with multiple objects, select them all and use Combine from the Arrange menu to make one object out of them), and then use the Create Arrow command in the Special menu to save the new arrowhead at the end of the list of arrowheads. It does not matter if you have the relative size of the new arrowhead correct, because you can modify this with the Arrowhead Editor.

In the next section, you will begin working with the pen shapes—Width, Angle, and Stretch— that make calligraphic effects possible in CorelDRAW!.

A Pen Shape for Calligraphic Effects

The Stretch and Angle settings in the Outline Pen dialog box are in a separate enclosed area subtitled "Calligraphy." The Calligraphy option allows you to create variable calligraphic "nibs" that can be highly effective with freehand drawings and text. If you adjust both of these settings in various combinations, you can approximate a freehand style of drawing.

In the following exercise, you will experiment with the nib shape settings, using some curves you will draw, to achieve both hand-sketched and comic-strip-style looks.

1. At Actual Size magnification, and with the rulers turned off, draw an approximation of the objects shown in Figure 11–20.

2. Select all the objects, group them using the Group command in the Arrange menu, set their Width to 2 points (the fourth width from the right in the Outline Pen fly-out), and turn off their fill by clicking on the X at the end of the on-screen palette.

3. Save this image with the File Save As command and the name Curves.

4. Activate the Outline tool and open the Outline Pen dialog box. The current Calligraphy settings for this are Stretch 100% and Angle 0.0 degrees.

5. Leave the Width value at 0.028 inch (2 points), but change the Angle and Stretch values to 42 degrees and 14%, respectively. This translates into a thin outline and a relatively narrow nib with the "pen" held at a 42-degree angle. The effects are shown in Figure 11–21.

11

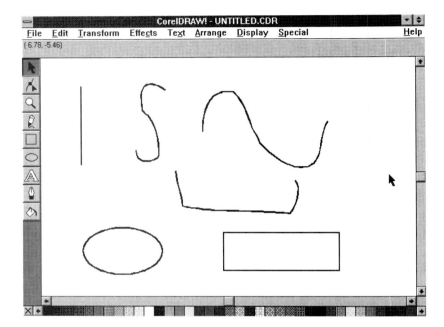

Objects on
which to test
the outline pen
Figure 11–20.

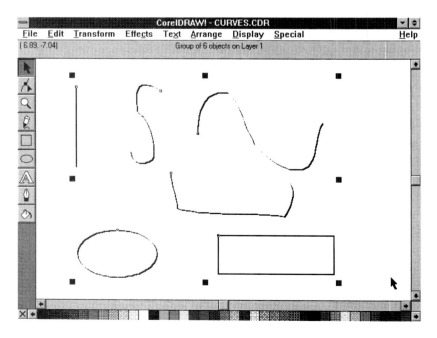

Outline Width
of 0.028 inch,
Angle of 42
degrees, and
Stretch of 14%
Figure 11–21.

TIP: It is easier to use the numeric entry boxes to achieve exact Angle and Stretch settings. Interactively using the mouse pointer in the Nib Shape display box is better suited to nibs that can be approximately sized by eye.

6. To vary line thickness, experiment with the stretch of the nib, expressed as a percentage of the nib width. Keep decreasing the Stretch value all the way to 2%, and then select OK. There doesn't seem to be much change. As the value in the Stretch numeric entry box decreases, you effectively flatten the nib in one direction; the black symbol representing a pen nib is broad in one dimension and extremely narrow in the other, which makes more extreme calligraphic effects possible. If you were to increase the Stretch value all the way to 100%, the curves of the image would have the same thickness everywhere, and no calligraphic effects could result.

7. Access the Outline Pen dialog box once more. Return the stretch to 50% and adjust the Angle of the nib from 42 to 0 degrees. You will recall that the Angle setting is analogous to the way you hold a calligraphic pen in your hand; at a 0-degree setting, the Nib Shape display box alters to show you a perfectly vertical nib.

8. Select OK to exit the dialog box. Now the areas that display the thickest and thinnest lines have shifted as shown in Figure 11–22 (by 42 degrees). Adjusting the Angle value is therefore a convenient way to control where thick and thin lines appear on any selected object.

9. Access the Outline Pen dialog box again and click on the Default button. This resets the Stretch and Angle settings to the default values of 100% and 0 degrees, respectively—a square nib with no variations in thickness. Now set Width to 0.06 inch, and then select OK. The curves are redrawn with a consistently thick outline, much like a cartoon character, as shown in Figure 11–23.

10. Experiment with Stretch and Angle settings at this outline width, too. For example, to obtain greater variation in line thickness, set Stretch at a reduced value, such as 4%. To change the placement of the thinner segments of the curve, try different angle settings.

11. Select New from the File menu and answer No to saving the changes to clear the screen.

11

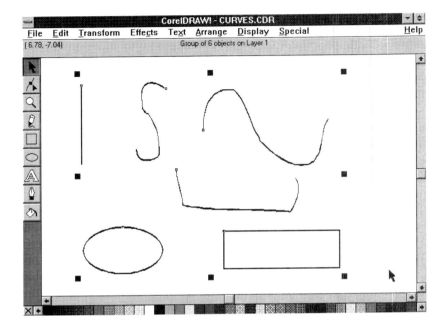

Outline Width of 0.028 inch, Angle of 0.0 degrees, and Stretch of 50%
Figure 11–22.

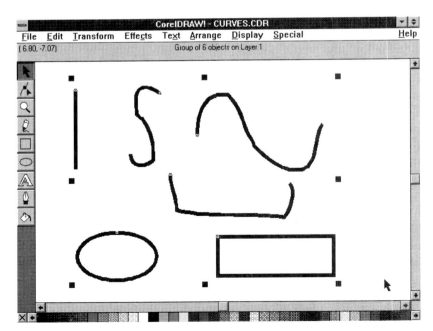

Outline Width of 0.06, Angle of 0.0 degrees, and Stretch of 100%
Figure 11–23.

The possibilities for creating custom calligraphic nibs should spark your imagination. An interesting use for an image sketched faintly at 0.01-inch width might be as a background illustration in a newsletter, where the text overprints the image without obscuring it totally. You have probably seen applications like this involving outlines of scanned photographs. Chapter 18 will give you more information on how to outline bitmapped and scanned images.

TIP: Avoid using 0.00-inch widths unless your draft printer is also the printer you will be using for your final output. As an Outline Width setting, 0.00 inch represents the thinnest line your printer is capable of printing. For PostScript printers, this is 1 pixel or 1/300 of an inch, but for a Linotronic or other high-resolution imagesetter, 0.00 inches could represent something even thinner. Because of the variations among printers, this setting does not truly represent a fixed width, and the screen does not display a WYSIWYG representation of it.

Angle settings are especially useful to help you fine-tune the exact location of thick and thin lines within a drawing. With precise, degree-by-degree control available, you can make sure that thinner areas of a selected curve are positioned exactly where you want them.

The Stretch settings represent the relative squareness or roundness of the nib, with 100% representing a square nib and 1% representing a long and narrow nib. As the Stretch percentage value decreases, the variation in line thickness of a drawn object increases.

Outline Pen Hints

The range of choices available to you makes the outline pen one of the richer areas of CorelDRAW!. The following sections contain selected hints for making the most of your choices and coordinating your settings with the type of work you are doing.

11

Defining an Outline Pen for Text

Do you want text in your drawings to appear normally? Or are you aiming for exaggerated or stylized effects? For a clean-cut look, it's best to create text without an outline, using the X in the Outline tool fly-out menu. When text has a visible outline, some characters appear to be drawn thicker, with the result that spaces within letters (such as in a small "a" or "e") are partially or wholly filled in. This is especially the case when you create text in small point sizes.

If your design calls for outlined text, a good way to maintain readability in smaller point sizes is to activate the Behind Fill option in the Outline Pen dialog box. As mentioned earlier, Behind Fill causes the outline to appear half as thick as it really is, because the other half of the outline is hidden behind the object's fill.

In some cases, you may really prefer a slightly "smudgy" graphic look of text with thick outlines. Let the purpose and design of your illustration be your guide in choosing how to outline text.

Varying Your Calligraphic Style

Unless you have a prior background in calligraphy, the wealth of width, angle, stretch, and corners settings available to you in the Outline Pen dialog box can be confusing. The following hints should help put you on the right track if you know the effect you would like to achieve.

Desktop publishers can create faint background illustrations from original artwork or scanned photos and then overprint them with text. The result is a visible but not distracting piece of artwork that enhances the mood of an article or feature. Recommended settings for this kind of graphics effect are Width, 0.03 inch or less; Stretch, 14% or less; and a variable Angle according to your tastes. Keep in mind that if you reduce the outline width setting below 0.02 inch (or 1.2 fractional points), you will not be able to see an accurate representation of the calligraphy on your screen. The outline will still print according to your specifications, however.

Illustrators, cartoonists, and other artists seeking a traditional hand-sketched look should set Calligraphy options to achieve the desired variation in line thickness. For finer lines, outline pen width should be fairly thin, below 0.05 inch; and for blunter strokes, above 0.06 inch. Stretch should be set to 1 to 2% for the maximum variation in line thickness, and closer to 100% for minimal variation. The fine-tuning possible with angle settings permits illustrators to place thicker or thinner lines at exact locations. Miter corner settings promote a more angular look, while rounded corner settings create a smoother appearance.

For those who are interested in extremely broad calligraphic strokes, consider setting Stretch above 100%, removing the fill of an object, and then varying the Angle settings. The example text that follows has a three-dimensional look because it was created at a Width of 0.06 inch, at an Angle of 75 degrees, and with a Stretch of 225%:

outline pen

Copying Outline Styles

In Chapter 10, you transferred text attributes from one text string to another using the Copy Style From command in the Edit menu. You can do the same with outline pen attributes.

You can imagine how useful the Copy Style From command can be if you need to copy outline pen styles to, or from, even larger blocks of text or groups of objects.

C H A P T E R

12

DEFINING OUTLINE COLOR

To define an object's outline completely in CorelDRAW!, you must define both the outline pen shape and the outline color attributes. You learned how to select attributes for the outline pen in Chapter 11; in this chapter, you will begin to define outline color. As you may recall, the outline pen allows you to draw with the characteristic style of a calligraphic pen, using "nibs" of various sizes. The outline color represents the colors and textures that flow from the pen.

CorelDRAW! offers you a choice between two different color systems—*Spot color* and *Process color*—for assigning color to an object's outline. In the Spot color system, each color is assigned a unique name or number. The Pantone Color Matching System, which is the standard of the printing industry, has licensed its Spot color specifications for use in CorelDRAW!. Spot color works best for images that contain only a few colors, such as headings in newsletters or single-color objects within black-and-white graphics. The Process color system, on the other hand, specifies colors in terms of a mix of primary colors or color properties. Process color is more appropriate to use when you plan traditional four-color printing of images that contain a large number of colors. You will find more information concerning color systems and color separation principles in Chapter 15, "Printing and Processing Your Images."

Your options for assigning outline colors do not end with Spot and Process colors, however. Unlike a hand-held pen, the CorelDRAW! pen not only dispenses "ink" in all colors of the rainbow, it can lay down an assortment of halftone screens for PostScript printing.

The exercises in this chapter will give you practice in specifying Spot color, Process color, gray shades, and halftone screen patterns for your object outlines. The CorelDRAW! window faithfully reproduces your settings, except in the case of halftone screens. Since you cannot preview an outline consisting of a halftone screen, you must print out your work on a PostScript printer in order to view it. See Chapter 15 for assistance with printing.

Defining an Object's Outline Color Attributes

Your first step in defining outline color attributes is to determine whether you want to define the attributes for existing objects or for objects not yet rendered. When defining outline color attributes for an existing object, you are in effect editing its current attributes. The changes you make apply to that object only, not to additional objects you may create later. When you define outline color attributes for a new object, on the other hand, you are changing default attributes. The object or series of objects that you draw next will incorporate automatically the newly defined outline color attributes.

TIP: Always work in full mode when you alter outline color attributes. Wireframe mode does not show you how the selected outline color looks. For most attributes, full color mode lets you see the result of your changes instantly.

An existing object can be either one that you have just drawn, or one that you have saved previously. To begin the process of defining outline color attributes for an existing object, proceed as follows:

1. Activate the Pick tool and select an object whose outline color attributes you wish to edit. Make sure that Edit Wireframe is turned off in the Display menu.

2. Click on the Outline tool. When the Outline tool fly-out menu appears, select the Outline Color icon, the first icon in the second row, which looks like a color wheel. The Outline Color dialog box appears, as shown in Figure 12–1. You will practice working with this dialog box later in this chapter; for now, click on Cancel.

TIP: If your Outline Color dialog box does not look like Figure 12–1, it has been previously used and left in another mode. You will see how to change this in a moment.

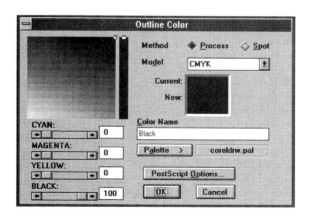

The Outline Color dialog box with the Process color settings
Figure 12–1.

12

Alternatively, if you have just drawn an object, it is selected automatically, as you will recall from Chapter 6. To invoke the Outline Color dialog box, follow step 1 above without activating the Pick tool.

TIP: If you have an item selected, you can immediately open the Outline Color dialog box by pressing the shortcut keys [Shift]-[F12].

The next section explains the process of defining default outline color attributes for objects that you haven't created yet.

Setting New Outline Color Defaults

When you click on an option in the Outline tool fly-out menu without first having selected an object, CorelDRAW! assumes that you want to change the standard or default attributes for objects that you draw in the future. Here's how to begin the process:

1. Click on the Outline tool and then proceed to select the Outline Color tool. The message box shown in Figure 12–2 appears, asking you which default settings you want to change.
2. Click on OK. The Outline Color for New Object dialog box appears. The contents of this dialog box are the same as those of the Outline Color dialog box; only the title is different. For now, click on Cancel.

The "New Object" Outline Color dialog box
Figure 12–2.

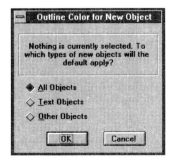

The next set of sections introduces you to the concept of Spot color and lets you practice assigning a Spot color to an existing or planned object. You gain access to the Spot color display as soon as you invoke the Outline Color or Outline Color for New Object dialog box.

Outlining with Spot Color

If you work with a PostScript printer, you can create color separations for Spot color and Process color that are ready to take to a print shop. You should base your choice of a color system (Spot or Process color) in CorelDRAW! on the number of colors in your picture. If an image contains more than four colors, you would probably find Spot color too expensive and time-consuming to produce, and should opt for Process color instead. If an image contains fewer than five colors, and you require close color matching, you should use the Spot color system to assign a unique Pantone color name to each color. Spot color is also the system to use with a PostScript printer, since it gives you access to special PostScript halftone screen patterns.

You define colors in CorelDRAW! using the Outline Color dialog box that you access from the Outline tool fly-out menu. This dialog box allows you to choose between Spot color and Process color, to select a color *model* (the method of defining color) as well as a color, and to select from among several options. As you can see from Figure 12–3, there are some differences between the Outline Color dialog box with the Spot color method selected (as shown in that figure), and the same

The Outline
Color dialog
box for Spot
color
Figure 12–3.

12

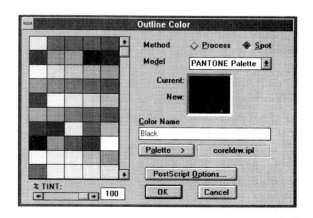

dialog box with the Process color method selected, as shown in Figure 12–1. This difference is largely a function of the color model. In the Process color dialog box, you can select Palette as the model and a palette similar to the one in the Spot color dialog box appears. The Spot color dialog box uniquely allows you adjust the percentage of tint and to select a PostScript halftone and its attributes (see Outlining with PostScript Halftone Screen Patterns later in this chapter). All versions of the Outline Color dialog box have a Palette button that opens the menu shown here:

The Palette menu allows you to add colors to or delete colors from the current palette, and to load a palette from your hard disk or save it to disk.

Once you have made changes in the Outline Color dialog box, those changes will be reflected in its settings the next time you open the dialog box. Therefore, you can make decisions on Spot vs. Process color, the model and the palette you want to use when you begin a drawing, and those changes will keep displaying in the dialog box until you change them.

The colors you select using the Spot color system are from the Pantone Matching System that is the standard for the printing industry. Since the colors that appear in the dialog box color display box are only approximations, you should use the Pantone Color Reference Manual to evaluate your choice of colors prior to printing. In addition, you can specify a percentage of the tint of any Spot colors you select. The effect of settings below 100% is to render a lighter shade of the selected color on your monitor or color printout.

In the following set of exercises, you will learn how to specify Spot colors for the outlines of your CorelDRAW! objects. If you are working with a color monitor, you will see your drawings come alive in vivid color. If you are working with a monochrome monitor, an exercise is included to show you how to set up your outlines in shades of gray.

The exercises in these sections assume that you understand how to invoke the correct dialog box for either a planned object or an existing object. If you need to review this process, refer to the section of this chapter entitled "Defining an Object's Outline Color Attributes" before continuing.

Assigning Spot Color Outlines

In the following exercise, you will assign Spot colors and shades of gray to the outline of an existing object.

1. From the Outline tool fly-out menu select the 2-point width (top row, fourth from the right), click on OK to have it apply to all objects, then, at Actual Size (1:1) magnification, quickly draw several curves as shown here:

   When you are done, drag a marquee around all of the objects to select them and choose Group from the Arrange menu.

2. To begin editing the existing outline color attributes, click on the Outline tool and the Custom Outline Color icon, or press [Shift]-[F12]. The Outline Color dialog box, shown in Figure 12–3, appears. If you have not altered the default selections, the dialog box still looks like Figure 12–1. Click on the Spot option button to change from the default Process color.

3. Click on the fourth color in the top row. The selected color appears in a color display box on the right of the dialog box. The % TINT numeric entry box shows a value of 100% (the default value). The Pantone identification name or number for this color, in this case "PANTONE Rhodamine Red CV," displays above the palette. If you have the Pantone Color Reference Manual and have a color monitor, you can compare what you see on the screen with what you see in the manual. There probably is a difference since most color monitors are not perfectly calibrated.

12

4. Click OK in the dialog box. Notice that the curves have changed from black to Rhodamine Red. If you are not working with a color monitor, you'll see a dithered gray.

5. Invoke the Outline Color dialog box again. This time, click on the black color near the bottom left, and set the tint value to 51%. The color preview window in the dialog box now displays a 51% gray shade.

6. Click OK in the dialog box. If you have a VGA or Super VGA display card, you will see an actual representation of a 51% gray shade in the drawing, as shown in Figure 12–4.

7. Access the Outline Color dialog box once more, reselect PANTONE Rhodamine Red (fourth color in the top row), and then return the tint value to 51%. You have just selected a lighter tint of PANTONE Rhodamine Red.

8. Select OK to exit the dialog box with the new outline color setting.

9. Save this as CURVES2 and clear the screen by selecting New from the File menu.

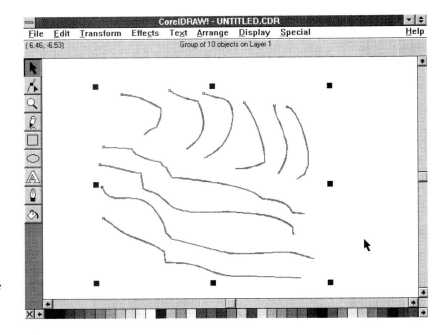

An outline at
51% gray shade
Figure 12–4.

In the next exercise, you will practice assigning new Spot color outline default values. These values apply automatically to objects that you create after assigning the new defaults.

Setting New Spot Color Outline Defaults

When you access the Outline Color dialog box with no objects selected, CorelDRAW! assumes that you intend to change the default outline color values. If this is not the case, select Cancel and select an object before trying again. In the following exercise, you will change defaults for both the outline pen and outline Spot color attributes, and then create new objects that exhibit those defaults automatically.

1. Begin with an empty page. Set the display magnification to Actual Size (1:1).

2. Without creating or selecting any objects, click on the Outline tool and on the Custom Outline Pen icon in the first row of the fly-out menu. The message box that you saw in Figure 12–2 appears, asking whether you want to change default outline pen values. Click on OK to select All Objects and access the "Outline Pen for New Object" dialog box.

3. When the Outline Pen for New Object dialog box appears, set the outline pen attributes as follows: Width 0.15 inch, Style solid line, Corners sharp (miter), Line Caps butt, Stretch 10%, Angle –45 degrees. Do not check either Behind Fill or Scale With Image.

4. Click the More button in the Color section at the top of the dialog box. The Outline Color dialog box appears.

5. Set up the new object outline color attributes as follows: Spot Method, Pantone Process, Blue CV Color (second box from the left in the second row), tint value 100%. Select OK twice to save these settings and exit both the Outline Color and Outline Pen dialog boxes.

6. Activate Show Rulers, make sure Edit Wireframe is off, and then click on the Text tool. Click in the lower left of your screen.

7. Open the Text roll-up window from the Text menu and select the following text attributes: No Justification, Banff Normal, 300.0 points. Click on Apply, roll up the text window, type a capital **A**, and press the [Spacebar] to activate the Pick tool and select the

12

character. If you followed all the steps up to this point, the text should have a default fill of black. Your screen should look like Figure 12–5, except that the color of the outline is blue. Remember that *all* of the new outline pen and color attributes you have selected apply to the new object automatically.

8. Clear the screen by selecting New from the File menu. Do not save your work.

If you create the same kinds of images regularly in your line of work, you probably have strong individual preferences for what you would like default outlines to look like. If you wish, start a new drawing on your own, setting up the outline pen and outline color default attributes that will apply to the basic elements in your drawing. You can edit settings for objects that should have different outline fills by selecting them after you draw them and accessing the appropriate dialog boxes. If you are not satisfied with the results of your outline pen or outline color attribute settings, you can make any adjustments during the drawing process.

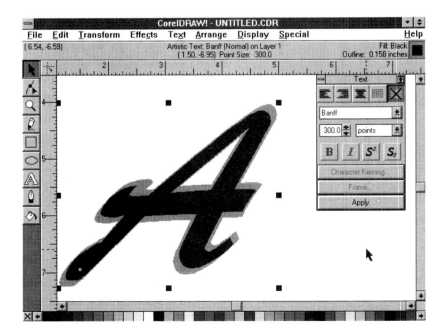

Letter created with new default Pantone Spot color outline
Figure 12–5.

You may find selecting a particular Spot color from the color palette difficult—it could be hard to find a particular Pantone color from the more than 600 that are shown. If you have a Pantone Color Reference Manual and/or know the Pantone name or number of a particular color, CorelDRAW! provides another way to select a Spot color by providing a list of Pantone color names as shown in Figure 12–6. This list is reached by selecting Names from the Model drop-down list box in the Outline Color dialog box. When you select a color on the list, the color is displayed in the color display box to the right of the list. Also, you can enter a few characters of a PANTONE name or number in the Search String box, and that name or number will be highlighted in the list while the color that name represents will be shown in the display box.

If you click on OK to leave the Outline Color dialog box you are returned to your drawing and the next time you select the Outline Color icon from the Outline fly-out menu, you will get the list of Pantone colors that you just left (Figure 12–6), not the Palette shown in Figure 12–3. If you want to return to the palette when you next select the Outline Color icon, select Pantone Palette as the model before leaving the Outline Color dialog box.

Using the Outline Pen Roll-Up for Outline Color

The Outline Pen roll-up, which you'll remember from Chapter 11, opens from the Outline tool fly-out menu (second icon from the left in the top row). It provides two ways to select or change outline color. The

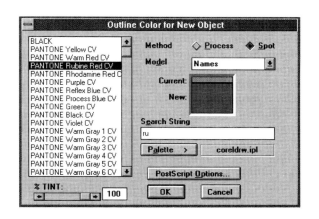

Outline Color dialog box listing Spot colors

Figure 12–6.

12

first is the color button (fourth bar up from the bottom), which opens
the color palette as shown here:

This color palette, although smaller, has the same colors to choose from
as the color palette in the Outline Color dialog box. Clicking on a color
in the roll-up palette, and clicking on Apply, will apply the color to the
outline of the selected object.

The second method of applying outline color from the Outline Pen
roll-up is to click on the Edit button (second from the bottom), to open
the full Outline Pen dialog box, and to then click on the More Color
button to open the Outline Color dialog box. This is, of course, the
same dialog box you get by clicking on the Outline Color icon in the
Outline tool fly-out menu, or by pressing F12.

If you own or use a PostScript printer, go on to the next section to learn
how to assign a PostScript halftone screen as an outline color. This
option is available only when you choose the Spot color method, and it
takes effect only if you have a PostScript printer. You cannot see it on
the screen.

Outline with PostScript Halftone Screen Patterns

If you work with a PostScript printer, you can elect to fill an outline
with a *halftone screen pattern* of the currently selected Spot color. This
option is available only when you have selected Spot color as your
outline color method. The CorelDRAW! window displays PostScript
halftone screen patterns as solid colors only; to see the patterns, you
must print the images on a PostScript printer.

The concept of a halftone screen is probably familiar to you already: it
is a method of representing continuous tone or color by patterns of
dots. Black-and-white and color photographs in newspapers and
magazines are examples of halftone images that you see every day.

You define a PostScript halftone screen by clicking on the PostScript Options command button in the lower-right of the Outline Color dialog box. CorelDRAW! offers ten different types of halftone screen patterns. You can vary the frequency (number of occurrences per inch) and angle of any screen to achieve dramatic differences in outline appearance, even within a single pattern. To see how a PostScript halftone really looks, however, you must print it; the CorelDRAW! window cannot display these screens.

Defining a PostScript halftone screen outline requires the following steps:

1. Select the Spot color (and tint, if desired) in which you want to print a screen pattern.

2. Click on the PostScript Options command button at the lower-right of the Outline Color dialog box.

3. Specify a halftone screen pattern from among the ten available patterns.

4. Select the frequency or number of occurrences of the pattern, per inch.

5. Determine the angle at which the pattern should print.

Since you cannot view the results of your selections on screen, this section does not feature any exercises. Following, however, are brief instructions for selecting a halftone screen pattern, frequency, and angle, and some guidelines you should keep in mind when working with these patterns. You can refer to Chapter 15 for more instructions on printing with PostScript printers.

Accessing the PostScript Halftone Screen Dialog Box

12

To begin defining a halftone screen outline, make sure you have selected the Spot color and tint in which you want to print your outline. Then click on the PostScript Options command button at the lower-right of the Outline Color dialog box. The PostScript Options dialog box shown in Figure 12–7 appears. This dialog box contains settings for pattern Type, Frequency, and Angle attributes.

The PostScript
Options dialog
box with
default settings
Figure 12–7.

Selecting the Halftone Screen Type

The Type option in the PostScript Halftone Screen dialog box features
10 halftone patterns that are available for your outline color work. Your
choices are Dot (the default), Line, Diamond, Dot2, Grid, Lines,
MicroWaves, OutCircleBlk, OutCircleWhi, and Star. To select a halftone
pattern type, scroll through the list until you see the name of the
desired pattern, and then click on the name to highlight it.

Selecting the Halftone Screen Frequency

The Frequency option in the PostScript Options dialog box allows you
to determine how many times per inch the pattern should occur within
the outline. The available range is from 10 to 100 per inch, and the
default setting is 60. The number you should select depends upon the
resolution of your ultimate output device; refer to Chapter 15 for more
details on frequency settings for PostScript halftone screens.

Setting the Halftone Screen Angle

The third option in the PostScript Options dialog box allows you to
specify the angle of the screen pattern when you print it. Keep in mind
that the halftone screen angle remains constant, no matter how you
transform an object. If you stretch, scale, rotate, or skew an object after
assigning it a halftone screen outline, you could alter its appearance

significantly. If you do not want this to happen, remember to change the screen angle after performing a transform operation, to match the offset of the transformed object. You will achieve the best results by setting your screen angle at 0, 45, 90, and 180 degrees.

In the next group of sections, you will begin defining Process color outline for objects in CorelDRAW!.

Outlining with Process Color

Process color is the term used for specifying color in terms of either a set of other colors, or a set of color properties. CorelDRAW! provides three methods or models for defining Process color: CMYK (cyan, magenta, yellow, and black), RGB (red, green, and blue), and HSB (hue, saturation, and brightness). Both CMYK and RGB define a color in terms of the constituent colors in the model while HSB defines a color in terms of color properties. For example, the color "brick red" is defined as 0% cyan, 60% magenta, 80% yellow, and 20% black in the CMYK model, or 80% red, 20% green, and 0% blue in RGB, or 15 degrees of hue, 100% saturation, and 80% brightness in HSB. You can use any of the three models you are most comfortable with, but CorelDRAW! will convert RGB and HSB to CMYK. Therefore, CMYK will be the primary focus of this book.

CMYK is the four-color standard for the printing industry. You can specify over 16 million colors by using various CMYK percentages. In general, you should specify Process color instead of Spot color when your drawing includes more than four colors and you plan to reproduce it through the four-color printing process.

CorelDRAW! supports color separation for Process as well as Spot color if you send your work to a PostScript printer. When you specify color in CMYK terms, your printer generates only four sheets (one each for cyan, magenta, yellow, and black percentages) for every image page, no matter how many colors the image contains. When you specify in Spot color terms, on the other hand, the printer generates a separate page for every single color used in the drawing. You will learn more about printing Spot and Process colors in Chapter 15.

To specify Process colors for an existing object, you select or create the object, click on the Outline tool, and click again on the Outline Color icon in the fly-out menu. When the Outline Color dialog box appears,

12

you select the Process option button and then choose a model to use in defining the color you want. If you pick CMYK, RGB, or HSB, you will be able to create a color by defining a mixture of the constituent colors or color properties, using a dialog box that looks like Figure 12–8. If you pick Palette or Names for the color model, you can select a color from a palette or from a list of names similar to the palette and list you saw with Spot color.

For each color model, the Outline Color dialog box looks a little different. The Outline Color dialog boxes for HSB and RGB look, and operate, very much like the one shown in Figure 12–8 for CMYK. In the upper-left corner of the dialog box is a color selector that consists of two boxes (one circle and one box in the case of HSB) filled with varying shades of color. By dragging a marker in each box you can define a Process color. The marker in the square box or circle can be moved in two directions (left or right and up or down) while the marker in the rectangular box can be moved only up or down. In the CMYK model the square defines percentages of cyan and magenta, while the rectangle defines the percentage of yellow (black is automatically defined). In the RGB model the square defines percentages of red and green while the rectangle defines blue. In the HSB model the circle defines the hue (it is specified in degrees from 0 to 360 around the circle) and the percentage of saturation (specified by the distance from the center) while the rectangle defines brightness.

Below the visual selector is a set of scroll bars and numeric entry boxes, for selecting the desired percentages of constituent colors or properties.

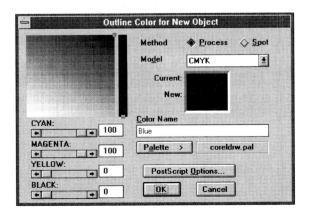

Outline Color
dialog box
Figure 12–8.

If you are using a Process color reference chart such as the TruMatch Colorfinder, you can look for a color in the chart and then enter the percentages that create that color.

In the following exercise, you will specify both the outline pen and outline Process color for a text string.

1. At Actual Size magnification with rulers turned off, select the Text tool, click in the middle of the left side, and type **CorelDRAW!**. Activate the Pick tool to select the text string.

2. Open the Text roll-up and select Banff normal, 70-point type. Click on Apply, and move or close the roll-up.

3. From the Fill tool fly-out menu, click on X to turn off the fill. From the Outline tool fly-out menu, open the Outline Pen dialog box. Select rounded corners and enter 0.083 inches (6 points) for Width, 14% for Stretch, 0 degrees for Angle, and click on OK.

4. When you are back on the drawing, your screen should look like Figure 12–9.

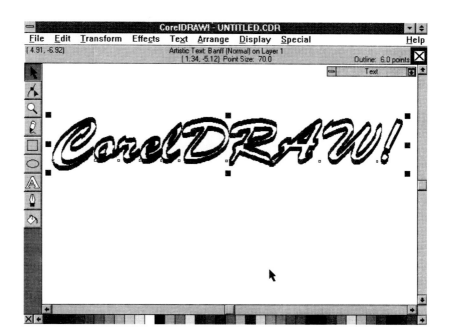

Text for testing a color outline
Figure 12–9.

12

5. Your settings have resulted in a moderately thick text outline, and by the calligraphic Pen Shape, an "artistic" look. The rounded corners setting adds a more polished look to the outlines of corners of angular letters. The black color does not do it justice, so you will change it now.

6. With the text string still selected, click on the Outline tool once more. This time, select the Outline Color icon in the second row of the fly-out menu to invoke the Outline Color dialog box. Notice that the current outline color is black.

7. If necessary, click on the Process option button to switch color selection methods. The options in the dialog box change instantly. Take a moment to again familiarize yourself with this dialog box. Move the markers in each of the visual selector boxes and notice how the color changes in the color display box, and how the percentages in the numeric entry boxes change as well. Using the scroll bar or your mouse and keyboard, set the following color mix: Cyan 40%, Magenta 40%, Yellow 0%, and Black 60%. The color display box shows a real-time approximation of changes to the color, as you scroll to or enter each specified value. When you have specified all of the values, the color display box shows a deep navy blue and the name confirms it.

8. Select OK to exit the dialog box. If you have a color monitor, the text string's outline displays as a deep navy blue, providing a contrast to the light background.

9. Press (Shift)-(F12) or click on the Outline Color icon in the Outline tool fly-out menu.

10. Select first RGB and then HSB from the Model drop-down list box, and notice that the Deep Navy Blue has been defined in each of these models. Then select Names as the model. The Outline Color dialog box changes to include a list box of the color names, as well as the standard display box and a Search String text box for finding a desired color. If you know a color name, enter it in the Search String text box. Then you can go to one of the color models and see or modify the color composition.

Next, define your own color and add it to the color palette. Leave the CorelDRAW! text string on your screen and the Outline Color dialog box open. You can use the text string to test your new color.

Defining a New Color and Adding It to the Palette

The color palette in the Outline Color dialog box for Process color displays 100 colors and 10 shades of gray. This is a far cry from the more than 16 million possible colors available with the CMYK model. The Outline Color dialog box's color selector is Corel's answer to this discrepancy. You have seen how you can define a new color with this color selector when you want to apply it to an object. But if you want to use a color over and over, say a special corporate color you've defined, you will want to add this color to the Outline Color palette.

In the following exercise you will truly define a new color. In the last exercise the color you entered was already on the palette and in the name list. The new color you will define is Deep Royal Blue.

1. Select CMYK from the Model drop-down list box.

2. Type in the numeric entry boxes, or use the scroll bars, to define a color mix of 100% cyan, 55% magenta, 0% yellow, and 45% black. The color display box will show the color but the Color Name text entry box is empty because the color is not defined.

3. Click on the Color Name text entry box and type Deep Royal Blue. Your dialog box should look like that shown in Figure 12–10.

4. Click on OK to return to your drawing and see your new color. More important, clicking on OK defined your new color and added it to the color palette and the name list. See for yourself.

12

Deep Royal
Blue being
defined
Figure 12–10.

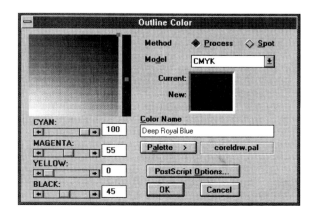

5. Press Shift - F12 to reopen the Outline Color dialog box and then select Palette as the model. The Outline Color dialog box will open with a new color at the bottom of the palette highlighted and the name Deep Royal Blue in the Color Name text entry box.

When it is nice to have a new color in the palette, having it at the very end of the palette is not very handy. CorelDRAW!, though, allows you to rearrange colors by dragging them around the palette. You can drag a color to any existing location and release the mouse button, and all the existing colors shift to the right and down to accommodate the new color.

6. Point on the new color you just defined, press and hold the mouse button while dragging the new color up to the top of the palette and then bringing it down to the sixth row, second color from the right. When you are there, release the mouse button. Now Deep Royal Blue (your new color) is right next to Deep Navy Blue, as shown in Figure 12–11.

7. Assure yourself that your newly defined color is in the list of named colors by selecting Names as the model.

   If necessary, click on the scroll bar beside the scroll box until you see Deep Royal Blue. The list is alphabetical, so you should see it immediately after Deep Rose, as shown in Figure 12–12.

8. Click on OK to close the dialog box and return to the drawing. Leave the text string on your screen to use in the next exercise.

Result of dragging Deep Royal Blue up next to Deep Navy Blue

Figure 12–11.

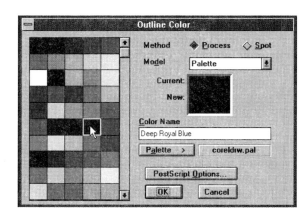

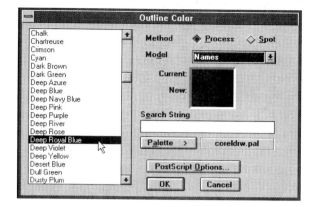

Newly defined
color in named
list of colors
Figure 12–12.

When specifying Process colors, you can include as many colors in the
picture as you like. When you finally print the image, the results will
still be separated into no more than four sheets.

In the next section of this chapter, you will learn a shortcut to
specifying outline color that will be useful if you usually print to a
black-and-white printer.

Outlining with Black, White, or Gray

When you worked with the outline pen in Chapter 11, the first row of
the Outline tool fly-out menu contained five preset outline widths that
you could select simply by clicking on the desired icon. The
arrangement of the second row of the Outline tool fly-out menu is
similar. Following the Outline Color icon is a series of seven symbols
that let you select a preset outline color (gray shade) quickly, without
having to set attributes in a dialog box. As Figure 12–13 shows, the
seven outline color options are white, black, and 10%, 30%, 50%, 70%,
and 90% gray.

To select one of these preset outline colors for an existing object, you
select the object, access the Outline tool fly-out menu, and then click
on the appropriate icon. To select one of these options as the default
outline color, you click on the desired icon in the Outline tool fly-out
menu without first selecting an object.

12

Preset black,
white, and gray
shades in the
Outline tool
fly-out menu
Figure 12–13.

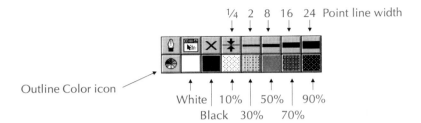

In the following exercise, you will select several of the preset outline
color options and apply them to the text string you created in the
previous exercise.

1. Recreate the CorelDRAW! text string if you did not leave it on the
   screen after the last exercise. Magnify the area containing
   CorelDRAW! as before.

2. Select CorelDRAW!, and then select the Outline tool. When the
   fly-out menu appears, click on the black square in the second row
   of the menu. The outline of the text string changes from dark blue
   to solid black.

3. Select the Outline tool again, and this time click on the 50% gray
   symbol (the third symbol from the right in the second row). Now
   the text outline shows a much lighter color, as in Figure 12–14.

4. Experiment with different preset outline color settings. Leave the
   text string on the screen for the final exercise.

Remember that you are not limited to these preset shades of gray if you
use a black-and-white printer. You can use either the Spot color or the
Process color system to define other shades of gray. To define shades of
gray using the Spot color method, access the Outline Color dialog box
and set shades of gray by clicking on black and setting the % tint in
increments of 1%. To define custom shades of gray using the Process
color method, define a percentage for black only, leaving cyan,
magenta, and yellow all at 0%.

You can also use the preset shades of gray in the Outline tool fly-out
menu in combination with the PostScript halftone screens.

Copying Outline Color and Pen Styles

In previous chapters, you have learned how to use the Copy Style From command in the Edit menu to copy text or outline pen attributes from one object to another. You use the same command to copy outline color attributes between objects, as you will see in the following exercise.

1. With the CorelDRAW! text string still on the screen from the previous exercise, zoom out to reduce the size enough to draw a rectangle around the string.

2. With the rectangle tool, draw a rectangle around the word "CorelDRAW!"; then turn off the fill by clicking on the X in the Fill fly-out menu. The result is a black rectangle around the text string. The rectangle is selected, by default.

3. Select the Copy Style From command in the Edit menu. When the Copy Style dialog box appears, click on both the Outline Pen and the Outline Color checkboxes, and then select OK. The pointer turns into an arrow containing the word "From?" to indicate that

Magnified text string with preset outline of 50% gray
Figure 12–14.

12

the next object you select will copy its outline attributes to the previously selected rectangle.

4. Click on the CorelDRAW! text string. The rectangle redisplays to show the same outline thickness and color as the text string, as shown in Figure 12–15.

   If your rectangle does not come out like Figure 12–15, it could be that the specifications on your text have been changed. They should be a 6 point line width, with a 50% gray outline color, and no fill.

5. Clear the screen by selecting the New command and not saving the changes.

For more practice with the Outline color tool, you can go back to the LANDSCA4.CDR file or any other landscape drawing that you created and edited in earlier chapters. The default outlines and fills or the objects in those files are black, but you can begin to differentiate objects by varying their outlines. You can give custom outlines to interior objects, or copy outline styles to multiple objects at one time.

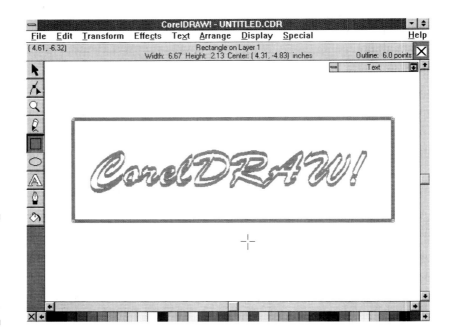

Rectangle with outline color and pen styles copied from text string
Figure 12–15.

CHAPTER

13

DEFINING FILL COLOR

In Chapters 11 and 12, you learned how to enhance your drawings by defining outline pen and outline color attributes for objects. The outline color attributes make up the "ink" that flows from a pen, while the outline pen is like the calligraphic pen or marker from which the ink flows.

This chapter introduces you to the CorelDRAW! Fill tool. The Fill tool, , as its icon suggests, functions like a paint bucket with a limitless supply of paint, capable of filling the interior of any leakproof object. A leakproof object is any object that is a closed path; all CorelDRAW! objects are leakproof, except straight lines and open curves. If you have drawn a curve object in which the two end nodes do not join, the object remains an open path, and you cannot fill it. When you select such an object, the words "Open Path" appear at the right side of the status line. (You can close an open path by joining its end nodes, as you will recall from Chapter 8, "Shaping Lines, Curves, Rectangles, and Ellipses.")

The Fill tool is similar to the Outline Color tool in that it can dispense Spot color, Process color, and PostScript halftone screen patterns. It can also dispense other types of fills that the Outline Color tool does not provide: fountain fills in any combination of colors, Bitmap and Vector Pattern fills from the CorelDRAW! library, and 42 different gray-scale PostScript texture fills. You will learn more about these types of fills in the "Custom Fountain Fills," "Bitmap and Vector Fill Patterns," and "PostScript Fill Textures" sections of this chapter.

The exercises in this chapter give you practice in specifying Spot or Process color, gray shades, PostScript halftone screen patterns, fountain fills, bitmap fills and vector pattern fills, and PostScript fill textures for objects. The preview window faithfully reproduces your settings, unless you have chosen a PostScript halftone screen or fill texture. Since you cannot preview these types of fills, you must print out your work on a PostScript printer in order to view it. See Chapter 15, "Printing and Processing Your Images," for assistance with printing.

Defining Fill Color Defaults

Before you define fill attributes for the interior of an object, you must determine whether you want to define the attributes for existing objects or for objects not yet rendered. When defining fill attributes for an existing object, you are editing its current fill. The color or name of the fill will appear in the status line when you select the object. The changes you make apply to that object only, not to additional objects you may create later. When you set new default fill attributes, on the other hand, you are specifying how objects you create in the future will be filled automatically. In this respect, the Fill tool works like the Outline tool.

Always work in full color mode when you alter fill attributes for new or existing objects. Except for PostScript textures and halftone screen patterns, the full color mode lets you see the results of your changes instantly.

Fill Color for Existing Objects

An existing object can be either a newly created object or an object that you have drawn previously. In general, it's a good idea to define fill color for one object at a time. If you define fill colors for multiple objects that you have selected using the (Shift) key technique, the fill colors of all of the objects change to match the fill of the last object you selected. If you select multiple objects using the marquee, the fill colors of all the objects change to match the fill of the most recently drawn object in the group.

To begin the process of defining fill attributes for an existing object, select the object and the Fill tool in the following way:

1. Activate the Pick tool and click on an object that has fill attributes you would like to edit. The current fill color of the object displays on the status line. Alternatively, if you have just drawn an object, it is automatically selected and available for further work, and you do not have to activate the Pick tool.

2. Click on the Fill tool in the CorelDRAW! toolbox. The Fill tool fly-out menu appears and looks like this:

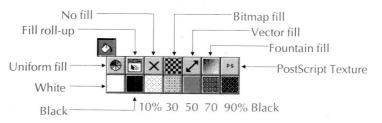

The first icon in the top row of the Fill tool fly-out menu is the Uniform Fill icon. This icon opens the Uniform Fill dialog box that lets you define custom spot and Process color fills and PostScript halftone screen patterns. The next icon opens the Fill roll-up window, which gives you access to the color palette and to certain

13

other tools in the Fill fly-out menu. The X icon causes an object to have a transparent (or no) fill. The last four icons in the top row of the fly-out menu let you access dialog boxes to apply and edit bitmap, vector, and fountain fills, and PostScript textures. The first two icons in the second row let you specify preset fill colors of white and black. The remaining icons in the bottom row let you specify one of five preset shades of gray as the fill.

3. Click on the icon that accesses the desired dialog box or specifies the desired preset fill shade, as described in the previous step. To remove the fly-out menu from the screen without making any selections, click anywhere outside the menu or press Esc.

The remaining sections in this chapter offer you practice in working with each dialog box and selecting fill attributes for each of the major types of fills. Whether you are setting fill attributes for selected objects or altering default attributes for objects you haven't drawn yet, the main steps involved are similar. The next section explains the minor differences in steps that change default fill attributes.

Defining New Default Fill Attributes

When you click on an option in the Fill tool fly-out menu without first having selected an object, CorelDRAW! assumes that you want to change the default attributes for objects that you will draw in the future. To begin defining new default attributes:

1. Click on the Fill tool without first creating a new object or selecting an existing one.

2. Click on the icon that accesses the desired dialog box or specifies the desired fill of black, white, or shade of gray. For any icon you select (except bitmap and vector fill patterns, which cannot be the default), the message box shown in Figure 13–1 appears, asking you whether you want to change the default settings. Only the title of the message box will differ, depending on which fly-out menu icon you select.

3. If you meant to select an existing object and edit its fill, click on Cancel; otherwise, click on OK. If you clicked on the first, next to last, or last icon in the fly-out menu (the Uniform Fill, Fountain Fill, or PostScript Textures icon), a dialog box appears. If you

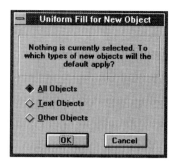

A sample New Objects message box for setting default fill attributes
Figure 13–1.

clicked on the Bitmap Fill or Vector Pattern icons (third and fourth from the right) you will get a message box telling you that these two fills cannot be used as defaults, like this:

If you clicked on any other icon, the next object or series of objects you draw will have the specified fill color automatically.

Next, look at Uniform Fill dialog box. This dialog box allows you to specify a fill color as a Spot color, PostScript halftone screen pattern, or Process color.

Defining Uniform Spot Color Fills

To fill an object with Spot color, Process color, or a PostScript halftone screen pattern, you use the settings in the Uniform Fill dialog box. This dialog box appears when you click on the Uniform Fill icon, the first icon in the Fill tool fly-out menu. You can also open the Uniform Fill dialog box with the shortcut keys Shift-F11. Its name, Uniform Fill, distinguishes it conceptually from Bitmap, Vector Pattern, Fountain,

13

and PostScript Texture fills, which involve multiple hues or patterns rather than a single color. Except for the title, the Uniform Fill dialog box is identical in appearance and function to the Outline Fill dialog box you worked with in Chapter 12.

You will recall from Chapter 12 that Spot color is the preferred color system when an image contains fewer than five colors or if you want to use PostScript halftone screen patterns. If you do not have a PostScript printer at your disposal and your work does not require Spot color or four-color printing, you can use either the Spot or Process color system to specify fill colors.

TIP: If you have a black-and-white display adapter and monitor, you can still specify Spot color fills, but your screen will not display them in color. Refer to the PANTONE Color Reference Manual to see the color you have selected.

As mentioned at the beginning of the chapter, an object must be a closed path in order for you to fill it. However, a closed path does not assure a solid object. If you combine two or more objects as you learned to do in Chapter 6, "Selecting, Moving, and Arranging Objects," "holes" result where the combined objects overlap. You can then create interesting design effects by surrounding the "holes" with outline and fill colors. Perform the following exercise to create a logo with transparent text, outline it, and assign a uniform fill Spot color to it. You will edit this logo throughout the chapter as you learn new ways to use the Fill tool fly-out menu. If you are working with a color monitor, you will see the example drawings come alive in living color! If you are working with a black-and-white monitor, you will see the specified colors as shades of gray.

1. To prepare the screen, set magnification at Actual Size (1:1). Activate the Snap To Grid command and set both Horizontal and Vertical Grid Frequency to 1 per pica. If the units boxes display a unit of measurement other than picas, click on their scroll arrows until the word "pica" displays. Activate both Edit Wireframe and Show Rulers from the Display menu; because of the grid settings, the rulers display in picas rather than in inches.

2. Before beginning to draw, set the default outline pen and outline fill attributes back to the original CorelDRAW! defaults. To do this, click on the Custom Outline Pen icon in the Outline tool fly-out menu. Select OK when the Outline Pen for New Object message box appears to ask you whether you want to set a new default value. Adjust settings in the Outline Pen dialog box as follows: black color, Width 0.003 inches, Corners sharp, butt Line Caps, no Arrows, solid line style, Angle 0 degrees, Stretch 100%. No checkboxes should be filled. Select OK to make these settings the default outline pen attributes.

3. Select the Ellipse tool, and position the pointer at the 24-pica mark on the horizontal ruler and the 33-pica mark on the vertical ruler. Draw a perfect circle from the center outward, starting from this point. Make the circle 22 picas in diameter or the largest circle you can draw, using the information on the status line to help you.

4. Activate the Text tool. Select an insertion point near the top of the circle, at the 24-pica mark on the horizontal ruler and the 25-pica mark on the vertical ruler. You do not have to position the pointer exactly, because you can align the text and circle later. Type a capital T and then choose Edit Text from the Edit menu. When the Text dialog box appears, continue typing **The World of Corel DRAW!** in the text entry window, one word per line, and select the following text attributes: Aardvark Bold, 40.0 points, Center justification. Click on the Spacing command button, set inter-character spacing to 20% and inter-line spacing to 115%, and then select OK twice. The text appears centered vertically and horizontally within the circle, as shown in Figure 13–2. If the text is not centered perfectly within the circle, then with the text still selected, activate the Pick tool and drag the text as necessary to center it.

Depending on the type of display and display adapter you have, the diameter of the circle and the point size you can fit in the circle may differ from what is described and shown here. Draw the biggest circle and use the largest type size needed to fill your screen at Actual Size magnification.

13

5. Click on both Show Rulers and Edit Wireframe in the Display menu again to deactivate them. You cannot clearly distinguish the

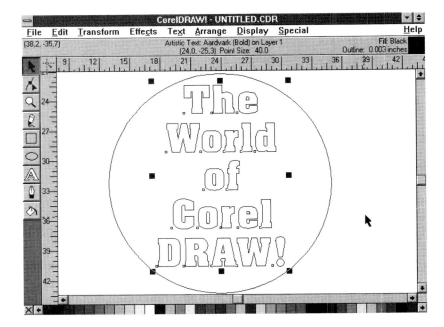

Centering a text string within a circle
Figure 13–2.

text from the circle now, because they have the same outline and fill colors.

6. Select the Preferences command in the Special menu (or press Ctrl-J). When the Preferences dialog box appears, adjust both of the numeric settings beside the Place Duplicate option to –2,0 picas and points. Make sure that you place a comma rather than a period after the 2. Duplicate objects that you create with this setting are offset from the original by the specified amount (in this case, 2 picas below and to the left of the original). Select OK to exit the dialog box.

7. Activate the Pick tool, select the circle, and then click on the Duplicate command in the Edit menu. A duplicate of the circle appears below and to the left of the original, and is selected immediately.

8. Change the fill of this duplicate circle to none by clicking on the X at the left of the color palette at the bottom of your screen.

9. Select both the original circle and the text string again using the Shift key, and click on the Combine command in the Arrange

menu. The message in the status line changes from "2 objects selected" to "Curve on Layer 1." The "Fill:" message at the right side of the status line displays a default fill of black, but the text now appears white, as shown in Figure 13–3. In combining the two objects, you have converted both the circle and the text string to curves. The area behind the text has become not white but transparent.

10. Select the Save As command in the File menu. When the Save As dialog box appears, type the name **FILL-1** in the File Name text box, and then select Save.

11. With the curve object still selected, click on the Fill tool and again on the Uniform Fill icon (you can also press (Shift)-(F11)). The Uniform Fill dialog box appears. Click on the Spot option button, and then select the top-left color in the palette, Pantone Yellow CV, and set the tint to 55%. Your settings should match those in Figure 13–4.

12. Select OK to exit the dialog box. Now you can see some contrast between the black outline and the fill colors, even if you do not

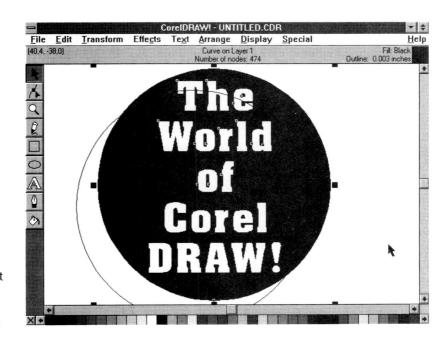

Combining two objects to form a curve object with transparent "holes"
Figure 13–3.

13

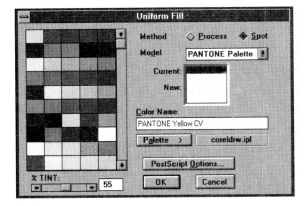

Setting for a
Spot color
uniform fill
Figure 13–4.

have a color monitor. The text has the same outline style as the circular shape, because CorelDRAW! treats the text curves as "holes" or edges within the single combined object. The outline is very thin, however, so you will thicken it in the next step.

13. With the curve object still selected, click on the Outline tool. Access the Outline Pen dialog box by clicking on the Custom Outline Pen icon (or by pressing F12). Change the Width setting for the outline pen to 5.0 fractional points. Place a checkmark in the Behind Fill option and then select OK to apply these settings to the object. Now you see a heavier outline around both the outer rim of the circle and the text, as shown in Figure 13–5. Because you activated the Behind Fill option, the "ink" of the outline doesn't completely clog up the transparent spaces in the text.

14. You are ready to give the finishing touches to the curve object. Click on the Outline tool once more, and select the Custom Outline Color icon (or press Shift-F12) to access the Outline Color dialog box. Select the Spot option button, select Names as the Model, and select Pantone 293 CV (in Versions 2.01 and above, type 293 in the Search String Text box), then set the tint to 52%. Click on OK to exit the dialog box.

15. Select the duplicate circle. Click on the Fill tool and the Uniform Fill icon to access the Uniform Fill dialog box. Select the Spot option; Names should still be the Model. Scroll to Pantone 281 CV (a dark purplish blue), and leave tint at 100%. Click on OK to select this setting and exit the dialog box.

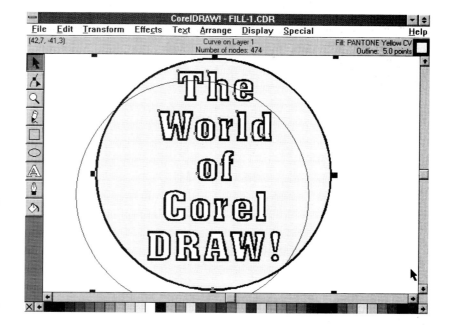

Outline
appearing
behind fill for
clearer text
appearance
Figure 13–5.

16. When you return to the image, you see that the circle that you thought was behind the combined text-circle curve object is really in front of it, and now covers part of the curve object. Choose To Back from the Arrange menu to fix this situation.

17. The image redisplays to show the background circle creating a dramatic "shadow" effect behind the curve object. The alignment is not quite right yet, however; white space may be visible behind the upper portion of the word "The." To remedy this situation, deactivate the Snap To Grid command and adjust the position of the background circle slightly so that it fills the word "The" completely. Now all of the transparent spaces behind the letters in the curve object have fill behind them.

18. To see this apparent fill more closely, turn on Full Screen Preview by pressing F9 . Your screen should look similar to Figure 13–6.

19. Again press F9 to turn off Full Screen Preview and group the curve object and the circle behind it, and then press Ctrl-S to save the changes you have made to this graphic. Leave the graphic on the screen to use in the next exercise.

13

Apparent fill of
transparent
areas using a
background
object
Figure 13–6.

The kind of object you have just created makes an excellent specimen
for outline and fill experiments of all kinds. You will continue to use
this graphic throughout the chapter. In the next section, you will add
an interesting design effect by specifying a PostScript halftone screen
pattern for the background circle in FILL-1.CDR.

Defining PostScript Halftone Screen Fill Patterns

When you choose the Spot color rather than the Process color system
in the Uniform Fill dialog box, another set of fill specifications becomes
available. If you work with a PostScript printer, you can fill an object
with a halftone screen pattern of the currently selected Spot color. You
will recall from your work with outline color in Chapter 12 that the
CorelDRAW! preview window displays PostScript halftone screen
patterns as a solid color; to see how they actually look, you have to
print them on a PostScript printer.

You define a PostScript halftone screen pattern by clicking on the PostScript Options command button at the lower-left corner of the Uniform Fill dialog box. CorelDRAW! offers ten different screen options. You can vary the frequency (number of occurrences per inch) and angle of any screen pattern to achieve dramatic differences in the appearance of a Spot color fill.

In the following exercise, you will assign a PostScript halftone screen pattern of a specified angle and frequency to the background circle in the FILL-1.CDR image and save the altered image under a new name. If you have a PostScript printer, you can print this image out once you have mastered the printing techniques covered in Chapter 15.

1. With FILL-1.CDR still on the screen, select the foreground curve and ungroup its component objects by clicking on the Break Apart command in the Arrange menu. Deselect all objects and then click on the outline of the curve object (the circle) that you combined earlier.

2. With the curve object selected, click on the Fill tool and the Uniform Fill icon in the Fill tool fly-out menu. When the Uniform Fill dialog box appears, click on the PostScript Options command button at the lower part of the dialog box. The PostScript Options dialog box appears.

3. Select the MicroWaves halftone screen type by scrolling through the Type list box until MicroWaves is highlighted.

4. Adjust screen frequency in the Frequency numeric entry box to 20.0 per inch. This is a very low frequency (the minimum is 10, the maximum 1000) and will display a dramatic pattern on a 300 dpi PostScript printer.

5. If necessary, use the scroll arrows to adjust the number in the Angle numeric entry box to 45 degrees. This will cause the screen pattern to tilt at a 45-degree angle.

6. When your settings match the ones in Figure 13–7, select OK to exit the PostScript Options dialog box. Click on OK again to exit the Uniform Fill dialog box and return to the screen image. You will not notice anything different, because the preview window cannot display PostScript patterns.

7. Select the Save As command in the File menu and type **FILL-2** in the File Name text box of the Save As dialog box. Select OK to save

13

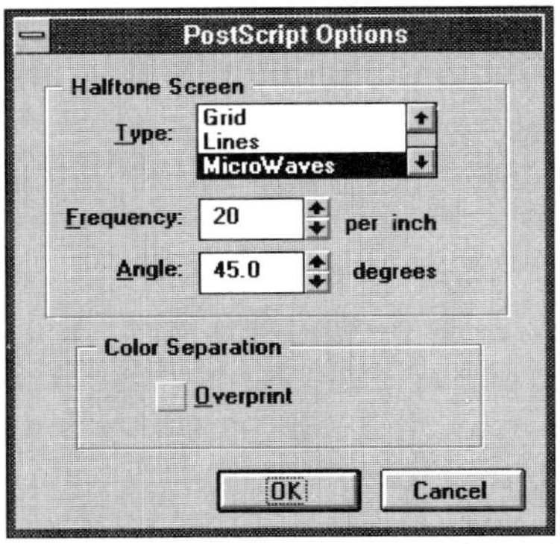

Defining a
custom
PostScript
halftone screen
pattern
Figure 13–7.

the file under this new name. After you complete Chapter 15, you
can print this file to see the results of your settings if you have a
PostScript printer. Your results should look like Figure 13–8.

When you assign PostScript halftone screen pattern fills to objects, base
your choice of frequency on the resolution of the PostScript printer you
will use. On any PostScript printer, low frequencies result in more

Printed image
of the PostScript
halftone screen
Figure 13–8.

dramatic pattern effects, while high frequencies result in the pattern being hardly visible. The resolution of the printer, not any absolute number, determines what constitutes a low or a high frequency. To achieve the same visual effect on different printers, you should vary the frequency assigned to a screen. For example, you should assign lower screen frequencies when the printer resolution is 300 dpi, and higher frequencies for Linotronic or other image-setting equipment at a resolution of 600 or 1270 dpi. Table 13–1 provides information on the number of visible gray levels for each printer resolution at a given screen frequency.

You can specify a PostScript halftone screen pattern as a default fill in the same way that you would specify a normal Spot color. In the next section, you will change the fill and outline colors of both of the objects in the original FILL-1.CDR file, using the Process color system instead of Spot color.

Defining Uniform Process Color Fills

As you will recall from Chapter 12, Process color is the term used for expressing colors as percentages of other colors or color properties. CMYK Process color is the industry standard for four-color printing. In general, you should specify Process color instead of Spot color when your drawing includes five or more colors or when you plan to reproduce it through the four-color printing process.

CorelDRAW! supports color separation for Process as well as Spot color if you send your work to a PostScript printer. When you specify color in

Printer Resolution and Number of Gray Levels Visible for PostScript Halftone Screen Patterns
Table 13–1.

Selected Frequency	Number of Gray Levels		
	300 dpi	600 dpi	1270 dpi
30 per inch	101	401	1600
60 per inch	26	101	401
100 per inch	10	37	145
120 per inch	7	26	101

13

CMYK terms, your printer generates only four sheets (one each for cyan, magenta, yellow, and black percentages) for every image page, no matter how many colors the image contains. When you specify color in Spot color terms, on the other hand, a separate page is printed for each color used in the drawing. Spot color is more exact for purposes of color matching than Process color but also more expensive to produce.

To specify Process colors for an existing object, you create or select the object, click on the Fill tool, and then click again on the Uniform Fill icon in the fly-out menu. When the Uniform Fill dialog box appears, you select the Process option button (this may not be necessary, since Process is the original default), choose one of the color models (CMYK, RGB, or HSB), and select a color with the visual selector or by entering percentages of the constituent colors. You can also choose a named color by selecting Names as the color model and choosing a color from the list box, or by selecting Palette as the model and clicking on a color. All of these alternatives are explained in Chapter 12. To specify default Process colors for objects that you plan to draw in the future, you access the Uniform Fill dialog box without first having selected an object.

In the next exercise, you will specify fill and outline color for the original FILL-1.CDR file using Process color instead of Spot color.

Assigning Process Color Uniform Fills

If you plan to generate color separations for an image in preparation for printing, remember to specify outlines and fills for all objects in terms of the same color system. In the following exercise, you will change fill color specifications for FILL-1.CDR from Spot to Process color.

1. Open the original FILL-1.CDR file that you created in the first exercise of this chapter. The curve object and background circle are currently combined; to make them accessible as separate objects, select them and apply the Break Apart command from the Arrange menu.

2. Magnify the image using the fit-in-window icon in the Magnification tool fly-out menu. Deselect all objects and then select the background circle.

3. With the background circle selected, press (Shift)-(F11) or click on the Fill tool and then the Uniform Fill icon. The Uniform Fill dialog

box appears, displaying the object's current Spot color fill as a named color.

4. Click on the Process option button. The contents of the dialog box change, as shown in Figure 13–9. CorelDRAW! attempts to define the Spot color in terms of a Process color. Here you see the same color in the display box, but the Color Name text box is blank in place of the "PANTONE 281 CV." Select CMYK as the Model, if necessary. Here you see a color definition of 100% cyan, 72% magenta, 0% yellow, and 38% black. Again, there is no name for the color.

5. Adjust the color values to Cyan 55%, Magenta 55%, and Black 75%. Leave Yellow at 0%. The color preview display box shows a very dark blue. Select OK to redisplay the background circle with the new fill color.

6. Use the marquee to select the foreground circle and text, and access the Uniform Fill dialog box again. Select the Process Method option button, set fill color values to Magenta 30% and Yellow 10% (leaving Cyan and Black at 0%), and then select OK.

7. Whenever you are preparing an image for four-color printing, make sure that *both* outline and fill colors are specified using the Process color system. In the present illustration, the outline color for the curve object is still specified with Spot color. To switch color systems for the circle's outline, press (Shift)-(F12) or select the Outline tool and the Custom Outline Color icon to access the Outline Color dialog box. Click on the Process Method option

The Uniform Fill dialog box with Process color selected
Figure 13–9.

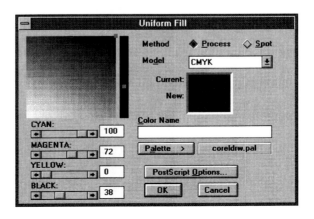

13

button, and set outline fill color values to Cyan 35%, Magenta 30%, and Black 10% (leaving Yellow at 0%). Click on OK to exit the dialog box and redisplay the image. If you turn on Full Screen Preview, the image should appear similar to Figure 13–10.

8. Select the Save As command in the File menu. When the Save As dialog box appears, type **FILL-3** in the File text box and then click on Save.

Specifying Process color uniform fills is easy; you will begin working with color separation for Process color in Chapter 15, "Printing and Processing Your Images." Many CorelDRAW! applications require only black and white graphics, however. In the next section, you will learn a shortcut for specifying fill color that will be useful if you usually print to a black-and-white printer.

Curve object with Process color outline and fill
Figure 13–10.

Filling with White, Black, or Gray

When you specified outline fill colors in Chapter 12, the second row of the Outline tool fly-out menu contained seven preset colors (white, black, and five shades of gray) that you could select quickly by clicking on the desired icon. The arrangement in the Fill tool fly-out menu is similar. There are seven icons in the Second row that allow you to select a preset color without having to set attributes in a dialog box. These seven options represent preset uniform fills in the following order: white, black, and 10%, 30%, 50%, 70% and 90% gray.

To select one of these preset uniform fill colors for an existing object, you simply select the object, access the Fill tool fly-out menu, and then click on the appropriate icon. If you had previously assigned a PostScript halftone screen fill to the selected object, the pattern remains the same but now has the new shade that is assigned to it.

To select one of the preset options as the default uniform fill, you click on the desired icon in the Fill tool fly-out menu, without first selecting an object. Again, if the previous default fill involved a PostScript halftone screen pattern, that pattern remains active but in the new default gray shade.

In the following exercise, you will assign black, white, or preset gray shade fills to the objects in the FILL-2.CDR file.

1. Open the FILL-2.CDR file. As you will recall, this is the file in which you assigned a PostScript halftone screen pattern to the background circle.

2. Adjust viewing magnification to fit-in-window and then select the curve object.

3. With the curve object selected, click on the Fill tool. When the Fill tool fly-out menu appears, select the 70% gray icon (the second icon from the right on the bottom row). After a moment, the curve object redisplays with a dark gray shade of fill.

4. Select the Outline tool and click on the 10% gray icon, the fourth icon from the left in the second row of the Outline tool fly-out menu. The curve object redisplays with a faint gray outline around the outside and the letters.

13

5. Select the background circle and click on the Fill tool and then the black icon. The background circle now contrasts with the 10% gray outline of the letters and with the original circle. Make sure the Behind Fill check box in the Outline Pen dialog box is checked, and then select Full Screen Preview. You should see an image similar to Figure 13–11.

6. To save this altered image, turn off Full Screen Preview and select the Save As command in the File menu. When the Save As dialog box appears, type **FILL-4** in the File text window and select Save.

Although the preview window cannot show it to you, the circle still contains a custom PostScript halftone screen fill in the MicroWaves pattern. When you reach Chapter 15, you can print out this file to see the effect of combining this pattern with the gray shades, if you have a PostScript printer.

Preset fills: curve object 80% gray, outline 10% gray, background circle black
Figure 13–11.

Fill Roll-Up Window

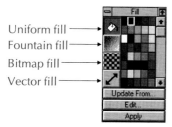

Uniform fill
Fountain fill
Bitmap fill
Vector fill

Like many other major functions, fill color has a roll-up window in CorelDRAW! 3 and on. The Fill roll-up window, shown on the left, is opened by clicking on the roll-up icon, second from the left in the top row of the Fill fly-out menu.

Like other roll-up windows, the Fill roll-up window stays open on your screen until you roll it up or close it. It provides access to the Uniform Fill, Fountain Fill, Bitmap Fill, and Vector Fill dialog boxes. It also allows you to edit the fill of an existing object. To use the Fill roll-up, you first click on one of the four buttons on the left side to specify the type of fill you want. Clicking the Edit button, near the bottom of the roll-up, opens the dialog box for the type of fill you have selected. Also, the display area to the right of the four fill-type buttons changes to reflect the type of fill. For uniform fill, this area is the current color palette. For the other types of fill it provides display boxes and buttons unique to those types.

Use the following exercise to try out the Fill roll-up with uniform fill. In later sections of this chapter you will use the roll-up with the other types of fill. You should still have FILL-4.CDR on your screen.

1. Click on the Fill icon to open its fly-out menu, and click on the Fill Roll-up icon (second from the left in the top row) to open the Fill roll-up window.

2. If necessary, click on the Uniform Fill button in the upper left of the roll-up to select that as the fill type.

3. With the Pick tool, use the marquee to select the text-circle combination (deselect the background circle if necessary).

4. Click on the Update From button in the roll-up and then click on the selected text/circle combination in your drawing. By using Update From, you are bringing these objects' fill characteristics into the roll-up.

5. Click on the Edit button in the roll-up to open the Uniform Fill dialog box. Spot color and the list of color names should still be selected. If they aren't, click on Spot color and select Names as the Model.

6. Click on PANTONE Warm Red CV as the new fill color, click on OK to close the dialog box, and click on Apply in the roll-up to change the fill of the curve object.

7. Open the Outline Pen flyout menu and click on the Pen Roll-up icon. When the Pen roll-up opens, click on the Update From button and click on the selected group of objects.

8. Click on the Color button in the Pen roll-up (fourth button from the bottom) to open the outline color palette. Click on PANTONE Yellow CV in the upper-left corner of the palette, then click on Apply to change the outline color.

9. Click on the background circle in your drawing to select it. Click on Update From in the Fill roll-up and then click on the background circle.

10. Click on PANTONE Reflex Blue CV—the first color in the second row of the Fill roll-up's color palette. The color of the background circle changes immediately; you don't have to use Apply. The resulting design is shown in Figure 13–12.

11. Save this new design as FILL-5.

Changes made with the Fill and Pen roll-ups
Figure 13–12.

In the next section, you will begin working with one of the most creative types of fills in CorelDRAW!: fountain fills, which involve a smooth transition of two different colors through the interior of an object.

Custom Fountain Fills

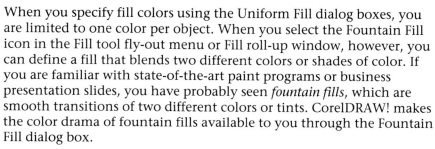

When you specify fill colors using the Uniform Fill dialog boxes, you are limited to one color per object. When you select the Fountain Fill icon in the Fill tool fly-out menu or Fill roll-up window, however, you can define a fill that blends two different colors or shades of color. If you are familiar with state-of-the-art paint programs or business presentation slides, you have probably seen *fountain fills*, which are smooth transitions of two different colors or tints. CorelDRAW! makes the color drama of fountain fills available to you through the Fountain Fill dialog box.

By adjusting settings in the Fountain Fill dialog box, you can fill any object with two different colors or tints in such a way that the colors blend evenly from one extreme to the other. CorelDRAW! allows you to create two different types of fountain fills: *linear* and *radial*. Think of the difference between these two fills as similar to the difference between drawing a circle or rectangle from one side to the other or from the center outward. In a linear fountain fill, the color transition occurs in one direction only, determined by the angle that you specify. In a radial fountain fill, the blend of start and end colors proceeds concentrically, from the center of the object outward or from the outer rim inward. Whichever type of fountain fill you select, you can specify colors using either the Spot color or Process color system. If you choose Spot color, you can also define PostScript halftone screen patterns to add an extra visual "punch" to your fountain fills.

The following exercises provide practice defining linear and radial fountain fills using Spot color, PostScript halftone screen patterns, and Process color.

Defining Linear Fountain Fills

13

When you specify a linear fountain fill, the start color begins at one edge of the object and the end color appears at the opposite side. In between is a smooth blending occurring along an imaginary line that extends from one edge to the other. The direction of the color blend depends on the angle of the fill, over which you have complete control.

You can also control the speed and the fineness of the display that defines the fountain fill in the CorelDRAW! window, by choosing Preferences from the Special menu, clicking on Display and adjusting the Preview Fountain Stripes settings. A low setting (2 is the lower limit) causes the fountain fill to display rapidly with a small number of circles. A high value (100 is the upper limit) causes the filled object to redraw very slowly in the preview window, but it also results in a very finely graded transition of color. For all output devices *except* PostScript printers, the Fountain Stripes setting also determines the resolution at which the fountain fill will print. You will have the opportunity to practice adjusting this setting, and viewing the results on the screen, in the "Fill Tool Hints" section of this chapter.

As with the outline pen and outline fill, you can define a linear fountain fill for existing objects or set defaults for objects that you have not yet created. To define a linear fountain fill for an existing object, you first select the object and then access the Fountain Fill dialog box by clicking on the Fountain Fill icon in the Fill tool fly-out menu. To define a linear fountain fill as the default fill for the next object you create, you click on the Fountain Fill icon without first selecting an object. The exercises in the next few sections use existing objects as examples. Once you enter the Fountain Fill for New Object dialog box, however, the techniques for specifying the fill are the same as when you work with an existing object. To open the Fountain Fill dialog box for either future objects or existing objects, you can also use the shortcut key F11 .

Spot Color Linear Fountain Fills

Theoretically, you can select any two colors as the start and end colors when you specify a linear fountain fill using the Spot color system. In practice, however, it's best to select two tints of the *same* color if you intend to send color separations of the resulting image to a commercial reproduction facility. The reason for this has to do with the way Spot color is physically reproduced, which makes it difficult to blend two discrete colors evenly.

In the following exercise, you will define a Spot color linear fountain fill for the objects in the FILL-1.CDR file, which you created earlier in the chapter.

1. Open the original FILL-1.CDR file you set up in the first exercise of this chapter, not one of the edited versions. If you have a color monitor, your screen displays a curve object containing a PANTONE Yellow CV Spot color at 55% tint and a blue PANTONE 293 CV outline at a 52% tint. A darker blue (PANTONE 281 CV) fills a circle behind the object. (To check the current fill colors for an existing object at any time, just ungroup and select the object, click on the Fill tool, and click on the Uniform Fill icon to display the Uniform Fill dialog box.)

2. Adjust the viewing area to a fit-in-window viewing magnification.

3. Select the combined objects. Apply the Break Apart command in the Arrange menu to separate them, and then deselect all objects and reselect the circle alone.

4. Click on the Fill tool and then on the Fountain Fill icon in the Fill tool fly-out menu, or press [F11]. The Fountain Fill dialog box displays, as shown in Figure 13–13.

The upper portion of the dialog box contains controls for the type of fountain fill (linear or radial), a display box showing the current fill, and the angle that determines the direction of the fill. In the middle left portion of the dialog box are controls for specifying the From and To colors of the fill. These include a color button that opens the current color palette, and a More command button that opens the Fountain Fill color dialog box. The default settings are Type Linear, Angle 90 degrees, From color Black, and To color

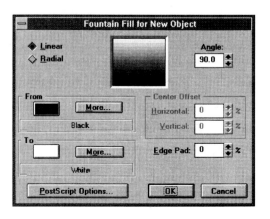

The (default)
Fountain Fill
dialog box
Figure 13–13.

13

White, and color Method Process. These settings would result in a fill that is white at the top, blending gradually into solid black at the bottom.

5. Leave the Linear Type and 90-degree Angle. Click on More for the From color and select Spot as the Method and PANTONE Yellow CV (first color in the list) at 100% tint. Similarly set the To color to PANTONE Yellow CV, but at 0% tint, which will look virtually white. Remember that when you define color using the Spot color method, both the start and end colors should be different tints of the same color.

6. Select OK to exit the dialog box with the new settings. The circle object now shows a darker yellow fill at the bottom, with a gradual transition to white at the top. If you have a black-and-white monitor, the transition in tones is similar to the one shown in Figure 13–14.

7. Access the Fountain Fill dialog box again (F11). This time, change the Angle setting to 45 degrees and then select OK to exit the

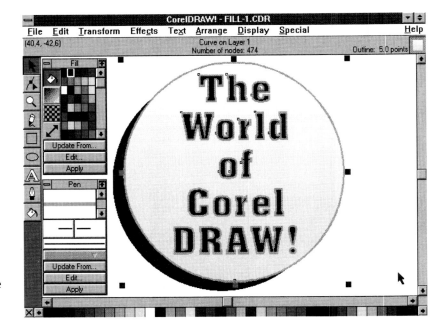

Spot color
linear fountain
fill at a
90-degree angle
Figure 13–14.

dialog box. Now, the curve object redisplays with a fountain fill that is lighter at the upper right and darker at the lower left.

8. For an interesting enhancement, create a fountain fill for the background circle that runs in the opposite direction from the fill for the curve object. To do this, select the background circle, then click on the Fountain Fill button in the Fill roll-up, and click on Edit. When the Fountain Fill dialog box appears, click on More for the From color, select Spot as the Method, set the color to PANTONE 281 (use the scroll bars) at a 100% tint. Similarly, set the To color to PANTONE 281 at a 30% tint. Change the Angle setting to 135 degrees, the exact opposite of the 45-degree setting you chose for the fill of the curve object. This will result in a fill running in the exact opposite direction than the fill for the foreground object.

9. Select OK to exit the dialog box and then click on Apply in the roll-up. When the objects are redrawn, you can see that the area behind the letters is a richer color at the upper right than at the lower left. This arrangement adds some visual tension to the mock logo as shown in Figure 13–15.

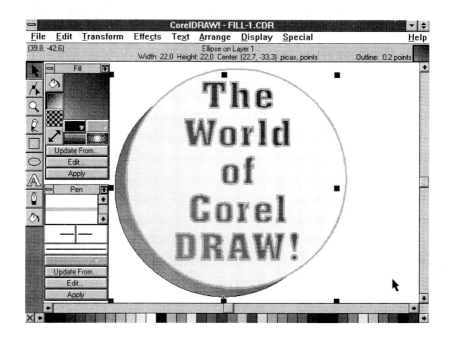

Background linear fountain fill at a reverse angle from foreground
Figure 13–15.

13

10. Group the foreground objects, and then select the Save As command from the File menu. When the Save As dialog box appears, type the filename **FILL-6** in the File text box, and then click on the Save command button to save the altered picture under this new name.

TIP: If you plan to use a commercial process to reproduce images that contain Spot color fountain fills, make the start and end colors two tints of the same color. If you do not plan to reproduce your images by a commercial process, however, this restriction does not apply.

When you select the Spot color method of assigning start and end colors, you can create a fountain fill from black to white by specifying colors as 0% or 100% black. Spot color is especially useful for black-and-white linear fountain fills if you are interested in assigning a PostScript halftone screen pattern to the object at the same time. In the next section, you will review the process of specifying a PostScript halftone screen pattern with a linear fountain fill.

Spot Color Linear Fountain Fills with PostScript Halftone Screens

You will recall from your work with outline fill colors in Chapter 12 that the preview window cannot show you how a selected PostScript halftone screen pattern will look when printed. You must actually print the object with such a fill on a PostScript device in order to see the results. The same is true of PostScript halftone screens when you combine them with fountain fills, which is possible when you use the Spot color system to specify start and end colors.

You cannot see the results of your work immediately when you select a PostScript halftone screen pattern with a linear fountain fill. Nevertheless, here are some tips that should help you achieve a better design on the first try:

✦ Set the angle of the PostScript halftone screen either at the same angle as the linear fountain fill or at an angle that complements it in a design sense. (You do not want the eye to travel in many directions at once.) Sometimes, you can determine the best angle only by experimentation; varying the angle of the halftone screen from the angle of the fountain fill can produce unexpected results.

✦ If you want the halftone screen to be visible when you print it, use a low frequency setting in the PostScript Halftone Screen dialog box. This is most important if the Fountain Stripes setting in the Preferences dialog box, which controls the fineness of the fountain fill itself, is high.

Go on to the next set of sections to experiment with fountain fills that radiate from the center outward or from the rim inward.

Defining Radial Fountain Fills

When you specify a radial fountain fill, the start color appears all around the outer area of the object and the end color appears at its center, or vice versa. The blending of colors or tints occurs in concentric circles. Because color density in radial fountain fills changes gradually in a circular pattern, a 3-D look is easy to achieve.

You cannot specify an angle when you select a radial fountain fill, but you can control the location of the fill's apparent center. You'll see one way to change the center of a radial fountain fill in this chapter and two others in Chapter 16, "Creating Special Effects" and Chapter 17, "Combining CorelDRAW! Features."

You can use either Spot color or Process color to define a radial fountain fill. When you use Spot color, you have the additional option of selecting a PostScript halftone screen pattern. The tips contained in the section "Spot Color Linear Fountain Fills with PostScript Halftone Screens" apply to radial fountain fills, too.

You can control both the speed and the fineness of the display that defines the fountain fill in full-color mode by adjusting the Fountain Stripes setting in the Preferences dialog box as discussed under Defining Linear Fountain Fills earlier in this chapter.

13

As with the linear fountain fill, you can define a radial fountain fill for existing objects or set defaults for objects that you haven't yet created. The exercises in the next few sections use existing objects as examples.

Spot Color Radial Fountain Fills

In the following exercise, you will define a black-and-white Spot color radial fountain fill for the objects in the FILL-4.CDR file that you created earlier in the chapter.

1. Open the FILL-4.CDR file. As you will recall from a previous section, the curve object in this file contains a preset uniform fill of 80% black. (Remember, you can find out the current fill specifications by accessing the Uniform Fill dialog box.)

2. Adjust viewing magnification to fit-in-window. Select the curve object and click in the Fountain Fill button in the Fill roll-up.

3. Click on Edit to open the Fountain Fill dialog box and then on the Radial option button. Notice that the Angle numeric entry box dims and is not accessible when the Radial option is selected. Click on More for the From color, select Spot as the Method, Black with 100% tint as the color, and then click on OK to return to the Fountain Fill dialog box. For the To color, also select Spot, 20% Black, and OK. Then, select OK again to exit the dialog box, and then click on Apply in the Fill roll-up. The curve object redisplays with a brighter area (the 20% black of the color range) in its center as you can see in Figure 13–16. The apparent play of light you achieve with this kind of fill creates a 3-D effect, making the surface of the "globe" appear to curve outward.

4. Select the Save As command in the File menu. When the Save As dialog box appears, type the name **FILL-7** in the File text box and then select Save.

As long as you choose the Spot color method of specifying color, you can select a PostScript halftone screen pattern with a radial fountain fill. The added 3-D effect possible with radial fountain fills can lead to quite dramatic results when you add a halftone screen.

You can change the center of a radial fountain fill to create an off-center highlight for the object. You'll look at one method next. Two other methods for accomplishing this effect are available; both are included among the techniques discussed in Chapter 17, "Combining CorelDRAW! Features."

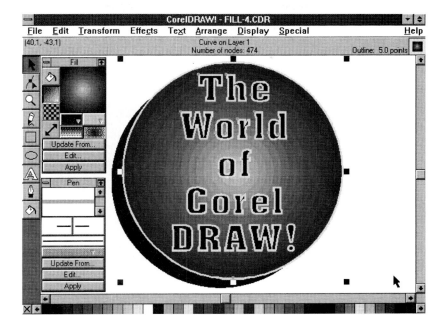

Spot color
radial fountain
fill with lighter
shade at center
Figure 13–16.

Edge Padding and Radial Offset

The Fountain Fill dialog box allows you to add edge padding and offset
the center of a radial fill. You may have noticed that when CorelDRAW!
creates a fountain fill, it is initially rectangular, filling an object's entire
boundary box. When the creation process is complete, the excess is
clipped off to fit the shape of the object, for example, the circles in this
chapter. As a result, the starting and/or ending bands of the fill may be
clipped off. *Edge padding* allows you to increase the percentage of an
object's boundary box that is to be occupied by the starting and ending
bands up to a maximum of 45%. Explore edge padding with the
following brief exercise.

1. With FILL-7.CDR still on your screen and the curve object still
   selected, click on Edit in the Fill roll-up to open the Fountain Fill
   dialog box.

2. Type **20** in the Edge Pad numeric entry box and click on OK and
   then on Apply. Your drawing should look like Figure 13–17.
   Compare this with Figure 13–16 and you will see the impact of
   adding 20% edge padding.

13

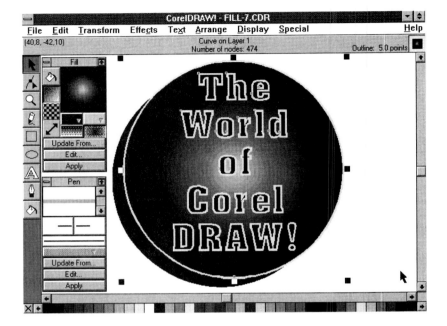

First and last bands of fountain fill set at 20% of the object
Figure 13–17.

The other function of the Fountain Fill Options dialog box is offsetting the center of a radial fill moving the center off center. Look at that next.

3. Again click on Edit in the Fill roll-up to open the Fountain Fill dialog box. (Be sure the Radial button is still selected.)

4. Type **20** in both the Horizontal and Vertical offsets. Click on OK, and then Apply .

5. You should see the center of the radial fountain fill offset to the upper-right corner, as shown in Figure 13–18.

6. Save the current image as FILL-8.

Bitmap and Vector Fill Patterns

CorelDRAW! has two more ways to fill objects: bitmap fill and vector patterns. Bitmap and vector refer to two methods of forming a graphic image in a computer. Bitmap images are formed by defining each point (or bit) in an image. Vector images are formed by defining the start, end, and characteristics of each line (or vector) in an image.

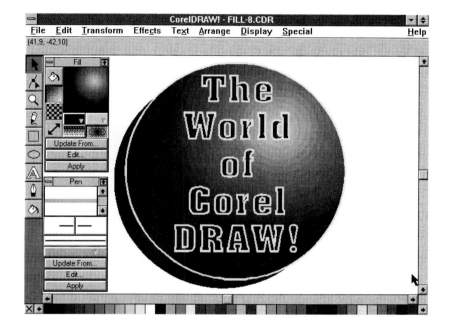

Center of a radial fountain fill offset 20 degrees to the right and 20 degrees up
Figure 13–18.

CorelDRAW! comes with a number of bitmap and vector images that can be used to construct fill patterns. You can create your own or modify existing bitmap and vector images and then use them in fill patterns.

Bitmap and vector patterns are formed by repeating an image many times—tiling—so each image is a single tile. CorelDRAW! provides the means of selecting existing bitmap and vector images, of sizing, editing, and offsetting both kinds of images, and of creating, importing, and coloring bitmap images.

Using Bitmap Fill Patterns

Bitmap images are the most numerous and the most easily manipulated, and CorelDRAW! provides the most capability to handle them. Look at bitmap fill patterns with the following exercise.

13

1. FILL-8.CDR should still be on your screen with the curve object selected.

2. Select the Fill tool and the Bitmap icon. The Two-Color Pattern dialog box will open.

3. Click on the display box and then on the fly-out window's scroll bar to scan through the more than 48 patterns that are included with CorelDRAW!. Then select the Corel image shown here:

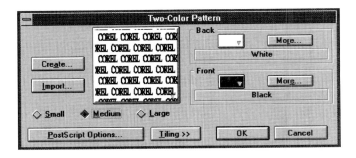

4. First click on Small, then Medium, and then Large to see the difference the three sizes make. Click on Tiling and type in your own sizes in the numeric entry boxes. The height and width do not have to be the same, but for most images you probably want them to be. The maximum size is 5 inches square.

The Tile Size is the size of each tile or image in the pattern. Different sizes work for different patterns. On some patterns, Small causes the images to looked "smudged," while on others, Large causes straight lines to have jagged edges. You need to pick the size that is right for the image and for what you are trying to achieve.

Clicking on either the Front or Back color buttons or the More buttons allows you to assign a color to either the Front (foreground—the word Corel in the selected pattern) or the Back (background). The default is a black foreground and a white background. The color buttons open the color palette, and More opens a color dialog box that is very similar to other color dialog boxes you have used in both this chapter and in Chapter 12. You can select between Spot and Process color, select a color from a palette, specify a % tint if you are using Spot color, and specify a custom process or a named color. Also, if you are using Spot color, you can select a PostScript halftone.

5. Select 50% Black for the Front by clicking on the color button and then on the first color in the second row of the palette. Keep the default White for the Back, and click on OK. You will return to your drawing and see the bitmap pattern provide the fill for the curve object. The text in the curve object is hard to read due to the lack of contrast among the new fill, the outline of the curve object, and the fill for the duplicate circle. Change the last two to improve the contrast.

6. Select the Outline tool and select the white icon to change the outline color to white.

7. Select the duplicate circle and the Fill tool, and select the black icon to change its fill to black. Your screen should look like Figure 13–19.

8. Save your current drawing with the filename FILL-9.

The Import command button in the Two-Color Pattern dialog box opens a file selection dialog box. If you select a file, the image is added to the set of images that you can access in the Two-Color Pattern dialog

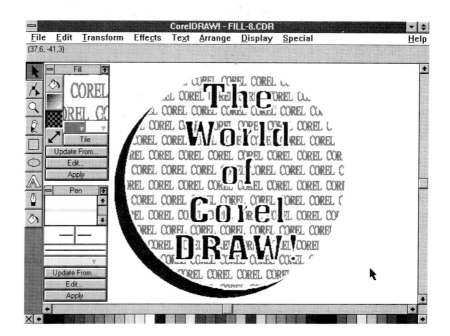

Medium-sized
bitmap fill
pattern
Figure 13–19.

13

box. You can offset (stagger) both the horizontal and vertical starting position of each image in the pattern, as well as offset neighboring rows or neighboring columns.

The Create button allows you to create a new bitmap image to use in constructing a fill pattern. When you activate the Create button, the Bitmap Pattern Editor opens as shown in Figure 13–20. The Bitmap Pattern Editor provides for three different sizes of drawings: 16 pixels ("dots" on your screen) square, 32 pixels square, and 64 pixels square. The more diagonal or curve elements in your image, the larger the size you will need. From a practical standpoint you should use the smallest size possible because the larger sizes take longer to draw and take more room on disk. To draw, click the left mouse button to make a pixel black and the right mouse button to make a black pixel white again. If you want to erase an unfinished drawing, change the size, say, from 16x16 to 32x32. You can then change the size back, and all of the pixels will be clear. When you are done with a drawing, click on OK, and the image will be saved as one of the bitmap images that are available from the Two-Color Pattern dialog box. You can then select it to create a fill pattern.

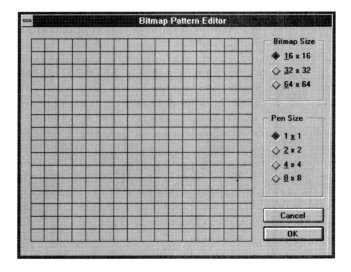

Bitmap Pattern
Editor
Figure 13–20.

Using Vector Fill Patterns

Vector images are more clear than bitmap, but they may take more time to draw and more storage space. Change the fill in the curve object to a vector fill in the following exercise.

1. With FILL-9.CDR still on your screen and the curve object selected, open the Fill tool fly-out menu and select the Vector Fill icon. The Full-Color Pattern dialog box will open as shown here:

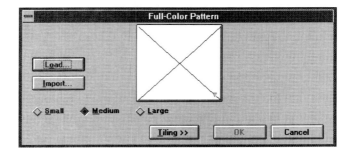

2. The Full-Color Pattern dialog box lets you open disk files with a .PAT extension. Click on the display box to look at the patterns that are available.

3. Select the Corel balloon pattern and click on OK. The balloon pattern will fill your drawing.

4. Click on Update From in the Fill roll-up menu, and click on the curve object in your drawing. Then click on Edit to open the Full-Color pattern dialog box. Select Small, then Medium, then Large. Notice that the default tile sizes in the numeric entry boxes are not square like bitmap patterns are. For now, select Medium, and click on OK and then on Apply. Your vector-filled drawing will appear as shown in Figure 13–21.

5. Save the changed drawing with the name FILL-10.CDR.

The Fill tool fly-out menu contains one more icon that you have not explored yet, but which unlocks the door to a very rich "palette" of patterns and graphic designs. This icon is the subject of the next section.

13

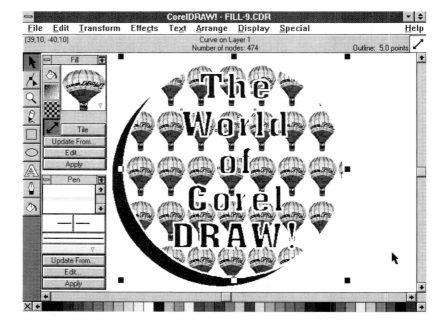

PostScript Fill Textures

The last icon in the Fill tool fly-out menu is the PostScript Textures
icon. If you print to a PostScript printer, you can select this icon to fill
selected objects with a choice of 42 different textures. This number is
deceptive; although only 42 basic patterns exist, you can alter the
parameters for each texture to achieve wide variations in appearance.

When you assign a PostScript fill texture to an object, the preview
window displays the object with a small gray "PS" pattern on a white
background. The Fill designation in the status line, however, indicates
the name of the particular texture assigned. Unfortunately, you cannot
view these textures until you print them. Chapter 15 contains more
information about printing these textures.

Because you cannot adequately see on the screen an object filled with a
PostScript texture, this section contains no practical exercise. It does
summarize the steps involved in defining a PostScript fill texture,
however: accessing the PostScript Texture dialog box, selecting a
texture, and adjusting parameters.

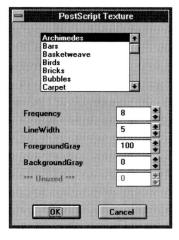

1. To begin the process of defining a PostScript fill texture, you select the object you'd like to fill, and then click on the Fill tool and the PostScript Textures icon at the extreme right of the Fill tool fly-out menu. The PostScript Texture dialog box shown in Figure 13–22 appears.

2. To select a texture, scroll down the list of texture names in the Name list box. The currently highlighted name is the selected texture.

3. Adjust each of the parameters in turn. The parameters vary, depending on the texture. You will often see references to Frequency, Foreground and Background Gray, Maximum or Minimum Size or Distance, and Random Seed (a built-in mathematical "chance" formula).

4. When you have adjusted parameters to your satisfaction, select OK to exit the dialog box and return to your drawing.

5. Print the filled object to see whether you need to adjust parameters further. Since the mathematical algorithms used to calculate the textures are very complex, some textures contain "chance" elements and may not print in a predictable way.

Working with PostScript fill textures is an adventure because of the *aleatory*, or chance, characteristics built into the mathematical formulas for the textures. Think of these textures as a way to bring more creative

PostScript
Texture dialog
box
Figure 13–22.

13

design elements into your drawing, even if your own drawing powers are limited.

Fill Tool Hints

The hints contained in this section by no means exhaust the many uses to which you can put the Fill tool. Rather, they represent tips to help you gain speed in your work or to introduce creative effects.

Copying Fill Styles

In previous chapters, you have learned how to use the Copy Style From command in the Edit menu to copy text, outline pen, or outline fill attributes from one object to another. You can use that same command and its associated dialog box to copy fill styles between objects, too. The following summarizes how to use this feature to best advantage:

1. Select the object or group of objects *to which* you would like to copy the fill attributes of another object.

2. Select the Copy Style From command in the Edit menu. When the Copy Style dialog box appears, activate the Fill checkbox by clicking on it. If you want to copy text, outline pen, or outline color attributes at the same time, activate those checkboxes, too.

3. Select OK to exit the dialog box. The pointer turns into an arrow containing the message "From?," indicating that you should select the object from which you want to copy the fill style.

4. Select the object whose style you want to copy to the selected object. The selected object redisplays with the new fill style.

The entire continuum of fill styles is available to you when you use this command. You can copy Spot or Process color uniform fills, PostScript halftone screen textures, preset shades of gray, bitmap or vector fills, or even PostScript textures. Use this command and dialog box as a handy shortcut to defining fill attributes for one or more objects.

Enhancing Preview and Printing with Fountain Stripes

You will recall that the Preferences—Display dialog box (accessible from the Special menu) contains many useful settings to customize the way CorelDRAW! displays your work. One of these settings, Fountain Stripes, applies to the use of linear and radial fountain fills.

CorelDRAW! displays a fountain fill by creating a series of concentric circles that begin at the highlighting box for the object and work their way inward. You have probably noticed this process each time the preview window redraws an object containing a fountain fill. The Preview Fountain Stripes setting in the Preferences dialog box lets you determine how many circles CorelDRAW! creates to represent a fountain fill. The number ranges from 2 to 100, with 2 representing two circles with coarse outlines, and 100 representing a high number of finely drawn circles. As you can imagine, the window redraws more quickly when Preview Fountain Stripes is set to a low number, and extremely slowly when the Preview Fountain Stripes setting is high. Furthermore, if you print to a device other than a PostScript printer, the number of circles you select in the Preview Fountain Stripes setting represents what will actually print. You can achieve some interesting effects by varying this setting, as you will see in the following exercise.

1. Open the FILL-7.CDR file you edited in an earlier section of this chapter. The curve object in this file contains a gray-shade radial fountain fill specified with Spot color.

2. Set the viewing magnification to fit-in-window.

3. Open the Display dialog box from the Preferences dialog box and the Special menu. Unless you have altered the settings since you first installed CorelDRAW!, the numeric entry box next to the Preview Fountain Stripes option contains the number 20.

4. Use the scroll bar to adjust this number downward to 2, the lowest setting possible. Select OK twice to return to the drawing.

5. Press F9 to redraw the image in Full-screen Preview. Notice how much more quickly the screen redraws now. Only two coarse concentric circles mark the fountain fill, however; as shown in Figure 13–23, the color transition is abrupt rather than smooth.

13

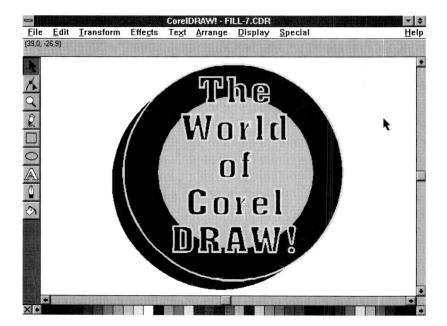

Radial fountain
fill with
Fountain Stripes
set at 2 (coarse)
Figure 13–23.

Depending on your design, such a setting could work to your advantage.

6. Open the Print & Preview dialog box once more. Adjust the Preview Fountain Stripes setting in the Preferences dialog box upward to 100, the highest setting possible. Select OK twice to return to your drawing.

7. Activate Full Screen Preview once more to redraw the image. This time, the redraw takes much longer, because of the high number of fine stripes used to recreate the fountain fill. The resulting blend of color is extremely smooth.

8. Select New to clear the screen. Do not save any changes.

If you do not have a PostScript printer, you can select a high setting for Fountain Stripes to maximize the printer output quality. If you do have a PostScript printer, you can set Fountain Stripes to a low number to speed up the redraw time in the preview window.

C H A P T E R

14

IMPORTING AND EXPORTING FILES

As more graphics applications for IBM-compatible computers become available, the need to transfer files between different applications becomes more acute. Connectivity, or the ability of a software program to import and export data to and from different file formats, is rapidly becoming a requirement for graphics applications. Whether your work involves desktop publishing, technical illustration, original art, or graphic design, it is essential to be able to export your CorelDRAW! graphics to other programs, to import clip art, and to polish your work from other programs.

CorelDRAW! offers you two different methods of connectivity. In Chapter 10, you learned how to use the Windows clipboard to transfer files between CorelDRAW! and other applications that run under Microsoft Windows. The Windows clipboard is not your only option for transferring files, however. CorelDRAW! has its own independent import and export utilities specifically for transferring data between different graphics formats. These utilities allow you to import graphics from and export them to a variety of drawing, painting, desktop publishing, and word processing applications, even though some of these programs may not run under Windows. The use of the Import and Export commands in CorelDRAW! is the subject of this chapter.

CorelDRAW! imports from and exports to both bitmapped and object-oriented applications. If you are unfamiliar with the basic differences between the two graphics formats, the next section will acquaint you with the advantages and disadvantages of each.

Bitmapped vs. Object-Oriented Graphics

CorelDRAW! users come from a variety of backgrounds. Some have many years of experience with electronic drawing and design; others are experts at word processing and desktop publishing, but have little experience with graphics applications. Still others have worked with many different paint (bitmap) programs, but CorelDRAW! represents their first drawing (object-oriented) application. Whatever your background, it is important to have a clear understanding of the differences between bitmapped and object-oriented graphics. You then have a firm basis for choosing how and when to import and export graphic files.

There are many different graphics file formats, but only two kinds of graphics: *bitmapped*, also known as *pixel-based*, and *vector-based*, also known as *object-oriented*. The differences between these two kinds of graphics involve the kinds of software applications that produce them, the way the computer stores them in memory, and the ease with which you can edit them.

Paint programs and scanners produce bitmapped images by establishing a grid of *pixels*, the smallest visual unit that the computer can address, on the screen. These applications create images by altering the colors or attributes of each individual pixel. This way of storing images makes inefficient use of memory, however. The size of an image (the number of pixels it occupies) is fixed once it is created, and is dependent on the resolution of the display adapter on the computer where the image first took shape. As a result, finished bitmapped images are difficult to edit when you transfer them from one application to another. If you increase the size of a finished bitmapped image, you can see unsightly white spaces and jagged edges. If you greatly decrease the size of a finished bitmapped image, parts of the image may "smudge" because of the compression involved. Distortion can also occur if you transfer bitmapped graphics to another computer that has a different display resolution.

Object-oriented graphics, on the other hand, have none of these limitations. They are produced by drawing applications such as CorelDRAW! and are stored in the computer's memory as a series of numbers (not pixels) describing how to redraw the image on the screen. Since this method of storing information has nothing to do with the resolution of a given display adapter, line art is considered to be *device-independent.* No matter what computer you use to create an object-oriented graphic, you can stretch, scale, and resize it flexibly without distortion. Object-oriented graphics also tend to create smaller files than bitmapped graphics because the computer does not have to "memorize" the attributes of individual pixels.

How can you use each type of graphic in CorelDRAW!? As you will learn in greater detail in Chapter 18, "Tracing Bitmapped Images," you can import bitmapped images in order to trace them and turn them into object-oriented graphics. Alternatively, you can simply import them and incorporate them into an existing picture. Your options for editing an imported bitmapped image do not end with the editing capabilities available in CorelDRAW!, however. When you need your finished work to issue from a paint application, or if you prefer to polish your artwork in pixel format, you can export CorelDRAW! graphics back to your favorite paint program.

If you work with other object-oriented drawing and design programs, you can import line art in order to enhance it with advanced features that only CorelDRAW! offers. You can introduce clip art and edit it flexibly. When you are finished editing, you can export CorelDRAW!

14

artwork back to your favorite object-oriented application or to the desktop publishing application of your choice. You can even export your CorelDRAW! graphics to a format that film recorders and slide scanners will be able to use to create professional-looking presentation materials.

CorelDRAW! supports an ever-growing number of file formats that include both pixel-based and object-oriented graphics. Table 14–1 lists all of the file formats you can import into CorelDRAW!, while Table 14–2 lists the file format to which you can export CorelDRAW! graphics. Both tables categorize each file format by format type, by graphics type—bitmapped (pixel) or object-oriented (line)—by file extension.

The first half of this chapter addresses the process of importing graphics files into CorelDRAW! and special notes on importing specific file formats. The second half of the chapter covers the process of exporting graphics to other programs, as well as notes pertinent to exporting each type of file format.

Importing Graphics: An Overview

The process of importing graphics into CorelDRAW! from other file formats always involves these three steps:

1. Select the Import command from the File menu.
2. Select one of the file formats listed in the Import dialog box.
3. Specify the directory and filename of the graphic you want to import.

Once you import the file, you have several editing options, depending on what kind of application it comes from. If the imported graphic originated in a paint program, you can trace it automatically or manually and turn it into a distortion-free, object-oriented image. You will find more information on the CorelDRAW! bitmap tracing features in Chapter 18.

When you select the Import command from the File menu, the Import dialog box shown in Figure 14–1 appears. The drop-down list box in

Program	Graphic Type	Import Formats	Extension
Adobe Illustrator	line/object	AI (EPS)	.AI, .EPS
Arts and Letters	line/object	AI (EPS), Clipboard	.AI, .EPS
ASCII Text	text	Clipboard, Paragraph text	.TXT
AutoCAD	line/object	DXF, HPGL, (PLT files)	.DXF
CorelDRAW!	line/object	CDR, Clipboard	.CDR
CorelTRACE!	line/object	CorelTRACE! EPS	.EPS
CorelPhoto-Paint!	pixel	PCX, PCC	.PCX, .PCC
CompuServe Bitmap	pixel	GIF	.GIF
Computer Graphics Metafile	line/object	CGM	.CGM
Excel (Graphs)		Clipboard	
GEM	line/object	GEM file	.GEM
Harvard Graphics	line/object	Metafile, CGM	.CGM
HP Plotter	line/object	HPGL	.PLT
IBM PIF	line/object	PIF	.PIF
Lotus 1-2-3	line/object	Lotus CGM, PIC	.PIC
Lotus Freelance Plus	line/object	CGM	.CGM
Macintosh	line/object	MAC PICT, AI	.PCT
Micrografx Designer, Graph Plus		Clipboard	
PC Paintbrush	pixel	PCX	.PCX
Targa	pixel	TGA	.TGA
TIFF (Scanners)	pixel	TIFF	.TIF
Windows Bitmap	pixel	BMP	.BMP
Windows Metafile	line/object	WMF	.WMF

CorelDRAW!
Import File
Formats
Table 14–1.

CABINET VISION   LINE/OBJECT   HPGL   .OUT

14

Program	Graphic Type	Import Formats	Extension
Adobe Illustrator 88, 3.0	line/object	AI, EPS	.AI, .EPS
Adobe Type 1 Font	line/object	PFB	.PFB
Ami Professional	line/object	EPS, WMF	.EPS, .WMF
Arts and Letters	line/object	EPS, WMF	.EPS, .WMF
AutoCAD	line/object	DXF	.DXF
Corel Photo-Paint!	pixel	PCX, PCC	.PCX, .PCC
CompuServe Bitmap	pixel	GIF	.GIF
Computer Graphics Metafile	line/object	CGM	.CGM
Delrina Perform	line/object	GEM	.GEM
Encapsulated PostScript	line/object	EPS	.EPS
GEM Artline	line/object	GEM	.GEM
HP Plotter	line/object	HPGL	.PLT
Macintosh	line/object	MAC PICT, AI	.PCT, .AI
Matrix Genegraphic Film Recorders	line/object	SCODL	.SCD
Micrografx Designer	line/object	CGM	.CGM
PageMaker 4.0	line/object	EPS, WMF	.EPS, .WMF
PC Paintbrush	pixel	PCX	.PCX
Targa Bitmap	pixel	TGA	.TGA
TIFF 5.0 Bitmap	pixel	TIFF	.TIF
True Type Font	line/object	TTF	.TTF
Ventura Publisher	line/object	EPS, GEM	.EPS, .GEM
Windows Bitmap	pixel	BMP	.BMP
Windows Metafile	line/object	WMF	.WMF
WordPerfect 5.x	line/object	EPS, WPG	.EPS, .WPG

CorelDRAW!
Export File
Formats
Table 14–2.

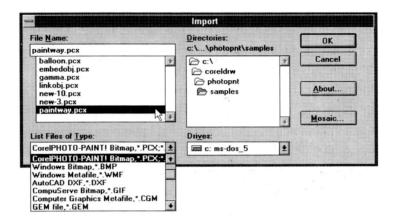

The Import
dialog box
Figure 14–1.

the bottom left of the dialog box contains the extensions of formats available for import. The following sections explain how to work with each of these controls.

Bringing in a File

To select the format for the file you wish to import, and actually bring the file into CorelDRAW!, follow these steps.

1. Select the Import command from the File menu. The Import dialog box will appear as shown in Figure 14–1.

2. In the Directories window, select the path to the directory that contains the file you want to import.

3. Click on the down arrow in the List Files of Type drop-down list box. If the type you want does not immediately appear in the fly-out, use the Scroll arrows to move through the list.

4. Select the filename you want and click on OK, or double-click on the filename. The image will begin importing to the CorelDRAW! page, as you see here.

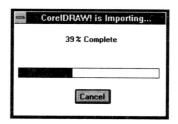

What happens to the image during the import process depends on the specific file format you have chosen. The following sections offer notes on importing each file format for which a CorelDRAW! filter exists.

Importing Bitmapped Graphics

CorelDRAW! can import bitmapped graphics in many different formats including PCX, TIFF, BMP, GIF, and others. The most common source of .PCX files is the ZSoft family of paint applications, although some other paint programs also allow you to save files in this format. TIFF files (extension .TIF) are generated by gray-scale scanners and by paint-and-draw programs that allow you to save bitmapped images with gray-scale information. Windows 3 and 3.1 Paintbrush is the primary source of .BMP files, and CompuServe is the source for GIF files.

Bitmapped images appear inside a rectangle in the editing window after you import them. You cannot break bitmapped images down into their component parts, because CorelDRAW! treats the entire bitmapped image as a single object. You can crop a bitmap after importing it, however, so that only a specified section is visible. You can also select, move, rearrange, stretch, scale, outline, and fill a bitmap as though it were any other type of object.

In some respects, imported bitmaps behave differently from other objects when you edit them. If you rotate or skew a bitmap, you can no longer see the original image in the preview window; it becomes a gray rectangle with a white triangle in the corner to indicate its orientation. A rotated or skewed bitmap will not print unless you output it to a PostScript printer.

The following sections describe the limitations on importing bitmaps as they apply to a specific file format.

PC Paintbrush .PCX Files

If the file you choose to import is in .PCX or .PCC format, CorelDRAW! will accept either the original .PCX or .PCC black-and-white format, or the newer color .PCX format. If you import a color .PCX file, CorelDRAW! will print it in color on a color printer, or convert it to shades of gray for a black-and-white printer. In the Import dialog box, the .PCC format can be chosen by selecting the option for "CorelPHOTO-PAINT! Bitmap, *.PCX, *.PCC". The .PCC extension is hidden behind the scroll bar, but is still available for use.

Windows Paintbrush .BMP Files

Files imported from Windows 3 and 3.1 Paintbrush in the .BMP format can be either black-and-white or color but the format will not convey gray-scale information. On a color printer, files with color will print in color or they will be converted to shades of gray for a black-and-white printer.

Scanned or Gray-Scale Bitmaps (TIFF)

Scanners and some paint programs save bitmapped images in the .TIF file format. CorelDRAW! will import saved gray-scale information with the TIFF format, so if your paint application allows it, you should save gray-scale paint images in this format if you intend to import them into CorelDRAW!.

Several different versions of TIFF formats are available. CorelDRAW! supports most of these. Extra time is needed to decompress and import a compressed TIFF file, however, and you may get errors from some compressed files. Although CorelDRAW! cannot display gray-scale bitmap information on your monitor screen, it saves this information. If you use a PostScript output device, the gray-scale information will be reproduced faithfully when you print the image.

Additional Bitmap Formats

CorelDRAW! can also import CompuServe .GIF files which conform to 89A Specification, as well as Targa TGA 16- and 24-bit files.

14

The following group of sections provides tips on importing and working with graphics files in each of the object-oriented formats that CorelDRAW! supports.

Importing Object-Oriented Graphics

The original release of CorelDRAW! allowed you to import three object-oriented graphics file formats: .CDR (the native CorelDRAW! format), Lotus .PIC graphs, and .AI and .EPS files created by Adobe Illustrator or clip art manufacturers. Since then, the ranks of supported object-oriented file formats have swelled to include .CGM, .GEM, .DXF, .PCT, .PLT, .PIF, and .WMF files. Table 14–1 lists each supported object-oriented file format.

Specific notes on importing and working with each file format are provided in the following sections. Keep in mind that software applications are being upgraded continually and that process may alter the way certain file formats interact with CorelDRAW!.

CorelDRAW! Files and Clip Art

As you will recall from Chapter 10, you can copy or cut and paste objects or images between different CorelDRAW! files using the Windows clipboard. The Windows clipboard limitations render this solution less than satisfactory, especially if you attempt to transfer images that contain many nodes or complicated attributes. A better solution in such cases is to import the .CDR file into the current graphic, using the Import command.

You can also use the Import command to import clip art in .CDR format. Corel Systems and ArtRight Software Corporation are among the clip art manufacturers who provide files in this format.

A file that you import in .CDR format appears as a group of objects. You can select the group, apply the Ungroup command in the Arrange menu, and then edit the objects normally.

Lotus .PIC Files

You can import graphic images in Lotus 1-2-3 .PIC format into CorelDRAW! and modify them. When you import a Lotus .PIC file,

CorelDRAW! groups the entire file. To manipulate individual objects within the imported graphic, select the graphic, apply the Ungroup command, and then edit objects normally.

Adobe Illustrator Files

A wide variety of clip art files is available in either Adobe Illustrator (.AI) or Adobe Illustrator's own Encapsulated PostScript (.EPS) format, which is different from the .EPS format used by other PostScript applications. If the extension of the file you want to import does not match the one generated automatically by CorelDRAW! (.EPS or .AI), just backspace over the incorrect extension and type the desired extension instead. CorelDRAW! will recognize the correct files.

CAUTION: Keep in mind that the CorelDRAW! .EPS Export filter allows you to save files in a format that most desktop publishing applications can use. However, you cannot edit these files in other graphics applications that use the .EPS format. In addition, the CorelDRAW! .EPS Import filter supports only the Adobe Illustrator version of .EPS. Therefore, if you export a CorelDRAW! file in .EPS format without having saved it as a .CDR file first, you will not be able to re-import it to make changes. Always save your work in CorelDRAW! before exporting it if you think you might need to edit it later.

CorelDRAW! imports an Adobe Illustrator-compatible image file as a group of objects. To edit individual objects in the imported file, select the group, apply the Ungroup command, and then select the desired object(s).

IBM Mainframe Graphics .PIF and .GDF Files

Files in the Base .PIF format are most familiar to graphics users in the mainframe IBM environment.

Not all information in a .PIF file transfers smoothly into CorelDRAW!. For example:

14

✦ You may sometimes need to scale and/or center the image on the page before you can edit it.

✦ Objects that are white in the .PIF file will not show up on the white CorelDRAW! page unless you place a page-sized colored rectangle in the background as contrast.

✦ Base .PIF specifications for "Set Background Mix," "Set Foreground Mix," "Call Segment," "Set Character Set," "Set Paper Color," and "Set Pattern Symbol" do not transfer into the CorelDRAW! format.

✦ Base .PIF "Line Types" specifications do not match CorelDRAW! outline pen line types on a one-to-one basis. .PIF line types 0 and 7 become solid; 1, 4, 2, 5, 3, and 6 become one of the dashed or dotted line styles available in CorelDRAW!; and line type 8 becomes a line type of None.

✦ Text strings from Base .PIF files come into CorelDRAW! as text in the CorelDRAW! Monospaced Font. If that is not available, Toronto is the next choice. If neither is available, the text will be assigned the font at the top of the font list.

As with most other line-art files, a graphic imported from a .PIF application arrives in CorelDRAW! as multiple grouped objects. To edit individual objects in the graphic, select the group, apply the Ungroup command in the Arrange menu, and then select the object you wish to manipulate.

Computer Graphics Metafile .CGM Files

CorelDRAW! includes an import filter for the object-oriented .CGM format, which appears in the Import dialog box as the Computer Graphics Metafile option. Unlike the other file formats discussed so far, the .CGM format has many variants because it is used by a wide variety of popular software applications, including Harvard Graphics, Lotus Freelance Plus, Zenographics Mirage, Arts & Letters, Micrografx Designer, ISSCO Display, and some CAD applications. A number of clip art libraries that make use of the .CGM format exist as well.

Since these programs all have different features, the limitations on transferring .CGM file information into CorelDRAW! vary from application to application, but two general limitations apply to all programs. The first limitation involves the size of the imported file relative to the CorelDRAW! page. As with Base .PIF files, if the imported .CGM file is larger than the page, adjust viewing magnification to fit-in-window and then select and scale the grouped image. You may then apply the Ungroup command to the image to break it into its component objects. The second general limitation with .CGM imports involves bitmapped graphics, which are supported in many applications that use .CGM file formats but which do not transfer into CorelDRAW!.

The following sections describe application-specific limitations on importing .CGM files into CorelDRAW!.

Harvard Graphics

Harvard Graphics treats colors and fills differently from CorelDRAW!, and you should keep some of these differences in mind when importing a .CGM file. Specifically, a filled shape saved in Harvard Graphics transfers into CorelDRAW! as two separate objects: an outline and a fill. You will need to group these two objects in order to edit them as a single entity. In addition, colored objects created in Harvard Graphics come into CorelDRAW! darker than in their original form. This problem is due to features of the Harvard Graphics environment and has no remedy at the present time. Circles, straight lines, and curves retain their original object identity when imported, but rectangles, ellipses, and arrows transfer into CorelDRAW! as curve objects. Text transfers into CorelDRAW! as text in Monospaced or the Toronto font, but only if you do not save the file in Harvard Graphics with a native Harvard Graphics font. If you opt to use a Harvard Graphics font, the text turns into curves when you import it into CorelDRAW!.

CorelDRAW! uses the Windows character set for most of its native fonts, but the extended character set for Harvard Graphics differs somewhat from the Windows set. If you use foreign-language or other special characters above ASCII 128 in Harvard Graphics, some may not transfer as expected.

Micrografx Designer

As you will recall from Chapter 10, you can transfer objects from Micrografx Designer images into CorelDRAW! through the Windows clipboard, as long as they do not run into the clipboard's limitations. If

14

you want to transfer complex objects or entire images into CorelDRAW!, however, you can use the Import command and dialog box instead, and import the file in .CGM format.

Most file information from the .CGM format transfers into CorelDRAW! as expected. Exceptions do exist, however. For example, circles and ellipses come into CorelDRAW! as curve objects, and both fountain fills and *hatching* fills (a series of lines of varying density) transfer as solid color fills. Although Micrografx Designer can use bitmapped graphics, these do not import into CorelDRAW!.

Lotus Freelance Plus

Some text-related information in Lotus Freelance Plus .CGM files may not transfer quite as expected. As with Harvard Graphics, for example, Freelance Plus uses a character set that differs slightly from the Windows character set. If text strings created in Freelance Plus contain characters above ASCII 128, you may notice some character substitutions. In addition, text transfers into CorelDRAW! in the Monospaced font.

Colors and fills created in Freelance Plus do not always come into CorelDRAW! as originally specified. For example, hatching fills transfer as solid color fills. More important, colors specified in the Freelance Plus .CGM file may not transfer accurately unless the printer installed for Freelance supports color printing. If a black-and-white printer was installed with Freelance Plus, colors may transfer into CorelDRAW! as gray shades.

As with Micrografx Designer, bitmapped graphics from Freelance Plus do not transfer into the CorelDRAW! file format.

Arts & Letters

Most of the file information that does not transfer well into the CorelDRAW! format has to do with object types. Circles, ellipses, and text come into CorelDRAW! as curve objects and can only be edited as such. Rectangles transfer over as connected straight line segments. And, as with other .CGM file formats, bitmapped objects saved in Arts & Letters do not transfer into CorelDRAW! at all. In addition, filled objects come into CorelDRAW! as two separate objects: an outline and a fill. This is the same situation you encounter with filled objects created in Harvard Graphics.

AutoCAD Data Exchange .DXF Files

You can import AutoCAD files into CorelDRAW! in .DXF format. The .DXF format retains more AutoCAD information than any alternative format; nonetheless, not all information resident in the AutoCAD .DXF file transfers into the CorelDRAW! format. The following sections give some examples.

3-D Information   In order to retain as much 3-D information from an AutoCAD file as possible, you should take special steps to prepare the file carefully before importing it. A recommended procedure is to save the AutoCAD 3-D file in .DXB format, then begin a new drawing and transfer the .DXB file to it, and finally save the file in .DXF format using the DXFOUT utility. You should also save the 3-D image in the specific view that you want to transfer into CorelDRAW!.

Because of the complexity of information stored in a 3-D AutoCAD image, the imported file may be much larger than will fit on the CorelDRAW! page. If this happens, adjust the viewing magnification to fit-in-window, then select the imported .DXF graphic and scale it downward.

Some precision is lost in the transfer of information, however. For example, CorelDRAW! does not support 3-D extrusion of circles, arcs, text, or polylines with dashed patterns.

Colors   When you save a 3-D file in AutoCAD according to the procedure just mentioned, color information is lost. You must respecify colors once the file has arrived in CorelDRAW!. In other cases, however, colors should match the 256-color scheme that AutoCAD uses for the IBM Professional Graphics Controller.

Lines, Outlines, and Fills   Since CorelDRAW! does not support variable widths on a single line, variable-width lines in AutoCAD are imported as single-width lines. The width of the line in CorelDRAW! is equal to the *minimum* width that the variable-width line had in AutoCAD.

Objects that are specified as invisible in AutoCAD come into CorelDRAW! with no outline and no fill. You can see these objects in the editing window but not in the preview window.

A point in AutoCAD transfers into CorelDRAW! as an ellipse of the smallest possible size. An extruded point (a point seeming to extend outward in 3-D format) comes into CorelDRAW! as a line segment with two nodes.

Text   Text generated in AutoCAD may appear stretched in CorelDRAW!, since CorelDRAW! attempts to keep the physical length of text the same. Some differences in text length may still occur, however.

If the point size or degree that text is skewed in the original AutoCAD file exceeds the limits allowed by CorelDRAW!, the text transfers over within the CorelDRAW! limits and may not match the original.

Non-standard characters imported into CorelDRAW! appear as a question mark (?), and some special characters are ignored. CorelDRAW! will match the AutoCAD fonts with the closest match in the font list. See the Help screen for "Import—AutoCAD (DXF)" for a complete list of matching fonts.

GEM Applications .GEM Files

CorelDRAW! supports the import of images created in the object-oriented .GEM format. This includes artwork from GEM Draw and GEM Artline as well as files created by Ventura Publisher. You will notice a few differences between the original file and its imported version in CorelDRAW! as follows:

✦ CorelDRAW! does not support the custom fill patterns (grids, ball bearings, and so on) offered in GEM applications. Objects containing these fills in the .GEM format transfer into CorelDRAW! with a tinted spot color fill of the same color as the original pattern fill.

✦ CorelDRAW! allows only ten levels of object grouping, but GEM applications allow more. If you import a file that has more than ten levels of object groups, some objects transfer over as ungrouped. The best solution is to regroup objects after importing the file.

✦ In GEM applications, you can mix line cap styles in the same line. For example, a line can be rounded at one end and flat on the other. In CorelDRAW!, however, you can mix line cap styles only if one end of the line or curve is an arrow. When you import a .GEM file that contains lines with mixed line cap styles, therefore, CorelDRAW! assigns the line cap style of the starting point to both ends of the line or curve.

✦ Text created in GEM Artline transfers into CorelDRAW! as curve objects. Text created in other GEM applications transfers as text. The Dutch, Swiss, and System fonts under GEM come into CorelDRAW! as Toronto, Switzerland, and Avalon, respectively. Text alignment and spacing settings are not maintained, but you can edit these features after importing the file. Text with underlines in GEM Draw, however, transfers into CorelDRAW! without underlines.

HPGL .PLT Plotter Files

HPGL files are created by various applications, notably AutoCAD, to drive a plotter.

Color is specified in HPGL files in terms of pen numbers. The CorelDRAW! CORELDRW.INI has a pen assignment list under the heading [CDrawHPGLPenColor]. An entry in this list might be

Pen3="Pen#3=Red",0,100,100,0

This assigns pen 3 to the color red, which has the CMYK color mix of 0% cyan, 100% magenta, 100% yellow, and 0% black. A pen number in an imported HPGL file not in the CORELDRW.INI file will be assigned to pen 1 (normally black). You can edit the CORELDRW.INI file and add or reassign pens.

Only HPGL objects Shade Rectangle Absolute, Shade Rectangle Relative, Shade Wedge, and Text will be filled in CorelDRAW!.

HPGL text is imported in the first CorelDRAW! Monospaced font and the text attributes can be modified in CorelDRAW!.

HPGL Lines are imported according to the following list:

14

#0	solid	#4,5	dot-dash
#1	dotted	#6	double dot-dash
#2	small dash	#7 and over	small dash
#3	large dash		

Fonts will be converted from Times, Helvetica, and Symbols to Toronto, Switzerland, and Greek/Math Symbols, respectively.

Macintosh PICT .PCT Files

Files created on the Macintosh computer in either PICT1 (black-and-white) or PICT2 (color) formats can be imported into CorelDRAW! beginning with version 1.2. The Macintosh PICT format (converted to IBM PC-compatible files with a .PCT extension) can contain both vector and bitmap objects. CorelDRAW! will import the vector objects and will attempt to import the bitmap objects.

PICT2 Color will be matched exactly. Fills are often Bitmap patterns and may not transfer perfectly. There could be some noticeable differences. PICT text will transfer into CorelDRAW! as editable text with matching fonts and styles where possible. Unsupported fonts will be converted to Toronto, underlined text will not be underlined in CorelDRAW!, and there may be differences in text alignment. If text is rotated in the PICT file, it will not come into CorelDRAW! since rotated text is stored as a bitmap object.

PICT files can contain more levels of nested groups than the ten levels allowed in CorelDRAW!. If you import a file with more than ten levels, some objects will transfer ungrouped. You can regroup them in CorelDRAW!.

The CorelDRAW! import filters offer you a rich world of possibilities. But the uses to which you can put CorelDRAW!'s advanced graphics features are even richer when you consider the software applications to which you can export your images. The remainder of this chapter covers the process and pitfalls of exporting CorelDRAW! files to other applications.

Exporting Graphics: An Overview

Connectivity is a two-way street. The ability to import any number of different file formats would be of limited use if you could not export your work to other applications as well. CorelDRAW! has an even greater number of export filters than import filters. After perfecting a masterpiece in CorelDRAW!, you can send it to your favorite paint program, object-oriented drawing software, desktop publishing application, or film-recording device.

In some cases, you may have a choice of more than one export format. Popular desktop publishing applications such as Xerox Ventura Publisher, and Aldus PageMaker, for example, accept .EPS, .CGM, .PCX, and .TIF graphics files. When several file formats are available, how do you determine which is the best for your needs? The notes on each type of export file format attempt to cover this issue, as well as to describe any features of the original CorelDRAW! artwork that transfer differently than expected.

The process of exporting a CorelDRAW! file to another application always involves these five steps:

1. Open the CorelDRAW! image file you want to transfer and save it before beginning the export procedure. If you want to export only certain objects rather than the entire file, select those objects.

2. Select the Export command from the File menu.

3. Select a file format from the choices in the Export dialog box.

4. Choose whether to export the entire file or selected objects only.

5. Specify the directory and filename for the graphic you want to export.

Depending on the export file format you choose, other choices in various secondary Export dialog boxes may also become available to you. Each of these will be detailed in the following sections.

Preparing for Exporting

If you are planning to export an existing file, open it before you select the Export command. If the page is empty when you attempt the export procedure, you'll find you can't select the Export command.

14

If you are preparing to export a new file or one you have imported and edited, always save the file as a .CDR image before exporting it. This is extremely important if there is any chance that you might need to edit the image again later. In several cases, potential problems or inconveniences may occur when you try to re-import an exported file that you never saved in CorelDRAW! format.

.EPS   The CorelDRAW! .EPS import filter supports several EPS Formats, including Adobe Illustrator, CorelTRACE!, and Arts and Letters. The .EPS export filter, on the other hand, supports the standard .EPS format used by desktop publishing applications such as Aldus PageMaker and Ventura Publisher. If you export a CorelDRAW! file to .EPS without saving it in normal .CDR format first, you will not be able to import it again later.

.PCX, .PCC and .TIF   If you export a CorelDRAW! image to a pixel-based format without saving it first, and then re-import it, the imported image will be pixel-based as well. You would have to retrace and edit it extensively before you could make changes.

If you want to export only a part of the CorelDRAW! file rather than the entire image, select the desired objects before beginning the export procedure. An option in the Export dialog box will allow you to specify the export of selected objects only.

The Export Dialog Box

When you select the Export command from the File menu, the Export dialog box shown in Figure 14–2 appears.

At the lower-left corner of the dialog box, the List Files of Type box contains the names and extensions of the file formats to which you can export the current file. Depending on the format selected, there are several secondary Export boxes for entering further options; these include Bitmap Export, Export EPS, HPGL Pen Color Selection, and Export AI, to name a few. One of these boxes will appear after you select the corresponding file type in the drop-down list and click OK. The following sections explain how to work with the controls in each of the secondary Export dialog boxes. Again, the availability of these options depends on the file format you select.

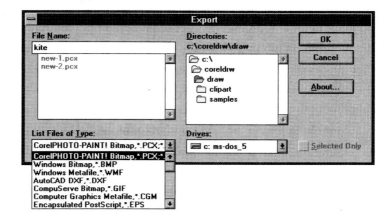

The Export
dialog box
Figure 14–2.

Selecting a File Format

To select and highlight the file format to which you will export the CorelDRAW! image, click on the file format name. If the name of the file format is not visible, scroll through the list box until you can see it, and then click on it.

"Selected Only" Option

This option is available for any export file format that you choose. It lets you choose to export only certain objects from your on-screen graphic. However, you must have one or more objects selected before the Selected Only option is available.

The Export box in Figure 14–2 indicates that no object has been selected, since the Selected Only option is not available.

Including an .EPS Image Header

An image header is a visual representation of a PostScript graphic on screen. The Image Header option is available only when you select the .EPS export file format for PostScript images and the Export EPS secondary dialog box appears, as shown in Figure 14–3. While not truly WYSIWYG, the image header helps you position or crop the .EPS image in desktop publishing applications such as Aldus PageMaker and

14

Export EPS
dialog box
Figure 14–3.

Ventura Publisher. If you choose to deactivate the Include Image Header option, you will not have a visual representation of an .EPS image in your desktop publishing application.

Choose the None option only if you plan to use the exported .EPS image in an application that cannot display an EPS image header. Versions of Ventura Publisher earlier than 2.0, for example, do not support the display of EPS image headers.

"All Fonts Resident" .EPS Option

When you activate this option in the Export EPS box, you tell CorelDRAW! to assume that all fonts used in your graphic are resident in the output device. Text strings in the exported graphic will be printed using the printer-resident fonts rather than the original CorelDRAW! fonts.

You should use the All Fonts Resident option if you have downloadable PostScript fonts and want to use them instead of CorelDRAW! fonts. You might also use this option when producing material that will be printed by a service bureau. Most laser service bureaus have access to all of the Adobe PostScript fonts and can substitute them for the CorelDRAW! fonts automatically.

Specifying a Bitmapped Graphics Resolution

After you have chosen a pixel-based export file format and then selected OK, you can choose the bitmap resolution from the Bitmap Export secondary dialog box. The available resolution is from 75 Dots Per Inch (DPI), up to 300 DPI. A higher resolution is the option to choose if you want to give the exported image the best possible appearance.

Because of the way a computer stores pixel-based graphics, however, an image that is large in CorelDRAW! can occupy an enormous amount of memory (up to 1 MB for a full-page image) when you export it at a high resolution. Rather than export the graphic at a lower resolution, consider using the Pick tool to scale the CorelDRAW! image down to the size it should be in the final application. For example, if you plan to export the graphic to a desktop publishing program and know the desired image size on the page, scale it down to that size before exporting it from CorelDRAW!. This precautionary action will also prevent you from having to resize the bitmap later, thereby causing its appearance to deteriorate.

Specifying an .EPS Image Header

Although an Encapsulated PostScript (.EPS) file is object-oriented, the image header that represents it is a pixel-based approximation. The Image Header option buttons in the secondary Export dialog box let you specify the resolution of the visible image header in the exported file.

The image header resolution you select does *not* affect the size of the actual PostScript graphic. If conserving memory and disk space is a concern, you should select the Low Resolution option for the smallest image header. If accurate representation is more important to you than memory conservation, however, select the High Resolution option to obtain an image header that is true to the proportions of the actual graphic. The size of the resulting .EPS files may exceed 64K if you select the High Resolution option.

14

Specifying the Filename and the Destination Directory

To specify the destination drive and directory for the exported image, double-click on the appropriate drive and directory in the Directories list box. Use the scroll bars if the desired directory is not visible. The path of the highlighted drive and directory appear above the box.

To name the export image file, double-click in the File Name box to select the default extension. Then type the desired filename; CorelDRAW! will restore the correct extension. Click on OK. You may get a secondary Export box, like this:

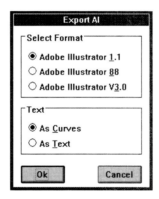

Select the needed options in the secondary Export box, and click OK to begin transfer of the image.

What happens to the image during the export process depends on the specific file format you have chosen. The following sections offer notes on exporting images to each available file format. Equally important, they explore the practical uses of exporting to various file formats.

Exporting to Bitmapped Graphics Formats

When you have a choice of several different export file formats, your primary concerns should be the end use to which you will put the exported graphic, the CorelDRAW! features that can or cannot be retained, and the convenience of working with the image in the export file format. The advantages of two of the bitmap formats supported by CorelDRAW!.PCX and .TIF are that they command wide support throughout the software industry and that the paint programs in which you edit them are usually easier to learn and use than most object-oriented drawing and design applications. The disadvantages are that they do not display well on monitors that support resolutions different from the resolutions in which the bitmaps were created, and that they are inconvenient to resize. If you design a bitmap on CorelDRAW! and then export it, however, your image will not suffer from this limitation.

The bitmap file formats are good choices for export to desktop publishing programs if you do not use a PostScript printer and cannot take advantage of the .EPS file format. However, one of the object-oriented formats such as .CGM is a better choice for desktop publishing applications. Unlike the bitmapped formats, the object-oriented formats are easy to resize without distortion and preserve more attribute information. You should select a bitmapped file format only when one of the following conditions applies:

✦ The application to which you are exporting accepts only bitmapped graphics.

✦ You plan to alter the CorelDRAW! graphic using techniques available only in the pixel-by-pixel editing environment of a paint program.

As you saw in Table 14–2 earlier in this chapter, CorelDRAW! 3 can export drawings in Windows BMP, CompuServe GIF, PC Paintbrush PCX 3.0, Targa TGA, and TIFF 5.0 formats. When you choose one of these formats from the File Export dialog box, the secondary Bitmap Export box opens as shown in Figure 14–4.

Unlike versions of CorelDRAW! prior to 3.0, you can now export full-color and gray-scale images with these bitmap formats. The files they create, if uncompressed, would be quite large—well over a megabyte. For that reason, you can compress some formats, and others, particularly PCX 3, are always compressed. Compression is good, so long as the program you are using to read the files can decompress them. For example, the compressed PCX 3 files written by CorelDRAW!

14

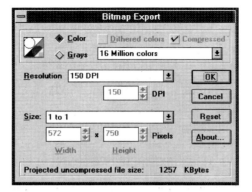

Bitmap Export
dialog box
Figure 14–4.

3 cannot be read by the Windows PaintBrush program that comes with Windows 3.1—you must use the BMP format which, even when compressed, creates huge files.

The next group of sections explores the advantages and disadvantages of exporting CorelDRAW! objects and images to each of the available object-oriented file formats.

Exporting to Object-Oriented Graphics Formats

As mentioned earlier in this chapter, object-oriented formats transfer color, outline, fill, and attribute information more accurately than is the case with bitmapped formats. In addition, object-oriented formats are *device-independent*, which means that their images look the same despite resizing or changes in the display resolution.

Your main concerns when choosing an object-oriented export format are the final use to which you plan to put the image and the kinds of information you cannot afford to lose during the export process. The following sections provide information on the uses and limitations of each type of export file format.

Encapsulated PostScript .EPS Format

The .EPS file format is the export format of choice when your CorelDRAW! image contains features that are available for PostScript

output devices only. Such features include PostScript halftone screen patterns and textures, and rotated or skewed bitmapped images. If you export a CorelDRAW! graphic containing both line art and bitmaps to the .EPS format, both types of graphics will transfer properly. The Graphics Metafile (.CGM) format, on the other hand, cannot accept bitmaps.

The main limitations of exporting to .EPS file format involve the treatment of complex curves, the bitmapped image header, and the fact that it is a one-way export from CorelDRAW!.

Complex Graphics   If the graphic that you want to export to .EPS format contains approximately 200 or more nodes per curve object, you may have trouble printing it in your desktop publishing, or other PostScript, application. The same difficulty may occur if your image is laden with PostScript textures, halftone screen patterns, combined objects, and fancy text strings.

Image Header   As explained previously, the image header in an .EPS graphic is an approximate bitmap representation made available for the purposes of positioning and cropping the graphic. It is not always convenient to work with this header, because it's not truly WYSIWYG.

One-Way Export   The Adobe-standard .EPS import format supported by CorelDRAW! works with Adobe Illustrator files only. If you export a CorelDRAW! graphic to the *standard* .EPS format and then decide you need to make changes, you will not be able to re-import the graphic to CorelDRAW!. The importance of saving your graphic in .CDR format in CorelDRAW! before exporting it cannot be overstated.

All in all, the .EPS file format offers you the best opportunity to transfer CorelDRAW! image information if you use a PostScript printer or imagesetter and a relevant application. Other object-oriented formats work nearly as well for other applications, as you will see in the following sections.

Adobe Illustrator 88's .AI Format

As you just read, the .EPS format that CorelDRAW! exports is different from Adobe Illustrator 88 and some Macintosh-based programs. For that reason, CorelDRAW! has the ability to export a file in the .AI format. It is *not* recommended that this format be used where you can also use .EPS, for example, with Ventura Publisher and Aldus PageMaker.

There are many limitations to the .AI format export. Among these are that fountain fills, PostScript textures, arrowheads, fitting text to a path, calligraphic pen effects, bitmaps, and individual character attributes are all not supported. Also avoid combined objects and exporting text that has been converted to curves in CorelDRAW!. If you want text as curves in the application to which you are exporting, select the "Send text as curves" option in the special .AI dialog box.

IBM .PIF Format

When you choose to export a CorelDRAW! graphic to the IBM mainframe .PIF graphics format, the Selected Only option, mentioned above, allows you to transfer just a portion of your graphic rather than the whole file. CorelDRAW! will transfer calligraphic outlines, special line caps, and fountain fills and the export filter translates these attributes into polygons and fills them accordingly. Some radial fills may not transfer exactly as they appear in CorelDRAW! and PostScript fills do not transfer at all.

Color information transfers to the mainframe format as the closest match to one of the 16 colors available in the .PIF graphic format.

Computer Graphics Metafile .CGM Format

The .CGM, or Computer Graphics Metafile, format represents not a single format, but rather a group of closely related object-oriented file formats. The application determines which file format will be used. Since there are so many versions available, each with its own characteristics, graphics information does not always translate in exactly the same way. The CorelDRAW! .CGM export filter cannot "know" automatically the software application to which you are planning to export a graphic. In general, however, most color, line thickness, and fill attributes transfer well.

The .CGM option is an excellent choice for exporting files to desktop publishing applications. The WYSIWYG representation of a .CGM file is much easier to work with than an .EPS header and takes the guesswork out of cropping and positioning graphics within a document. If you do not work with a PostScript printer, or if your CorelDRAW! graphics do not contain PostScript-only attributes, you might prefer the .CGM option to the .EPS format.

Windows Metafile .WMF Format

The .WMF format, like the .PCX, .TIF, and .EPS formats, was one of the earliest export options in CorelDRAW!. This object-oriented format makes a CorelDRAW! graphic available to a wide variety of Microsoft Windows applications. This export format does not transfer PostScript-only features, so it is best suited for graphics that do not contain such features. In addition, if the artwork in your graphic has many outline and fill attributes, many curves and nodes, or complex text, the exported .WMF file might become very large and not be acceptable to some programs. In this case, try using the .CGM export filter instead.

Exporting to Film Recorders (SCODL)

SCODL, which stands for Scan Conversion Object Description Language, is an image-description language that many popular film recorders use to create object-oriented slides at high resolution. Some ink-jet and thermal printers also make use of this language and its associated .SCD file format. The SCODL export option first became available with CorelDRAW! release 1.1. When you select the SCODL option in the Export dialog box, the additional options Include All Artistic Attributes and Selected Objects Only become available for selection.

In general, CorelDRAW! will export these outline attributes: Corner types, Calligraphic pen effects, Line caps and Fountain fills. Some features not supported are PostScript Textures, Bitmaps, and two-color and full-color Pattern fills. PostScript effects can be exported using special equipment such as Agfa-Matrix Adobe PostScript RIP. Some service bureaus now use this or similar equipment.

If you are new to the world of film recorders and slide generation equipment, you may be interested in the following tips that will help you create a SCODL (.SCD) export file that will not produce visual surprises.

Aspect Ratio Considerations

The graphic that you plan to export to SCODL format should have the same width-to-height aspect ratio as the film that will be used to create your slide. In most cases this will be the aspect ratio of 35 mm film, which is 0.67. On an 8 1/2-by-11-inch page, this translates into 7.33-inch width by 11-inch height (or 11-inch width by 7.33-inch height in landscape format). The easiest way to ensure that a graphic will conform to the aspect ratio required for slidemaking is to open the File menu, choose the Page Setup command, and select Slide in the Page Size panel. At this time you can also select the paper color. Click on Paper Color, and a secondary dialog box will appear to present color options. Alternatively, you can activate the Show Rulers command in the Display menu to help you fit the graphic within the appropriate dimensions.

Fountain Fill Tips

The SCODL format does not support fountain fills as CorelDRAW! understands them. Recall that when you watched a fountain fill redisplay in Chapter 13, the fill began as a rectangle equal to the space occupied by the highlighting box that surrounded the object. The fill outside the object boundary disappears as the redraw of the object proceeds. SCODL does not recognize the last step in this process. As a result, linear fountain fills export to SCODL correctly *only* for rectangles. Radial fountain fills do not, however, export correctly for perfect circles.

If the graphic from which you want to create a slide contains fountain fills for other types of objects, there is a way to work around the problem. You can overcome this limitation by creating a *mask* that includes a background rectangle with a fountain fill. If you performed the "World of CorelDRAW!" series of exercises in Chapter 15, you are already familiar with the principles of a mask. In summary,

1. Create the object to which you want to assign a fountain fill.
2. Create a rectangle that is larger than the object you created in the last step. Place it on top of the previous object so that it covers the object completely.

3. Use the Combine command in the Arrange menu to combine both objects into one object. This creates a transparent "hole" with the shape of the first object.

4. Assign the same color fill to the combined object that you assigned to the background color of the drawing. Assign an outline of NONE to the object.

5. Create another and slightly smaller rectangle, and place it on top of the combined object so that the transparent "hole" is completely covered. Assign any desired fountain fill to this rectangle.

6. Use the To Back command in the Arrange menu to place the filled rectangle behind the combined object. The result is that the fountain fill shows through the transparent hole.

7. Apply the Group command in the Arrange menu to group the two objects and treat them as a unit.

This may seem like a complicated solution, but SCODL understands it perfectly and delivers a flawless fill in your slide if you follow the directions carefully.

Exporting Graphics to .WPG WordPerfect Format

CorelDRAW! allows you to export images to WordPerfect using the .WPG format. A good use of this feature is to create clip art libraries for use in WordPerfect 5.0 or 5.1.

After you select the .WPG format, and specify the filename and directory in the Export dialog box, a second dialog box containing color options displays on your screen, as shown here:

You have a choice of 16 or 256 colors. Select the option button that best matches your display adapter's capabilities, the output device you will be using, and the colors in your drawing, and then select OK.

14

The following kinds of information do not transfer into the WordPerfect environment:

✦ PostScript halftone screens and textures

✦ Radial or linear fountain fills

✦ Text as text (WordPerfect converts it to curves)

✦ CorelDRAW! line type settings of none

✦ Bitmaps

In addition, you cannot rotate a drawing once it is in .WPG format, or it will not print properly from within WordPerfect.

AutoCAD .DXF Format

CorelDRAW! allows you to export as well as import files using the AutoCAD .DXF format. The .DXF files tend to be memory-intensive, however, so it may happen that a complex drawing that occupies only 20-30K in CorelDRAW! can take up half a megabyte or more in the AutoCAD format. Make certain that your hard drive contains enough free space to accommodate potentially large files.

A few CorelDRAW! features either export to .DXF format differently than expected, or do not transfer at all. For example, text preserves its appearance but turns into curves in AutoCAD format. Calligraphic outlines preserve their visual appearance as well, but the .DXF filter interprets them as polygons rather than as lines. Colors match fairly closely, as the .DXF format uses a 256-color scheme.

More important, the present .DXF filter supports the transfer of *outlines only*. This means that no fills at all are exported with the AutoCAD format. If you require fills for certain objects, you must add them using the CAD application.

GEM Applications .GEM Format

CorelDRAW! allows you to import and export graphics using the .GEM graphics format. There is an important difference between the import and export filters, however. You can import .GEM files from both GEM Draw and GEM Artline, but you can export only to GEM Artline,

Delvina Perform, and Ventura Publisher versions 2.0 and above. The present GEM export filter does not support export to GEM Draw. As always, save your drawing in CorelDRAW! format before exporting it if you think you might need to edit it later.

There are a few limitations in what kinds of features you can transfer, for example, GEM applications support only 16 colors, so colors may not match exactly. In Xerox Ventura Publisher, colored images display as black-and-white unless you have a VGA or compatible display adapter. Another limitation concerns the number of nodes in an exported file. GEM applications can handle a maximum of 128 nodes, so you should limit the size or complexity of your drawings accordingly. If your drawing contains more than 128 nodes, it may transfer, but the GEM application may segment curves into multiple sub-paths (see Chapter 8) and the object will appear differently.

HPGL Plotter .PLT Format

You can export CorelDRAW! image *outlines only* in the HPGL format, for plotters with a .PLT extension. When you do, a second dialog box appears as shown in Figure 14–5.

The HPGL Pen Color Selection dialog box allows you to make a number of choices for settings unique to plotters. These are: Stretch factor, for horizontal and vertical scaling in the range of 0 to 1000%; and Pen Color Selection, which allows you to choose from among the color

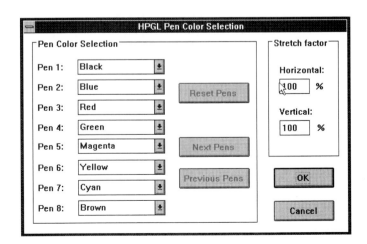

HPGL export
dialog box
Figure 14–5.

14

pens that have been defined in the CORELDRW.INI file (see "HPGL .PLT Plotter Files" earlier in this chapter).

Solid lines exported in the HPGL format are given the HPGL default line thickness of 0.3 mm. A dotted line is given a 0.5 type pattern, and a dashed line is given a 3 type pattern. Text is exported as HPGL fonts and is editable. If you want the text to appear as it does in CorelDRAW!, edit the CORELDRW.INI file and set Export Text As Curves to a value of 1. The text will then export as line segments, and will not be editable. Finally, HPGL export does not support bitmaps, calligraphic pens, fountain fills, or PostScript halftone textures.

Macintosh PICT2 and .PCT Format

You can export to the Macintosh in the PICT2 color file format. If you want to export calligraphic pens or line caps, you must edit the CORELDRW.INI file and set the Calligraphic Clipboard value to 1.

All text takes on the current text attributes active in the Mac application. If you want the exact appearance of CorelDRAW! fonts, you must edit CORELDRW.INI and set the Export Text As Curves value to 1.

Bitmaps and PostScript textures cannot be transferred to PICT, and there is no font correspondence between the two packages. Color transference will depend on the color capability of the Macintosh. One using 8-bit color is limited to 256 colors and will be mapped to CorelDRAW! colors as well as possible. A Macintosh with 24-bit color will be virtually identical to CorelDRAW!'s color. Radial fills and text without fill do not transfer properly to PICT.

C H A P T E R

15

PRINTING AND PROCESSING YOUR IMAGES

No matter how sophisticated an image may look on your computer monitor, you can judge its true quality only after it has traveled from your hard drive to the outside world. The means by which graphics travel from your computer to your intended audience is a question of output, and until recently, output meant printer and paper. In today's world, however, paper is only one possible means by which your artwork can reach the outside world. As you learned in

Chapter 14, film negatives, videotape, and 35 mm slides are equally valid output media. CorelDRAW! offers you your choice of all these media and their associated output devices.

If print media remain your preferred end products, you can output your images using the Print command in the File menu. CorelDRAW! allows you to print selected objects within an image, scale your image to any desired size, print oversize images on multiple tiled pages, print from selected layers, or print to a file that you can send to a service bureau. If you work with a PostScript printer, even more advanced printing functions are available to you. You can prepare color separations for process color images, add crop marks and registration marks, print in film negative format, and add file information to your printouts. With a PostScript printing device, you can also reproduce the dotted and dashed outlines, custom halftone screens, and PostScript textures you learned to create in Chapters 12 and 13.

If you want your image produced as slides or used in presentations, refer to Chapter 14. You will use the Export command, not the Print command, to generate your output. CorelSHOW!, discussed in Appendix C, allows you to assemble the slides, charts, and drawings you've created in CorelDRAW! into professional presentations.

The first part of this chapter describes the output devices and media that CorelDRAW! supports. The middle portion of the chapter guides you step-by-step through the process of printing, using the Print Options and Print Setup dialog boxes. The concluding sections of the chapter contain tips to help you achieve satisfactory printing results, based on the type of printer you use.

Output Devices

In considering how your images will travel from your computer to your audience, you are actually concerning yourself with both equipment and the product of that equipment, or with both *output device* and *output medium*. The output device you work with determines what media you can produce, or what the end product of your work will be. For example, all printers produce paper output. PostScript printers and imagesetters, however, also allow you to prepare your images as color separations or in film negative format, so that you can eliminate costly steps in the commercial printing process. CorelDRAW! supports some printing devices better than others. As you may recall from Chapter 1, Windows provides drivers for many different printers and plotters, but not all of them work equally well with CorelDRAW!. The following list shows the printing devices that CorelDRAW! supports best, in the order in which you are likely to reproduce the fullest range of CorelDRAW! features.

✦ PostScript Plus black-and-white printers, color printers, and imagesetters (Linotronic)

✦ HP LaserJet with Adobe-licensed PostScript controller boards and plug-in cartridges

✦ Older PostScript printers compatible with the original Apple LaserWriter

✦ HP LaserJet printers and 100% compatibles

✦ HP DeskJet

✦ HP PaintJet

The PostScript Plus printers, older PostScript printers, and printers with genuine Adobe-licensed PostScript controller boards are the only ones in this list that let you generate output using PostScript printing options.

You can print your CorelDRAW! images with other printers, too, but the results may vary depending on the complexity of your images and the characteristics of a given manufacturer's device. With some of the following printers, your output may match your expectations exactly. With others, you may experience problems that are hard to predict because of the variety of standards in the industry.

✦ HP LaserJet clones that are not 100% compatible

✦ HP LaserJet printers, compatibles, and clones with PostScript-compatible controller boards and plug-in cartridges not licensed by Adobe

✦ Genuine HP Plotters

✦ HP Plotter clones and other plotters

✦ Dot-matrix printers

The "Hardware-Specific Tips" section of this chapter contains information about designing your images to obtain the best output results for the printer that you use. It also describes the kinds of limitations you are most likely to encounter with a specific type of printer and provides suggestions on how to solve them. The "Complex Artwork on PostScript Printers" section provides tips specific to working with PostScript printers.

In the next section, you will learn about general steps you can take before you print to ensure trouble-free output.

Preparing to Print

Before you select the Print command, you should make certain that your printer is correctly installed to run under Windows. You should also adjust several default settings in Windows in order to customize printing for the special needs of CorelDRAW!. Two of these other settings, called *Printer Timeouts*, determine how long Windows waits before sending you messages about potential printer problems. The settings you need to review are all in the Windows Control Panel.

TIP: If you work with a PostScript printer, you should be using Windows' own printer driver or a Windows-compatible PostScript driver that came with your printer (for example, the UltraScript PostScript interpreter from QMS).

Another adjustment you should make is to disable the Windows Print Manager. You do this by de-selecting the Use Print Manager check box in the Printers dialog box, reached from the Control Panel. The short sections that follow will guide you through the process of reviewing and editing your printer setup.

Printer Installation and Setup

If you did not specify the correct printer and port when you installed Microsoft Windows, you will not be able to print in CorelDRAW!. To check whether your printer is correctly installed to run under Microsoft Windows, follow these steps:

1. From CorelDRAW!, press [Ctrl]-[Esc] to open the Task List and double-click on Program Manager.

2. From the Windows Main group, double-click on the Control Panel icon. The Control Panel window appears, as shown in Figure 15–1.

3. Double-click on the Printers icon, shown in the lower-left corner of Figure 15–1. The Printers dialog box will open and display a list of installed printers. An example of a Printers dialog box appears in Figure 15–2. The Installed Printers list box should contain the name of the printer you are going to use, and this name should be highlighted. If the name of your printer is in the list box but is not highlighted, click on it with the mouse, click on OK to return to the Control Panel, and skip to step 5.

4. If the name of your printer is missing in the Installed Printers list box, select Add. An extensive list of printers appears. Use the scroll bar to find the printer you want (they are in alphabetical order) and then double-click on it (or highlight it and select Install). You will be asked to insert one of the original Windows Install disks so that the printer's software driver can be copied to your hard disk. When your printer appears in the Installed Printers list box, select Connect, click on the port to which the printer is attached (LPT1, COM1, and so on), and then click on OK. Repeat these steps for all the printers you have. When you are done, click on close to return to the Control Panel.

5. If your printer is connected to a serial port, double-click on the Ports icon in the Control Panel. Select the port to which the printer is connected (COM1 through COM4), and click on Settings. The Settings for Com 1 (or whatever port you selected) dialog box will open as shown in Figure 15–3. Make sure that the

The Control Panel window
Figure 15–1.

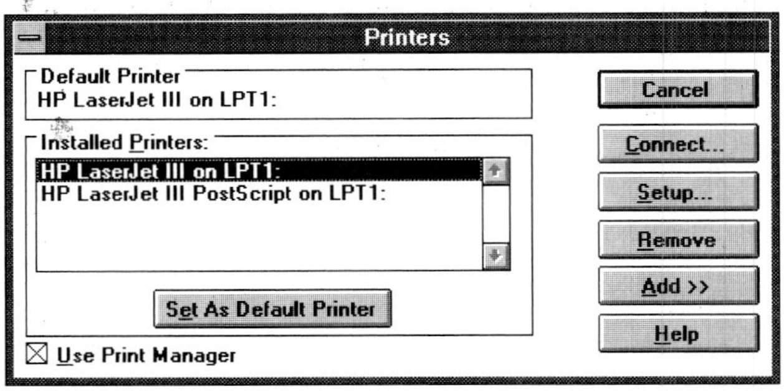

The Printers
dialog box of
the Control
Panel
Figure 15–2.

Baud Rate, Data Bits, Parity, and Stop Bits are correct for your printer. More settings are available by clicking on the Advanced button to open on Advanced Settings dialog box. Refer to your printer manual if necessary. When you are finished, click on OK to return to the Control Panel.

If you need to alter your printer installation after performing this check, refer to your *Microsoft Windows Version 3.1 User's Guide* and see the chapter that discusses the Control Panel and gives the necessary instructions.

Printer Timeouts

After checking for correct printer and port assignments, you should customize the Printer Timeouts settings, found under the Printers icon in the Control Panel. These settings define how long Windows waits before sending you messages about potential printer problems. The default Printer Timeouts settings installed with Microsoft Windows may be adequate for average Windows applications, but you should customize them to improve printing performance in CorelDRAW!. To edit Printer Timeouts:

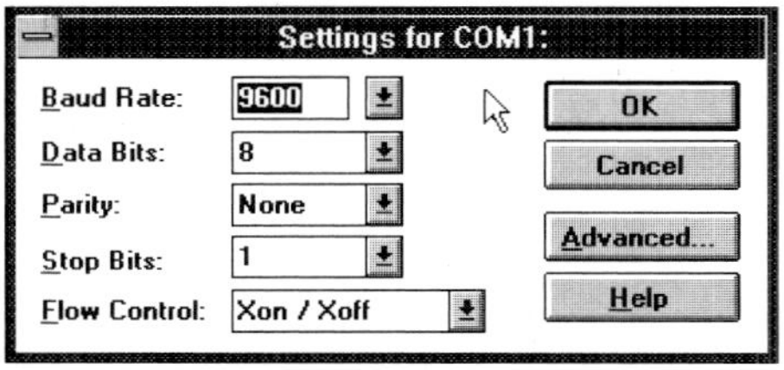

The Settings for
COM1 dialog
box of the
Control Panel
Figure 15–3.

1. From the Control Panel, double-click on the Printers icon again. With your printer selected, click on Connect. The Connect dialog box will open as shown in Figure 15–4.

2. The Timeouts section of the dialog box shows two settings: Device Not Selected and Transmission Retry. The Device Not Selected setting determines how long Windows waits before informing you that the printer is not connected properly, not turned on, or otherwise not ready to print. Leave this setting at its default value of 15 seconds, because if the printer is not ready to perform, you want to find out as soon as possible.

3. Adjust Transmission Retry from its default value of 90 seconds to 600 seconds (equal to 10 minutes), as is shown in Figure 15–4. The Transmission retry value determines how long the printer waits to receive additional characters before a timeout error occurs. Although 45 seconds may be long enough for most software that runs under Windows, it is not always adequate for graphics applications such as CorelDRAW!. The output file that CorelDRAW! sends to your printer can contain complex information, requiring more time to transmit.

4. The Fast Printing Direct to Port check box should be left checked, its default mode. When it is checked, Windows bypasses MS-DOS interrupts and sends your output directly to the printer. The only time you would want to clear the check box is if you are using print spooler software that requires MS-DOS interrupts to control printing. Otherwise, clearing the check box will slow down your printing.

By verifying your printer setup and Timeouts settings each time you run CorelDRAW!, you can prevent potential printing and

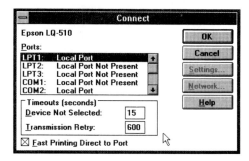

Adjusting
Printer Timeouts
Figure 15–4.

communications problems before you even attempt to print. You can eliminate one more potential printing pitfall by disabling the Windows Print Manager, about which you will learn in the next section.

Disabling the Print Manager

Windows is installed to print all files through the Print Manager. The Print Manager is a program that captures printing instructions and sends them to the printer. The printer then runs in the background, so that you can continue working in your application without interruption. The Print Manager doesn't always work efficiently with graphics files, however. For this reason, you can avoid printing problems if you disable the Print Manager. When the Print Manager is disabled, the printing operation runs in the foreground; you must wait until printing is complete before you can continue with your work. Printing takes place faster this way than when the Print Manager is enabled, however.

To disable the Print Manager, use the following:

1. If necessary re-open the Control Panel and double-click the Printers icon. The Printers dialog box will again appear.
2. Look at the check box in the lower-left corner labeled Use Print Manager. If it is checked, click on it.
3. Click on Close to return to the Control Panel, and then double-click on the Control-menu box to close the Control Panel.
4. Click once on the Program Manager Control menu to open it, choose Switch, then double-click on CorelDRAW!.

Now that you have customized Windows' printer settings to improve printing performance in CorelDRAW!, you are ready to explore the options in the Printer Options dialog box. The next series of sections lets you experiment with the choices available to you when printing.

The Print Options Dialog Box

To begin the process of printing in CorelDRAW!, you select the Print command in the File menu. An image must be on the screen before you

15

can select this command. The options Selected Objects Only, Scale, Fit to Page, Tile, and Print to File are available for use with all printers.

If you use a PostScript printer, you can also include date and file information on the printout, prepare spot or process color separations, and print crop and registration marks with your graphic. You can also print the image in film negative format, change the default screen frequency for proofing images, or print using fonts resident in the host printer rather than the native CorelDRAW! fonts.

The following sections each explore one printing option or one aspect of the printing process. So that you can practice printing using the options in the Print Options dialog box, you will open a clip art image from the CLIPART directory, and then use it in the exercises that follow. If you are using a version of CorelDRAW! earlier than 3.0 you will need to import the clip art image according to the instructions used in Chapter 14.

Using Mosaic

Mosaic is a separate program supplied with CorelDRAW! that provides visual access to CorelDRAW! files. Mosaic can be started either from the Program Manager, by double-clicking on the Mosaic icon in the Corel Graphics group, or from within CorelDRAW!. In this case, you'll start Mosaic from CorelDRAW!—it is less obvious but handier for the purposes here.

The piece of clip art you will use, if you are using CorelDRAW! version 3, is named KIDS.CDR. It is in the MISC clip art directory. With the following instructions, start Mosaic and use it to bring this piece of clip art into CorelDRAW!.

1. Starting with a blank screen in CorelDRAW!, click on the Open option from the File menu. Choose the Options button which allows you to access additional features.

2. Click on the Mosaic button. The program CorelMOSAIC 3 loads and the Mosaic window opens, as shown in Figure 15–5.

3. From the File menu, click on the Open Directory option. The Open Directory dialog box opens as shown in Figure 15–6. Your current directory may be different from the one shown in Figure 15–6. Use the Directory list box to locate the MISC clip art directory.

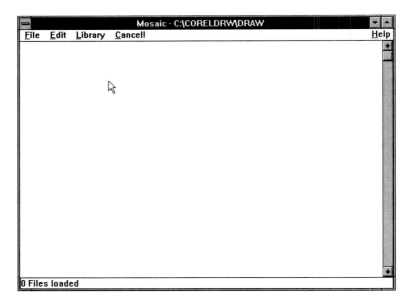

Mosaic window
Figure 15–5.

4. Highlight the MISC subdirectory and click on OK. A pictorial directory will open displaying a small image for each file in the directory, as shown in Figure 15–7.

5. Click twice (do not double-click) on the downward pointing scroll arrow, and then double-click on the KIDS.CDR image. After a few moments, you'll see the KIDS.CDR image appear in your CorelDRAW! window as in Figure 15–8.

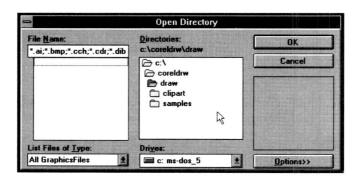

Mosaic Select
Library dialog
box
Figure 15–6.

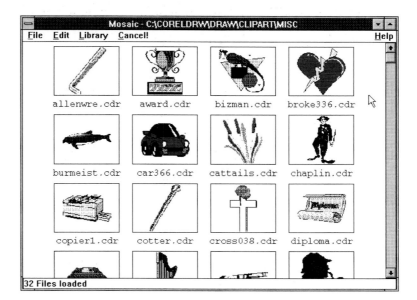

Mosaic pictorial
directory
Figure 15–7.

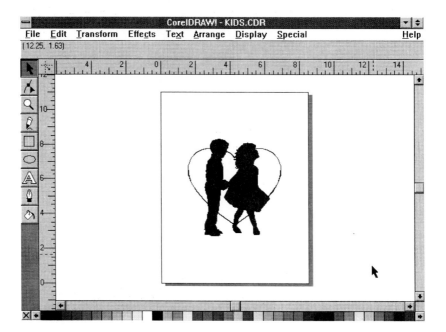

KIDS.CDR in
CorelDRAW!
Figure 15–8.

Now that you have an image ready for printing, you can select the Print command and become acquainted with the Print Options dialog box.

Selecting the Print Command

Select the Print command from the File menu. The Print Options dialog box appears. If you have a non-PostScript printer, it will look like Figure 15–9.

For non-PostScript printers, there are eight options in this dialog box: Selected objects only, Copies, Fit To Page, Tile, Scale, Fountain Stripes, Print to File, and Printer Setup. For PostScript printers, as shown in Figure 15–10, there are the same eight options plus eight other options: Print As Separations, Crop Marks & Crosshairs, Film Negative, Print File Info, All Fonts Resident, Flatness, Screen Frequency, and For Mac. In addition, you can select multiple options for any given print operation, as long as all of the ones you choose are available for your printer.

Before you experiment with the printing options, go on to the next section to learn how to check the printer setup.

Checking Print Setup

Whenever you print, it is advisable to develop the habit of checking the printer setup *before* you select any print options. The Print Setup dialog box, which you access by clicking on the Print Setup command button in the Print Options dialog box, contains controls that allow you to define the desired number of copies, the paper size and orientation, and the brand name of your printer. Alternatively, you can open the Print Setup dialog box directly from the File menu by choosing the Print Setup option. The other items in the Print Setup dialog box vary,

The Print
Options dialog
box,
non-PostScript
Figure 15–9.

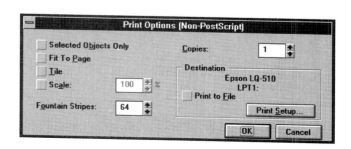

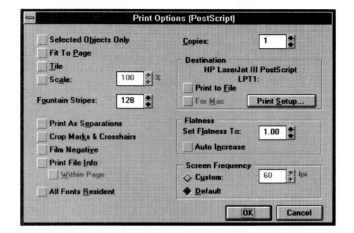

The Print
Options dialog
box, PostScript
Figure 15–10.

depending on the printer you selected using the Printer icon in the
Control Panel. For example, the Print Setup dialog box shown in
Figure 15–11 shows the controls available for a PostScript printer.

Some of the variable controls are important to know about because
they help you avoid possible pitfalls when you attempt to print
complex images. Later on, in the series of sections following
"Hardware-Specific Tips," you will find hints on adjusting these settings
to prevent or minimize printing problems. Take a moment to explore
the contents of *your* Print Setup dialog box and of any nested sub-dialog
boxes that are accessible by clicking on special command buttons.
When you are ready, click on the Cancel command button of the Print
Setup dialog box. Click again on the Cancel button of the Print Options
dialog box to return to the image on your screen.

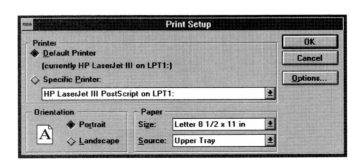

Printer Setup
options for a
non-PostScript
printer
Figure 15–11.

Each of the next series of sections presents a single option in the Print Options dialog box and allows you to test it using the KIDS.CDR file you saved earlier in the chapter. The non-PostScript options are presented first, for the convenience of those who do not work with a PostScript printing device.

Printing Only Selected Objects

There are several reasons why you might choose to print only selected objects within a picture, rather than the entire graphic:

◆ You want to save printing time and need to check only a portion of the image.

◆ Your picture contains a great deal of fine detail, such as in a technical illustration, and you want to examine certain areas for accuracy.

◆ Some of your picture elements contain complex or PostScript-only features.

◆ You have experienced printing problems and want to locate the object or objects that are causing the trouble.

Whatever your reason, you can print just the selected objects within a picture by activating the Selected Objects Only checkbox in the Print Options dialog box. You must select the desired objects before you select the Print command, however, or you will receive an error message. Practice printing selected objects in the KIDS.CDR file now.

1. If the Print Options dialog box is still on your screen, click on Cancel to exit it and return to the KIDS.CDR file.

2. Select any object in the image; the status line shows you that all of the objects in the picture are grouped. Click on the Ungroup command in the Arrange menu to ungroup all of the objects.

3. Using the Pick tool, select just the heart by clicking on its border; it's selected if the status line changes to "Number of nodes:4".

4. Leave the heart selected and click on the File Print command. When the Print Options dialog box appears, review your Print

Setup, and then click on the Selected Objects Only check box. A check appears in the check box.

5. Select the OK command button to begin the printing process. After a short time, the image of the heart should emerge from your printer. Leave the KIDS.CDR image on your screen for the next exercise.

As you learn about the other options in this dialog box, you will think of effective ways to combine one or more of them with Selected Objects Only. Assume, for example, that you are working with a complex technical illustration and need to proof just a small area. If you activate both the Selected Objects Only and Fit To Page options, you can print the selected objects in magnified format in order to proof them more easily.

TIP: When you print complex, memory-intensive images, it is a good practice to use the Select All command in the Edit menu to select all objects before you click on the Print command, and then print with the Selected Objects Only option activated. Some objects in a memory-intensive image may be left out; by using the Select All command and the Selected Objects Only option, you minimize this problem.

In the next section, you will learn about a way to print proofs of a graphic that is larger than the page area.

Tiling a Graphic

You can choose from several different methods of sizing a graphic in CorelDRAW!. The most obvious method is to use rulers when creating objects. Another method involves defining a custom page size with the Page Setup command and the Page Setup dialog box. You can also use the Pick tool to scale an image to the desired size *after* you have created it.

Posters and other applications, however, require images that are larger than any paper size available for your printer. Even if you print final versions of these images on a Linotronic or other imagesetter that has fewer restrictions on paper size, how do you obtain accurate proofs?

The answer is through *tiling* the image. Tiling refers to the process of printing an oversize image in sections that fit together precisely to form the complete picture. If, for example, you create a poster that is 11 inches wide by 17 inches high and select Tiling as a printing option, the image will print on four 8 1/2-by-11-inch sheets (or on some multiple of whatever size paper you use for your printer).

In the following exercise, you will enlarge the page size for KIDS.CDR, scale the image to fit the page, and print the entire image with the Tile option enabled.

1. With the KIDS.CDR image still on your screen, click on the Select All command in the Edit menu to select all of the objects in the picture. Then select the Group command in the Arrange menu to keep all objects together.

2. Activate the Show Rulers command in the Display menu, and then select the Page Setup command in the File menu. When the Page Setup dialog box appears, click on the Landscape and the Tabloid option buttons to activate them. Selecting Tabloid will result in a page that is 17 inches wide by 11 inches high in landscape format. Click on the OK command button to exit the dialog box. Your page is now approximately twice as large as the graphic. The rulers show you the change in page size, as shown in Figure 15–12.

3. With the Pick tool active, position the cursor at the upper-left corner boundary marker of the selected, grouped image. When the pointer turns to a crosshair, drag the mouse until you have scaled the image to fit the upper-left corner area of the page. Do the same for the lower-right corner boundary marker.

4. Move the scaled image so that it is centered on the enlarged page, and then select the Print command from the File menu.

5. When the Print Options dialog box appears, deselect any options that are currently active, and then click on the Tile option to activate it. Select OK. If you get a window advising you that the printer and page orientations do not match, click on Yes to have the printer adjusted automatically. After a few moments, the image begins to print. Depending on the algorithm your printer uses, the number of sheets used for tiling may vary.

6. When the file has finished printing, deactivate the Show Rulers command, return to Portrait orientation and letter size paper in

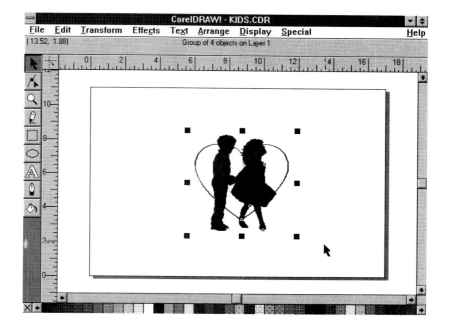

Changing page
size through the
Page Setup
dialog box
Figure 15–12.

the Page Setup dialog box, and then select Open from the File menu. Do not save the changes you have made to the picture. When the Open File dialog box appears, double-click on KIDS.CDR to re-open this file in its original state. Leave the current on the screen for the next exercise.

Since most printers do not print to the edge of the page, you may need to use scissors or a matte knife to cut and paste the tiled pieces together exactly. Still, this method gives you a fairly exact representation of your image as it will print on the imagesetter. If your cutting and pasting skills are also exact, you may be able to use the tiled version of the image as the master copy for commercial printing.

Number of Copies

You can enter the number of copies you want printed at one time in the Print Options dialog box. This can be a number from 1 through 10,000 and it overrides the number entered in the Print Setup dialog box.

Scaling an Image

There is a difference in CorelDRAW! between scaling an image on the screen with the Pick tool and defining a scaling value in the Printer Options dialog box. When you scale an image visually, you are altering its actual dimensions. When you adjust values for the Scale option of the Printer Options dialog box, however, you change only the way the file prints, not its actual size.

Perform the following exercise to print the KIDS.CDR file at a reduced size, using the Scale option:

1. With the KIDS.CDR file on the screen, click on any outline within the image. As the status line informs you, the entire image is grouped.

2. Select the Print command from the File menu. When the Print Options dialog box appears, deselect any options that are currently active, and then click on the Scale check box. The value 100% (actual size) appears in the associated numeric entry box as soon as you enable this option.

3. Using the bottom scroll arrow, scroll to the lowest value available. This should be 10%, as shown here:

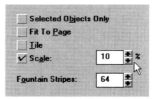

Depending on your printer, you may not be able to print as samll as 10%. If this is the case, increase the scale until your printer accepts the image.

4. Click on OK to begin the printing process. Again, depending on your printer, the image will probably print centered on your page, but it may be slightly offset.

5. Leave the current image on the screen for further work.

You have seen how you can reduce the scale of an image to a lower limit of 10% of original size. You can also increase the scale of an image to an upper limit of 1000% of original size. If you expand the scale of an image beyond the dimensions of the page, however, remember to activate the Tile option as well.

In the next section, you will experiment with another printing option that involves image size.

Fitting an Image to the Page

Like the Scale option, the Fit To Page option in the Printer Options dialog box does not affect the actual size of the graphic. When you select this option, CorelDRAW! automatically calculates how much it must increase the scale of the graphic or selected object(s) in order to make it fill the entire page. In the following exercise, you will combine the Fit To Page option with the Selected Objects Only option you learned about previously.

1. Select any outline within the KIDS.CDR image; since the entire image is grouped, you select all objects automatically.

2. Click on the Ungroup command in the Arrange menu, and then click on any white space to deselect all objects. Select the 3 objects that make up the boy and girl by drawing a marquee around them.

3. With the boy and girl selected, click on the Print command in the File menu. When the Print Options dialog box appears, deselect any options that are currently active, and then activate the Selected Objects Only option.

4. Click on the Fit To Page option to activate it, and then select OK to begin printing. After a few moments, the boy and girl appear on the paper, filling the entire sheet as shown in Figure 15–13.

5. Leave the KIDS.CDR image on the screen for the next exercise.

As mentioned earlier, you can use the Fit To Page option along with Selected Objects Only when you want to blow up details within a complex graphic, such as a technical illustration.

In the next section, you will experiment with printing an image to a file.

Boy and girl
selected and
printed with Fit
To Page
Figure 15–13.

Printing to a File

There are two common reasons why you might choose to print an image to a file.

✦ You are creating files to send to a service bureau for output on a Linotronic or other imagesetter.

✦ Your printer is busy and you prefer to copy the print information directly to the printer at a later time.

To print to a file, you select the Print to File option in the Print Options dialog box and name the output file. Printer output files created in applications that run under Windows bear the extension .PRN. CorelDRAW! then displays another screen, prompting you to set printing parameters specific to the printer that will eventually print the file.

The following exercise assumes that you are going to send an output file to a service bureau for use on a PostScript imagesetter. In order to do this, you do not need to have a PostScript printer, but you must

15

have a PostScript printer driver installed in your Windows directory. If
you do not have a PostScript driver installed, use the Add command in
the Printers dialog box of the Control Panel. Refer to the discussion
under "Checking Print Setup" earlier in this chapter for assistance.
Once you have the PostScript driver set up, practice printing the
KIDS.CDR image to a file in the following exercise:

1. With the KIDS.CDR file on the screen, deselect all objects in the
   image, and then select Print from the File menu. When the Print
   Options dialog box displays, deselect any options that are
   currently active.

2. Click on the Print to File option. (Do not click on the Print Setup
   option, because any changes you make at this point will be
   ignored. A dialog box similar to the Print Setup dialog box, but
   with a different name, will pop up automatically after you finish
   specifying an output filename.)

3. If you are going to print on a printer or imagesetter controlled by a
   Macintosh computer, select the For Mac option. Without this
   selection, the print files you produce will not work on a
   Macintosh. Select OK; a second dialog box appears with the title
   Print To File, as shown in Figure 15–14. This dialog box looks and
   operates similar to the Open File dialog box.

4. If the filename KIDS is not already in the File Name, type it, and
   then select OK. CorelDRAW! adds the file extension .PRN
   automatically to designate this as a printer output file. A third
   dialog box appears; the contents vary depending on the type of
   printer that will receive the output file. Figure 15–15 shows a
   dialog box set up for a PostScript printer, which is the most

The Print To
File dialog box
for specifying
an output
filename
Figure 15–14.

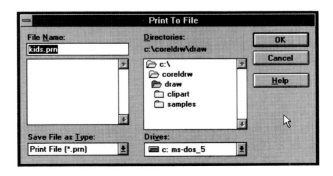

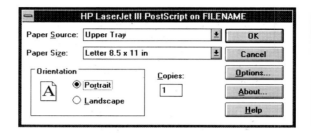

common choice if you are sending an output file to a service bureau. If you are printing a file for use by an other printer, the dialog box you see on your screen will be different.

5. Make the changes you need in the dialog box and click on OK to begin the process of printing to a file.

6. When printing is complete, select New to clear the image from the screen without saving any changes.

When printing an image to a file, you can combine several options. For example, if you are creating color separations for commercial printing, you might choose to activate the Print As Separations, All Fonts Resident, and Print to File options at the same time.

The next group of sections introduces you to print options that apply specifically to PostScript printers. Since you may use some of these options in combination, the sections are ordered according to task, rather than according to their appearance in the Print Options dialog box.

Printing File Information with a Graphic in PostScript

If you are like most illustrators and designers, you probably revise a graphic several times, renaming it with each revision so that you can choose the best version later. You are therefore familiar with the bewilderment of viewing multiple printouts of the same graphic and not knowing which sheet represents which version.

CorelDRAW! provides a convenient solution to this common frustration, available to you if you print to a PostScript device. By activating the Print File Info option in the Print Options dialog box,

15

you can print the filename, date and time of printing with your image. This information appears in 10-point Courier *outside* the left margin of your *page*, not of your graphic (unless you select the Within Page option). If you activate the Print File Info without the Within Page option, choose a page size in the Page Setup dialog box that is smaller than the nominal page size. For example, if your graphic fits on an 8 1/2-by-11-inch page, select a 10-by-14-inch or Tabloid page size before you print. This step is necessary because file information is visible *only* if you reduce Page Size below the size of the paper in your printer tray. If you are using 8 1/2-by-11-inch paper, for example, you must use the Page Setup dialog box to define a custom page size of smaller dimensions, and then fit the graphic within that page. You can practice defining a custom page size and printing file information in the following exercise. You'll start by separating out the sitting woman and using her as the subject for printing for the rest of the chapter. This will reduce your printing time.

1. Open the CAR366.CDR file, which is also in the MISC clip art directory. The car graphic will appear, as shown in Figure 15–16.

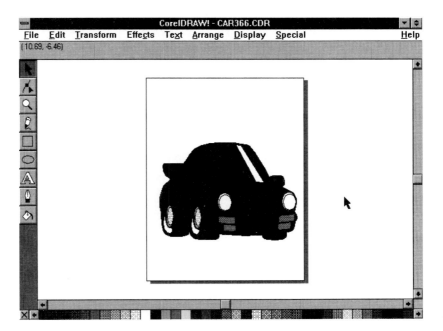

Car366 image
Figure 15–16.

2. Select the Page Setup command in the File menu. Click on Landscape orientation and on Custom Page Size in the Page Setup dialog box, and define a page 6.0 inches wide (the Horizontal value) and 4.0 inches high (the Vertical value). Then select OK to exit the dialog box and return to your picture, which is now larger than the new page size.

3. Scale the picture down to fit on the new page size and move the picture so that it fits entirely within the page and is reasonably centered.

4. Click on the Print command and activate the Print File Info option in the Print Options dialog box. Click on Print Setup, select Landscape orientation, make sure that the other settings are as you need them, and then click on OK to return to the Print Options dialog box. Click on OK again to begin printing. After a few moments, the image emerges from your printer. The filename, date, and time of printing appear in 10-point Courier just beyond the left boundary of the custom page, at a 90-degree angle to the image as shown in Figure 15–17.

Car366 printed with file information
Figure 15–17.

5. Leave this image on the screen for subsequent exercises.

Since CorelDRAW! generates object-oriented art, you can scale your images without distortion. It is therefore convenient to change page size so that you can print file information for your own use. Another common use for the Include File Info option is in conjunction with the Print As Separations and Crop Marks & Crosshairs options, which you will learn about in the next section.

Color Separations, Cropping, and Registration Marks with PostScript

When you began to specify outline fill and object fill colors in Chapters 12 and 13, you learned about the differences between Spot color and Process color in the commercial printing process. If you have a PostScript printer or plan to send output files to a PostScript imagesetter, you can reduce your commercial printing expenses by generating color separations on paper or in a file. This reduces the number of intermediary steps that commercial printers must perform to prepare your images for printing.

Put simply, *color separation* is the process of separating the colors that you specify for an entire image into the primary component colors. When you generate color separations using the Process color system (CMYK), the output is four separate sheets, one each for the cyan, magenta, yellow, and black color components of the image. The commercial printer uses the four sheets to create separate overlays for each color, in preparation for making printing plates.

When you generate color separations using the Spot color system, the output is one sheet for each color specified in the image, and the commercial printer creates overlays for each color. This process becomes very expensive as the number of spot colors in an image increases, so it is a good idea to use the Process color system if you plan to have more than four colors in a given image.

When you generate color separations using the Print As Separations option in the Print Options dialog box, it is also important to include *crop marks* and *registration marks* (called crosshairs by CorelDRAW!). You can see examples of these marks in Figure 15–18. Crop marks are small horizontal and vertical lines printed at each corner of the image to

a.

b.

c.

Process color
separations for
CAR366
(a) magenta,
(b) yellow,
(c) black
Figure 15–18.

show the exact boundaries of the image. A registration mark, two of which appear at the inside of each corner of an image, are crossed lines with a circle. Both crop marks and registration marks assist the commercial printer in aligning color separation overlays exactly; if misalignment were to occur, the final printed product would display a host of color distortions. When you activate the Print File Info option, CorelDRAW! prints the color for the page, together with the halftone screen angle and density, which appear beyond the crop marks at the left side of the image with the filename, time, and date information.

CAUTION: Just as with File Information, you can see crop marks and registration marks from your printer only if you define a custom page size that is smaller than the size of the paper you are using unless you select the Within page option. The exception to this rule is if you are printing to Linotronic or other imagesetting equipment.

In the following exercise, you will generate PostScript color separations for the car in the CAR366.CDR file using the Print As Separations, Crop Marks & Crosshairs, and Print File Info options. This particular file uses only three colors (magenta, yellow, and black) even though this is using the four color mode. If you send files to a PostScript imagesetter but do not have a PostScript printer for your draft copies, you may perform this exercise with the Print to File option activated as well.

1. With the CAR366.CDR image still on the screen, turn on Preview Selected Only. Select the image and from the Arrange menu, choose Ungroup. Click in any white area to deselect the grouped object. Then, select various objects in turn, pressing F9 to see just that object on the previous screen, magnifying portions of the image if necessary for more accurate selection. When you select a color object, open the Uniform Fill dialog box and check the process color values that have been specified.

2. After you have observed the fill colors of various objects, choose Select All from the Edit menu and then Group from the Arrange menu to regroup the car. Then select the Print command in the File menu. When the Print Options dialog box appears, deselect any options that are currently active. Then activate the Print As

Separations options. You will see that Crop Marks & Crosshairs, Film Negative, and Print File Info get selected automatically when you select Print as Separations. Click on Film Negative to turn it off. If your own draft printer is not a PostScript printer, you can select the Print to File option. (If you select Print to File, do not bother to check your print setup yet. Changes you make in the Print Setup dialog box will not take effect until that dialog box opens automatically later in the process. You will specify print setup automatically after you specify an output filename.)

3. Select OK. A second dialog box, the Color Separations dialog box, now appears, as shown in Figure 15–19. In the upper-left corner of the dialog box is a list box containing the names of the three process colors. (If you were preparing to print an image using the spot color method, you would see specific color names here instead.) Under Screen Angles are four screen angle values, one for each of the process colors. Do *not* alter these values unless you are very experienced in four-color printing and know exactly what you are doing. These angles are preset to ensure the best possible color alignment and registration. At the bottom of the dialog box is separate:, followed by two option buttons: All Colors and Selected Colors. For this exercise, leave All Colors selected, or click on this option if it is not selected already. For future reference, you can choose to print separations for either one color or a few colors at a time. To do so, just click on the Selected Colors option button

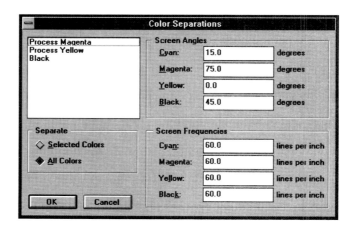

The Color
Separations
dialog box
Figure 15–19.

and then on a desired color or colors in the list box. To highlight more than one color, click on the name of the first color, press and hold ⌈Shift⌉, and click on each additional color.

4. Select OK to save these settings and exit the Color Separations dialog box. If you are printing directly to your own PostScript printer, CorelDRAW! now begins printing the separations. The printing of color separation sheets takes longer than simply printing the file normally. In several minutes, three sheets of paper appear. The first shows the color values for magenta, the second for yellow, and the third for black. As shown in Figure 15–18, each sheet also contains crop marks, registration marks, filename and date information, and color and screen information.

5. If you chose to print to a file, the Print to File dialog box appears when you exit the Color Separations dialog box, prompting you to name the output file. Type **COLORSEP** and select OK; CorelDRAW! adds the extension .PRN automatically. The Printer Setup dialog box now appears, bearing the title "PostScript Printer on FILENAME."

6. Adjust the file printing parameters as necessary; then click on the Options command button in the right-hand column of the PostScript Printer on FILENAME dialog box. Make sure that send Header with Each Job is specified. Then, select OK twice to begin printing the file to the specified drive and directory. You can then send the file to a PostScript service bureau for output.

7. Leave the CAR366.CDR image on the screen for the next exercise.

CAUTION: If you fill objects with any PostScript halftone screen pattern other than the default pattern, your custom settings will have no effect when you print color separations for the objects because CorelDRAW! uses the halftone screen function to calculate color separation angles. This limitation applies only to the objects for which you print color separations. If you require separations for only a few objects, therefore, you are free to assign PostScript halftone screen patterns to the remaining objects. If you assign non-default screens to objects for which you must print color separations, your screen assignments have no effect.

Keep in mind that you can combine any number of options when you specify color separations. For example, you can tile separations for an oversize image, include file information, make selected objects fit the custom page size exactly, or scale the selected image for printing. If you are sure that the current image is in a final version, you can also print it in film negative format, as you will do in the next section.

Film Negative Format with PostScript

In commercial black-and-white or color printing, the transfer of the image or of color separations to film negative is one of the last steps to occur before the printing plates are made. Think of the difference between a snapshot and the negative from which it was produced: colors in the negative appear inverted and backward. The same thing happens when you activate the Film Negative option in the Print Options dialog box. White image backgrounds fill with printer toner, dark areas in the original image print as light, and the image is reversed horizontally. If you print in this format with Print File Info or Crop Marks & Crosshairs activated, even the file and color separation screen information is printed backward.

Use of the Film Negative option can save you money, but only if you are certain that the color separations in the image (if any) are in final form and will not need any further color correction or screen angle adjustments. If you intend to send a film negative file to a service bureau for output on a high-resolution imagesetter, ask the bureau management whether they can output your file in film negative format automatically. Many imagesetters can print your color separation file as a film negative just by flipping a switch. This might be preferable if your aim is to achieve a higher output resolution than that provided by your own 300 dpi laser printer.

In the following exercise, you will print one color separation screen for the CAR366.CDR file in film negative format. If you have your own PostScript laser printer, you can print this screen directly onto paper. If you use PostScript only to send files to a service bureau, steps are provided so that you can print the film negative format to a file.

1. With the CAR366.CDR file open, select the same grouped objects that you printed as color separations in the previous exercise. Then click on the Print command in the File menu.

2. Make sure that the print options that you used in the previous exercise—Print As Separations, Print File Info, Crop Marks & Crosshairs—are still active. (If you printed to a file in the previous exercise, make sure that the Print to File option is still active, too.) Then, click on the Film Negative option and select OK. The Color Separation dialog box appears, as before.

3. You do not need to print out all four color separation sheets to see how the Film Negative option works, so click on the Selected Colors option button at the bottom of the dialog box. Highlight the Process Yellow option in the process colors list box, and then click on the OK command button.

    If you are printing directly to your printer, the color separation now begins to print. In a few moments, the color separation sheet for process yellow appears in film negative format, as shown in Figure 15–20. The image in the figure shows only the graphic and its file information, but your output sheet is covered with toner all the way to the edges of the printable page area. If you elected to print to a file, the Print to File dialog box appears, prompting you to enter a filename.

Color separation sheet for process yellow printed in Film Negative format
Figure 15–20.

4. If you are printing to a file, type **NEG-YEL** in the File text box, and then click on the Print command button. The Printer Setup dialog box (PostScript Printer on FILENAME) now appears, as in the previous exercise.

5. Click on OK to generate your file. When you finish printing, leave the image on the screen, with the grouped objects selected.

You need not limit yourself to printing in film negative format when you are working with a spot or process color image. You can also use this printing option with black-and-white images.

In the next section, you will learn more about the Default Screen Frequency option and how it affects your printouts.

Fountain Stripes

You can use the Print Options dialog box to control the number of stripes used to create a fountain fill on both PostScript and non-PostScript printers. This is a number from 2 through 250. You may want to change the number of fountain stripes for either of two reasons: to increase the smoothness of the fill and get rid of banding, you would increase the number of stripes; to increase the speed of printing, you would decrease the number of stripes. The "normal" number of fountain stripes depends on the resolution of your printer. For a 300 dpi laser printer, the normal value is 64, while for a 1270 dpi imagesetter it is 128. A value below 25, while fast to print, produces obvious banding. On the other end, around 100 for a 300 dpi laser printer, you can add fountain stripes without any gain in the smoothness of the image but with a decided increase in print time. You need to try out a series of values and see which are correct for your output device.

Flatness Setting for PostScript

The Flatness setting allows you to reduce the complexity of the curves in a drawing and thereby improve the likelihood of being able to print the drawing and also reduce the printing time. As you increase the Flatness setting, curves become less smooth with more straight ("flat") segments and, therefore, less attractive in some applications.

15

PostScript printers have upper limits on the number of curve segments they can handle and check for this limit. When a print image exceeds this limit, the image won't be printed. The normal Flatness setting is 1. If you are having problems printing a complex image, increase the Flatness setting in increments of 3 or 4 until you can print. By about 10 the curves are obviously less smooth. You can choose values from 0.01 to 100. Settings below 1 increase the curvature (decrease the flatness).

Screen Frequency for PostScript

The Default Screen Frequency value appears in the PostScript Halftone Screen dialog box. As you may recall from Chapters 12 and 13, you can access this dialog box whenever you assign a spot color to an outline or object fill. The frequency of the default screen pattern determines how fine the halftone resolution will appear on the printed page. Each type of PostScript printer has a default screen frequency, with the most common being 60 lines per inch for 300 dpi printers and 90 or more for high-resolution imagesetters. The standard setting for Default Screen Frequency in the Print Options dialog box is Device's, because in most cases it is best to let the printer you are using determine the screen frequency.

You can override this standard value, however, by clicking on the Custom option button and entering the desired value in the associated numeric entry box. Thereafter, *all* of the objects in your image will have the custom screen frequency. The most common reasons for altering this value are:

✦ You want to create special effects such as the Fill patterns that result from altering the halftone screen settings, as discussed in Chapter 13.

✦ You experience visible "banding" effects while printing objects with fountain fills and want the color transitions to occur more smoothly.

In the first case, you would increase the default screen value for the selected printer, while in the second, you would decrease it. If you have a 300 dpi PostScript printer, perform the following brief exercise to compare how reducing the default screen frequency alters the appearance of your output.

1. With the CAR366.CDR image open and the same objects selected, click on the Print command in the File menu. The Print Options dialog box appears.

2. Make sure that the Print As Separations option and the associated other options are activated. Deselect any other options that show check marks in their respective check boxes. Then click on the Custom option button in the Screen Frequency section of the dialog box. If you have a 300 dpi PostScript printer, the number 60 appears in the numeric entry box next to Custom. This is the default screen frequency for your printer.

3. Change the Custom value to 45 lines per inch, and then click on OK.

4. When the Color Separations dialog box appears, click on Selected Colors and highlight Process Yellow, as you did in the previous exercise. These settings will cause only the color separation for the color yellow to print.

5. Click on the OK command button of the Color Separations dialog box to begin printing. After a few moments, the color separation sheet appears. If you compare this output sheet with the one produced in the "Color Separations, Crop Marks, and Registration Marks with PostScript" section, you will not notice a big difference, but if you look closely you will see that the dot pattern of the 45-lines-per inch screen printout appears coarser.

6. Select New from the File menu to clear the screen of the CAR366.CDR file. Do not save any changes to the image.

If you alter the default screen frequency in order to proof an image, be sure to change the frequency back to Device's before sending the final output file to a service bureau. Otherwise, your image will not appear to have a much higher resolution than what your printer could offer.

Note, however, that if you assign *custom* PostScript halftone screen patterns to an object while drawing, any changes you make to the *default* screen frequency at printing time will have no effect on the screen frequency of that object. In the next section, you will become familiar with the uses of the All Fonts Resident printing option. Since the example image does not contain any text, you will not have an exercise, but the principle of the option is quite straightforward.

All Fonts Resident for PostScript

15

The All Fonts Resident option in the Print Options dialog box is designed with the occasional user of Adobe PostScript fonts and laser service bureaus in mind. As you are aware, CorelDRAW! comes supplied with 153 different fonts and style combinations. Although these are of very high quality, they do not contain the "hints" (program instructions) that allow genuine Adobe PostScript fonts to print at extremely small sizes with very little degradation. Therefore, if you use text with a small typesize in a drawing, you might choose to substitute equivalent Adobe PostScript fonts for the CorelDRAW! fonts at printing time. You activate the All Fonts Resident option to instruct the PostScript printer to substitute the correct fonts.

The All Fonts Resident option is intended for temporary use. If you have purchased downloadable fonts from Adobe and *always* want your printer to automatically substitute Adobe fonts for CorelDRAW! fonts, you should alter the [PSResidentFonts] section of your CORELDRW.INI file according to the instructions in the next section under PostScript Printer and Controller. If you use the All Fonts Resident option when you send output files to a laser service bureau, make sure that the service bureau has all of the necessary PostScript fonts downloaded. If you specify a PostScript font that is not in the host printer's memory, the font will print as Courier instead.

In the final sections of this chapter, you will find tips for smooth printing based on the type of printer you are using and the features of your artwork.

Hardware-Specific Tips

Even if you closely follow all recommended printing procedures, such as checking the Printer Setup options or setting Transmission Retry at 600 seconds, you may encounter printing difficulties on occasion. Some difficulties involve settings for your specific printer type, while others may involve features of the artwork you are trying to print. This section deals with printing problems that could be dependent on hardware and makes suggestions for solving them. The final section, "Complex Artwork on PostScript Printers," deals with printing problems that might be related to features of the artwork itself.

TIP: Regardless of the type of printer you use, you may sometimes encounter one of several error messages indicating that you should cancel the printing process. In most cases, click on the Retry command button. Repeated attempts to print often force the data through your printer.

PostScript Printers and Controllers

CorelDRAW! is designed for the PostScript Plus type of printer, with its 11 resident fonts families and 2 or 3 MB of RAM. It also runs on older versions of PostScript printers that contain only four font families, but you may experience slower performance or other limitations if the memory in your printer is not sufficient. If this happens, check with your printer dealer to see whether a memory upgrade is possible. If you run CorelDRAW! with an older model of PostScript printer, you should edit your CorelDRAW! CORELDRW.INI file to notify the program that certain PostScript fonts are not available. To do this, proceed with the following steps.

1. From the Program Manager, open the Notepad application, double-click on the CORELDRW.INI filename in the directory where you installed CorelDRAW! to begin editing this file.

2. Go to the [PSResidentFonts] section of the CORELDRW.INI file and look at the listings of fonts that are followed by the number 3 at the end of the line. These are PostScript Plus fonts, not available for the older models of PostScript printers.

3. Change each 3 to a 0. This tells CorelDRAW! to always substitute CorelDRAW! fonts for the PostScript fonts when you print the file to a PostScript printer.

4. Save these changes to the CORELDRW.INI file and exit Notepad.

5. Exit and then restart CorelDRAW! to cause your changes to take effect.

In today's market, a number of so-called PostScript-compatible controllers and plug-in cartridges are available for the HP LaserJet and compatible printers. You should be aware that there is a distinction between genuine PostScript controller boards and cartridges (licensed by Adobe), and PostScript-*compatible* controller boards and cartridges that are only as compatible as their interpreters. If your LaserJet printer is equipped with a genuine Adobe PostScript controller board or cartridge, you should be able to print everything that would be possible on a genuine Adobe PostScript printer. This is not necessarily true for a printer equipped with a PostScript-compatible controller board or cartridge, although some of these components work extremely well.

If you have a genuine PostScript printer or if your printer has a genuine PostScript controller board or cartridge, the following tips should help you prevent printing problems when running CorelDRAW!. Potential problems are organized according to whether your printer is connected to a parallel or a serial port.

Parallel Printers

Printer or job timeout problems are common with PostScript printers that are parallel-connected. To avoid such problems, check for the following:

✦ The Print Manager should be turned off (see the "Preparing to Print" section of this chapter).

✦ Make sure that your printer is set up for batch processing mode, not interactive mode. Interactive mode does not permit the printing of imported bitmaps.

✦ See whether you can change Wait timeout directly from the printer as well as from the Windows Control Panel. Many PostScript printers provide utilities that let you specify these times independent of any software application.

✦ Set the Job timeout, Device Not Selected, and Transmission Retry settings as recommended in the "Preparing to Print" section of this chapter.

You will find additional tips related to printing complex artwork with PostScript printers in the "Complex Artwork on PostScript Printers" section at the end of this chapter.

Serial Printers

Although most PostScript printers attach to IBM-compatible computers with a parallel cable (the faster and preferred printing method), some printers require the use of a serial cable. To ensure trouble-free printing with a serially connected printer, compare your printer setup with the following checklist:

✦ Use the Ports icon in the Control Panel and make certain that the settings are correct. (Refer to your printer manual.) Make sure that hardware handshaking ("Flow Control") is active.

✦ Check your printer cable. Some long or unshielded serial cables do not always transmit all available data with graphics applications.

HP LaserJet Printers and Compatibles

Since the HP LaserJet and compatible printers connect to your computer by means of a parallel rather than a serial cable, you should refer to the "Parallel Printers" section under "PostScript Printers and Controllers." Printers that are guaranteed to be 100% LaserJet compatible perform equally well with the genuine HP LaserJet. Printers that are HP LaserJet clones and that do not guarantee 100% compatibility may present erratic problems, which vary with the printer driver and manufacturer.

If your LaserJet or compatible is an older model and you have only 512K of memory, you may find that you are unable to print full-page graphics with complex features such as outlines and fountain fills. Many LaserJet-type printers split a graphic that is too large for memory and tile it over several sheets. If you plan to print large graphics regularly, see whether you can expand your printer's memory. If this is not possible, try reducing the size of the graphic on the page. Since object-oriented graphics can be scaled up or down without distortion, this should be a satisfactory solution. As a last resort, reduce the printing resolution of the graphic to 150 dpi, or even 75 dpi, in the Printer Setup dialog box.

HP DeskJet and PaintJet

The HP DeskJet is a black-and-white inkjet printer that is almost completely compatible with the HP LaserJet. There are different versions of the software driver for this printer, however. Check to make sure that you have the latest model driver when printing graphics from

CorelDRAW!. In addition, avoid designing large filled objects or layered objects; the ink for the DeskJet is water-based and could run or smear if you layer it too thickly.

15

Genuine HP and Other Plotters

The Windows driver for plotters seems to be written specifically for the HP Plotter line. The HP Plotter supports only hairline outlines and no fills for objects that you create in CorelDRAW!. If you have a clone from another manufacturer, the Windows driver may not work well for you when you print images from CorelDRAW!. Contact your plotter manufacturer to see if a driver for CorelDRAW! is available.

Dot-Matrix Printers

The results of printing CorelDRAW! graphics on dot-matrix printers are very erratic, owing to the large number of printer types available and the many different drivers written for them. Some dot-matrix printers cannot print complex files at all, while others print part of a page and stop. Dot-matrix printers that have multicolor ribbons do not lay all colors down on the page in the same order. This can result in muddy colors that do not match what you see on your screen. Depending on the problem, you may wish to contact your printer manufacturer to see if a driver for Windows is available.

Complex Artwork on PostScript Printers

The term "complex" artwork, when applied to CorelDRAW!, can include a variety of features. Among them are curves with many nodes, multiple fountain fills in an image, PostScript halftone screens and textures, and text converted to curves. Many printing problems that are traceable to the complexity of features are encountered chiefly with PostScript printers. This happens because the PostScript language has certain internal limits. When these are exceeded, the affected object may not print at all or may print incorrectly. For example, objects that contain more than 200 to 400 nodes may cause your PostScript print job to crash. If you are having this problem, try increasing the Flatness setting in the Print Options dialog box by increments of 3. As was discussed earlier, this reduces the number of nodes in curves, and after only a couple of increments, improvement becomes noticeable.

You might not experience a problem with the same object if you are printing to an HP LaserJet printer, because the HP LaserJet does not recognize nodes; it interprets all graphic images simply as collections of pixels. Some PostScript printer manufacturers, such as QMS, allow you to run PostScript printers in LaserJet mode. If you have such a printer, try switching to LaserJet mode and printing your "problem" image again. If the file prints correctly, it is safe to guess that an internal PostScript limitation is causing printing problems in PostScript mode.

Downloadable PostScript Error Handler

You may not be aware (since it is undocumented) that both CorelDRAW! 3 and Windows 3.1 include error handlers that help you diagnose PostScript printing problems. As of this writing, Corel's is better. To understand how an error handler works, you need to know that PostScript prints the "bottom" or first-drawn object in the image first, followed by each succeeding layer. When you download the error handler and try to print a problem file, the printer begins with the first object and prints as far as it can. When the printer encounters an object that is problematic, it stops and prints out the objects completed so far, together with an error message. Although the messages are in PostScript code language, they are, in many cases, intelligible enough for you to decipher what the basic problem might be. The purchase of a relatively inexpensive PostScript manual, of which several are available, can help you even further.

To download the PostScript error handler to your printer and keep it resident there until you turn the printer off, follow these steps:

1. From the Print Options dialog box, click on the Printer Setup command button.

2. From the Print Setup dialog box, click on the Options command button to access the Options dialog box.

3. From the Options dialog box, click on Advanced. From the Advanced Options dialog box, make sure the box beside Print PostScript Error Information is checked.

This setting has no effect if you send a file to a service bureau, since most service bureaus use their own error handlers.

The PostScript error handler should be helpful in fixing problems that already exist within a graphic. However, there are other measures you can take to design a graphic that will cause no printing problems. The following sections explain a few of these measures briefly.

Printing PostScript Textures

The 42 PostScript textures described in Chapter 13 were created with highly complex mathematical algorithms. Sometimes, you may not be able to make an object with a PostScript texture print correctly. If this happens, try adjusting the parameters to avoid extremely dense patterns. If the image does not print at all, try removing excess objects. PostScript textures can be so memory-intensive that they do not tolerate many other objects within the same graphic. In general, you should use these textures as fills in a limited number of objects within a given graphic. Short text strings used as headlines (but not converted to curves) are among the best applications for PostScript texture fills.

If you are a desktop publisher, you may sometimes find that a page containing a CorelDRAW! graphic with PostScript textures does not print. Try removing everything from the page except the PostScript texture graphic, and then attempt to print the page again. Sometimes a page becomes too complex for PostScript if it contains both PostScript textures and other elements.

Printing Complex Curve Objects

As previously mentioned, the current version of PostScript may give you difficulty when you try to print images that contain objects with more than 200 nodes. If you suspect that an object has too many nodes and could be causing problems, click on it with the Shaping tool. The number of nodes contained in the object appears on the status line. If the number of nodes seems too high or approaches the danger zone, reshape the object and eliminate any unnecessary nodes.

When you drag one or more control points of a curve object outward by a great distance, the boundary markers of the object may extend much further outward than you can see. If you print a file containing many curve objects and some objects just do not print, it may be that you have not selected them. One remedy is to click on the Select All command in the Edit menu before you begin to print, and then activate Selected Objects Only in the Print Options dialog box. This procedure ensures that all objects in the graphic are selected, no matter how extensively you may have reshaped them.

Printing Fountain Fills

A common complaint when printing fountain-filled objects on PostScript printers is that "banding" effects can occur. In other words, the edges of each fountain stripe are clearly visible and do not blend into the next stripe smoothly. This occurs more often with 300 dpi printers than with Linotronic or other imagesetters that have a higher resolution. With LaserJet and compatible printers, solving this problem is easy: you simply increase the Fountain Stripes value in the Preferences dialog box to create a smoother blend. When you alter this value with a PostScript printer, however, it affects your preview window only, not the way the image prints.

To reduce banding effects on Fountain Fills when you print to a 300 dpi PostScript printer, with CorelDRAW! versions 2.0 and above, increase the value for Fountain Stripes in the Print Options dialog box by 10 or 20. With earlier versions of CorelDRAW! click on the Custom Default Screen Frequency option button in the Print Options dialog box, and reduce the frequency to a number between 30 and 45 lines per inch according to your taste. This procedure results in a somewhat coarser dot pattern, but definitely improves the smoothness of color transition in a Fountain Fill.

TIP: If you alter the default screen frequency for a draft printout on a 300 dpi printer, remember to change the Default Screen Frequency setting back to Device's before you create an output file to be sent to a high-resolution imagesetter. Also keep in mind that when you alter the default screen frequency, your image should contain no objects that have a non-standard halftone screen pattern.

300 dpi Printers vs. High-Resolution Imagesetters

15

It may sometimes happen that your graphic prints on your own 300 dpi PostScript printer, but causes a high-resolution imagesetter to crash. This occurs because at higher resolutions, the amount of information in a file multiplies. It is possible that your graphic exceeds certain internal PostScript limits at these higher resolutions, but didn't at the lower resolution. To avoid such problems, try reducing the resolution at which the imagesetter prints, using the Default Screen Frequency setting in the Printer Setup dialog box. Alternatively, you can define a custom default screen frequency for the imagesetter before you create the output file. If you do so, make certain that your custom frequency is lower than that of the imagesetter. These measures help reduce the amount of data in fills and outlines.

C H A P T E R

16

CREATING SPECIAL EFFECTS

The Effects menu is shown in Figure 16–1. It is used to produce dramatic effects. For example, with the Envelope feature, you can cause text within the envelope to conform to any shape you make the envelope. In CorelDRAW! an envelope is a box that surrounds text or graphics. You can pull the envelope in different directions, thereby distorting the shape as you might with putty. Any object contained within will follow the shape of the envelope. Figure 16–2 shows an example.

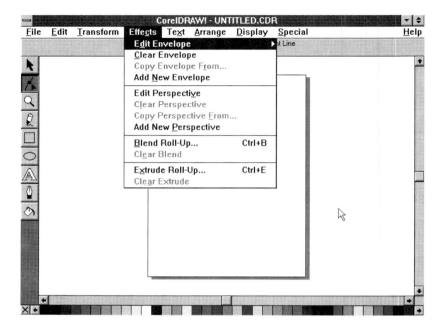

The Effects
menu
Figure 16–1.

Example of
Envelope effect
Figure 16–2.

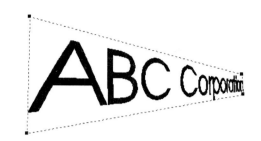

Example of
Perspective
effect
Figure 16–3.

Another special effect is the *Perspective* feature. It allows you to create depth in text or a graphic by stretching the borders of the object. The object seems to fade away into the distance. You can create a simple 3-D effect or a more complex version, such as seen in Figure 16–3.

The third special effect is the *Blend* feature. This allows you to blend one object into another, as shown here:

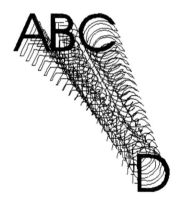

You define the beginning and ending points, and CorelDRAW! will fill in the blend steps.

Finally, the fourth special effect is the *Extrude* feature. This feature gives depth to objects. An example of an open path extruded surface is shown here:

If your computer is not turned on, turn it on now and bring up CorelDRAW!.

You will explore these special effects beginning with the Envelope feature.

Using an Envelope

An envelope is a bounding box with eight handles on it that surrounds the text or graphic. You pull the handles to reshape the object within the envelope.

You have four editing modes available that determine how the envelope can be reshaped. Three of the modes allow you to change the shape of a side of the envelope in a specific way. The first mode allows you to pull the side in a straight line, the second in a curved line, the third in a line with two curves. The fourth envelope editing mode is unconstrained. It allows you to pull in any direction, and to change a line to a curve.

As you move the handles, the envelope changes shape. When you let go of the handle, the contents of the envelope are reshaped to conform to the new shape.

You will now create and duplicate some text to use for the first three editing modes.

Creating and Duplicating Text

To prepare for the first exercise, you need to create a piece of text and then duplicate it twice.

1. Click on the Text tool and then click on the page, at about the middle left.

2. Type **Happy Birthday**, select the text, open the Text roll-up, and change the type size to 60 points, and the font to Cupertino. Click on Apply to change the text.

    Now you will copy the text twice so that there are three copies, one for each of the first three editing modes.

3. Make sure the text is still selected, and change the magnification so that you can easily see the words.

4. From the Edit menu, select Duplicate for the first copy.

5. Press Ctrl-D to duplicate another copy. The three copies will be stacked on top of each other with the edges of the bottom copies peeking out, as shown here:

Now you will move them apart.

6. Place the mouse pointer on an edge of the selected text. Press and hold the mouse button while moving the box outline to the bottom of the page. Center the outline horizontally on the page. When you release the mouse button, the selected copy of the text will be moved from the stack onto the page.

7. Click on the top of the stack to select the next text object. Repeat step 6 but move the second copy from the stack to the top of the page. The last copy will remain at the center of the page.

8. Space the three text units so that you can easily work with each one. Figure 16–4 shows an example of the screen with the three copies rearranged on the page.

Now you are ready to work with the first envelope editing mode.

Straight Line Envelope

The Straight Line editing mode allows you to pull envelope handles in a straight line. You can move one handle at a time.

As in all of the first three editing modes, the handles can be moved only in a restricted way: Handles located in the center of the sides move left or right; handles located in the top- and bottom-center move up or down; corner handles move up or down, or left or right. (In the fourth mode, all handles move in any direction.)

The easiest way to understand the feature is to try it out. Follow these steps:

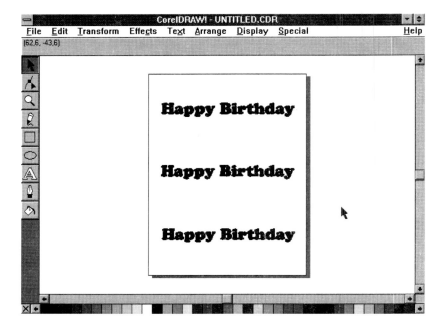

Text to be used
for illustrating
envelopes
Figure 16–4.

1. If the top text object is not selected, select it by clicking on it so that the selection box surrounds it.
2. Select Edit Envelope from the Effects menu.
3. Choose the first editing mode, Straight Line, as shown here:

   The envelope will appear on the screen surrounding the selected text. You can see the eight handles.
4. Pull the top-middle handle up, as shown here:

5. Pull the bottom-center handle up, like this:

You can see how the text conforms to the new straight line. Next you will see how the Single Arc editing mode differs.

Single Arc Envelope

The Single Arc editing mode allows you to create an arc by pulling the handles up, down, right, or left. You can only pull one handle at a time.

As above, the handles can be moved only in a restricted way: Handles located in the center of the sides move left or right; handles located in the top- and bottom-center move up and down; corner handles move up or down, or left and right.

Follow these steps to try it out.

1. Click on the Pick tool, then select the second text copy by clicking on it so a selection box surrounds it.
2. Select Edit Envelope from the Effects menu. Choose the second option, Single Arc, shown here:

3. Pull the top-middle handle up.
4. Pull the bottom-middle handle up, as shown here:

You can see how the Straight Line and Arc editing modes differ. Now you will try out the third editing mode.

Two Curves Envelope

The third choice allows you to create two curves by pulling one of the eight handles. You can only move one handle at a time.

Again, the handles can be moved only in a restricted way: Handles located in the center of the sides move left or right; handles located in the top- and bottom-center move up or down; corner handles move up or down, or left or right.

Follow these steps to try it out.

1. Click on the Pick tool, and click on the third text object so it is selected.

2. Select Edit Envelope from the Effects menu. Then choose the third item, Two Curves, shown here:

The envelope will surround the third text object.

3. Pull the top-middle handle up. Then pull the bottom-middle handle up, as shown here:

You can see how two curves are created out of the line, shaping the text in an entirely different way. These three envelope editing modes have an additional feature that can be used to constrain the shapes.

Using Ctrl and Shift with Envelopes

The above three envelope editing modes can be used with Ctrl or Shift with surprising results. You can cause three effects to take place:

✦ If you hold down Ctrl while you drag on a handle, the opposite handle will move in the same direction.

✦ If you hold down Shift while you drag on a handle, the opposite handle will move in the opposite direction.

✦ Finally, if you hold both Shift and Ctrl while dragging a handle, all four corners or sides will move in opposite directions.

You can use these keys with any of the first three Edit Envelope options. Try the Ctrl method now with the first text object on your screen.

1. Click on the top text image so that the envelope and handles appear on the screen.
2. Press ⌃Ctrl while dragging the top-middle handle down, as shown here:

You can see two immediate effects: First, the top and bottom sides move in the same direction. You expected that. Second, and unexpectedly, the lines are *not* being shaped according to the Straight Line edit mode that was earlier applied to this particular text object. Instead, the lines are being shaped according to the Two Curves edit mode, the last mode applied to another text object. Whenever you apply a new editing mode to any envelope on the page, all new edits will be assigned the new mode as well. If you need to change the shape of an object while retaining the original edit mode, simply reselect that mode before making your changes.

Now you will try the Shift method with the second text object.

1. Click on the middle text object so that the envelope and handles appear on the screen.
2. Select Edit Envelope from the Effects menu and then Single Arc from the submenu.
3. Press Shift while dragging the top-right handle out to the right.

The left and right sides will move in opposite directions, as shown here:

The Shift-Ctrl method is just as easy.

1. Click on the bottom text object to select it.
2. Select Edit Envelope from the Effects menu and then Two Curves from the submenu.

3. Press Shift-Ctrl while dragging the top-right handle to the right.

The top and bottom and both sides all move in opposite directions, as shown here:

These techniques are particularly useful when you are changing the shape of drawings, as in circles or rectangles, and you want one or all of the dimensions to be altered to the same degree.

Now you will explore the fourth envelope editing mode.

Unconstrained Envelope

The Unconstrained editing mode is the most dynamic of the four modes. The handles can be moved in any direction, and they contain control points that can be used to fine-tune and bend the objects even more dynamically. Unlike the first three Edit Envelope options, the Unconstrained mode lets you select several handles and move them as a unit.

To experiment with this, first clear the page of its contents.

1. Select New from the File menu. Click on No when asked about saving the current screen contents.

2. Select the Text tool and click on the middle left of the page.

3. Type **Not Constrained**. Select the text, and from the Text roll-up, change the type size to 70 points and the font to Bangkok. Click on Apply.

4. Select Edit Envelope from the Effects menu. Choose the fourth submenu option, Not Constrained:

You will see the text object surrounded by the envelope and its handles. Since you are using the Shaping tool, the handles become nodes.

5. Pull the top-middle handle or node up, and then the bottom-middle node down, as shown here:

You can see that a pair of control points appeared first on the top-, and then on the bottom-middle node. These control points, like Shaping tool control points, allow you to alter the shape by exaggerating and bending the curve.

6. Place the pointer on the left control point of the bottom-middle node and pull it down. (To experiment with it, move it down and then back up so that you will see what happens with the handle.)

7. Click on the top-middle node to select it. Place the pointer on the right control point of the top-middle node and pull it up, as shown here:

Now, suppose you want the last letters to curve up at the end.

8. While holding Shift, click on first the bottom-middle node and then the bottom-right node. Now you can treat all three selected nodes.

9. Hold down the mouse button and pull the bottom-middle node down, as shown here:

One way that you can use the Unconstrained edit mode is to modify text to conform to a shape, for example, text within a circle or oval. First you create the circle, oval, or whatever shape you want as a border and move the text with its envelope within the border. You then manually move the control points of the text so that they correspond with the border shape. Then if you don't want the border to appear, you can delete it.

Continue to experiment until you are comfortable with the Unconstrained edit mode. Then you can move on to more Envelope features.

Adding a New Envelope

Sometimes you may want to use more than one of the editing modes on an object. Adding a new envelope allows you to do this. You apply an envelope and shape the object with it. Then you add a new envelope, which replaces the first envelope while retaining its shape. With the new envelope, you select a new editing mode and change the shape again.

To try this out,

1. Clear the screen by selecting New from the File menu. Click on No when asked if you want to save the screen contents.

2. Select the Text tool and click on the middle left of the page.

3. Type **New Envelope**, select the text, and from the Text roll-up, set the type size to 80 points and select the Penguin font. Click on Apply.

4. Attach an envelope by selecting Edit Envelope from the Effects menu. Choose the Straight Line editing mode.

5. Click on the top-left handle and drag it up.

6. Click on the bottom-right handle and drag it down, as shown here:

Now you will apply a new envelope and change the shape using another editing mode on top of the Straight Line editing mode.

1. From the Effects menu, select Add New Envelope.
2. From the Effects menu, select Edit Envelope. From the submenu, select the Single Arc editing mode.

   You will use (Shift) to move the opposite handles in opposite directions.
3. While pressing (Shift), drag the upper-left handle up.
4. While pressing (Shift), drag the bottom-right handle to the right, as shown in Figure 16–5.

One way that a new envelope can be used is with certain fonts that do not bend or reshape themselves exactly as you want. You can form the basic shape with one of the first three edit modes, and then apply the Unconstrained edit mode to fine-tune the text. In this way you can manually form the letters with more precision than you might get with the font alone.

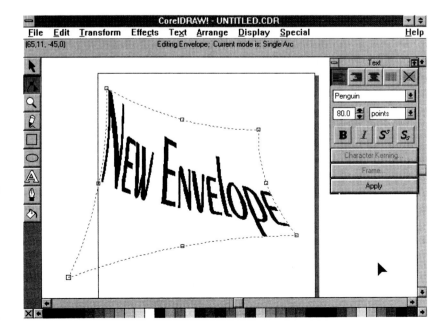

Using Add New Envelope to reshape a text object within the borders of a previous envelope
Figure 16–5.

Sometimes you might want to start over again. Clearing an envelope allows you to do that.

Clearing an Envelope

The Clear Envelope command removes the current envelope and all shape changes that occurred with it. If you have applied more than one most recent, only the previous one will be removed.

To clear the last envelope from the current text object, select Clear Envelope from the Effects menu. The drawing will be returned to the previous Straight Line edit mode. However, if you have applied a perspective (perspectives are discussed shortly) to the object after applying the most recent envelope, the perspective must be removed before you can clear the envelope.

(Note that the Clear Transformations command, found on the Transform menu, removes all envelopes, restoring the drawing to its original shape. If you have applied perspectives, they will also be removed and the original shape restored.)

Now you can copy an envelope to a new object.

Copy Envelope From

The Copy Envelope From command allows you to copy the envelope and its current shape to a new object. The new object does not need its own envelope. To try out this feature, you will first create a new object.

1. Click on the Ellipse tool. Draw a circle below the text, using the Ctrl key.
2. Select Copy Envelope From in the Effects menu.

   The pointer will be turned into a special "FROM?" arrow. You will move the arrow to the source of the envelope, which is the text.
3. Move the arrow to the text "New Envelope," and click on it.

The destination object will be reshaped with the new tool, as shown in Figure 16–6.

Now you will explore another dynamic feature, Perspective.

16

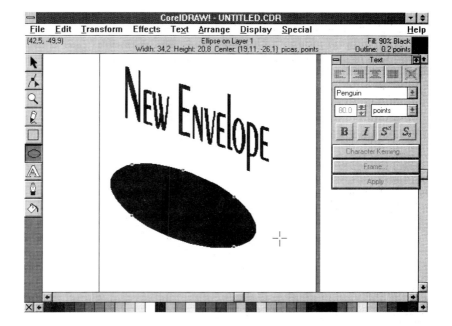

Using Copy
Envelope From
to reshape a
second object,
in this case, a
circle
Figure 16–6.

Creating Perspective Effects

Perspective gives an object a sense of depth, as if the object were moving away from you. This effect can be applied from one- or two-point perspective views. Figure 16–7 shows the two kinds of perspective.

The one-point perspective, on the top, gives the effect of moving away from you in a straight line. The two-point perspective, on the bottom, distorts the view so that the object is moving away and being twisted in the process.

You will see how these two points are applied.

Using One- or Two-Point Perspective

You apply perspective in much the same way that you change the shape of an envelope. A perspective bounding box with handles surrounds the object. You can drag the handles to shorten or lengthen the object, giving the perspective you want.

Examples of
one-point and
two-point
perspectives
Figure 16–7.

Follow these steps to try it out.

1. Clear the screen by selecting New from the File menu. Click on No when asked if you want to save the screen contents.
2. If the rulers are not showing, click on Show Rulers in the Display menu to display them. Place a horizontal guideline at 9 inches, and a vertical guideline at 1 inch.
3. Select the Text tool and click at the intersection of the guidelines.
4. Type **Moving Away**, select the text, and with the Text roll-up, set the type size to 60.0 points and the font to Toronto. Click Apply when you are done.
5. Select Edit Perspective from the Effects menu.

    The pointer will change to the Shaping tool arrow. When you place it on the handles, it will change to crosshairs. You will move the handles according to the coordinates, which tell the location of the pointer. The coordinates are shown in the upper-left corner of the status line.

You will now change the shape of the text object. To change to one-point perspective, drag the handle either up, down, right, or left, that is, vertically or horizontally. In the instructions you'll find below and in the next several exercises you will see sets of coordinates. These are meant as guidelines and are approximate. The coordinates are in inches and always have the horizontal displacement before the vertical.

6. Click on the bottom-right handle and drag it vertically straight down until the coordinates are approximately 5.7 and 8.0.

7. Drag the bottom-left handle vertically straight down until the coordinates are approximately 1.0 and 6.0, as in Figure 16–8.

Now you will alter the shape to add the two-point perspective. You do this by dragging the handles either toward or away from the center of the object. If you drag toward the object, the shape is pushed under; if pulled away from the object, the shape is pulled out toward you.

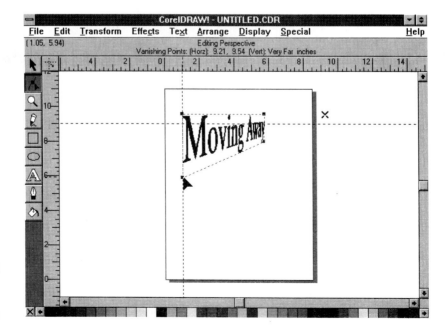

Example of one-point perspective created by dragging the handles straight down
Figure 16–8.

8. Drag the handles as close as possible to the following coordinates, as shown in Figure 16–9.

> Upper-right corner: 6.9, 9.0
>
> Bottom-right corner: 6.6, 8.0
>
> Bottom-left corner: 2.0, 6.5

You should see two X symbols known as vanishing points, which you will learn about next.

Using the Vanishing Point

In Figure 16–9, just off the page on the right, is the horizontal vanishing point. On the bottom of the page is the vertical vanishing point. Each of these points is marked with an X.

You can change the perspective by moving the vanishing point itself. By moving the vanishing point toward the object, the edge closest to the point becomes vertically shorter; the edge becomes vertically longer when the point is moved away from the edge.

Example of two-point perspective created by dragging the handles diagonally toward or away from the center of the object **Figure 16–9.**

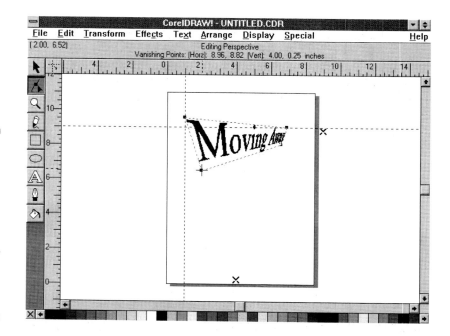

16

When you move the vanishing point parallel to the object, the far side will remain stationary while the side nearest the point moves in the direction you drag the vanishing point.

Try these steps to see what the vanishing point can do:

1. Place the pointer on the horizontal vanishing point (it becomes a crosshair) and move it left and down, toward the text object, as shown here:

2. Move the vanishing point in the opposite direction, toward the right, away from the bounding box.

Take a moment now to play with the vanishing point. When you are satisfied, you can explore some of the other Perspective features.

Clearing a Perspective

Clear Perspective, similar to Clear Envelope, removes the most recent perspective applied to an object. If you've applied more than one perspective, only the last one is removed.

If you've applied an envelope over a perspective, you must first remove the envelope before the perspective can be removed. Before you remove the envelope, be sure to duplicate the object in order to retain the shape you have created with the envelope. Then you can restore the shape by using the Copy Envelope From command after the perspective is removed.

Notice that Clear Transformations in the Transform menu will clear all perspectives and envelopes from an object at once. This is used when you want to restore an object to its original shape.

Now remove the perspective from the current object by selecting Clear Perspective from the Effects menu. The perspective bounding box will be removed, and the shape will be restored. Now you will apply another perspective to the object.

Editing a Perspective

When you edit a perspective, you simply apply another bounding box to an object, or you may simply activate the Shaping tool if the object already has a bounding box.

1. Select Edit Perspective from the Effects menu. A new bounding box will be applied, and the Shaping tool is selected.

   You will now change the shape again.

2. Drag the handles to the following coordinates, or close to them, as shown below.

   > Upper-left handle: 1.0, 9.0
   >
   > Upper-right handle: 7.0, 8.0
   >
   > Lower-left handle: 1.0, 5.0
   >
   > Lower-right handle: 7.0, 6.0

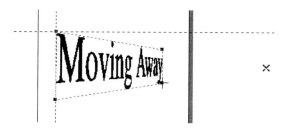

Now you will add another perspective.

Adding a New Perspective

You can add a new perspective to an object on top of one that already exists. This allows you to change the perspective, within the limits of the perspective already applied.

To see how this is done,

1. Select Add New Perspective from the Effects menu. A new bounding box will be applied to the object. Now you will change the perspective again.

2. Drag the handles to the following coordinates, or close to them, as shown in Figure 16–10.

16

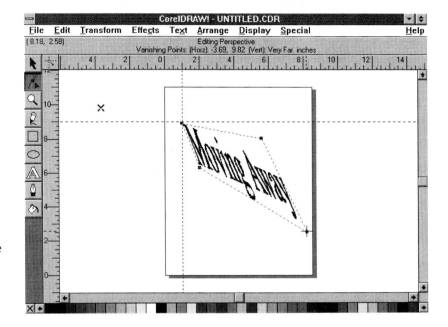

Changing shape
with Add New
Perspective
Figure 16–10.

Upper-right handle: 5.6, 8.0

Lower-left handle: 2.0, 6.3

Lower-right handle: 8.2, 2.5

Now you will apply this perspective to a new object.

Copy Perspective From

When you select the Copy Perspective From option, you use the shape of one object to change the perspective of another one. You will create a form to which the perspective will be applied.

1. Select the Ellipse tool and draw a perfect circle under the text object.
2. Select the Copy Perspective From command from the Effects Menu. The From? arrow will appear.

3. Move the tip of the From? arrow to the outline of the text object, and click on it. The circle will be redrawn with the new perspective.

4. Use the Pick tool to drag the circle over the text object. (It doesn't matter if the reshaped circle isn't the same size as the text.)

5. Click on No Fill (the X) in the bottom-left corner of your screen.

6. The results should look like Figure 16–11.

Now you will explore the Blend feature.

Blending Objects

The Blend command causes one object to be blended into another by a number of connecting images. For example, you can turn a square into a circle with 20 intermediate images. You can also use this feature to create highlights and airbrush effects. The images can be of different colors, line weights, fills, and so on.

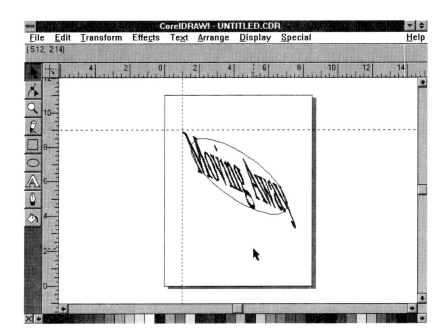

The circle reshaped with a copied perspective

Figure 16–11.

Before the objects are blended, you must fill them and place them where you want them on the screen. And, of course, first you must create the objects to be blended.

1. Select New from the File menu to clear the page. Click on No when asked whether you want to save the file.

2. Select the Text tool and click on the upper-left area of the page.

3. Type **Happy**, select the text, and from the Text roll-up, set the type size to 60 points, and set the font to USA-Black. Click on Apply.

4. While the text object is still selected, click on the yellow in the palette at the bottom of your screen as the fill for the word "Happy."

5. Again select the Text tool, and click on the lower center area of the page.

6. Type **Birthday**, select the text, and with the Text roll-up, set the type size to 60 points, and the font to USA-Black. Click on Apply.

7. Click on the leftmost blue in the palette at the bottom of your screen for the word "Birthday."

Now you are ready to blend the two.

Blending Two Objects

Blending is done with the Blend roll-up window. To blend the objects you must first select the two objects. Then you simply open the Blend roll-up window, tell CorelDRAW! how many steps are needed between the two objects, and click on Apply.

1. Select the Pick tool and then marquee-select the two objects by dragging a dotted rectangle around both objects. You must be careful that both objects are selected. If not, you will not be able to use the Blend command.

2. When both objects are selected, select Blend from the Effects menu. The Blend roll-up window will appear:

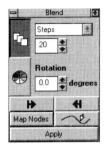

You now tell CorelDRAW! the number of intervening steps between the two objects. It assumes 20 steps, which is acceptable for this example. You can also indicate the degree of rotation and whether to map matching nodes. You'll do these in a minute.

3. Accept the 20 steps and 0 degrees of rotation by clicking on Apply. You will see the two objects blended on the screen, as in Figure 16–12.

Next you will see what the rotation can do.

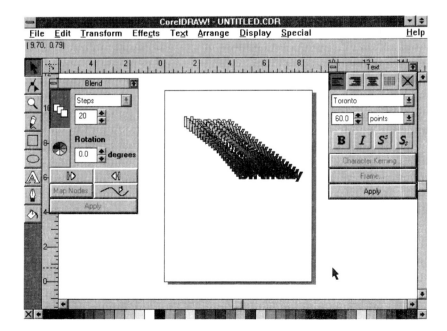

Blending of "Happy" into "Birthday" with no rotation
Figure 16–12.

Rotating the Blended Objects

You can cause the blended objects to be rotated by putting a degree of rotation in the Blend roll-up window. You cause the intervening steps to be rotated counterclockwise, if a positive number is entered; clockwise, if a negative number is entered.

The Blend roll-up window allows you to specify the degrees of rotation to be used in the intervening steps. Let's see how this is used.

1. Choose Clear Blend from the Effects menu to remove the current Blend effects. You will be left with the two unblended selected objects.

2. Change the degree of rotation to 95.0 in the Blend roll-up window and click on Apply.

The effects of the blending will appear on the screen, as shown in Figure 16–13.

Now you will try out clockwise rotation. To see how this is done,

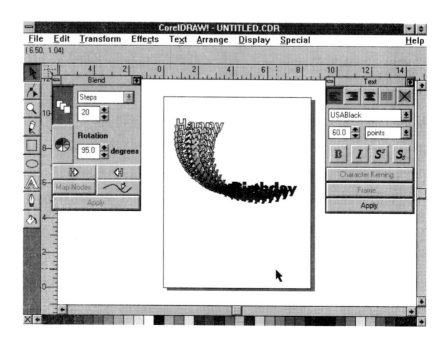

"Happy" blended into "Birthday" with 95 degrees of rotation

Figure 16–13.

1. Again, choose Clear Blend to remove the current Blend effects. You will be left with the two selected objects.

2. In the Blend roll-up window, type **–90.0** for the degree of rotation and click on Apply. The results look something like Figure 16–14.

One other rotation feature can be used to create interesting effects.

Mapping Matching Nodes

By varying the beginning nodes of both of the objects, you can create some unexpected results. The nodes identify where the blend is to begin and to end. You will try two different ways of identifying the nodes.

1. Begin with a new screen by selecting New from the File menu. Click on No.

2. Select the Rectangle tool, and create four different-sized rectangles on your screen, as in Figure 16–15. Make sure that all four

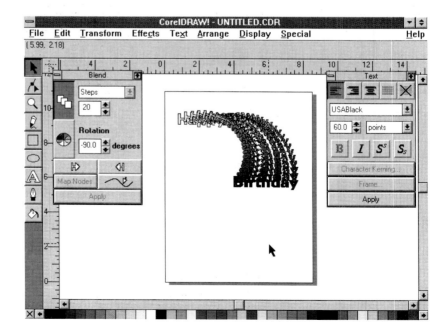

A blended arc created with –90 degrees of rotation
Figure 16–14.

16

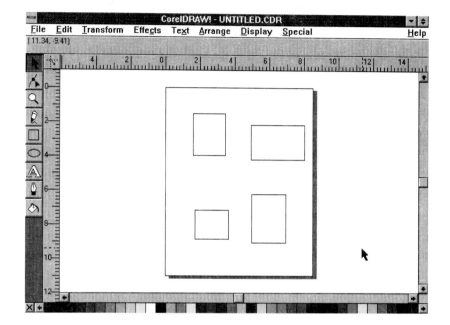

Placement of
rectangles on
the page
Figure 16–15.

rectangles are unfilled. Click on the X in the bottom-left corner of
your screen for no fill.

3. Press ⟨Spacebar⟩ for the Pick tool and marquee-select the two
rectangles on the left.

4. In the Blend roll-up window, click on the Map Nodes button.
Enter 20 Blend steps and 90 (positive) degrees of rotation. The
pointer will become an arrow and one of the selected objects will
have nodes displayed on each corner.

5. Select the upper-left corner node by moving the arrow to that
node and clicking on it. The second object's nodes will be
displayed.

6. Select its upper-left corner node by moving the arrow to that node
and clicking on it.

7. Click on Apply in the Blend roll-up.

You will now see one result of Map Matching Nodes.

8. Marquee-select the second two objects.

9. Click on Map Nodes in the Blend roll-up.

10. With the arrow, click on the lower-right node of the first object.

11. Click on the upper-left node of the second object and click on Apply in the Blend roll-up. The blend will occur as in Figure 16–16.

You can continue to experiment with Map Nodes, adding a different degree of rotation if you want to see its effects. When you are finished, you can look at the last major feature found on the Effects menu the Extrude feature.

Extruding Objects

Extruded objects appear to have depth. You can use the Extrude feature on text, closed shapes, or open paths. The results can be very dramatic.

There are three ingredients to the Extrude feature that affect the results: the depth and direction of the extrusion, the spatial alignment of the extruded object, and the shading and coloring of the extruded object. Each of these will be investigated separately.

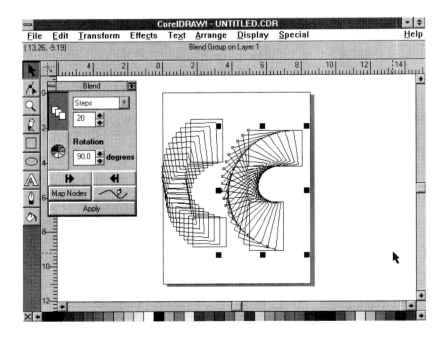

Examples of blends with two types of Map Nodes

Figure 16–16.

16

First you will create the objects to be extruded.

1. Renew the screen by selecting New from the File menu. Click on No. Also, close the Blend roll-up.
2. Click on the Text tool and click in the upper-left quadrant of the page.
3. Type **T**, select the letter, and from the Text roll-up, select 120 points, and select Nebraska font. Click on Apply.
4. Re-select the Text tool, and click to the right of the first T (Figure 16–17 shows the placement of the items). Repeat step 3.
5. Repeat these steps a third time below the first T.
6. Click on the Pencil tool and draw a wavy line in the lower part of the page. Your screen should look something like Figure 16–17.

Now you are ready to experiment with extruding.

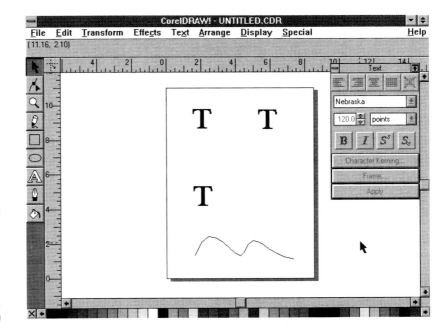

Placement of objects for experimenting with the Extrude feature
Figure 16–17.

Extrude Roll-Up Window

Extruding is controlled by the Extrude roll-up window, which you open
from the Effects menu. The Extrude roll-up opens in its depth and
direction mode which you can see here:

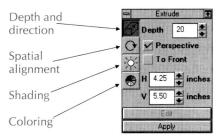

Depth and
direction

Spatial
alignment

Shading

Coloring

The depth and direction mode is one of four modes that the Extrude
roll-up can be in. These modes, which are activated by the four buttons
on the upper left of the roll-up, perform the following functions:

✦ Depth and direction allows you to determine the depth of the
   extrusion, the location of the vanishing point, whether the
   vanishing point is in front of or behind the object, and whether the
   extrusion is in a perspective or orthogonal (parallel) view.

✦ Spatial alignment allows you to rotate the extruded object in any of
   three dimensions.

✦ Shading allows you to determine the location of the light source
   and its intensity.

✦ Coloring allows you to determine if the extruded object will use the
   same coloring as the original object, or whether the extruded
   portion and its shading should be different (and what those
   different colors should be).

Selecting these modes significantly changes the options available in the
Extrude roll-up, as you will see in the following sections.

Depth and Direction

Depth and direction is the default mode for the Extrude roll-up
window—the window automatically opens in this mode. Should you be

16

in another mode and want to return to this mode, you can do so by clicking on the depth icon in the upper-left of the Extrude roll-up.

Examine the Extrude roll-up window now by following these instructions:

1. With the Pick tool, click on the topmost *T* to select it.
2. From the Effects menu, choose Extrude roll-up.

The Extrude roll-up will open, as you can see in Figure 16–18. When it does, the selected *T* is placed in Edit mode.(You can tell it's in Edit mode because of the wireframe that extends behind the letter. The wireframe shows where the eventual extrusion will go.) Had you not selected the T before opening the Extrude roll-up, you could have selected it afterwards and then clicked on the Edit button near the bottom of the Extrude roll-up.

There are four sets of controls in the Extrude roll-up when it is in depth and direction mode. At the top there is the Depth counter that controls

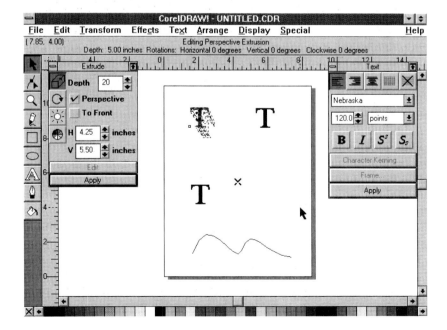

The Extrude roll-up with the selected T in Edit mode
Figure 16–18.

the depth of the extrusion. Below it is a check box for type of extrusion: perspective (if checked) or parallel (if not checked). The next check box lets you move the vanishing point in front of the object (if checked), or leave it behind the object (the default). Finally, there are horizontal and vertical counters that let you move the vanishing point from its default at the center of the page.

Perspective and Parallel Extrusions

You normally see an extrusion in a perspective view—it gets smaller as it extends away from you. Therefore, the Perspective checkbox is checked by default. If you turn off this checkbox, the extrusion will be orthogonal, meaning that the lines forming the extrusion will be parallel to each other. See this for yourself with this exercise:

1. Click on Apply in the Extrude roll-up. The wireframe behind the T on the left is filled in to form a short extrusion, which narrows as it extends toward the center of the page—it is in a perspective view with a centered vanishing point, as you can see here:

2. Click on the right-hand *T*, deselect on the Perspective check box in the Extrude roll-up, and click on Apply. An extrusion is created behind the *T*, extending undiminished all the way to the center of the page—it is very obviously not in perspective, as shown here:

Changing the Depth

The Depth counter is available only if you are working with an extrusion in perspective, and it determines how far toward the vanishing point the extrusion extends. You can think of this counter number as the percentage of the distance between the object and the

16

vanishing point that is occupied by the extrusion. The depth counter can go from –99 to 99. Negative numbers mean that the extrusion extends away from the vanishing point, while positive numbers are toward the vanishing point. A value of 99 makes the extrusion extend all the way to the vanishing point, and a value of 0 creates no extrusion. A value of 0 is not a valid entry.

Reselect the *T* on the left (it must be in perspective) and change the depth with these steps:

1. With the Pick tool, click on the left-hand *T* to select it.

2. Click on the Edit button in the Extrude roll-up. This is not necessary to change the depth, but it will allow you to see the wireframe of the extrusion as it is changed.

3. Click on the up arrow of the Depth counter to increase the depth to 70. As you are doing this you will see the wireframe extending toward the center of the page.

4. When the depth is at 70, click on Apply. A new extrusion will appear, as shown in Figure 16–19.

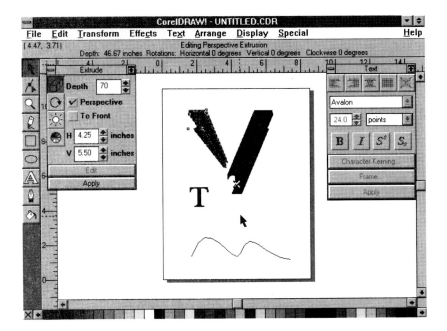

Original extrusion with Depth changed to 70
Figure 16–19.

5. Drag across the Depth counter's numeric entry box and type –40. Click on Apply. The extrusion now extends in front of the object—a negative extrusion, as you can see here:

Making the Vanishing Point the "Front"

The To Front checkbox allows you to change the order of the extrusion. Normally, the object is in front (closest to the viewer) with the extrusion behind it and the vanishing point furthest back. When checked, the To Front check box changes this order to place the vanishing point "in front" (without actually moving it on the page), the object next, and the extrusion last and closest to the viewer. The extrusion, then, increases in size as it moves away from the object and toward the viewer. See the results of turning on To Front with this exercise:

1. Drag across the –40 in the Depth counter, type **40**, and click on Apply to change the depth and display the result.

2. Click on To Font and again on Apply. The result is shown here:

The result is very subtle. The object (the original letter *T*)—the "face" of the extrusion—has moved to the other end of the extrusion, toward the vanishing point. In a normal view, you are "in front" and the vanishing point is away from you. With To Front checked, the vanishing point, which hasn't changed on the page, is now the "front," and you are in the "back."

3. Click on To Front to deselect the Check box, then click on Apply to change back to a normal view.

Moving the Vanishing Point

You can move the vanishing point on the page in two ways: by adjusting the Horizontal and Vertical counters in the Extrude roll-up, or by using the mouse to drag the X that indicates the vanishing point. Try both techniques:

1. The T on the left should be selected, with the depth set to 40, and To Front not checked.

2. Change the Horizontal and Vertical counters in the Extrude roll-up so they both have a value of 6.5. You can do this either by clicking on the up arrows, or by dragging across the numbers and typing the new value. Click on Apply.

By moving the vanishing point, you've made the extrusion shift to follow it, as you can see in Figure 16–20. If you rotate the vanishing point around the object, the extrusion will also rotate. If you move the vanishing point away from the object, the extrusion will extend out

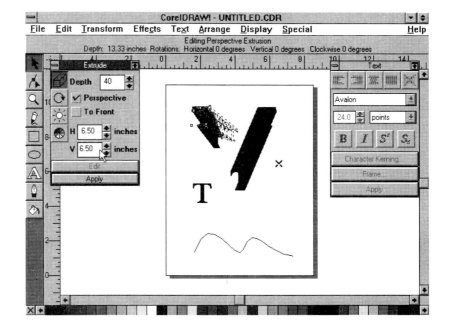

Moving the vanishing point with the counters
Figure 16–20.

following the vanishing point (although the depth value doesn't change—it is a percentage, so it merely re-scales the extrusion).

3. Drag the vanishing point to the upper-right corner of the page. Again, the extrusion will follow, as shown here:

Clearing an Extrusion

It you have an extrusion that you want to remove without getting rid of the original object, you cannot just press Del, which would get rid of everything, including the object. You must use the Clear Extrusion option in the Effects menu.

1. Click on the extruded *T* on the right. Press Del, and the entire object and extrusion is removed from the page.

2. Click on the extruded *T* on the left. From the Effects menu, choose Clear Extrude. The extrusion is removed, leaving the original selected object.

3. Press on Del to also remove that letter, and get ready for the next exercise.

Spatial Alignment

The second mode in which you can place the Extrude roll-up is spatial alignment. You change to spatial alignment mode by clicking on the second button in the left column of the Extrude roll-up. Try that now, and the Extrude roll-up will change to include the 3-D rotator that you see here:

The 3-D rotator has six arrows that allow you to move the currently selected object in any of six directions—two in each of three planes. When you click on an arrow, the object is rotated five degrees in the direction of the arrow. In the center of the sphere is an X button that allows you to clear the current rotation. The 3-D rotator does not change the vanishing point, only the object and its extrusion. Try the 3-D rotator now with this exercise:

1. Click on the remaining *T* to select it, and click on Apply from the Extrude roll-up window to create an extrusion. This also places the selected object into edit mode.

2. Click several times on the upward-pointing arrow above the X on the sphere. The wireframe representing the extrusion will rotate upward—the face of the extrusion, the original letter, moves up, while the other end of the extrusion moves down, as you can see here:

3. Click on Apply to fill in the wireframe and complete the rotation.

4. Click on the X in the center of the sphere, and then click on Apply to remove the rotation and return the extrusion to its original position.

5. Click several times on each of the arrows on the rotator to observe their behavior. Click on the center X after each, to return the extrusion to its original position.

With the 3-D rotator, you can look at the extruded object from literally any angle.

Shading and Coloring

You may have noticed both on your screen and in the figures and illustrations in this part of the chapter, that the extruded surfaces were hard to see, and the extruded effect therefore was not very clear. The reason for this was that both the original letter and the extrusion were black, and so there was no differentiation between them. You can change this by altering the shading and coloring of the extrusion. The last two modes, and the last two buttons on the left of the roll-up window, provide this capability. Try them now, starting with the remaining *T* selected:

1. Click on the color wheel icon to place the Extrude roll-up window in coloring mode. The roll-up's appearance will change, as you can see here:

The default coloring scheme is Use Object Fill. In other words, the object's fill color is used as the color for the extrusion. This is why both are presently black.

2. Click on Solid Fill to make the extrusion a solid (not shaded) color that is independent from the original object.

3. Click on the color button just under, and to the right of, Solid Fill. The current color palette will open. Click on the second gray from the right in the second row, and click on Apply.

The extruded object now has clear differentiation, as shown here:

16

This two-color scheme is nice, but you can improve on it with shading. When you select the Shade option, you can specify a range between two colors or shades for the extrusion. You will get a linear fountain fill along the extrusion, with the From color nearest to the original object, and the To color at the vanishing point.

4. Click on Shade to give the extrusion a shaded fill.

5. Click on the From color button, and select the same gray you chose above. Then click on the To color button, and choose the middle black in the top row of the palette. Click on Apply. The extrusion changes to this:

To give your extrusion even more life, you can put a spotlight on it and change the location of that light.

6. Click on the third button in the left column of the Extrude roll-up window. The Extrude roll-up changes once more, this time to include a device for setting the light source, a slider to control the intensity, and an On/Off switch:

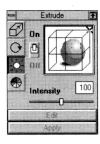

7. Click the On/Off switch to turn the light source on. Then click on the upper-left corner of the wireframe around the sphere to place

the light source (represented by the X) there. Next, drag the intensity control to 150.

8. Click on Apply. The extrusion will be redrawn like this:

Now you will experiment briefly with how an open path can be used **in** a creative way with extrusions.

Applying Extrusions to Open Paths

Open paths can be used to create some interesting effects with extrusions. In this case you will create a ribbon from your wavy line.

1. Click on the wavy line to select it.
2. Click on the color wheel in the Extrude roll-up. Then click on Shade, if it isn't selected. Make the From color a black, and the To color a gray. Click on Apply. Your wavy line will change to a shaded ribbon, like this:

When you are finished, leave CorelDRAW without saving your test files. They can easily be created again.

You can see that the Effects menu offers many dramatic ways to enhance your text and drawings. Chapter 19 introduces more special effects that you can use with CorelDRAW!, and combines many of the other features you've learned about CorelDRAW!.

C H A P T E R

17

COMBINING COREL DRAW! FEATURES

The previous chapters in this book concentrated on teaching you a specific set of skills. The key word is concentrated, *for the exercises throughout the book built on skills you had already learned, even as you mastered new ones.*

This chapter, however, takes a different approach. It assumes that you have mastered all of the basic skills in CorelDRAW! and are ready to explore applications that combine many different techniques. In this chapter you will find ideas, and perhaps some of these ideas may inspire you in your own work. However, you will not find a comprehensive catalog of every possible technique or special effect of which CorelDRAW! is capable. The three major exercises that make up this chapter feature text in the sample illustrations, because no other software for the PC allows you to turn text into word pictures as magnificently as CorelDRAW!.

This chapter is composed of three major sections, each containing one exercise in designing a graphic. The title of each section describes the graphic; the introduction to each exercise describes briefly the main CorelDRAW! techniques that help you create the graphic. If you need to review certain techniques, you can refer back to the chapter or chapters that first introduced these skills. Bon voyage!

Integrating Clip Art and Line Art

In the following exercise, you will design a poster that integrates a clip art image with line art—in this case, text. You can use this exercise to review text editing, stretch and scale, and outline and fill techniques (Chapters 4, 7, 9, 11, 12, and 15). Since the poster format is 11 inches by 17 inches, you also can brush up on the page setup, printing, and tiling skills you learned in Chapter 15. The end result of your exercise should look similar to Figure 17–7.

NOTE: The instructions that follow assume that you are using CorelDRAW! version 2.0 or later. If you have an earlier version of CorelDRAW!, you cannot perform this exercise exactly as written. However, you can import another image and try your hand at merging it with the text described here.

To create the poster:

1. Starting with a blank screen, turn on the Show Rulers command in the Display menu. Also make sure both the Edit Wireframe and the Snap To Grid options are turned off for this exercise.

2. From your CELEBRAT clip art directory, double-click on the HAT066.CDR file to open it.

3. Select Page Setup from the File menu, select Tabloid (11x17), assure that Portrait is selected, and click on OK. In the Grid Setup dialog box reached from the Display menu, type **17** in the vertical grid origin numeric box to move the vertical zero point to the top of the page, and click on OK to return to the drawing.

4. Drag two horizontal guidelines down to 4 inches and 11 inches on the vertical ruler and drag a vertical guideline to 4 1/2 inches on the horizontal ruler.

5. Drag the hat image up and to the right until the upper-right corner of the dotted frame that forms when you drag the object is in the upper-right corner formed by the guidelines and the page edge. Drag the lower-left boundary marker until the bottom edge of the boundary marker is at 11 inches vertical. Your screen at this point should look like Figure 17–1.

6. Save and name the image. Select Save As from the File menu, and type **dance** in the file text box. Then press Enter or click on the OK command button to save the file and return to the CorelDRAW! screen.

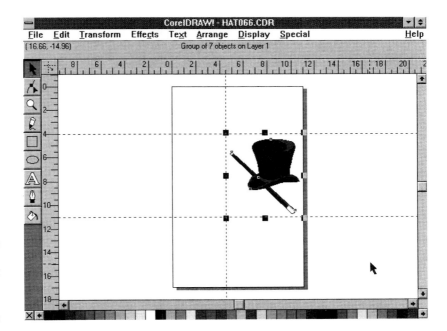

Incorporating a piece of clip art into a poster
Figure 17–1.

17

7. Select the Zoom-In tool from the Magnification tool fly-out menu, and magnify just the part of the page to the left of the hat.

8. Activate the Text tool and select an insertion point at 6 inches vertically and 2.25 inches horizontally. Type **8th** and then activate the Pick tool. Open the Text roll-up and set text attributes to Center Justification, Paragon Normal, 250.0 points. Click on Apply. The text re-appears at the insertion point.

9. Move the text to the position shown in Figure 17–2. Press Ctrl-S to save the changes you have made to the file.

10. With the text string still selected, click on the Outline tool and then on the Custom Outline Pen icon in the fly-out menu. The settings for this text string should be: Black Color, Width 0.01 inches, solid line style, sharp Corners, butt Line Caps, Stretch 100%, and Angle 0 degrees. Both the Behind Fill and Scale With Image options should be inactive. Click on the OK command button to save these settings for the text.

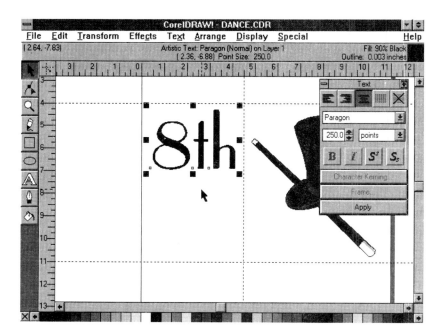

Moving "8th" into position
Figure 17–2.

11. Click on the Fill tool and then on the 50% gray icon in the fly-out menu. This is the third icon from the right in the second row. The screen shows the change in the fill color of the text. Since the outline of the text is black, however, the word stands out. Save your changes by pressing ⌷Ctrl⌷-⌷S⌷.

12. Activate the Text tool again and select another insertion point at 9.5 inches vertically and 2.25 inches horizontally. Type **Annual** and activate the Pick tool. In the Text roll-up, set text attributes to Center Justification, Paragon Normal, 125.0 points, and click on Apply.

13. Move "Annual" to the location shown in Figure 17–3.

14. With the "Annual" text string still selected, Choose Copy Style From in the Edit menu. In the Copy Style dialog box, check the boxes for Outline Pen, Outline Color, and Fill, but not Text Attributes. Click on OK. The From? pointer will appear. Click it on the "8th" text string you entered earlier.

17

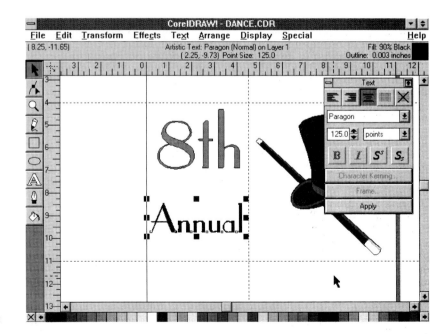

Moving "Annual" into position beneath "8th"
Figure 17–3.

15. Scroll your screen so you can see the bottom 1/3 of the poster. Also, roll up the Text roll-up window.

16. Activate the Text tool once more and select a third insertion point at 12.5 inches vertically and 5.5 inches horizontally. Type **DINNER-DANCE** and press Ctrl-T to open the Artistic Text dialog box. Set text attributes to Center Justification, Paragon Normal, 100 points. Click on the Spacing command button and set Inter-Character spacing to 10% and Inter-Word spacing to 120%, and then select OK twice. The text string re-appears at the insertion point.

17. Activate the Pick tool to select the text automatically. Move this text string to the position shown in Figure 17–4.

18. With the "DINNER-DANCE" text string still selected, click on the Copy Style From command in the Edit menu. Activate only the Outline Pen, Outline Color, and Fill checkboxes, and then select OK. When the From? pointer appears, click on the "Annual" text string to copy its outline and fill attributes to the currently selected

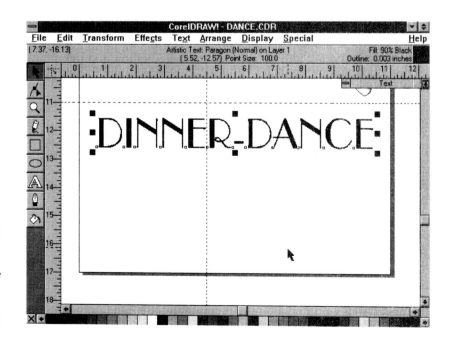

Aligning "Masked Ball" with the handle of the mask

Figure 17–4.

text string. Make certain to click on the *outline* of the object from which you want to copy the style, or you will see an error message.

19. Activate the Text tool once more and select another insertion point at 14 inches vertically and 2 inches horizontally. Type **Olympic Hotel 7pm**, press ⌷Enter⌷, and then type **Saturday, July 25th**. Press ⌷Ctrl⌷-⌷T⌷ to open the Artistic Text dialog box. Set text attributes to Center Justification, Paragon Normal, 100 points. Click on the Spacing command button and set Inter-Character spacing to 10%, Inter-Word spacing to 110%, Inter-Line spacing to 110%, and then select OK twice to display the text.

20. Activate the Pick tool to select the new text string automatically. Move this text string to the position shown in Figure 17–5.

21. With "Olympic Hotel..." still selected, choose Copy Style From in the Edit menu. Make sure Outline Pen, Outline Color, and Fill are turned on, and Text Attributes is turned off, and then click on OK. The From? pointer will appear. Click it on the "Dinner-Dance" you entered earlier.

17

Moving "Presented By:" into position
Figure 17–5.

22. Scroll your screen so you can see the top third of it.

23. Activate the Text tool once more, and select an insertion point at 5.5 inches horizontally and 1 inch vertically. Type **SEATTLE** on the first line of the text entry window, then press Enter and type **SYMPHONY** on the second line. Press Ctrl-T to open the Artistic Text dialog box. Set text attributes to Center Justification, Paragon Normal, 130 points. Click on the Spacing command button. Set Inter-Character spacing to 10% and Inter-Line spacing to 110% of point size, and then select OK twice.

24. Activate the Pick tool to select the new text string automatically. Drag the text string to the position shown in Figure 17–6.

25. Click on the Fill tool and then on the 90% Black Fill icon on the far right to fill the selected text with 90% black.

26. Click on the Magnification tool and again on the Show Page icon and then press Ctrl-S to save your changes. Select Full Screen Preview F9. Your final poster should look like Figure 17–7.

27. Select New from the File menu to clear the screen.

Aligning
SEATTLE
SYMPHONY
Figure 17–6.

SEATTLE
SYMPHONY
8th
Annual

DINNER-DANCE

Olympic Hotel 7pm
Saturday, July 25th

The completed
poster
Figure 17–7.

You may choose to print this oversize poster on your own printer. If you do, be sure to activate the Tile option in the Print Options dialog box. This will result in your poster being printed on four separate sheets, each containing one quarter of the graphic. If your printer does not have enough memory to print this graphic at 11-by-17 inches, try scaling the image down. Then, change the page size to 8 1/2-by-11 inches, using the Page Setup command in the File menu.

To add to your CorelDRAW! applications gallery, continue with the next exercise. There, you will create a color design that takes advantage of the CorelDRAW! features that fit text to a path and mirror images.

Fitting Text to a Path

If you have followed this book from the first chapter onward, you have learned nearly every available CorelDRAW! drawing technique. One important (and very creative) technique remains: fitting text to a path using the Fit Text To Path command in the Text menu. You can cause a text string to follow the outline of *any* object, be it a circle or an ellipse, a rectangle or a square, a line, a curve, a complex curved object, or even another letter that has been converted to curves.

Once you have fitted text to an object, you can delete that object without causing the text to lose its newly acquired shape. If you edit text attributes later, however, the text may change its alignment. You can remedy this simply by fitting text to the same path again. You can also make the curve object transparent by selecting the X (none) icon for both the object's outline and its fill.

Fit Text To Path Roll-Up

Beginning with CorelDRAW! 3, fitting text to a path is controlled by a roll-up window. This is a significant improvement over version 2.x, which used a less interactive (and less flexible) method.

You open the Fit Text To Path roll-up by selecting Fit Text To Path from the Text menu. There are actually two Fit Text To Path roll-up windows, depending on whether you are fitting text to an open line or open curve, or to a closed rectangle or ellipse. If you are fitting text to an open line or curve, the roll-up is shown on the left below. If you are fitting text to a closed rectangle or ellipse, the roll-up is shown on the right.

The top two roll-up windows share two drop-down list boxes. The list box at the top of the roll-up lets you determine the orientation of the text, while the second list box lets you select the distance that the text will sit above or below the path of the object. Also, both roll-ups have a check box for moving the text to the opposite side of the path. The difference in the two roll-ups is in how to align the text on the object. For an open object, you have a drop-down list of alignment possibilities, whereas closed objects have a four-sided button to set their alignment. Each of these elements will be discussed in the next several sections. Figure 17–8 shows several examples of fitting text to a path that will be referred to in these sections.

The Orientation of the Text

The orientation of the text is its degree of rotation, or skew, as it follows the path it is fitted to. There are four options for orientation in the drop-down list. Most of the examples in Figure 17–8 show the first (default) orientation; in this orientation, the letters rotate to follow the path. Figure 17–8f shows the second orientation, Figure 17–8e shows the third, and Figure 17–8g shows the fourth orientation.

The Distance of the Text from the Path

The second drop-down list box offers five alternative settings for the text's distance from its path. Figure 17–8a and 8f show the first alternative, in which the text sits right on the path (the baseline of the

a.

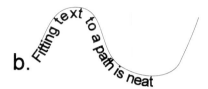

b.

c.

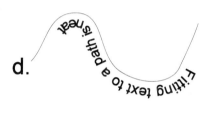

d.

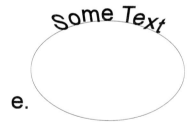

e.

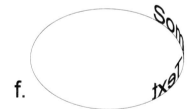

f.

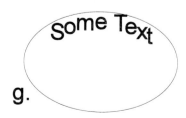

g.

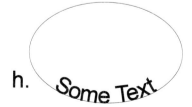

h.

Examples of
fitting text to a
path
Figure 17–8.

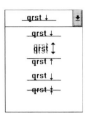

text is on the path, and the descenders are beneath it). Figure 17–8b and 8g show the third alternative: the text sits underneath the path. Figure 17–8e and 8h show the fourth alternative, in which the text sits slightly above the path (only the descenders are on the path). Figure 17–8c shows the fifth alternative (the path going through the text). Figure 17–8d shows the second alternative, in which the text can be pulled away from the path either with the mouse or with the Fit Text To Path Offsets dialog box shown here:

Aligning the Text on the Path

For open paths, the third drop-down list box provides three alternatives for aligning text on a path. Figure 17–8b shows the first alternative, in which the text is aligned with the left end of the path. Figure 17–8a and 8d show the second alternative, in which the text is centered on the path, and Figure 17-8c shows the third alternative, in which the text is aligned with right end of the path.

For closed-path rectangles and ellipses, the text is aligned to the middle of one of four sides, by clicking on the corresponding side of the four-sided button that is displayed. The text is rotated as it is moved to the right, bottom, or left side. It is, therefore, upside-down on the bottom. If you want to flip the text to the other side of the path, click on the Place on other side check box in the Fit Text To Path roll-up. Figure 17–8g and 17-8h have this box checked.

Using Fit Text to Path

In the following exercise, you will design a stylized "rainbow" image that consists of a series of scaled and aligned wedges. You will then fit the word "Rainbow" to a curve, combine the text string with a background object to create a mask, and overlay the transparent letters on the rainbow colors. The result after stretching and mirroring the mask and rainbow is shown in Figure 17–18. If you have a color monitor, your results will appear more vivid than the one shown in the figures. If you have a black-and-white display adapter and monitor, you can achieve a similar "rainbow" effect by filling the wedges with the gray shades indicated in parentheses in the following steps.

1. Starting with a blank screen, select Page Setup from the File menu. When the Page Setup dialog box appears, click on the Landscape and Letter option buttons, and then select OK. This results in a page that is 11 inches wide and 8 1/2 inches high.

2. To prepare the CorelDRAW! screen for the exercise, activate the Show Rulers and Edit Wireframe commands. Make sure that Snap To Grid is activated, that the Vertical Grid Origin is set to 8.5 inches and that both Horizontal and Vertical Grid Frequency are set to 8 per inch.

3. Set new outline and fill defaults so that all of the objects you draw will be standardized. First, click on the Outline tool and again on the X (for none) icon in the first row of the fly-out menu. The Outline Pen for New Object dialog box appears, asking whether you want to define outline pen settings for objects you haven't drawn yet. Select OK to set no outline as the new default for all objects.

4. Click on the Fill tool and then on the black fill icon. The Uniform Fill for New Object dialog box appears, asking whether you want to define fill colors for objects you haven't drawn yet. Select OK to define a default fill color of black for all new objects.

5. Activate the Ellipse tool, then position the pointer at the 3 1/4-inch mark on the horizontal ruler and the 6 1/2-inch mark on the vertical ruler. Press and hold (Ctrl)-(Shift) and drag the mouse downward and to the right until the status line shows a width and height of 3 inches. As you may recall from Chapter 4, the use of (Ctrl) and (Shift) together results in a circle drawn from the center outward. When you release the mouse button, the circle appears with the node at the top, as shown in Figure 17–9a.

6. Create a 90-degree wedge from this circle, as you learned to do in Chapter 8. Activate the Shaping tool and position the Shaping pointer at the node of the circle. To turn the circle into a pie wedge, press and hold (Ctrl) and drag the node in a clockwise direction until you reach the 9 o'clock position (90 degrees on the status line). (Hold the tip of the Shaping pointer *inside* the rim of the circle as you drag, or you will see an open arc instead of a

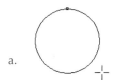
a.

b.

17

Creating a pie
wedge from a
circle and
rotating it
Figure 17–9.

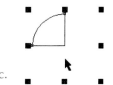
c.

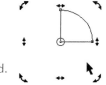
d.

wedge.) Release the mouse button when you reach the 9 o'clock position. The wedge appears, as in Figure 17–9b.

7. Activate the Pick tool to select the wedge automatically. Notice that the highlighting box is much larger than the wedge, just as in Figure 17–9c. CorelDRAW! continues to treat the wedge as though it were a full circle.

8. Click again on the outline of the wedge to enter rotate/skew mode. Position the pointer at the arrow markers in the upper-right corner, press and hold Ctrl, and rotate the wedge in a clockwise direction until the status line indicates an angle of –90 degrees. Remember to release the mouse button before you release Ctrl; otherwise, the wedge may not snap to the exact –90-degree angle. The curve of the wedge now faces upward and to the right, as shown in Figure 17–9d.

9. Click again on the wedge outline to return to stretch/scale mode. You are ready to increase the scale of the wedge and leave a copy of the original. Position the pointer at the boundary marker in the upper-right corner and scale the wedge upward and to the right, until the status line value reaches approximately 116.7%. When you reach the desired point, continue to hold the mouse button, but press the right mouse button or the + key on the numeric keypad to leave a copy of the original. Then, release the mouse button. The original wedge remains in position, and a scaled version overlays it, as in Figure 17–10.

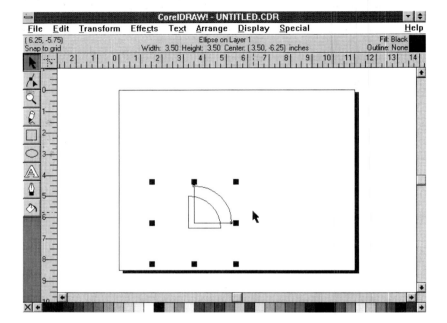

Scaling a
wedge and
leaving a copy
of the original
Figure 17–10.

10. Press [Ctrl]-[R] (the Repeat key combination) five times to create five additional wedges, each larger than the previous one. Your screen should show a total of seven wedges, resembling Figure 17–11.

11. Your next step is to align the wedges so that they form one-half of a rainbow. Click on the Select All command in the Edit menu to select all seven wedges, and then select the Align command in the Arrange menu. When the Align dialog box appears, click on both the Horizontally Center and Vertically Center option buttons, on the Align to Center of Page check box, and then select OK. The wedges realign with a common corner point in the center of the page, as shown in Figure 17–12.

12. With the seven wedges still selected, click on the Reverse Order command in the Arrange menu. You will not see a visible change at this point, but you have positioned the larger wedges in the back and the smaller wedges in the front. When you turn on the preview window later in the exercise and begin to assign fill colors to the wedges, you will see each wedge as a ribbon-like band.

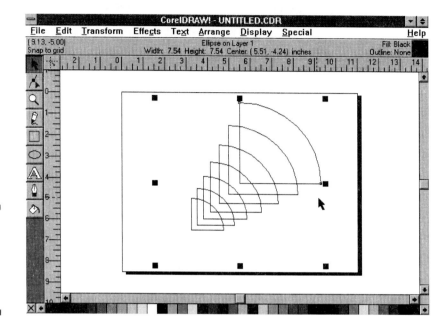

A series of scaled wedges created using the Repeat key combination
Figure 17–11.

17

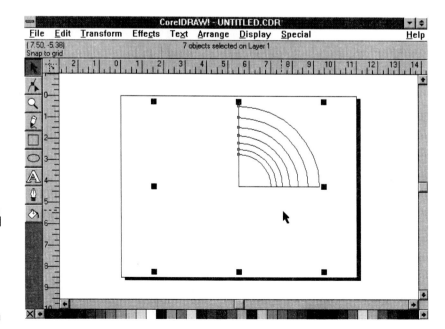

Wedges aligned using Horizontal and Vertical Center options
Figure 17–12.

13. Select the Save As command from the File menu. When the Save As dialog box appears, type **RAINBOW1**, and then press `Enter` or click on Save.

14. To design the other half of the rainbow, you simply create a horizontal mirror image of the currently selected image. Click on the Stretch & Mirror command in the Transform menu to access the Stretch & Mirror dialog box. Then activate both the Horz Mirror command button and the Leave Original checkbox, and then select OK. The mirror image of the seven wedges appears and fits tightly against the original group of wedges, as shown in Figure 17–13.

15. You can now begin to assign fill colors to the wedges of the "rainbow." Activate the Preview Selected Only command in the Display menu. Adjust magnification to fit-in-window by clicking on the fit-in-window icon in the Magnification tool fly-out menu.

16. Deselect all of the wedges by clicking on any white space. Then, select both the largest wedge on the left half of the "rainbow" and the smallest wedge on the right half. To select both of them, click on each of their curve outlines while holding `Shift`. The editing

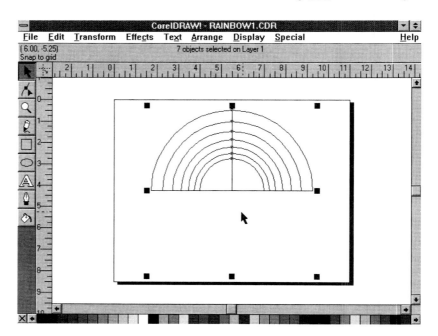

Original seven wedges with a horizontal mirror image
Figure 17–13.

window, shown in Figure 17–14a looks as though all of the wedges were selected, because the highlighting box of the largest wedge surrounds all of the objects. However, the preview window, reached by pressing F9 and shown in Figure 17–14b, shows you that only two wedges are selected.

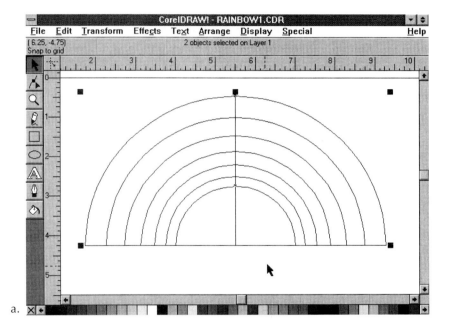

Selecting pairs of wedges in Wireframe (a.) and in Preview Selected Only (b.)
Figure 17–14.

17. With the two wedges selected, click on the Fill tool and again on the Uniform Fill icon. When the Uniform Fill dialog box displays, select Process color, CMYK as the Model, and set color values to 0% Cyan, 100% Magenta, 75% Yellow, and 10% Black. Select OK; the two opposite wedges now redisplay with a red fill, the hue of which varies depending on whether you have an EGA or VGA display adapter. (If you have a black-and-white monitor, set black to 80% and leave all other colors at 0%.)

18. Deselect the previous wedges. Then select the second-largest wedge on the left half of the "rainbow" and the second-smallest wedge on the right half, and then press Shift - F11 to access the Uniform Fill dialog box once more. If you have a color monitor, set process color values to 0% Cyan, 60% Magenta and 100% Yellow, and 0% Black, and then select OK. The two wedges now show a bright orange fill. (If you have a black-and-white monitor, set black to 40% and leave all other colors at 0%.)

19. Continue in the same way with the next five pairs of wedges. If you have a color monitor, assign colors as follows: third pair, 100% yellow; fourth pair, 40% cyan and 60% yellow; fifth pair, 100% cyan, 40% yellow, and 20% black; sixth pair, 100% cyan, 100% magenta, and 10% black; seventh pair, 100% magenta and 50% black. Leave the colors not mentioned at 0%. Check your colors by pressing F9. (If you have a black-and-white monitor, assign 15% black to the third pair, 40% black to the fourth, 30% black to the fifth, 75% black to the sixth, and 100% black to the seventh.) When you are finished, turn off the Preview Selected Only feature and press F9. The two halves of the rainbow show an opposite sequence of colors, as you can see by the black-and-white representation in Figure 17–15.

20. Press F9 and click on the Select All command in the Edit menu to select all 14 wedges, and then apply the Group command from the Arrange menu. This prevents you from accidentally moving or editing an individual wedge apart from the group.

21. Click on the Show Page icon in the Magnification tool fly-out menu to display the full page.

22. Now you are ready to prepare the text that will eventually overlay the rainbow as a transparent mask. First, activate the Ellipse tool and position the drawing pointer at the 2 1/2-inch mark on the

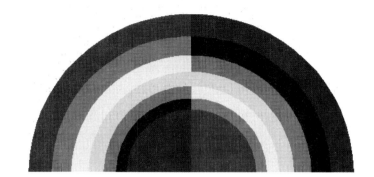

horizontal ruler and the 1-inch mark on the vertical ruler. Drag the
mouse downward and to the right and draw a circle 6 inches in
diameter. Remember to use Ctrl (but *not* Shift) to obtain a circle
rather than an ellipse. The circle overlays most of the "rainbow"
for now, but you will delete it when it has served its purpose.

23. Activate the Text tool and select an insertion point in any white
    space on the page. Type **Rainbow** and press Ctrl-T to open the
    Artistic Text dialog box. Set text attributes to Aardvark Bold, 105.0
    points, and a Justification of None. Click on the Spacing command
    button and set Inter-Character spacing to 10%, and then select OK
    twice to re-display the text on the page.

24. Activate the Pick tool to select the text string automatically. Use
    Shift to also select the circle you have just drawn. Then, press
    Ctrl-F or click on the Fit Text To Path command in the Arrange
    menu.

25. When the Fit Text To Path roll-up opens, make sure that all of the
    defaults in the roll-up are set: rotated text orientation (the top
    alternative in the top drop-down list); text sitting on the path (the
    first alternative in the second drop-down list); the top quadrant in
    the four-sided button; and Place on other side not checked. After
    verifying these settings, click on Apply. After a few seconds, the
    text appears right side up but on the circle, as shown in
    Figure 17–16.

26. Deselect the text to leave only the circle selected, and then press
    Del to delete the circle. The text retains its new shape.

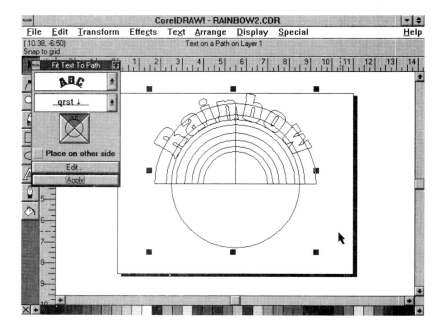

Fitting text to a
circle
Figure 17–16.

27. Click again on the outline of the text string to select it, and then fill the text with white by clicking on the Fill tool and again on the white icon in the second row of the fly-out menu.

28. Create the rectangle that will become the background of the mask. Activate the Rectangle tool and position the drawing pointer at the zero point on both the horizontal and vertical rulers. From this point, draw a rectangle 7 3/4 inches wide and 3 3/4 inches high, dragging downward and to the right.

29. Press the (Spacebar) to select the rectangle automatically. Give the rectangle a white fill by clicking on the Fill tool and then on the White icon in the fly-out menu. Make the edge of the rectangle also transparent by clicking on the Outline tool and again on the No Fill icon on the first row of the fly-out menu.

30. Select the text string and move it on top of the rectangle. Position it so that the bottom of the text string is 1/4 inch above the lower edge of the rectangle.

31. To center the text horizontally on the rectangle, select both objects, click on the Align command in the Arrange menu, and

17

choose the Horizontally Center option button. Select OK to leave the Alignment dialog box and redisplay the newly aligned objects.

32. With both the text and the rectangle still selected, move both objects into the empty space at the bottom of the page, out of the way of the rainbow wedges. Then, select the Reverse Order command from the Arrange menu to place the text behind the rectangle.

33. Press F9 to turn on Full Screen Preview. You cannot see the rectangle because it is white, and you cannot see the text because it has a white fill and is behind the rectangle. Press F9 again to return to the editing window and, with the text and rectangle both selected, click on the Combine command in the Arrange menu. When the two objects combine, their common area, the text, becomes transparent "holes" in the white rectangle.

34. Move the newly combined object back over the grouped rainbow wedges and align the bottom edge of the curve object with the bottom edge of the wedges.

35. Press F9 for Full Screen Preview. With the white rectangle invisible against the page, all you can see are the rainbow colors behind the transparent text string, as shown in Figure 17–17.

TIP: The object that is in the background when you combine two objects determines the fill color of the combined object. If you see white letters over a transparent rectangle, you forgot to place the text behind the rectangle. Select Undo from the Edit menu, use the Reverse Order command in the Arrange menu to bring the rectangle to the foreground, and then combine the two objects again.

36. Return to the editing window and then adjust viewing magnification to fit-in-window. Select both the combined object and the wedges and apply the Group command from the Arrange menu.

37. Create a mirror image of the grouped object. With the group still selected, click on the Stretch & Mirror command from the Transform menu. When the Stretch & Mirror dialog box appears, click on *both* the Horz Mirror and Vert Mirror command buttons, and make sure that a checkmark appears in the Leave Original

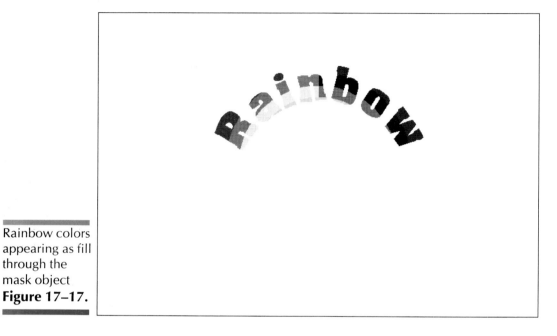

Rainbow colors
appearing as fill
through the
mask object
Figure 17–17.

checkbox. Select OK; an upside down and backwards version of the
"Rainbow" text displays beneath the original, as shown in the
full-screen preview in Figure 17–18. This object is selected
automatically in the editing window.

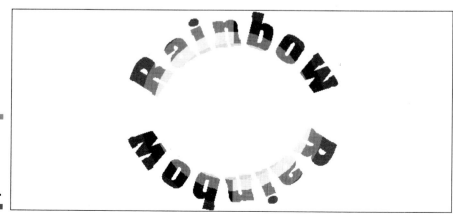

Rainbow with
vertically
flipped mirror
image
Figure 17–18.

38. Press Ctrl-S to save the changes to your work, and then select New from the File menu to clear your screen.

The main emphases in this last exercise have been on fitting text to a path, working with color effects, creating a mask, aligning objects, repeating operations, and creating mirror images. In the next and final sample application, you can achieve 3-D effects using fountain and contrasting fills, outlines, and repeated scalings.

Polishing Your Skills

The "FAX" image in Figure 17–25 has a vibrant, 3-D look; the graphic represents the power of facsimile to quite literally "broadcast" to the world. Several special effects techniques contribute to the dynamic quality of the image:

✦ Text fitted to a curve

✦ Text objects with drop shadows (shadows placed behind and offset from the original)

✦ A "globe" with an off-center radial fountain fill

✦ Repeated duplication and expansion of a text string

✦ Judicious use of contrasting fills

✦ Inclusion of a backdrop that makes the image seem to burst beyond its boundaries

You already have practiced the basic skills that make all of these special effects possible. In the exercise that follows, you will recreate this image, using the Leave Original and Repeat keys, fountain fill and node editing techniques, and the Duplicate, Fit Text To Path, Group, and Page Setup commands. For a review of shadow and fountain fill techniques, see Chapter 13.

1. Starting with a blank screen, select Page Setup from the File menu. When the Page Setup dialog box appears, make sure that Landscape and Letter options are still selected, and then select OK.

2. To prepare the CorelDRAW! screen for the exercise, activate the Snap To Grid command in the Display menu, select the Grid Setup

command, set both Horizontal and Vertical Grid Frequency to 8 per inch, and set the Vertical grid origin to 8.5 inches. Activate the Show Rulers and Edit Wireframe options as well.

3. Change the default outline type to a hairline by clicking on the Outline tool and then on the hairline icon in the first row of the fly-out menu. When the New Objects dialog box appears, click on All Objects and then on OK.

4. Change the default outline color to black by clicking on the Outline tool and then on the black icon in the second row of the fly-out menu. The New Objects dialog box appears; select All Objects and OK as you did in the previous step.

5. Create a small circle to which you will fit text. To do this, activate the Ellipse tool and position the crosshair pointer in the center of the page at 5.5 inches horizontal and 4.25 inches vertical. Press and hold Shift and Ctrl and draw a perfect circle 0.75 inches in diameter. When you complete the circle, remember to release the mouse button before you release Shift and Ctrl to ensure that you create a circle rather than an ellipse.

6. Now enter the text that you will fit to this circle. Activate the Text tool and select an insertion point about an inch above the circle. The exact location does not matter, because when you invoke the Fit Text To Path command later, the text will snap to the circle no matter where it is. Type FAX in all capital letters. Open the Artistic Text dialog box. Set text attributes to a justification of None, Frankfurt Gothic Heavy, Normal, 30.0 points. Click on OK to re-display the text on the page.

7. Press the spacebar to activate the Pick tool; the text string is selected automatically, since it was the last object you drew. While holding down Shift, select the circle as well.

8. With both objects selected, press Ctrl-F or click on the Fit Text To Path command in the Arrange menu. The Fit Text to Path roll-up will open, if it hasn't already. Accept the defaults and click on Apply. The text wraps around outside of the circle, centering itself at the top. The result is shown in Figure 17–19 (your image will be smaller).

9. Deselect the text string using Shift, and then press Del to delete the circle. The text remains curved, even though the circle is no longer there.

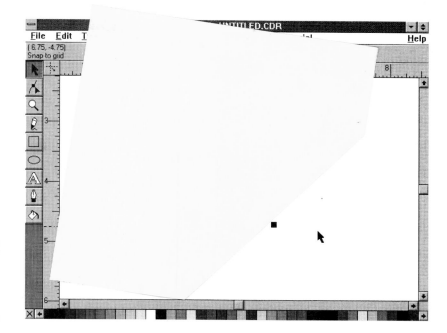

Magnified view
of text fitted to
a small circle
Figure 17–19.

10. Double-click on the text string to enter rotate/skew mode, and rotate the text by 45 degrees in a clockwise direction.

11. Move the text to the lower-left corner of the page approximately 1/2 inch from the bottom and left page edge.

12. Now you are ready to begin creating a text pattern. Turn off Snap to Grid and, with the Pick tool still active, position the pointer at the upper-right corner boundary marker of the text object and begin to scale the object from this point. As soon as the dotted outline box appears, click the right mouse button or press and release ⊞ on the numeric keypad (to leave a copy of the original). Continue scaling the text until the status line indicates a value of approximately 129%. Then, release the left mouse button. A larger-scaled version of the text string appears on top of, and offset from, the original. You can see the proportions more clearly if you temporarily change magnification to fit-in-window.

13. Select the Show Page icon from the Magnification tool fly-out menu to return to a full-page view. Then press Ctrl-R, the Repeat

key, ten times, to repeat the scaling and duplication of the text. Ten scaled replicas of the text string overlay one another, each one larger than the previous one. The last text string exceeds the boundaries of the page, as shown in Figure 17–20.

14. Leaving the most recently created text string selected, click on the Preferences command in the Special menu. Make certain that the Place Duplicate values are both at 0.25 inches, and then select OK. These values determine the placement of a duplicate object relative to the original.

15. Press Ctrl-D to create an exact duplicate of the top text string, offset 1/4 inch above and to the right of the original. The duplicate is selected as soon as it appears.

16. Press F9 for the preview window. All of the text strings appear with black fills. Press F9 again to return to the editing window and click on the Select All command in the Edit menu, and then on the Group command in the Arrange menu to group all of the text strings. Then, select the white fill icon in the Fill tool fly-out menu, and turn off Edit Wireframe. The text strings redisplay with

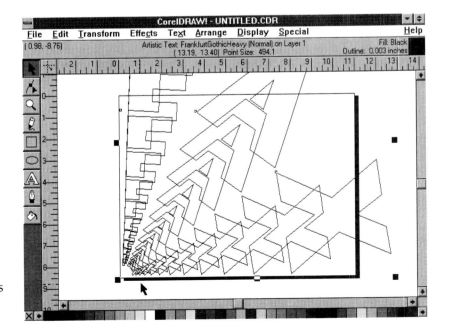

Scaled and repeated text strings exceeding the page boundaries **Figure 17–20.**

a fill of white, making it easier to distinguish them from one another.

17. With all text strings still selected, click on the Outline tool and then on the Custom Outline Pen icon to access the Outline Pen dialog box. Change the settings to Width 0.01 inch and turn on Scale With Image. Then select OK. The text strings redisplay with a medium outline of uniform width.

18. Ungroup and deselect all text strings, and then select only the last text string you created (the top). Click on the Fill tool and again on the Fountain Fill icon to access the Fountain Fill dialog box. Choose a linear fountain fill, and an angle of 45 degrees. For the From color, click on More, select Spot color, then Black at 0% Tint, and click on OK. Similarly, for the To color, click on More, select Spot color, and Black at 100% Tint, and click on OK. Click on OK again to make this fill pattern take effect.

19. Now create a drop-shadow effect. Press Tab to select the text string in the layer just below the text string with the fountain fill. Assign a fill of black to this object by clicking on the Black Fill icon on the far left of the palette at the bottom of your screen. Select the Zoom-Out icon from the Magnification fly-out menu to see your whole work. Figure 17–21 shows the result of your selection.

20. Continue pressing Tab to select each text string in the reverse order from which it was created. Fill the text strings in the following sequence, starting with the largest text string after the drop shadow: 90% black, 80% black, 70% black, 60% black, 50% black, 40% black, 30% black, 20% black, and 10% black. Fill one more text string with 10% black and the remaining (smallest) text strings with white. You can quickly apply these shades by using the color palette at the bottom of the screen, beginning with the second black from the left. The resulting gradation of fills and the drop shadow make the repeated text strings seem to leap out of the screen, as shown in Figure 17–22.

21. To group all text strings so that you cannot separate them accidentally, click on Select All in the Edit menu, and then on the Group command in the Arrange menu. Then, move the group upward and away from the left side of the page. You will bring the group back later, but for now you need room to create more objects.

17

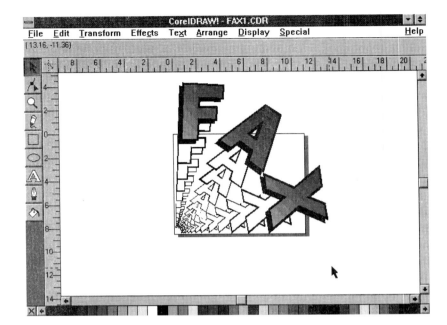

Drop-shadow effect using duplicated text and black fill
Figure 17–21.

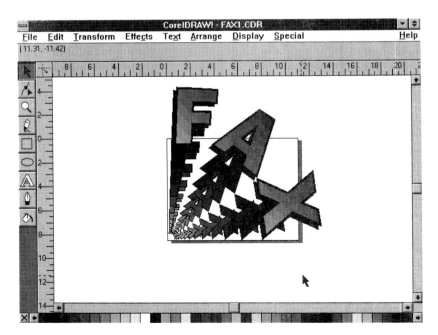

Gradation of fills, leading to a 3-D effect
Figure 17–22.

22. Activate the Ellipse tool and position the pointer 4 1/2 inches from the top of the page and 3/4 of an inch from the left margin. Press and hold ⌈Ctrl⌉ and draw a circle 3 inches in diameter, starting from the upper-left area of the rim. Use the status line as a guide.

23. Turn the circle into a 3-D globe by giving it a radial fountain fill. To do this, activate the Pick tool to select the circle automatically, and then click on the Fill tool and again on the Fountain Fill icon. When the Fountain Fill dialog box appears, use the More buttons to select the Spot method, change the From color to black (Black, Tint 100%) and the To color to white (Black, Tint 0%). Select a radial fountain fill, but leave the other settings unaltered. Select OK to make the fountain fill take effect. The globe reappears with a white highlight in the center and the fill gradually darkening toward the rim.

24. Prepare to create an off-center highlight so that the light source seems to be coming from above and to the right of the globe. Activate the Pencil tool and draw a short line segment above and to the right of the globe. Select both the line segment and the globe and click on the Combine command in the Arrange menu to combine these into one object. Redo the fountain fill by repeating step 23. Whenever the window redraws from now on, CorelDRAW! extends the first stage of the fountain fill as far as the line segment, as shown in Figure 17–23. This means that you can control the placement of the highlight on the globe by moving the nodes of the line segment with the Shaping tool.

25. If you wish to change the placement of the highlight on the globe, activate the Shaping tool and move the uppermost node of the line segment in a clockwise or counterclockwise direction. You can move either or both nodes; experiment until you find the placement you want.

26. Now, make the line segment invisible. Activate the Pick tool to select the combined object automatically, and then click on the Outline tool and again on the White Outline Fill icon in the second row of the fly-out menu. The line segment seems to disappear from the preview screen, but you can still use it to manipulate the highlight on the globe.

27. Create a rectangle that will form a backdrop for the rest of the image. Activate the Rectangle tool and begin a rectangle at the

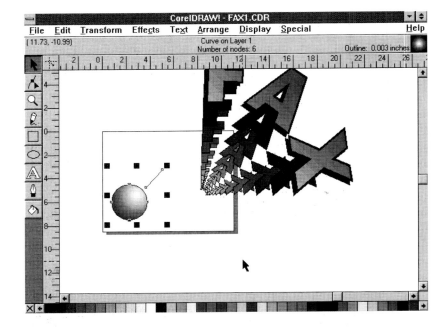

Changing the center of a radial fountain fill by combining line segment with globe
Figure 17–23.

1-inch mark on the horizontal ruler and the 1 1/2-inch mark on the vertical ruler. Extend the rectangle downward and to the right until you reach the 7 1/2-inch mark on the horizontal ruler and the 7 1/4-inch mark on the vertical ruler, and then release the mouse button. The window shows that this object lies on top of all the other objects, obscuring them from your view.

28. Activate the Pick tool to select the rectangle automatically, and then click on the To Back command in the Arrange menu. Now, the globe appears as the top layer.

29. With the Outline and Fill tools, assign a black outline of 2.0 fractional points, and a fill of 20% gray, to the rectangle.

30. To make the globe stand out in 3-D from the background, select it and assign an outline 0.01-inch wide, using the Outline Pen dialog box.

31. Select the FAX grouped text strings and move them on top of the globe, so that they seem to be emerging directly from the highlight. To make certain that the text strings are the top-layer

object, click on the To Front command. This also hides the line segment that you used as a "handle" to change the center of the globe's fountain fill as shown in Figure 17–24.

32. Adjust viewing magnification to fit-in-window by clicking on the fit-in-window icon in the Magnification tool fly-out menu. With the grouped object still selected, scale the text strings down until the status line displays a value of approximately 47%. Redo the fit-in-window magnification and select Full-Screen Preview. Thanks to the insertion of the background rectangle, the text strings still seem to thrust outward in 3-D, as shown in Figure 17–25.

33. Click on the Select All command in the Edit menu and then on the Group command in the Arrange menu to group all of the objects in the image.

34. Select Save As from the File menu. When the Save As dialog box appears, type **FAXTRANS**, and then press [Enter] or click on Save.

35. Select New from the File menu to clear the screen.

17

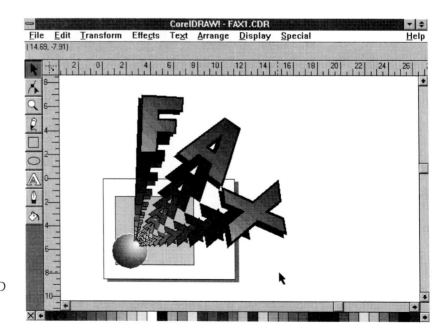

Grouped text strings overlaid on the globe highlight for 3-D
Figure 17–24.

"FAX" illustration using fountain fill, drop shadows, and a background frame to enhance 3-D effects
Figure 17–25.

If you have performed all three of the exercises in this chapter, you are well on the way to understanding how to combine many different CorelDRAW! features, tricks, and techniques. Perhaps these exercises have stimulated you to create your own original designs, or given you new ideas for embellishing existing ones. Whatever your field, your work in this tutorial has given you the tools to create more effective illustrations, documents, presentations, and designs. CorelDRAW! makes it all possible!

C H A P T E R

18

TRACING BITMAPPED IMAGES

In Chapter 14, you learned about the two types of graphics that you can import into CorelDRAW!: bitmapped images and object-oriented art. When you import an object-oriented image, you can edit it just as you would any picture created in CorelDRAW!. Bitmapped images, however, contain no objects for you to select; they consist entirely of a fixed number of tiny dots, called pixels. If you enlarge or reduce the size of the bitmap without converting it to a

617

CorelDRAW! object, distortion or unsightly compression of the pixels results. The solution is to *trace* the bitmap in CorelDRAW! and turn it into a curve object. You can then change the shape of its outline and the color of its fill, edit it normally, and print it, all without distortion. CorelDRAW! offers you three different methods for tracing an imported bitmap. The newest and most sophisticated of these is the CorelTRACE! batch autotracing utility, available with version 1.2 and later. You will be amazed at the speed and accuracy with which this product, similar to Adobe Streamline, can turn even the most complex bitmap into a finished curve object ready for editing. Turn to the section "Tracing with CorelTRACE!" to learn more about how to use this exciting feature.

If you have a version of CorelDRAW! earlier than 1.2, you can choose between manual tracing and the semiautomatic Autotrace feature. These methods are less rapid than the newer CorelTRACE! and require more work on the part of the user, but they offer you a high degree of control over the curves that result from your tracing.

Creating a Bitmapped Image

CorelDRAW! treats a bitmapped image as a unique object type, separate from other object types such as rectangles, ellipses, curves, and text. Unlike all of the other object types, bitmaps must be created outside of CorelDRAW!.

There are several ways to secure a bitmapped image for importing into CorelDRAW!. The easiest method is to import a finished clip-art image or a sample file having either a .PCX, .TIF, or .BMP extension (see Chapter 14). The next easiest method is to scan an existing image from a print source, such as a newspaper or magazine. Alternatively, you can sketch a drawing by hand, and then scan the image in .PCX or .TIF format. Finally, you can create your own original pixel-based images with CorelPhoto-Paint!.

Once the bitmapped image is available, you are ready to import it into CorelDRAW!. You will practice importing bitmapped images in the next section.

Importing a Bitmapped Image

You may recall from Chapter 14 that CorelDRAW! accepts three bitmapped file formats for import: .PCX, .TIF, and .BMP. The .PCX format is native to the ZSoft PC Paintbrush and Publisher's Paintbrush family of paint software and also used in CorelPHOTO-PAINT!, the .TIF format is the one that most scanners support, and .BMP is the Windows Paint file format. If the bitmap you want to import is in another format, you can convert it to .PCX or .TIF using an image conversion program such as Inset Graphics' Hijaak or Symsoft's HotShot Graphics.

To import a bitmap, you use the Import command in the File menu and select the appropriate bitmap file format in the Import dialog box.

The standard CorelDRAW! package includes several .TIF sample files in the Sample directory. In the following exercise, you will import one of the sample .TIF files.

18

1. Starting with a blank CorelDRAW! screen, open the Display menu and make sure that Show Rulers and Edit Wireframe are turned off. With Edit Wireframe off, the Show Bitmaps option is automatically dimmed. Show Bitmaps is only active when editing in Wireframe.

2. Select the Page Setup command from the File menu and make certain that the page is set for Portrait format and that the Page size is Letter. Click on the OK command button to save this setting.

3. Select the Import command from the File menu. The Import dialog box appears.

4. Open the List Files of Type drop-down list box and select TIFF 5.0 Bitmap.

5. In the Directories box, specify the drive and directory that contains the CorelDRAW! sample files. (If you have not installed or used the sample files, see Appendix A.)

6. To open the OUT_PLAY.TIF file, double-click on the filename in the Files list box, or highlight the filename and click on OK. After a few seconds, the image appears, centered on the page and surrounded by a selection box, as shown in Figure 18–1. The status line displays the message "Bitmap on Layer 1."

7. Select the Save As command from the File menu. When the Save As dialog box appears, change the directory to the one in which you save your CorelDRAW! drawings Name, type **AUTTRACE** in the File text box, and then choose OK.

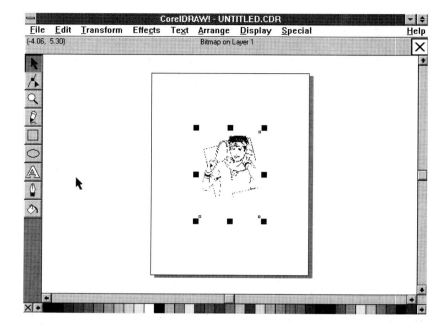

A bitmapped
image,
OUT_PLAY.TIF,
imported for
tracing
Figure 18–1.

Autotracing an Imported Bitmap

As mentioned earlier in the chapter, CorelDRAW! lets you turn an
imported bitmapped image into a resolution-independent curve object
by tracing the image. You can trace a single bitmapped image either
semiautomatically, using the Autotrace feature, or manually. (If you
have version 1.2 or later, you can also use the fully automatic
CorelTRACE! batch autotracing utility described later in this chapter.
Manual tracing is an excellent choice if you desire total control over the
appearance and placement of the outline curves. If you find it
cumbersome to use the mouse for tracing long paths manually,
however, use the Autotrace feature instead. You have less control over
the results, but you will spend less time manipulating the mouse.

The Autotrace feature becomes available to you when the bitmap object
is selected. Autotrace is semiautomatic in the sense that the software
draws the actual curves for you, but you must define a number of
parameters before tracing begins. You control the shape of the outline
pen, the color of the outline fill, the interior fill of the object, and the
smoothness of the curves.

In the following exercise, you will use Autotrace to trace portions of the AUTTRACE.CDR image that you imported earlier from the OUT_PLAY.TIF file.

1. With the image still on screen, make sure the bitmap object (the image of the tennis player) is still selected. Then adjust magnification to fit-in-window.

2. All black-and-white bitmap objects are imported with a preset outline color of black, and a preset fill of None. You can adjust the Outline Pen settings as desired, but to have those settings apply to your traced objects, you must first deselect the bitmap. For the bitmap itself, the fill color applies to the background, the outline color applies to the bitmap pixels that are turned on, and outline width has no meaning. Deselect the object, click on the Outline tool and then on the hairline icon in the first row of the fly-out menu. This will result in hairline curves of a very fine width. Click on OK to apply this default to all objects. With the object still deselected, click on the Fill tool and on the X (the no fill icon). Again, accept this as the default for all objects. Now reselect the bitmap.

3. Now you will crop the bitmap just enough to tighten the frame, so that no empty space extends beyond any of the objects in the image. With the bitmap still selected, activate the Shaping tool and position it over the middle boundary marker along the bottom edge of the rectangular frame. When the pointer turns into a crosshair, press and hold the mouse button and drag the bottom edge of the boundary marker upward. As you drag, the status line displays the percentage by which your cropping is diminishing the height of the bitmap frame. Release the mouse button when the status line displays the message, "Bitmap: Crop bottom: 19%" and provides an even margin all around. When you have finished, the status line displays all four cropping percentages, as shown in Figure 18–2.

4. Choose the Preferences command from the Special menu and then click on Curves. In the Preferences—Curves dialog box, adjust the settings as follows: Autotrace Tracking, 10 pixels; Corner Threshold, 8 pixels; Straight Line Threshold, 3 pixels; and AutoJoin, 10 pixels. These settings will result in smoother curves, smooth (rather than cusp) nodes, curves rather than straight line

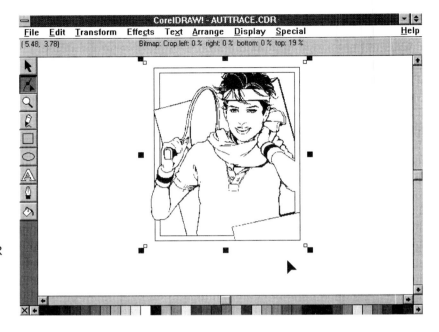

AUTTRACE.CDR
showing a
cropped bitmap
Figure 18–2.

segments, and curve segments that snap together when they are as far as 10 pixels apart, as shown in Table 18–1. Click on OK twice to make these settings take effect.

5. Turn on Preview Selected only in the Display menu. Select the Magnification tool and then the Zoom-In tool when the fly-out menu appears. Magnify only the woman's head. Your editing window should look similar to Figure 18–3.

6. Now you are ready to begin Autotracing. Make sure that the bitmap is still selected, and then select the Pencil tool. Notice that the pointer looks different than usual; instead of being a perfectly symmetrical crosshair, it has a wand-like extension on the right. This is the Autotrace pointer. It appears only when you activate the Pencil tool with a bitmap object selected. The phrase "AutoTrace on Layer 1" appears on the status line, indicating that you are now in Autotrace mode.

7. Position the wand of the Autotrace pointer near the bottom of the woman's left (your right) ear, and then click once. After a moment, a closed curve object appears, completely enclosing the contours of

Option	Determines	Settings	
		Low no. (1-3)	High no. (7-10)
Freehand Tracking	how closely Corel follows your freehand drawing	many nodes	few nodes
Autotrace Tracking	how closely the Autotrace pointer follows bitmap edges	rough curve	smooth curve
Corner Threshold	whether a node is cusped or smooth	cusp nodes	smooth nodes
Straight Line Threshold	whether a segment should be a curve or a straight line	more curves	more lines
Autojoin	how close together two line or curve segments must be in order to join	less joining	more joining

Guidelines for setting options in the Preferences—Curves dialog box
Table 18–1.

18

Magnified view of the woman's head
Figure 18–3.

the woman's face, as shown in Figure 18–4. Press F9 and you'll see the traced line similar to Figure 18–5. If you do not achieve the same result, select Undo from the Edit menu and try again.

8. Position the Autotrace pointer along the woman's hairline, but a little above the point where the woman's hair goes over the headband on your right, and click. Some seconds later, another curve appears. This curve outlines something the woman is carrying.

   Keep in mind that Autotrace does not give you the same high degree of control available with manual tracing.

9. Select the Zoom-In tool from the Magnification tool fly-out menu and zoom in on the woman's hair. Then position the intersection point of the Autotrace pointer inside one of the closed regions that represent the highlights of the hair, and click. A closed curve object appears quickly.

10. Create a few more highlighting curves in the same way and move around the face, tracing the objects you see.

Autotracing a closed region of the woman's face—Editing Screen

Figure 18–4.

Autotracing a closed region of the woman's face—Preview Screen
Figure 18–5.

11. Press [Shift]-[F4] to show the full page. Select the Pick tool and click on the bitmap somewhere other than where you were tracing. Press [Del] to remove the bitmap and see your handiwork. Depending on the areas you traced, your screen should look something like Figure 18–6.

12. Save your changes to the image by pressing [Ctrl]-[S] .

13. Select New from the File menu to clear the screen.

TIP: If you have trouble selecting a region that results in the curve you need, try pointing at the desired region using the wand of the Autotrace pointer instead of its center point. You will find that you can aim the wand more accurately when you are working in a magnified view.

As you saw in the previous exercise, the results of the Autotrace feature depend on your choice of the area to outline and on exactly how you

18

Result of tracing
the upper part
of the bitmap
Figure 18–6.

position the Autotrace pointer. Even if you use Autotrace in tracing the same area twice, CorelDRAW! may change the number and positions of the nodes each time. The path that an Autotrace curve takes can sometimes seem to be quite unpredictable, especially if the subjects within the bitmap have overlapping or connected pixels. With practice, you will gain skill in positioning the Autotrace pointer for the best possible results.

Tracing Manually

You don't have to be a superb drafter to trace a bitmap with precision in CorelDRAW!. By magnifying the areas you trace and adjusting the Lines and Curves settings in the Preferences dialog box, you can trace swiftly and still achieve accurate results. To trace a bitmap manually, you deselect the bitmap just before you activate the Pencil tool. This action prevents the Pencil tool from becoming the Autotrace pointer.

Manual tracing is faster and easier than using Autotrace if the imported bitmap contains multiple subjects with no clear separations between the pixels that compose these subjects. Most commercial clip art fits this description. Using the manual method avoids the problem of Autotrace curves that extend beyond the subject with which you are working. As a result, you usually need to do less editing after your initial manual tracing than after using Autotrace.

Just as when you use the Autotrace feature, you can define the default shape of the outline pen, the outline color, the interior fill of the object, and the smoothness of the curves before you begin tracing. In the following exercise, you will manually trace portions of the OUT_PLAY.TIF file.

18

1. Once again import OUT_PLAY.TIF as you did earlier.

2. When the bitmapped object appears, adjust magnification to fit-in-window. Also, make sure Snap To Grid, Show Rulers, and Edit Wireframe are turned off, and Preview Selected Only is turned on.

3. Deselect the object, click on the Outline tool and then on the hairline icon in the first row of the fly-out menu. This will produce hairline curves of a very fine width. Accept this setting as the default for all objects.

4. Click on the Fill tool and again on the none icon to change the object fill color to none. This prevents any closed paths that you trace from filling with an opaque color and obscuring other traced areas that lie beneath. (You can edit the fill colors of individual objects later.) Again, accept this as the default and then reselect the object.

5. Crop the bitmap so that only the woman's head is visible. With the bitmap still selected, select the Shaping tool and position the pointer directly over the boundary marker at the lower-left *corner* of the bitmap object. When the pointer turns into a crosshair, depress and hold the mouse button and drag this corner upward and to the right. Release the mouse button when the status line reads, "Bitmap: Crop left: 44% bottom 44%", as in Figure 18–7.

6. The bottom of the bitmap "frame" needs additional cropping. Position the Shaping tool directly over the *middle* boundary marker on the bottom of the bitmap. When the pointer turns into a crosshair, press and hold the mouse button and drag this marker up. Release the mouse button when the status line reads, "Bitmap: Crop bottom 61%."

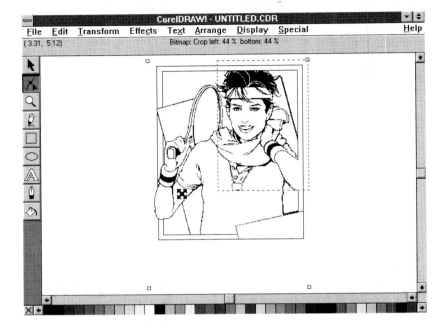

Cropping a
bitmap in
preparation for
manual tracing
Figure 18–7.

7. Position the Shaping tool directly over the top-right boundary marker. When the pointer turns into a crosshair, press and hold the mouse button and drag the marker down and to the left. Release the mouse button when the status line shows that you have cropped the top of the image 6% and the right of the image 9%, as shown in Figure 18–8. Then again adjust magnification to fit-in-window.

8. Select the Preferences command from the Special menu and click on Curves. Adjust the settings as follows: Freehand Tracking, 1 pixel; Corner Threshold, 10 pixels; Straight Line Threshold, 1 pixel; and AutoJoin, 10 pixels. These settings will result in curves that closely follow the movements of your mouse. You will generate smooth (rather than cusp) nodes, curves rather than straight-line segments, and curve segments that snap together when they are as far as 10 pixels apart. These settings promote ease of editing should you need to smooth out the traced curves later. Click on OK twice to save these settings.

9. Deselect the bitmap object, and activate the Pencil tool (if you see the Autotrace pointer instead of the regular Pencil pointer, you

Cropped image of woman's head in preparation for enlarging and manual tracing
Figure 18–8.

haven't deselected the bitmap). Position the Pencil tool anywhere along the outline of the face, then depress and hold the mouse and trace all the way around the face. End the curve at the starting point. Should you make any errors, you can erase portions of the curve by pressing the [Shift] key as you drag the mouse backward. If you end the curve within 10 pixels of the starting point, the two end nodes snap together and form a closed path, as shown in Figure 18–9. If the end nodes are farther apart than 10 pixels, the curve remains an open path. To close the path, activate the Shaping tool and draw a marquee around the two end nodes, double-click on one of them to invoke the Node Edit menu, and select Join.

10. Trace the outline of the woman's nose as an open path.

11. Magnify just the area around the mouth and trace two closed paths: one around the outer lips, and the other around the mouth opening. Similarly, magnify each eye and trace them both. Don't worry about being exact; you can always reshape your curves later.

A manually
traced closed
curve
Figure 18–9.

12. Use the Zoom-Out tool to return to the previous magnification
    showing the woman's head and neck. Then, activate the Pick tool
    and select the entire bitmap object. Remember that unless the
    bitmap is selected, you cannot enter Autotrace mode.

13. To enter the Autotrace mode, activate the Pencil tool again with
    the bitmap selected. Position the Autotrace pointer inside one of
    the highlighted areas of the hair and click to trace a curve around
    this tiny area automatically.

14. Using Autotrace, trace a few more highlights of the woman's hair
    and face. When you have finished, your screen should look
    roughly similar to Figure 18–10. Save the image at this point under
    the filename MANTRACE.

15. Select the Pick tool and click on the bitmap somewhere other than
    where you were tracing. Press Del to remove the bitmap and see
    your handiwork. Depending on the areas you traced, your screen
    should look something like Figure 18–11.

16. Save the changes you have made by pressing Ctrl-S, and then
    select New from the File menu to clear the screen.

Combining
Autotracing
with manual
tracing to create
highlights
Figure 18–10.

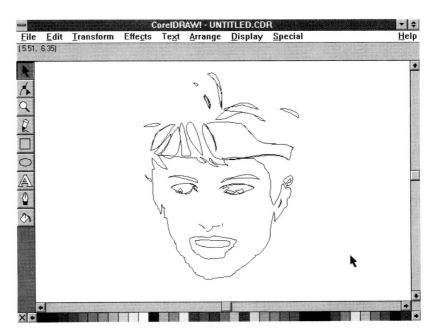

Traced image
without bitmap
Figure 18–11.

As you have just seen, it is possible and sometimes even preferable to combine both the manual and Autotrace methods when tracing complex bitmap images. Manual tracing is best for obtaining exact control over the placement of curves in bitmaps that contain several subjects close together, as is the case with most clip art. The Autotrace method is useful for tracing small closed regions like the highlights of the woman's hair in the previous exercises. The Autotrace method is also more convenient to use when the bitmap image has a single, clearly defined subject with sharp contours.

Whether you use the Autotrace feature, manual tracing, or a combination of both methods, you can always edit the curve objects you create.

Tracing with CorelTRACE!

A third method of tracing bitmapped images is available to you—one that is more rapid, sophisticated, and efficient than either the manual or Autotrace method. The CorelTRACE! batch tracing utility, similar to Adobe Streamline, allows you to trace one or more bitmaps automatically at high speeds and save them in the Adobe .EPS format. You can choose from two default methods of tracing, or customize tracing parameters to suit your needs. CorelTRACE! is provided with sample files in which you can practice changing the tracing parameters. When you are finished tracing files, you can edit the resulting vector-based images in any drawing program that can read the Adobe .EPS file format.

The following sections provide instructions for preparing to use CorelTRACE! for selecting and tracing bitmaps, and for customizing and editing tracing parameters.

Preparing to Use CorelTRACE!

CorelTRACE! is installed in the same directory and windows group where you installed CorelDRAW!. Before you begin using CorelTRACE! for the first time, check the amount of memory available on your hard drive. When you trace bitmaps using CorelTRACE!, temporary files are generated on your hard drive. If you trace large bitmaps, or more than one bitmap during a session, you are almost certain to require several megabytes of hard drive space for these temporary files. A good

18

recommendation is to have at least 5 MB of space free, and 10 MB is not too much.

If your hard drive does not have enough space available, you can either remove unnecessary files or, if you have one, specify a different hard drive where CorelTRACE! can place the large temporary files it generates. For example, if CorelDRAW! and CorelTRACE! are installed in drive C: and you wish to locate temporary files in the TRASH directory of drive D:, you would first open your AUTOEXEC.BAT file in a text editor. Then you would either add the following line, or else edit any existing "set temp=" line to match the following:

```
set temp=d:\trash
```

This statement tells Windows always to place temporary files in the specified drive and directory. Be sure to reboot you computer after you edit the AUTOEXEC.BAT file in order to make your changes take effect, and be sure that the directory exists on the specified hard drive.

CAUTION: Never select the Windows directory as the directory in which to store the temporary files that Windows applications generate. Errors could result that might cause your system to crash unexpectedly.

Loading CorelTRACE!

Unless you have over 2 MB of memory, do not run any other Windows applications in the background while you are running CorelTRACE!. CorelTRACE! requires a large amount of memory to work efficiently. If you run other applications concurrently, CorelTRACE! may not run or may function very slowly.

To load CorelTRACE!, follow these steps:

1. Load Windows to start the Program Manager.
2. Double-click on the CorelTRACE! icon. The opening screen appears and is then replaced by the main dialog box shown in Figure 18–12.

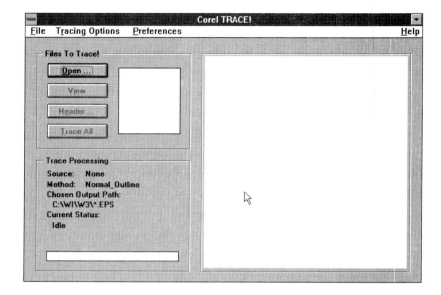

The
CorelTRACE!
main dialog box
Figure 18–12.

The main dialog box of CorelTRACE! contains four items in the menu bar: a File menu, a Tracing Options menu, a Preferences menus, and a Help menu. To obtain information on running CorelTRACE!, click on the Help menu or press the [F1] function key at any time. To begin the process of specifying and tracing files once the main dialog box displays, click on the Open button.

Opening Files To Trace

In order to trace one or more bitmaps, you must open the files in CorelTRACE! by clicking on the Open button. When you do this, the Open One Or More Files To Trace! dialog box appears, as shown in Figure 18–13. This dialog box is similar to the Import dialog box in CorelDRAW!, which you read about in Chapter 14. There are, though, two additional command buttons and an additional check box. The command buttons allow you to display a file's header, and to display (View) a miniature image of the file itself. The Auto View check box allows you to automatically view all files as you select them. Viewing files is slow, so Auto View is generally not a good idea. The header supplies such information about the bitmap file as its size, resolution, and color content, as you can see in Figure 18–14.

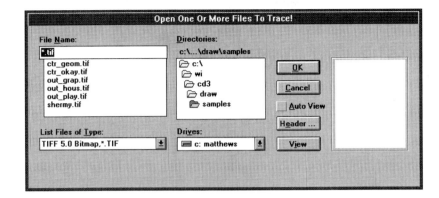

Open One Or
More Files To
Trace! dialog
box
Figure 18–13.

Tracing a Bitmap with CorelTRACE!

Tracing one or more bitmaps involves several steps:

1. Click on Open and specify the source directory of the files you want to trace, using the Directories list box if necessary.

2. Select one or more files to trace. To do so, click on their names in the Files list box while holding down Ctrl. Then click OK.

3. To specify a directory for converted (output) files, open the File menu and choose Output Options. The resulting dialog box will

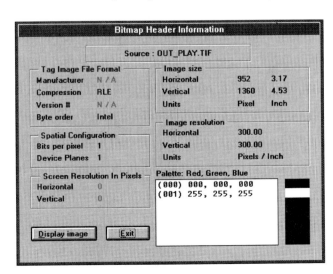

Bitmap file
header
Figure 18–14.

also let you choose between automatic and prompted replacement of existing filenames.

4. Edit the Tracing Options, if desired, by selecting an option from the Tracing Options menu.

5. Click on the Trace All command button to begin tracing the selected file(s).

In the following exercise, you will tell CorelTRACE! to batch trace (trace one after another) two bitmap files. The sample TIFF files used in the exercise were installed automatically if you installed the sample files with CorelDRAW!. If you wish, you can substitute any two bitmapped graphics files of your own.

1. Click on Open. If you did not install the sample files with CorelDRAW!, change to a drive and directory where your .PCX or .TIF files are located. If you did install the sample files with your software, make certain that the .TIF files shown in Figure 18–13 appear in the files to Trace! dialog box. If necessary, change the entries in the List Files of Type and the Directories list boxes.

2. While holding ⌈Ctrl⌉, click on the OUT_HOUS.TIF and OUT_PLAY.TIF filenames in the Files Names list box at the left side of the dialog box. Click on OK and both filenames will appear in the Files To Trace! list box.

3. Check the Chosen Output Path statement at the bottom of the dialog box. If you want CorelTRACE! to send the traced files to a different directory than the one specified, click on the Output Options command in the File menu. The Output Options dialog box appears, as shown in Figure 18–15.

4. Check the option settings in the "On name conflict" area of the Output Options dialog box. These settings determine what happens if you attempt to retrace a bitmap for which an output file of the same name already exists. If you select "Always replace," CorelTRACE! overwrites the existing file automatically. If you select "Always prompt," CorelTRACE! warns you about the conflict and lets you rename the output file before proceeding.

5. Check the Output directory setting. This determines the destination directory of the traced .EPS file. To change the current

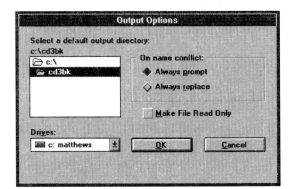

The Output
Options dialog
box
Figure 18–15.

output directory, double-click on the parent directory and select a
new one.

6. Select the OK command button to save your Output Options
   settings and return to the main CorelTRACE! dialog box.

7. Check the Tracing Method statement on the left side of the dialog
   box. The default tracing option is Normal_Outline. If the option
   that appears in your dialog box is Normal_Centerline or something
   else, open the Tracing Options menu and click on the
   Normal_Outline option. This tells CorelTRACE! to trace a line
   around each of the black or white regions of the bitmap image,
   and then fill each area with black or white to match the original
   bitmap. The Outline method is best for tracing bitmaps with thick
   lines, many fills, and a hand-sketched look. The Centerline
   method, on the other hand, is best for architectural or technical
   illustrations that have thin lines of fairly uniform thickness and no
   fill colors. See the next section of this chapter for more details on
   the differences between the Outline and Centerline methods of
   tracing.

8. As a last step before you click on the Trace All command button,
   open the Preferences menu.

   The Preferences menu provides three options:

   ◆ Trace Partial Area brings up an image of the bitmap after you
     start CorelTRACE!, and allows you to identify the area to trace
     by manipulating a bounding box.

✦ View Dithered Colors lets you choose between pure colors or shades of gray, and dithered colors or shades of gray, for viewing purposes. This does not affect the traced image, only what you see on the screen.

✦ Color Reduction provides a means of reducing the number of colors or shades of gray in the traced image. This provides for faster tracing and smaller files.

9. Click on the Trace All command button to begin tracing the two sample files. After a few seconds, the window on the right side of the screen contains the first of the two bitmaps. When the tracing is complete, the first bitmap disappears automatically and is replaced by the second bitmap. The traced image of the second bitmap remains on the screen after the tracing is complete, as shown in Figure 18–16. Status information about the tracing is shown on the left side of the window.

10. Select the Exit command from the File menu to exit CorelTRACE! and return to the Program Manager. Now you can load CorelDRAW!, import one or both of the traced files, and edit them just as you would any other object-oriented image.

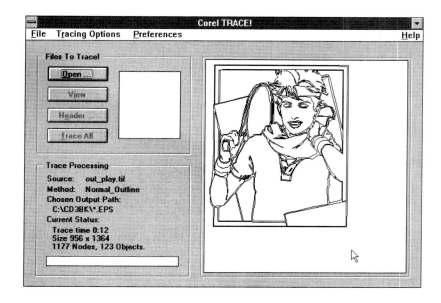

The traced bitmap upon completion
Figure 18–16.

The preceding exercise gave you a brief glimpse of what CorelTRACE! can do. In the next section, you will learn more about how you can customize the options that determine the smoothness, fineness, and clarity of the curves during the tracing process.

Customizing Your Tracing Options

The Tracing Options menu in the CorelTRACE! main dialog box contains two preset tracing options, Outline and Centerline. If you wish, you can modify the parameters associated with these two options to define up to eight custom tracing methods. When you modify a tracing option, you can save your result as a new option in the Tracing Options menu, using one of the eight blank menu positions. In the following sections, you will find out more about the two preset methods, Normal_Outline and Normal_Centerline, and when you will want to choose each method to obtain the best results.

Normal Outline Tracing

When you select Normal_Outline as the tracing method, CorelTRACE! seeks out the *outlines* of black or white areas and traces around them. Every curve becomes a closed object that is then filled with black or white, a color, or a gray shade to match the original bitmap as closely as possible. This method is most appropriate when the images that you trace contain many filled objects or have lines of variable thicknesses.

Normal Centerline Tracing

When you select Normal_Centerline as the tracing method, CorelTRACE! seeks out the *center* point of lines in a bitmap and traces down the middle of those lines. No attempt is made to close paths or fill them. The resulting accuracy and attention to fine detail makes this tracing method the best choice for scanned images of technical or architectural drawings. Normal_Centerline is also appropriate for tracing drawings in which line thicknesses are fairly uniform.

Defining a Custom Tracing Method

What if the image you want to trace contains both filled areas and line art? In CorelTRACE!, you can adjust a variety of tracing options by selecting the Edit Option command in the Tracing Options menu.

Follow these steps to access this command and define a custom tracing option.

1. Load CorelTRACE! from the Program Manager.

2. Without selecting any files, open the Tracing Options menu and click on one of the blank (. . .) menu options. The Tracing Options dialog box shown in Figure 18–17 appears. Using this dialog box, you can edit any of the displayed tracing parameters, then save the resulting combination under a unique name that will appear as an option in the Tracing Options menu. You can define up to eight additional tracing options using this dialog box.

3. Position the pointer in the Option Name text box at the upper-left corner of the dialog box and type the name of the new tracing option you are about to define.

4. Edit the tracing options as desired, referring to the descriptions that appear farther on in this section.

5. When you are finished editing, select the OK command button to save the tracing option under the new name that will now appear in the Tracing Options menu, as shown in Figure 18–18. The name of the new tracing option, and the settings that define it, also appear in the CORELDRW.INI file.

Information about tracing methods that you define is saved in the CORELDRW.INI file. Keep a backup copy of your CORELDRW.INI file so that you can restore your custom tracing options in the event that

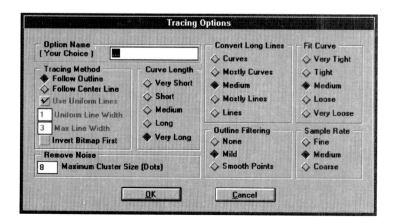

The Tracing
Options dialog
box
Figure 18–17.

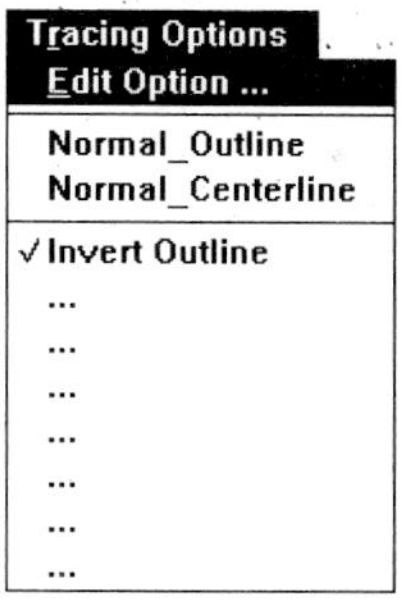

Tracing Options
  Edit Option ...

  Normal_Outline
  Normal_Centerline

✓ Invert Outline

  ...
  ...
  ...
  ...
  ...
  ...
  ...

The Tracing
Options menu
Figure 18–18.

18

you reinstall Windows, or lose your original CORELDRW.INI file due to some other cause.

Each of the eight parameters in the Tracing Options dialog box has a special function in the tracing process.

Tracing Method, Line Width   This tracing parameter is important only if you want to trace an image based on the Centerline rather than the Outline method. If you click on the Follow Center Line checkbox, the checkbox fills in and the Line Width options become available. The number in the Max Line Width option defines the maximum width, in pixels, that you want CorelTRACE! to treat as a line. If areas in the bitmap contain higher numbers of pixels grouped together, CorelTRACE! treats them as closed objects rather than as lines. The valid range for Line Width is from 2 to 99 pixels or dots. If you select 0 or 1, the setting defaults to a value of 3.

Invert Bitmap First   When the Invert Bitmap First checkbox is checked, this option is active. CorelTRACE! will convert black areas of the bitmap to white, and white areas to black.

Curve Length   This parameter determines the maximum length of each curve segment within the traced image. If you select Very Short or Short, each segment may be short, but the number of nodes in each segment remains high. As a result, the curves will fit the outline of the bitmap very closely. If you select Long or Very Long, on the other hand, the traced image will have smoother curves, but they will follow the bitmap more loosely. Select the desired option based on the characteristics of your input file and the way you want the resulting object-oriented picture to look.

Convert Long Lines   Your setting for this option determines whether CorelTRACE! treats a particular curve segment as a straight line or as a curve. If you select the Curves option, for example, CorelTRACE! will convert all traced segments to curves. If you select Lines, CorelTRACE! will convert all traced segments to straight lines. The other settings permit a mixture of curve and straight line segments in the traced drawing. If you frequently trace technical illustrations or other drawings that are made up of mostly straight lines, consider creating a custom tracing option that converts all segments to straight lines.

Fit Curve   This parameter affects how closely CorelTRACE! follows the outline of the bitmap when tracing it. A Very Tight setting results in a curve that follows the bitmap closely, while a Very Loose setting results in a looser curve. You should always set this option to the *opposite* of the setting chosen for the Sample Rate option. For example, if you select Very Loose for Fit Curve, choose Fine for Sample Rate.

Sample Rate   The Sample Rate option determines how closely CorelTRACE! matches its curve segments to the original bitmap. A setting of Fine results in a close match with many nodes, while a setting of Coarse results in a less exact match with fewer nodes per curve segment. Set this option in conjunction with the Fit Curve option, as described under Fit Curve earlier in the chapter.

Outline Filtering   Sometimes a bitmap image contains rather jagged outlines. You can select the Smooth Points option from the Edge Filtering selections to tell CorelTRACE! to smooth those outlines when tracing. Selecting the Mild option causes CorelTRACE! to smooth the outlines to a less extreme degree.

Remove Noise   Many scanned images contain unwanted flecks that are not truly part of the images themselves. The Remove Noise option lets you tell CorelTRACE! when to consider clumps of pixels as unwanted flecks and when to treat them as part of the picture. The number which you enter in the Maximum Cluster Size box determines the *minimum* pixel cluster size that CorelTRACE! will consider to be a part of the *picture*. All pixel clusters smaller than or equal to the specified number will be ignored during the file conversion and tracing process. You can set this option to any number between 2 and 999. When you are tracing a poorly scanned image, set the number slightly higher; when you are tracing a "clean" file, keep the number low. You'll rarely need to set this option above 10.

Option Name   As mentioned previously, you can define and name up to eight tracing options beyond the two standard options provided with CorelTRACE!. To save a modified tracing option under a new name, you must be sure to type a name in this text box *before* you select OK to exit the Tracing Options dialog box. Otherwise, the new settings will be valid only during the current session of CorelTRACE!.

If you trace and import many bitmaps, you probably tend to trace the same kinds of files over and over again. Defining custom Tracing Options to fit the kinds of files you trace most often can be a powerful time-saving tool.

Editing an Existing Tracing Option

Once you have defined a tracing option, you can alter its parameters permanently using the Edit Options command in the Tracing Options menu. This command always applies to the *currently selected* tracing option. You must therefore select the option you wish to edit *before* you click on the Edit Option command.

To edit an existing tracing option,

1. With the CorelTRACE! main dialog box open, click on the Tracing Options menu, then on the name of the option you wish to edit. The name of this option will now appear on the left as the Method, showing that it is the currently selected tracing option.

2. Now, select the Edit Option command from the Tracing Options menu. The Tracing Options dialog box for the currently selected tracing option appears.

3. Edit the tracing options as desired, then select OK to save the new settings permanently.

TIP: If you want to edit Normal Outline or Normal Centerline, first re-save it under a new option name, then edit that option.

Editing parameters for existing tracing options, like defining new tracing options, helps you save time when you import traced graphics into CorelDRAW! and edit them. For example, if you know in advance that you need to invert colors of a particular bitmap or that you require a larger or smaller number of nodes in the traced graphic, you can change tracing parameters to give you the desired results automatically.

C H A P T E R

19

USING CORELCHART!

CorelCHART!, which is new with CorelDRAW! 3, is a stand-alone program for creating charts. Charts let you view information in pictorial form and are commonly used in publications and presentations. Many people find information presented visually, rather than numerically, easier to understand.

CorelCHART! can create 12 basic chart types using data imported from spreadsheet and database programs, or entered directly into CorelCHART!. Each basic chart type is available in up to seven formats.

Charts can be customized with titles and other text labels. Graphics can be imported, or created with CorelDRAW! or CorelCHART!, and added to the charts. Customized charts can be saved and repeatedly used as *chart templates*—that is, preformatted starting points for new charts. The chart templates for each basic chart type includes the chart format, the color palette, and graphics. CorelCHART! comes with an assortment of templates for each basic chart type. You can also create and save your own templates.

The exercises in this chapter will demonstrate how to create a new chart; how to import data for the chart; how to add titles, labels, and graphics to your charts; how to modify the chart objects; and how to use chart templates. The different types and formats of charts will also be covered.

Charting Basics

The objective of charts is to present information in a graphic form that makes the information easier to understand, and highlights the message the information is carrying. Not all charts accomplish this objective. It is, therefore, important to learn not just how to create charts, but how to create effective charts.

Each value that will be plotted on the chart is called a *data point*. Data points are grouped in *data series* and *data categories*. Data series are groups of related data points. In a chart of sales figures from several sales offices, the data points (sales figures) for one office are one data series. The data categories are groups containing one data point from each data series, taken at one interval. If the chart of sales figures reflects monthly sales, then one data category could be the sales from all the offices for one month.

Figure 19–1 shows a vertical bar chart. This chart shows the attendance at a series of conferences in four cities, over a period of four years. The four years of attendance for each city constitute one data series. Each year constitutes one data category. This chart makes it easy to see the differences among the cities (the data series) in any year (the data category).

Figure 19–2 shows the same data as Figure 19–1, except that the data series and data categories have been reversed. Each year is now a data series, and each city a data category. This chart highlights the differences among the years (the data series) in any one city (the data category). When creating your charts, the relationship you want to emphasize will determine how you define your data series and data categories.

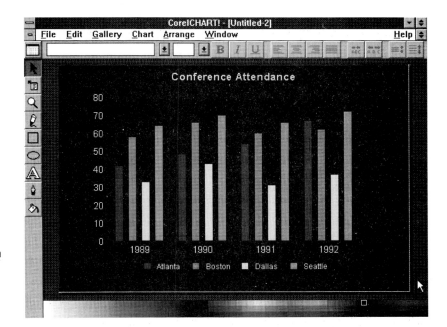

Conference
attendance with
each city as a
data series
Figure 19–1.

19

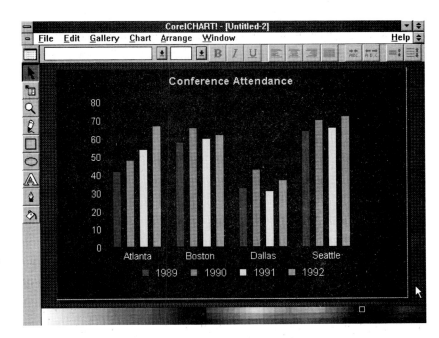

Conference
attendance with
each year as a
data series
Figure 19–2.

CorelCHART! can create both *two-* and *three-dimensional* charts. Two-dimensional (2-D) charts have two axes. The horizontal (X-) axis is usually the category axis. Each data category is plotted along the category axis. The vertical (Y-) axis is the data axis. Each data point is plotted against the data axis. The data axis will usually have a scale indicating the range of values for the data points. Three-dimensional (3-D) charts have an additional axis, the Z-axis, which is at a right angle to the X- and Y-axes, and adds depth to the chart.

Starting CorelCHART!

CorelCHART! is a separate program included with CorelDRAW! 3. It is installed in the Corel Applications group along with CorelDRAW!. To start CorelCHART!, open the Corel Applications group window and double-click on the CorelCHART! icon. Figure 19–3 shows the initial CorelCHART! screen after the title logo. As you can see, it is very similar in appearance to the CorelDRAW! window.

Text ribbon

Chart/Data
Manager toggle

Pop-up menu

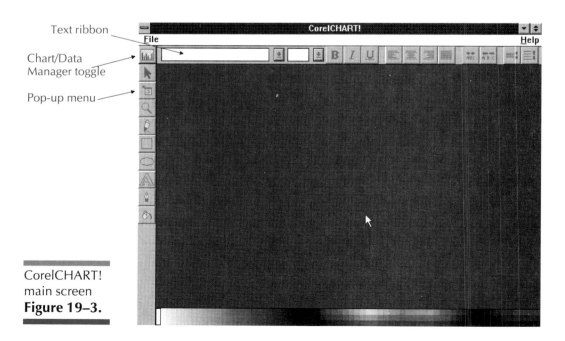

CorelCHART!
main screen
Figure 19–3.

Across the top of the screen, below the menu bar, is the *text ribbon*. The text ribbon is a set of drop-down list boxes and command buttons that you use to select the text attributes—the font, size, and other characteristics—for the text used in your charts. The text ribbon is similar to CorelDRAW!'s text roll-up, and is used in a similar manner.

On the left side of the screen is the CorelCHART! toolbar. Many of the tools operate much like their CorelDRAW! counterparts. The first tool at the top of the toolbar is used to switch between the chart window and the data window. The tool changes appearance based on which window is currently active. The tools are explained in this table:

19

Tool	Description	Function
	Chart View	Makes the chart window the active window when in the Data Manager.
	Data Manager	Makes the Data Manager the active window when in Chart View.
	Pick	The pick tool is used to select elements in a chart.
	Pop-up Menu	The pop-up tool is used to access the chart menus.
	Zoom	Presents a fly-out menu to change the magnification of the chart.
	Pencil	Presents a fly-out menu with four drawing modes: straight lines, polygons, freehand lines, and arrows.
	Rectangle	Draws rectangles in the same manner as its CorelDRAW! counterpart.
	Ellipse	Draws ellipses and circles in the same manner as its CorelDRAW! counterpart.
	Text	The text tool is used to add text to a chart.
	Outline	Sets the line characteristics used to outline objects.
	Fill	Fills the selected object with the selected color and pattern.

On the bottom of the screen is the color palette. To use the palette, simply select the chart element you to want to change, and then click on the desired color in the palette. The color of the selected element will change to the chosen color. To undo any color change, choose Undo in the Edit menu. Undo will only reverse the last action taken, so it must be used before you continue working with the chart.

Creating a New Chart

When CorelCHART! is started, only the File and Help menus are available. The File menu is used to either load an existing chart or to create a new chart. This exercise will create a new blank chart. In the next exercise, data will be added to the chart with the Data Manager.

1. From the File menu, choose New. The New dialog box, shown in Figure 19–4, will be presented. On the left is the Gallery list box, which is a listing of the basic chart types. To the right of the Gallery list box is the Graph Types list box. This is a pictorial display box, containing specific templates for the basic chart type chosen in the Gallery list box. Both a basic chart type and a

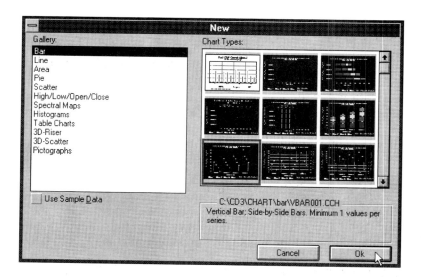

New dialog box
Figure 19–4.

template must be chosen for a new chart. The various chart types will be covered in detail later in this chapter.

2. For this exercise, click on Bar in the Gallery list box, then click on the chart template in the lower-left corner of the Chart Types pictorial display box, and click on OK. This chart template will create a Vertical Bar chart. A window for the chart and a window for the Data Manager are opened, as shown in Figure 19–5. The Data Manager is the element of CorelCHART! that is used to enter or import data for the chart. It also is used to format and prepare data for charting.

NOTE: If you are using version 3.0A of CorelCHART!, you are going to notice some differences in the screen shots, which were taken with version 3.0B. You should be able to find the equivalent functions in both versions.

19

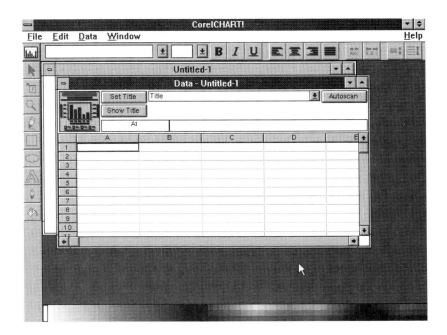

The Data
Manager
Figure 19–5.

Using the Data Manager

The Data Manager presents a grid of rows and columns that will hold the data for the chart. The Data Manager is arranged similar to a spreadsheet—data is stored on it in rows and columns—but the Data Manager cannot calculate values using the data. The Data Manager simply stores the numbers and text that will be used to create a chart. Only one Data Manager can be open, even though more than one chart can be open at a time.

The box where a row intersects a column is called a *cell*. Cells are usually referenced by the cell address, which is the column letter and the row number, in that order. The first cell in the upper-left corner of the Data Manager is A1, meaning column A, row 1. Each cell can contain one value. The value may be a data point to be charted, or text for a label.

Cells are selected by clicking on the cell—the selected cell then becomes the *active cell*. The active cell will have a heavier line surrounding it. A rectangular group of contiguous cells is called a *range*. Ranges of cells are selected by clicking on the cell that will be one of the corners of the range, and dragging the mouse until the desired range is highlighted. Ranges are referenced by the addresses of the cells in the upper-left corner and the lower-right corner, separated by a colon. A range of cells from A1 (in the upper-left corner) to B2 (in the lower-right corner) would be referred to as A1:B2.

In the upper-left corner of the Data Manager window is an icon showing the type of chart the Data Manager will create. At the top of the Data Manager window is a drop-down list box, which is used to *tag* the contents of each cell. The information in each cell is tagged so CorelCHART! will know which values are to be plotted, and which values are instead to be used for labels like row and column headers, titles, and other chart elements. The drop-down list box, shown below, presents a list of the tags available.

Most of the tags are self-explanatory. The Data Range tag is used to define the range of cells containing the data points to be plotted on the chart. The other tags define cells containing text for the chart's titles.

To the left of the drop-down list box are two command buttons. The top command button is used to attach the currently selected tag to the selected cell(s) in the Data Manager. The lower command button is used to highlight the cell(s) in the Data Manager that are tagged with the currently selected tag. The text on these two buttons will change to reflect which tag is currently selected.

To the right of the tag list box is the Autoscan command button. When Autoscan is selected, the Data Manager is scanned for a range of cells containing data. If a range of cells containing data is found, the first row and column are tagged as the row and column headers. The rest of the range is tagged as the data range. Any text below the data range is tagged as subtitles and footnotes.

Below the tag drop-down list box is the Contents Box. The Contents Box is used to enter and edit the contents of cells. When you select a cell and start to type information into it, the information will be entered in the Contents Box. When Enter or Tab, or one of the Arrow Keys is pressed, the information is entered in the selected cell. When you select a cell, the contents of that cell will be placed in the Contents Box, where it can be edited. To the left of the Contents Box, the address of the active cell is displayed. If a range of cells is selected, the address of the cell in the upper-left corner of the range is displayed.

Entering Data with the Data Manager

Data for charting can be entered directly into the Data Manager, as the next exercise shows. The data will represent attendance at a series of conferences.

1. Select cell A1 and type **Conference Attendance** in the Contents Box. Press Enter.
2. Use the Arrow Keys or mouse to move to cell **B2**.

3. In cell B2 type **1989**. Press the ⌑Tab⌑ key to move to the next cell in the row, C2. In cell C2 type **1990**. Repeat this step until cells B2:E2 contain the dates 1989 to 1992.

4. Use the Arrow Keys or mouse to move to cell A3.

5. In cell A3 type **Atlanta**. Press the ⌑Tab⌑ key to move to cell B3.

6. In cell B3 type **42**. Press the ⌑Tab⌑ key to move to the next cell in the row, C3. In cell C3 type **48**. Repeat this step until cells B3:E3 contain the numbers **42**, **48**, **54**, and **67**.

7. Select cell A1. In the drop-down list box, select Title. Click on the Set Title command button to the left of the drop-down list box. This will tag the selected cell as the title for the chart.

8. Select the range of cells B2:E2. In the drop-down list box, select Column Headers. The command buttons are now labeled Set Column Headers and Show Column Headers. Click on Set Column Headers to tag the selected range as the column headers for the chart.

9. Select cell A3. In the drop-down list box, select Row Headers. The command buttons are now labeled Set Row Headers and Show Row Headers. Click on Set Row Headers to tag the selected cell as the row header for the chart.

10. Select the range of cells B3:E3. In the drop-down list box select Data Range. The command buttons are now labeled Set Data Range and Show Data Range. Click on Set Data Range to tag the selected range as the data to be charted.

11. Click on the Chart View tool at the top of the toolbar to view the chart. Figure 19–6 shows the chart created from the information in the Data Manager.

12. Use the File Manager to save the chart and your data.

In this chart there is one data series, the attendance in Atlanta. Each year is one data category.

Importing Data with the Data Manager

The Data Manager also allows you to import information from spreadsheets and databases to use in charts. CorelCHART! can import data in the file formats shown in this table:

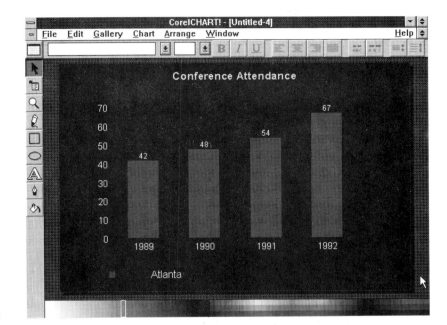

Conference
Attendance in
Atlanta
Figure 19–6.

File Format	Extension
ASCII (Comma Separated Value)	.CSV
ASCII (Space Separated Value)	.TXT
ASCII (Tab Separated Value)	.TXT
dBase	.DBF
Excel	.XLS
Harvard	.CHT
Lotus	.WK1, .WK3

The steps to import an Excel worksheet are as follows:

1. To import data, the Data Manager must be the active window. If it is not, click on the Data Manager tool in the toolbar, or choose Edit Chart Data in the Edit menu.

2. From the File menu, choose Import Data. The Import File with File Type dialog box, shown below, will be presented. In the lower-left corner is a drop-down list box for selecting the file type to import. For an Excel worksheet you want "Excel *.XLS" in this drop-down list box.

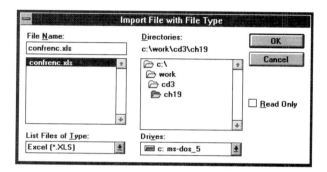

3. Select the file to import and click on OK. The imported data will replace any data already in the Data Manager.

4. The imported data needs to tagged before it will be charted properly. The imported data is tagged in the same manner as the data in the previous exercise. Select the cell with the title, and tag it as the Title. Select the range containing the row headings, and tag it as the Row Headings. Select the column headings range, and tag it as the Column Headings. Select the range with the data, and tag it as the Data Range.

5. To see the new chart, switch to Chart View by clicking the Chart View tool. The example data used here is shown in Figure 19–7.

Customizing Charts

CorelCHART! provides a number of ways to customize your charts. Text can be formatted by selecting a different font, color, size, placement, and style. Labels can be added to emphasize elements of your chart. Graphics, including arrows, can also be placed on the chart.

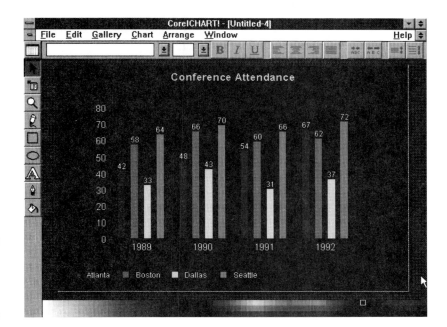

Conference
Attendance
chart
Figure 19–7.

Formatting Text

Text is formatted with the text ribbon, which is at the top of the
CorelCHART! screen, below the menu bar. This exercise will use the
text ribbon to format the chart title.

1. To format text, the chart window must be the active window. Click
   on the Chart View tool in the toolbar, if necessary.

2. Select the chart title, Conference Attendance, by clicking on it.

3. Select a new font for the title with the font drop-down list box
   shown here:

19

4. For this exercise, select Avalon by double-clicking on it.

5. The size of the text is set with the size drop-down list box, which is to the right of the font drop-down list box. Select 24 in the size list box by double-clicking on it.

6. The text is already formatted as bold. Add an underline by clicking on the underline button, further to the right along the text ribbon.

Figure 19–8 shows the conference attendance chart with the new chart title.

Adding Labels

You have already seen how to define text for chart titles and headings using the Data Manager. Other text, such as labels to draw attention to a specific element of the chart, can be added using the chart toolbar. This exercise will add a label and an arrow to identify the largest attendance on the chart.

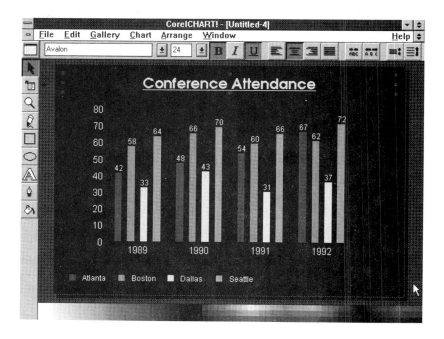

New chart title
Figure 19–8.

1. To add labels to the chart, the chart window must be the active window. Once again, click on the Chart View tool in the toolbar, if necessary.

2. Select the Text tool in the chart toolbar by clicking on it. The mouse pointer will turn into a crosshair.

3. Click on the chart in the approximate location where you want the text to be placed. The text can be moved after it has been added to the chart.

   This label will identify the largest attendance on the chart—which is 72, the attendance in Seattle in 1992—so click on the area above the chart on the right side. The I-beam insertion point will appear at the point you clicked on. Type **Best Attendance**, and then click on the Pick tool. The text you just typed will reflect the current text attributes (font, size, etc.) you selected in the Text ribbon for the title. The attributes can be changed with the text ribbon while the new text is selected.

4. If the text needs to be larger or smaller, it can be adjusted in two ways. The first is to select the text and then use the type size drop-down list box to change the size of the text. The other method is to select the text and use the edit handles to increase or decrease the size of the text box.

5. When you are satisfied with the appearance of the text drag it into its final location with the mouse.

6. Next, add an arrow to the chart to point out the bar representing the best attendance. Click on the Pencil tool in the toolbar. The Pencil tool has a fly-out menu for selecting the type of line to draw. Click on the arrow tool in the fly-out menu.

7. Click on the point where you want the arrow to start (this will be the end without the arrowhead). Drag the mouse to set the length and direction of the arrow. When the line is where you want it, release the mouse button. An arrow will appear with the arrowhead where you ended the line. The arrow can be moved by choosing the Pick tool in the Chart toolbar, selecting the arrow, and dragging it with the mouse.

Figure 19–9 shows the conference chart with the label and arrow described in this exercise.

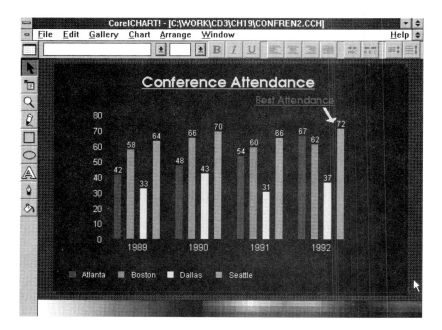

Chart with
annotation
Figure 19–9.

Adding Graphics

You can add graphics to your charts by creating them with
CorelCHART!'s drawing tools, or by importing them from other
programs. Graphics created with CorelDRAW! can be placed directly
onto a CorelCHART! chart.

Graphics and text are placed on the chart in layers, in a manner similar
to CorelDRAW! drawings. The chart layer, which contains all the
information on the Data Manager, is the bottom layer. All other layers
are placed above the chart layer. The label "Best Attendance" and the
arrow you added in the previous exercise are both above the chart layer.
The next exercise will add a simple graphic to the chart, using
CorelCHART!'s drawing tools. The graphic will appear behind the chart
title. To do this, you will first create the background graphic and then
create a new chart title to be placed above it.

1. To modify the chart, the chart window must be the active window.
   Click on the Chart View tool in the toolbar, if necessary.

2. Since the existing chart title will be covered by the graphic, you can turn it off. In the Chart menu, choose Display Status. The Display Status dialog box shown here will open:

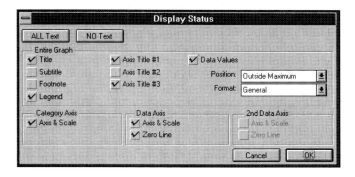

3. To turn off the chart title, click on the Title option button so there is no longer a check mark in the box, and then click on OK.

4. Now you will create an ellipse, using the Ellipse tool. Select the Ellipse tool from the toolbar. The mouse pointer will turn into a crosshair.

5. Place the mouse pointer in the area that will be the left side of the ellipse (see Figure 19–10). The ellipse can be moved with the Pick tool after it is created, so the exact placement isn't critical.

6. Drag the mouse to the right and down. When you like the shape and size of the ellipse, release the mouse button.

7. Select the Pick tool in the Chart toolbar, and drag the ellipse into position above the chart.

8. Since the ellipse was created after the text and arrow that you added earlier, it is on top of the text. To move the ellipse behind the text, leave the ellipse selected, pull down the Arrange menu, and choose To Back.

9. Now you need to add a new chart title. Select the Text tool in the toolbar and recreate the chart title, using the same steps covered previously.

Figure 19–10 shows one way the chart could appear. You should experiment with the Fill tool and the color palette to see the effects they can create.

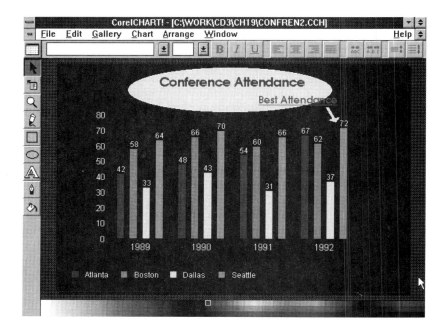

Ellipse added
Figure 19–10.

Graphics can also be imported into CorelCHART!. Imported graphics can be in a number of different formats which are shown in this table:

File Format	Extension
Adobe Illustrator 88, 3.0	.AI, .EPS
AutoCAD	.DXF
CompuServe GIF	.GIF
Computer Graphics Metafile	.CGM
CorelPhoto-Paint!	.PCX, .PCC
CorelTRACE!	.EPS
GEM	.GEM
HP Plotter HPGL	.PLT
IBM PIF	.PIF
Lotus PIC	.PIC

Mac PICT	.PCT
Targa Bitmap	.TGA
TIFF 5.0 Bitmap	.TIF
Windows Bitmap	.BMP
Windows Paintbrush	.PCX, .PCC
Windows Metafile	.WMF

Modifying Chart Elements

In the previous exercises you have modified charts by adding text and graphics to them. Charts can also be modified by changing the objects on the charts. In a Bar chart, the width of the bars, the distance between bars, and the shape of the bars can all be modified. The options for modifying chart elements are in the Chart menu; the exact options displayed will vary, depending on the type of chart being modified. For example, when a Bar chart is the selected chart, the Chart menu will contain options that modify the bars on the chart. When a Pie chart is selected, the Chart menu will contain options for modifying segments of the pie.

The commands in the Chart menu can be accessed in three different ways. For each method, you first select the chart object to be modified. You can then choose the desired option from the Chart menu, using the mouse or keyboard; or you can also select the Pop-up menu tool in the toolbar. When the Pop-up menu tool is selected, a pop-up menu containing the same options as the Chart menu will be presented next to the selected object. The pop-up menu will contain only the options that can be used with the selected object. Figure 19–11 shows the pop-up menu presented when one of the bars is selected. The submenu selects the amount of space between each bar.

Pop-up menus can also be used *without* selecting the Pop-up menu tool. Pressing the right mouse button while a chart object is selected will bring up the same menu.

Figure 19–12 shows the example chart with the bar thickness set to Maximum, and the marker Shape set to Triangle. Experiment with the different combinations CorelCHART! provides to discover what effects you prefer for your own charts.

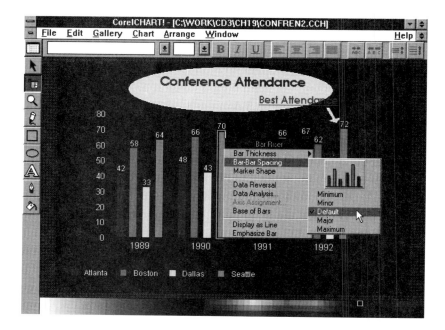

Pop-up menu
and sub-menu
Figure 19–11.

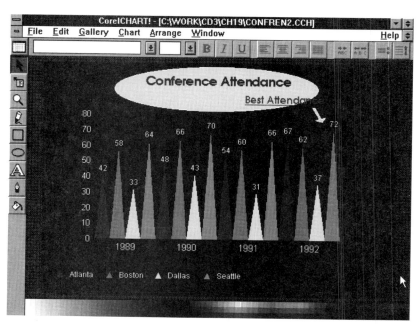

Triangle markers
Figure 19–12.

Creating Chart Templates

Any chart you design can be used as a chart template. You can insert your template in the Chart Types pictorial display box in the New dialog box, so it will be available when you are creating a new chart. You can also use a chart as a template after you have created it as a regular chart.

To include your chart template in the New dialog box, you must save it to the directory where CorelCHART! stores the other chart templates. In the directory containing your Corel applications, there will be a subdirectory named CHART. The CHART subdirectory will itself contain a series of subdirectories, one for each type of chart. The chart templates are stored in these directories. Figure 19–13 shows the path to the chart templates, as displayed in the File Manager. Any chart saved to these directories will be available in the Chart Types pictorial display box.

A chart template is simply a regular CorelCHART! chart. When it is loaded as a template, the existing data, including text, is ignored and

19

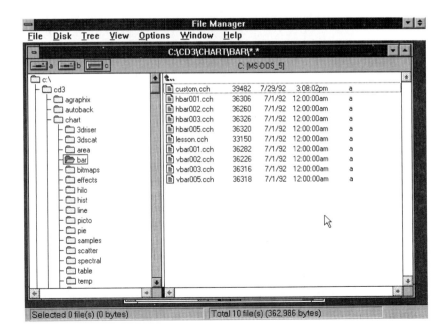

Path for chart templates
Figure 19–13.

only the chart type, graphics, color palette, and other modifications are presented.

Placing a template chart in the CorelCHART! directories simply makes it readily available when you are creating a new chart. However, any chart can be used as a chart template, no matter where it is located. If you want to use a chart as a template after you have saved it as a regular chart, follow these steps:

1. In the File menu, select Apply Template. The Open Chart dialog box, shown below, will be presented.

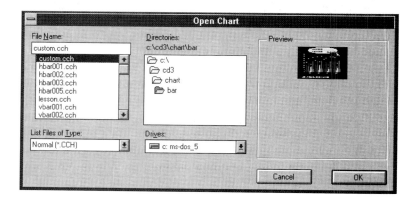

2. Select the drive and directory containing the chart file you want to use, and then select the file in the File Name list box.

3. Click on the filename and then click on OK, or just double-click on the filename.

The selected chart file will apply its format characteristics to the current chart.

Chart Types

CorelCHART! can create 12 basic chart types, with most of these chart types available in several formats. Each chart type and format will present your data in a different pictorial form. The chart type that best presents your data will depend upon the kinds of relationships you are illustrating.

Bar Charts

Bar charts are used to show how values compare with one another, and change over time. Each bar represents one data point—the value in one cell of the Data Manager. Bar charts can be configured as Vertical Bar Charts, as shown in Figure 19–14, or as Horizontal Bar Charts, as shown in Figure 19–15.

Vertical and Horizontal Bar charts have seven formats. The Bar, Line, and Area charts have the same set of formats. These formats will be covered in detail in this section, and mentioned only briefly in the sections on Line and Area charts.

The available formats are:

✦ *Side by Side Bars* The bars representing each data point are placed next to each other. Figure 19–14 is a Side by Side Bar chart.

✦ *Stacked Bar* Each bar in the data category is placed on top of the previous bar, rather than next to it. Each overall bar represents the

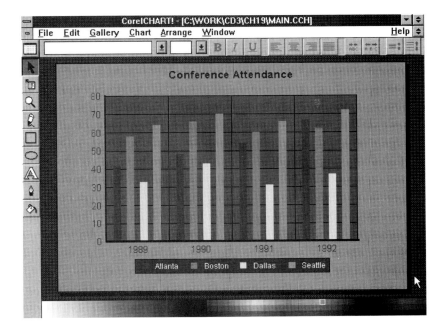

Vertical Bar chart
Figure 19–14.

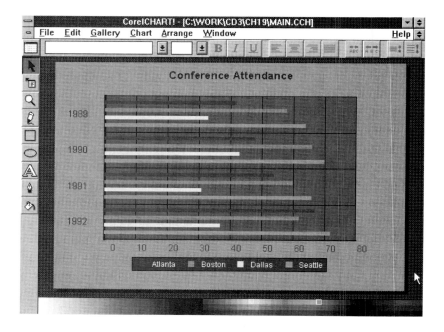

Horizontal Bar
chart
Figure 19–15.

sum of values for one data category. The Stacked Bar chart is used to compare sums of data points between categories, and to see the relative contribution of each data point. Figure 19–16 shows the conference data as a Stacked Bar chart.

✦ *Dual-Axis Side by Side* The charts shown so far have had one Category axis (the X- axis) and one Data axis (the Y- axis). The Dual-Axis Side by Side format has two Data axes. In a Horizontal Bar chart, one Data axis is at the bottom of the chart and the other Data axis is at the top of the chart. Some of the data series are plotted against the bottom Data axis, and the other series are plotted against the top Data axis. In a Vertical Bar chart, one Data axis is on the left side and the other Data axis is on the right side. Figure 19–17 shows the conference attendance as a Vertical Dual-Axis Side by Side chart.

✦ *Dual-Axis Stacked* Identical to the Dual-Axis Side by Side chart explained above, except that each bar in the data category is placed on top of the previous bar, rather than next to it. Each bar represents a sum of data points.

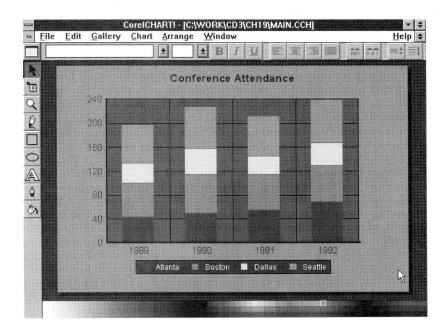

Stacked Bar
chart
Figure 19–16.

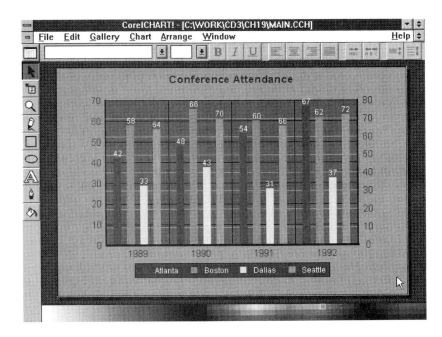

Vertical
Dual-Axis chart
Figure 19–17.

19

✦ *Bipolar Side by Side* The Bipolar Side by Side chart divides the chart into halves, horizontally for a Vertical Bar chart and vertically for a Horizontal Bar chart. There are two Data axes; each starts at the center of the chart, and increases in value towards the edge of the chart. Figure 19–18 shows a Vertical Bar Bipolar Side by Side chart of the conference data. As you can see, the baseline for the Data axes is the center of the chart, and values increase as they approach the top and bottom of the chart. The Horizontal Bar Bipolar Side by Side chart is similar, except that the data values increase as they get closer to the left and right sides of the chart.

✦ *Bipolar Stacked* Identical to the Bipolar Side by Side chart explained above, except that each bar in the data category is placed on top of the previous bar, rather than next to it.

✦ *Percent* A Percent chart is a type of stacked bar chart. In the Percent chart, the sum of all the numbers in each data category is represented as 100%. Each number in the data category is shown as a percentage of the total, rather than its actual value. Figure 19–19

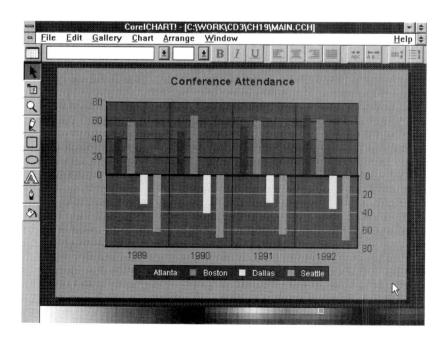

Vertical Bipolar Side by Side chart
Figure 19–18.

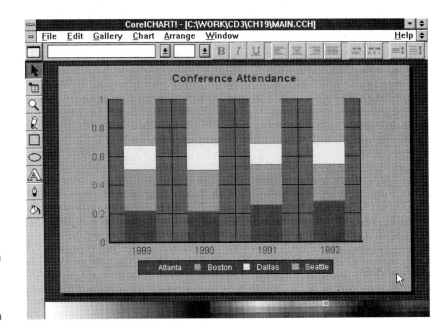

Vertical Bar
Percent chart
Figure 19–19.

19

shows the conference data as a Vertical Bar Percent chart. (Note that this chart's Y-axis scale runs from 0 to 1, rather than 0 to 100.)

Line Charts

Line charts are primarily used to show the change over time in a series of values. Each data series is plotted side by side, allowing you to readily observe trends between the data series. A marker is placed at each data point, and the markers in each data series are connected. Line charts can be either vertical or horizontal. Figure 19–20 shows the conference data plotted as a Vertical Line chart.

Vertical and Horizontal Line charts offer seven formats that are similar to the ones available with Bar charts. The Line chart formats are:

✦ *Absolute* Each data value is plotted at its actual value on the Data axis. The values in each category are plotted in line with each other on the Category axis. Figure 19–20 is an Absolute Line chart.

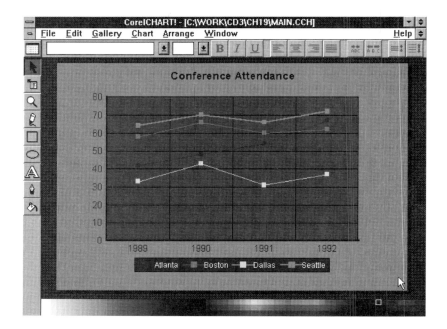

Vertical Line
chart
Figure 19–20.

✦ *Stacked* The Stacked Line chart is similar to the Stacked Bar
chart—each value is plotted above the previous value in the data
category, and the largest marker represents the sum of the values.

✦ *Bipolar Absolute* This is an Absolute Line chart in a Bipolar format,
similar to the Bipolar Bar charts described in the previous section.
The data is presented in the same manner as the Bipolar Side by
Side Bar chart.

✦ *Bipolar Stacked* A Stacked Line chart in the Bipolar format. Data is
presented in the same manner as the Bipolar Stacked Bar chart.

✦ *Dual-Axis Absolute* An Absolute Line chart in the Dual-Axis Format.
Data is presented in the same manner as with the Dual-Axis Side by
Side Bar chart.

✦ *Dual-Axis Stacked* A Stacked Line chart in the Dual-Axis format. Data
is presented in the same manner as the Dual-Axis Stacked Bar chart.

✦ *Percent* Shows each value as a percentage of the total, in the same
manner as the Bar Percent chart.

Area Charts

Area charts are similar to Line charts. The difference is that Area charts fill the areas between the lines with a color or pattern. Area charts can also be vertical or horizontal, and offer formats similar to Bar and Line charts. Figure 19–21 shows the conference data as a Stacked Area chart.

The Area chart formats are:

✦ *Absolute* Each data value is plotted at its actual value on the Data axis. The values in each category are plotted in line with each other in the Category axis.

✦ *Stacked* The Stacked Area chart is similar to the Stacked Bar or Line chart—each value is plotted above the previous value, and the largest value marker represents the total of all the values in the data category.

✦ *Bipolar Absolute* This is an Absolute Area chart in a Bipolar format, similar to the Bipolar Bar charts described previously. The data is

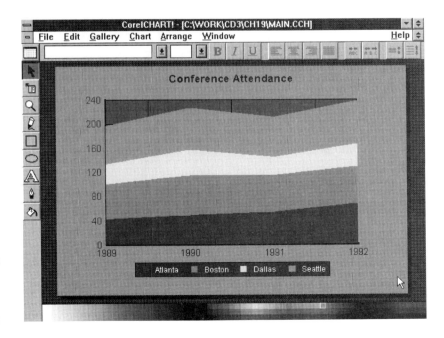

Stacked Area chart
Figure 19–21.

19

presented in the same manner as with the Bipolar Side by Side Bar chart.

✦ *Bipolar Stacked* a Stacked Area Chart in the Bipolar format. Data is presented in the same manner as with the Bipolar Stacked Bar chart.

✦ *Dual-Axis Absolute* An Absolute Area chart in the Dual-Axis Format. Data is presented in the same manner as with the Dual-Axis Side by Side Bar chart.

✦ *Dual-Axis Stacked* A Stacked Area chart in the Dual-Axis format. Data is presented in the same manner as with the Dual-Axis Stacked Bar chart.

✦ *Percent* Shows each value as a percentage of the total, in the same manner as the Bar Percent chart.

Pie Charts

Pie charts show the percentage distribution of your data. The entire pie represents 100 percent of one data series. Each data point is plotted as a wedge, representing a percentage of the total. Figure 19–22 shows the conference data as Multiple Pie Charts. Each Pie represents the data from one year.

Pie charts have six formats:

✦ *Pie* A single Pie chart, as described above.

✦ *Ring Pie* Identical to the basic Pie chart, except that the pie is shaped like a ring with a hole in the center.

✦ *Multiple Pies* Uses several Pie charts together, to represent several data series.

✦ *Multiple Ring Pies* Like the Multiple Pie chart, but with Ring-Shaped pies.

✦ *Multiple Proportional Pies* Each pie is sized in relation to the other pies. The pie that represents the largest total value will be the largest pie. The pie that represents the smallest total value will be the smallest pie.

✦ *Multiple Proportional Ring Pies* Like the Multiple Proportional Pies, but using Ring pies.

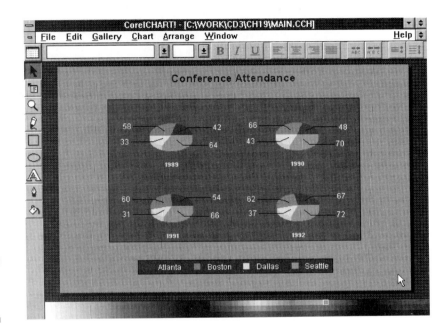

Multiple Pie
charts
Figure 19–22.

Scatter Charts

Scatter, or XY charts, show the relationship between pairs of numbers
and the trends they represent. In each pair of numbers, one is plotted
on the category axis, the other on the data axis. A marker is placed on
the chart at the point where the value on the category axis intersects
the value on the data axis. Figure 19–23 is a Scatter chart, showing the
hypothetical relationship between hours of sleep and units of
production.

The Scatter chart has four formats:

◆ *Scatter* The basic Scatter chart, as described above.

◆ *X-Y Dual Axes* The basic Scatter chart with two data axes.

◆ *X-Y with Labels* The basic Scatter chart with the data points labeled.

◆ *X-Y Dual Axes with Labels* A Dual Axes Scatter chart with the data
points labeled.

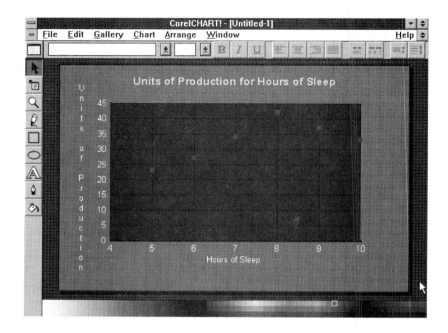

Scatter chart
Figure 19–23.

High/Low/Open/Close

The High/Low/Open/Close chart is a type of Line chart. It is also known as a Stock Market chart. A common use for a High/Low/Open/Close chart is to show opening, low, high, and closing prices for shares of stock. Figure 19–24 shows the high and low prices for two different stocks, over a period of four days.

The High/Low/Open/Close chart has six formats:

- *High/Low* Plots just the highest and lowest values.

- *High/Low Dual-Axes* Plots the highest and lowest values with dual axes.

- *High/Low/Open* Plots the highest, lowest, and starting values.

- *High/Low/Open Dual-Axes* Plots the highest, lowest, and starting values with dual axes.

- *High/Low/Open/Close* Plots the highest, lowest, starting, and ending values.

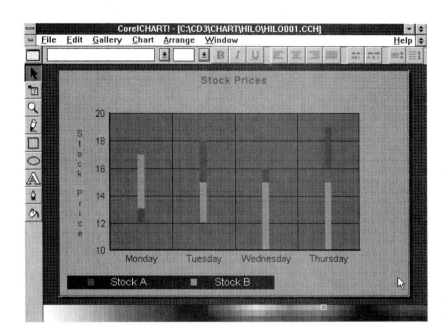

High/Low chart
Figure 19–24.

✦ *High/Low/Open/Close Dual Axis* Plots the highest, lowest, starting, and ending values with dual axes.

Spectral Maps

Spectral Maps are used to show relationships between sets of data. In Spectral Maps a range of values, not a data series, is marked with colors or patterns. Spectral Map charts are like topographic maps, where elevation ranges are marked with different colors. Spectral Maps have only one format. Figure 19–25 shows the conference data as a Spectral Map.

Histograms

Histograms are use to show how often values occur in a set of data. For example, if a temperature was recorded over a period of time, a Histogram could be used to show how often each temperature was recorded. Figure 19–26 shows what such a histogram might look like. Histograms have two formats:

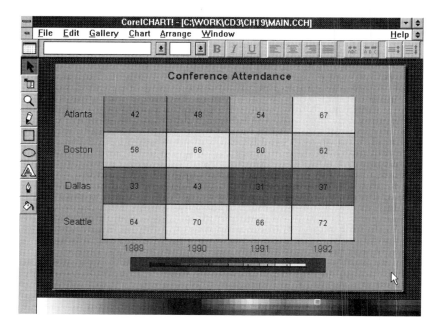

Spectral map
Figure 19–25.

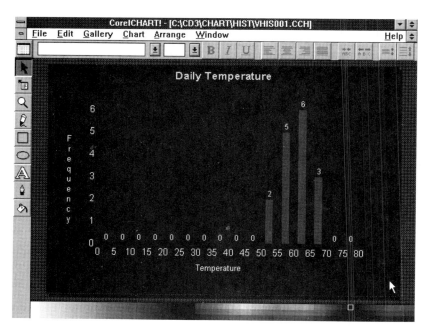

Histogram
Figure 19–26.

◆ *Vertical Histogram* Like a Vertical Bar chart, the bars are oriented vertically.

◆ *Horizontal Histogram* Like a Horizontal Bar chart, the bars are oriented horizontally.

Table Charts

Table charts present the data in a row and column format, similar to the way the data is contained on the Data Manager. Table charts have only one format, shown in Figure 19–27.

19

3-D Riser

The 3-D Riser chart is the general name for a 3-D Bar chart. Each bar represents one data point. Figure 19–28 shows a 3-D Riser chart with octagon bars. The 3-D Riser has four formats:

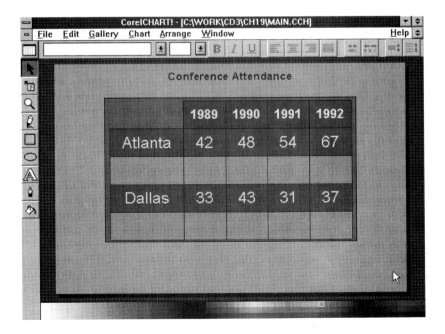

Table chart
Figure 19–27.

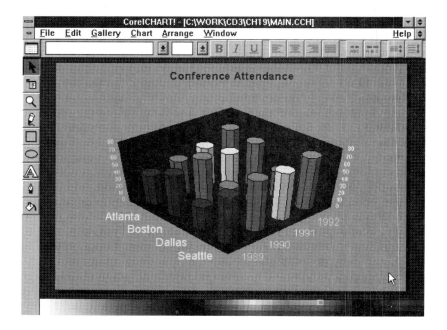

3-D Riser chart
Figure 19–28.

✦ *3-D Bars*   Each bar is rectangular.

✦ *Pyramids*   Each bar is a pyramid.

✦ *Octagons*   Each bar is an octagon.

✦ *Cut-corner Bars*   Each bar is rectangular with a cut corner.

3-D Scatter

The 3-D Scatter chart is similar to the 2-D Scatter chart with the addition of a third axis. Figure 19–29 shows a 3-D Scatter chart. The 3-D Scatter chart has two formats:

✦ *XYZ Scatter*   Like the 2-D Scatter chart, with a third data series.

✦ *XYZ Scatter with Labels*   A XYZ Scatter chart with data labels.

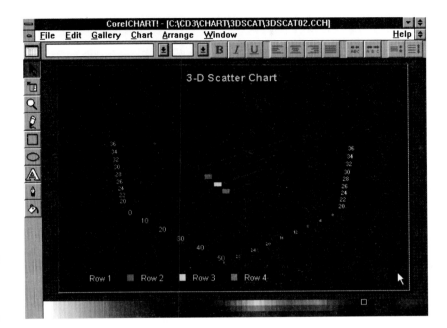

3-D Scatter
chart
Figure 19–29.

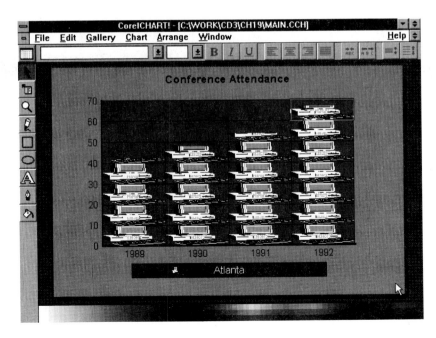

Pictograph
Figure 19–30.

19

Pictographs

A Pictograph uses a graphic element to replace the plain bars in Bar charts and Histograms. Figure 19–30 shows the conference data from Atlanta, using the image of a computer in place of a solid bar.

A P P E N D I X

INSTALLING CORELDRAW!

This appendix guides you through the process of installing CorelDRAW!. If you or someone else has installed your software already, you do not need to use this appendix.

This section contains detailed instructions on installing CorelDRAW!. Before you install CorelDRAW!, you must install Windows and ensure that it is working properly. Refer to the documentation that came with your Windows software for full instructions on installing Windows correctly.

System Requirements

Before you begin the installation procedure, review the hardware and software requirements explained in this section. You can help ensure trouble-free operation of CorelDRAW! 3 by checking to see that your system meets all requirements.

Computers and Hard Drive Space

Your computer should be based on an 80386 or 80486 microprocessor with a hard disk drive and at least one floppy disk drive. You can use an 80286-based computer if you have a minimum of 4 megabytes (MB) to run in Windows protected mode. (Windows real mode is not supported.) Your hard disk must have at least 29 MB of space available for a full installation using Windows 3.1, and at least 30 MB of space for a full installation with Windows 3.0. This disk space is needed because CorelDRAW! 3 is really a collection of five extensive programs, and CorelDRAW! itself generates large temporary files each time you run the software. The size of these temporary files can vary, depending on the complexity of your graphics and the number of bitmapped images you import (each bitmap generates a temporary file). However, you should ensure that the temporary files have plenty of room to work.

If you do not have this much space available on your hard drive, you can perform a minimum installation, which requires approximately 12 MB of disk space. Alternatively, if you are an experienced CorelDRAW! user, you can customize your installation by selectively installing programs, features, and graphic sample files.

Monitors and Display Adapters

Windows, not CorelDRAW!, determines which monitor and display adapter choices are available to you. Not all graphics adapters work well with CorelDRAW!, however. For best operation, you should have a color or monochrome graphics monitor, supported by either Windows 3.0 or 3.1, with at least VGA resolution. A color monitor and appropriate video display adapter are highly recommended to take full advantage of CorelDRAW!'s full-color mode.

Drawing Devices

You must have a mouse or another drawing device, such as a graphics tablet, in order to run CorelDRAW!. If you use a graphics tablet instead of a mouse, choose one that has the activation button on the side rather than on the top. This type of design gives you the best results because it minimizes unwanted movement on the screen.

This book assumes that most users work with a mouse instead of some other type of drawing device. References to a mouse therefore apply to any drawing device.

Output Devices

Using the Print and Export commands in the File menu, you can output your CorelDRAW! images to paper (standard printers) or to formats used by film recorders and slide generation equipment. Chapter 14, "Importing and Exporting Files," discusses output to 35mm slide generation or presentation equipment in greater detail. If you normally print your images to paper, however, you will achieve the best results with the following types of printers:

✦ PostScript printers, imagesetters, and PostScript controller boards and plug-in cartridges licensed by Adobe Systems

✦ HP LaserJet series or 100% compatible printers

✦ HP PaintJet and DeskJet printers

Although Windows supports other printers as well, many of these cannot reproduce complex CorelDRAW! images exactly as expected. In addition, a few of the most complex CorelDRAW! features can only be output on PostScript printers. For more information on printer limitations, see Chapter 15, "Printing and Processing Your Images."

Memory Requirements

The minimum memory to run CorelDRAW! 3 is 2 MB. This allows you to access Windows 3.1 Object Linking and Embedding (OLE) capabilities and to make use of the True Type fonts available in Windows 3.1. Increasing the memory size beyond 2 MB will speed the running of the program; 4 MB or more of memory is recommended.

Operating System and Windows Requirements

The combination of DOS 5.0 and Windows 3.1 is recommended to make full use of CorelDRAW!'s extended memory and OLE capabilities.

A

CorelDRAW! 3 will work with Windows 3.0 and with earlier releases of DOS, but you won't have the use of CorelDRAW!'s True Type fonts, which are available with Windows 3.1. Windows 3.0 font support is provided by using Adobe Type Manager, another program you will have to purchase. Additionally, Windows 3.0 does not fully support OLE.

Installing the Software

The SETUP program for CorelDRAW! 3 installs CorelDRAW! program files, fonts, sample files, and clip art onto your hard disk. Depending on your choice of installation method (Full, Minimum, or Custom), you can install some or all of the other five programs that make up the total CorelDRAW! 3 ensemble: CorelCHART!, CorelSHOW!, CorelPhoto-Paint!, CorelTRACE!, and CorelMOSAIC!. See the section on "Computers and Hard Drive Space" for the corresponding disk space requirements.

The directions that the SETUP program gives you vary according to which installation method you choose. The Full and Minimum installation methods require the least interaction on your part, and are recommended for new users of CorelDRAW!. If disk space is a concern, you might do the Minimum installation initially, and then later selectively add other CorelDRAW! programs using the Custom installation method, as your needs and disk space allow.

Before you begin, decide on the name of the hard disk directory in which you want to install CorelDRAW! 3, and have the Windows Program Manager on your screen. The following example assumes you will perform a Full installation.

1. Insert CorelDRAW! Disk 1 into the floppy drive from which you want to install CorelDRAW!. This book assumes that you are installing the software from drive A, but you can use any drive.

2. Click on the Program Manager's File menu, choose Run, and type **a:setup** in the Command Line text entry box. (If you are installing CorelDRAW! from a different floppy drive, type that drive name instead of "a:".) Click on OK.

3. After a short period, the initial installation window appears on your screen. Press ⎡Enter⎤ or click on Continue to proceed with the installation.

4. The next window provides buttons for the three installation methods, Full (the default), Minimum, and Custom. If you are unsure of your installation method, you can choose any button and explore some of its features before committing to the corresponding method. For example, choosing the Custom installation method accesses its menu of choices, as shown in Figure A–1. If you decide not to continue with the Custom installation, click on the Back button to return to the previous window with the three installation buttons.

5. To continue with the Full installation method, press ⎡Enter⎤ or click on the Full button. You are now given the choice of installing CorelDRAW! to the C:\CORELDRW directory on your hard drive. If this is satisfactory, press ⎡Enter⎤ or click on Continue. If you want the CorelDRAW! files copied to another destination, backspace over this default path and type your path name in the text entry

A

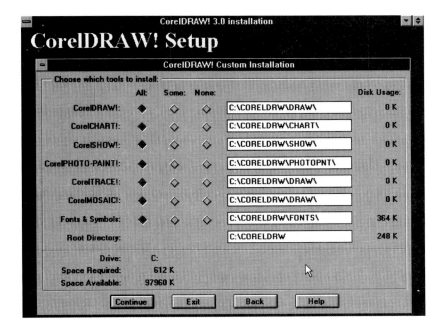

Corel Custom
Installation
window
Figure A–1.

box. Press Enter or click on Continue to continue with the installation.

6. CorelDRAW! now begins copying files to the destination you established in the previous step. When prompted, insert CorelDRAW! disk #2 in drive A. Press Enter or click on OK. Continue to insert the remainder of the installation disks when prompted. Depending on the speed of your computer, the installation process will take approximately 30 minutes.

7. SETUP finishes by creating a Program Manager application group called Corel Graphics, as shown in Figure A–2.

This completes the automatic installation procedure.

You should decide whether you want to make automatic backup copies of your drawings when you run CorelDRAW!. If you do not, use Windows Notepad to edit the [CDrawConfig] section of your CORELDRW.INI file, which is located in the directory where you installed CorelDRAW!. Change a line in the section that reads "MakeBackupWhenSave=1." If you do not want CorelDRAW! to make

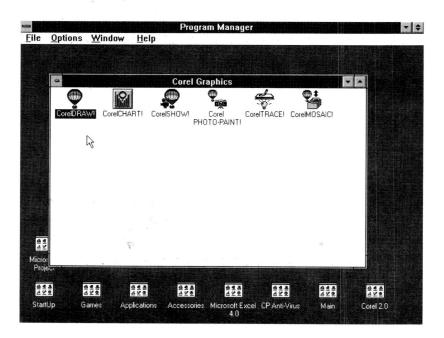

Corel Graphics group window
Figure A–2.

backup copies of your illustrations, edit this line so that it reads "MakeBackupWhenSave=0."

Creating a Directory

You need a directory in which to store the drawings created with CorelDRAW!. When you installed Windows and CorelDRAW!, directories were automatically created in which the program, font, and other files that came with Windows and CorelDRAW! are stored. While you could use these directories to store your CorelDRAW! drawings, it is unwise to do so for two reasons. First, when you get an update to Windows or CorelDRAW! you will want to remove the old program files and replace them with the new ones. The easiest way to do that is to erase the entire directory with a single command. If your drawing files were in the directory at the time, you would lose them. Second, if you want to do some file maintenance with either DOS or the Windows File Manager, the large number of product-related files will make looking for drawing files difficult.

Therefore, create a new directory now to hold your drawing files. You can name your directory anything you want as long as the name is from one to eight characters long and does not include the following characters:

+ ; , * ?

This book will use DRAWINGS as the example directory in which drawings will be stored. Your directory can be a full directory branching off the root directory, or a subdirectory within either the Windows or the CorelDRAW! directory. For simplicity this book will assume that the DRAWINGS directory is a full directory off the root directory. Its path then is \DRAWINGS. Use these instructions to create this directory either from the DOS prompt or from the Windows File Manager.

At the DOS prompt:

1. Type **cd**\ and press Enter to make sure you are in the root directory.
2. Type **md**\ **drawings** and press Enter to create the new DRAWINGS directory.

From Windows:

1. Double-click on the File Manager icon located in the Program Manager's Main application group.
2. Select the File menu and choose the Create Directory option.
3. Type **c:\drawings** in the Name text entry box. Press Enter or click on OK to create the new DRAWINGS directory.

The only remaining step is to start CorelDRAW! and begin using it. Do that now by following the directions in Chapter 1, "Getting Acquainted with CorelDRAW!".

A P P E N D I X

KEYBOARD AND MOUSE SHORTCUTS

This appendix contains an alphabetical listing of the CorelDRAW! operations that you can perform using keyboard shortcuts. Descriptions of the tasks you may wish to perform appear in the left column, and their keyboard shortcuts appear in the right column.

This quick reference list does not include the CorelDRAW! operations that you perform using the mouse only. However, if the word "click" or "drag" appears in the right column as part of the key combination, you must click or drag the mouse to complete the specified action. If a particular tool must be active in order to carry out the action, its icon appears within the description in the left column.

Action	Key Combination
Activate Ellipse tool	`F7`
Activate Fountain Fill dialog box	`F11`
Activate Outline Color dialog box	`Shift`-`F12`
Activate Outline Pen dialog box	`F12`
Activate Pencil tool	`F5`
Activate previous tool (▐ active)	`Spacebar`
Activate Rectangle tool	`F6`
Activate Pick tool (other tool active)	`Spacebar`
Activate Shaping tool	`F10`
Activate Text tool	`F8`
Activate Uniform Fill dialog box	`Shift`-`F11`
Activate Zoom-In tool	`F2`
Activate Zoom-Out tool	`F3`
Add New Envelope	`Alt`-`C` + `N`
Add New Perspective	`Alt`-`C` + `P`
Align multiple selected objects (▐ active)	`Ctrl`-`A`, `Alt`-`A` + `A`
Align selected text with baseline (▐ active)	`Ctrl`-`Z`, `Alt`-`X` + `L`
Arc, convert circle to, in 15-degree increments or Constrain Angle in Preferences (▐ active)	`Ctrl` + drag node outside circle
Back one layer	`Pg Dn`, `Alt`-`A` + `N`

Action	Key Combination
Blend Roll-up	`Ctrl`-`B`, `Alt`-`C` + `B`
Break apart selected combined objects (⬛ active)	`Ctrl`-`K`, `Alt`-`A` + `K`
Clear Envelope	`Alt`-`C` + `C`
Clear Perspective	`Alt`-`C` + `L`
Clear Transformations to selected object (⬛ active)	`Alt`-`T` + `C`
Combine selected objects (⬛ active)	`Ctrl`-`C`, `Alt`-`A` + `C`
Convert selected object to Curves (⬛ active)	`Ctrl`-`V`, `Alt`-`A` + `V`
Copy Envelope From	`Alt`-`C` + `R`
Copy Perspective From	`Alt`-`C` + `F`
Copy selected object to clipboard (⬛ active)	`Ctrl`-`Ins`, `Alt`-`E` + `C`
Copy Style From one object to another	`Alt`-`E` + `Y`
Create Arrow	`Alt`-`S` + `A`
Create Pattern	`Alt`-`S` + `C`
Cut selected object to clipboard (⬛ active)	`Shift` + `Del`
Delete (clear) newly drawn or selected object	`Del`, `Alt`-`E` + `L`
Dialog box, move to next field in	`Tab`
Dialog box, move to previous field in	`Shift`-`Tab`
Draw circle (⬛ active)	`Ctrl` + drag
Draw circle from center outward (⬛ active)	`Ctrl`-`Shift` + drag
Draw ellipse from center outward (⬛ active)	`Shift` + drag

Action	Key Combination
Draw line in 15-degree increments or Constrain Angle in Preferences dialog box (⟦🖉⟧ active)	[Ctrl] + drag
Draw rectangle from center outward (⟦🖿⟧ active)	[Shift] + drag
Draw square (⟦🖿⟧ active)	[Ctrl] + drag
Draw square from center outward (⟦🖿⟧ active)	[Ctrl]-[Shift] + drag
Duplicate selected object (⟦🖰⟧ active)	[Ctrl]-[D], [Alt]-[E] + [D]
Edit attributes of selected characters (⟦🖊⟧ active)	[Alt]-[X] + [C]
Edit Envelope	[Alt]-[C] + [D]
Edit Perspective	[Alt]-[C] + [V]
Edit attributes of newly drawn or selected text	[Ctrl]-[T], [Alt]-[E] + [X]
Edit Wireframe turn on/off	[Shift] + [F9], [Alt]-[D] + [E]
Ellipse Tool	[F7]
Erase portions of curve as you draw (⟦🖉⟧ active)	[Shift] + drag backwards
Exit CorelDRAW!	[Ctrl]-[X], [Alt]-[F4], [Alt]-[F] + [X]
Export current selection	[Alt]-[F] + [E]
Extract	[Alt]-[X] + [X]
Extrude roll-up	[Ctrl]-[E], [Alt]-[C] + [X]
Fit-in-window view	[F4]
Fit Text To Path Roll-up (⟦🖰⟧ active)	[Ctrl]-[F], [Alt]-[X] + [T]
Forward one layer	[Pg Up], [Alt]-[A] + [O]
Fountain Fill dialog box	[F11]

Action	Key Combination
Full Page view	`Shift`-`F4`
Full Screen Preview, turn on/off	`F9`
Grid Setup, specify	`Alt`-`D` + `I`
Grid, Snap To, turn on/off	`Ctrl`-`Y`, `Alt`-`D` + `S`
Group multiple selected objects (⬆ active)	`Ctrl` + `G`, `Alt`-`A` + `G`
Guidelines Setup	`Alt`-`D` + `L`
Import File	`Alt`-`F` + `I`
Leave Original	`+` on numeric keypad, or right mouse button in Version 2.01 and on
Maximize CorelDRAW! window	`Alt`-`Spacebar` + `X`
Merge-Back	`Alt`-`X` + `M`
Minimize CorelDRAW! window	`Alt`-`Spacebar` + `N`
Move CorelDRAW! window	`Alt`-`Spacebar` + `M` + arrow keys + `Enter`
Move Object dialog box	`Ctrl`-`L`, `Alt`-`T` + `M`
Move selected object in increments of 15-degree angles or Constrain Angle in Preferences dialog box (⬆ active)	`Ctrl` + drag outline
New (clear screen)	`Alt`-`F` + `N`
Open File	`Ctrl`-`O`, `Alt`-`F` + `O`
Page Setup	`Alt`-`F` + `G`
Paste object from clipboard	`Shift` + `Ins`, `Alt`-`E` + `P`

B

Action	Key Combination
Pencil tool	[F5]
Preferences, edit	[Ctrl]-[J], [Alt]-[S] + [E]
Preview Selected Only, turn on/off	[Alt]-[D] + [O]
Preview window, turn on/off	[F9], [Alt]-[D] + [P]
Print File	[Ctrl]-[P], [Alt]-[F] + [P]
Print Merge	[Alt]-[F] + [M]
Quit CorelDRAW!	[Ctrl]-[X], [Alt]-[F4], [Alt]-[F] + [X]
Rectangle tool	[F6]
Redo last undone operation	[Alt]-[Enter], [Alt]-[E] + [E]
Refresh Window	[Ctrl]-[W], [Alt]-[D] + [W]
Repeat last operation on selected object (⬆ active)	[Ctrl]-[R], [Alt]-[E] + [R]
Reverse Order of multiple selected objects (⬆ active)	[Alt]-[A] + [R]
Rotate & Skew selected object (⬆ active)	[Ctrl]-[N], [Alt]-[T] + [R]
Rotate selected object in 15-degree increments or Constrain Angle in Preferences dialog box (⬆ active)	[Ctrl] + drag corner node
Save current image	[Ctrl]-[S], [Alt]-[F] + [S]
Save As, name current image	[Alt]-[F] + [A]
Scale selected object in 100% increments (⬆ active)	[Ctrl] + drag corner node

Action	Key Combination
Scale selected object, leave original (⬚ active)	Drag corner node + ⊞ on numeric keypad, or right mouse button
Select All objects	Alt-E + A
Select multiple objects (⬚ active)	Shift + click
Select next object in picture (⬚ active)	Tab
Select previous object in picture (⬚ active)	Shift-Tab
Shaping tool	F10
Show Bitmaps in editing window	Alt-D + B
Show Color Palette, turn on/off	Alt-D + C
Show Full Screen Preview, turn on/off	F9
Show Grid, turn on/off	Alt-D + I + Alt-S
Show Page view	Shift-F4
Show Rulers, turn on/off	Alt-D + R
Show Status Line, turn on/off	Alt-D + H
Skew selected object in 15-degree increments or Constrain Angle in Preferences dialog box (⬚ active)	Ctrl + drag middle node
Snap To Grid, turn on/off	Ctrl-Y, Alt-D + S
Snap To Guidelines, turn on/off	Alt-D + G
Straighten selected text (⬚ active)	Alt-X + S
Stretch & Mirror selected object (⬚ active)	Ctrl-Q, Alt-T + S
Stretch selected object in 100% increments (⬚ active)	Ctrl + drag middle node

B

Action	Key Combination
Stretch selected object, leave original (⬚ active)	Drag middle node + ⊞ from numeric keypad or right mouse button
Text tool	F8
To Back, move selected object (⬚ active)	Shift-Pg Dn, Alt-A + B
To Front, move selected object (⬚ active)	Shift-Pg Up, Alt-A + F
Undo last operation	Alt-Backspace, Alt-E + U
Ungroup selected group (⬚ active)	Ctrl-U, Alt-A + U
Wedge, convert circle to, in 15-degree increments or Constrain Angle in Preferences dialog box (⬚ active)	Ctrl + drag node inside circle
Zoom-In	F2
Zoom-Out	F3

A P P E N D I X

INTRODUCING CORELSHOW! AND CORELPHOTO-PAINT!

CorelSHOW! and CorelPhoto-Paint! are two exciting products first made available with CorelDRAW! 3. CorelSHOW! assembles drawings and graphics from other products to produce presentations, which can be slide presentations, computer screen shows, documents (such as brochures), or overhead transparency presentations. CorelPhoto-Paint! combines traditional paint capabilities with photograph enhancement features.

Appendix C introduces these products by briefly discussing the features they offer, how you get started using them, and how to use their principal tools.

Introducing CorelSHOW!

CorelSHOW! lets you integrate drawings, charts, and other art for the purpose of creating a presentation. CorelSHOW! has few editing or artistic tools of its own. Rather, it gathers art from other OLE (Object Linking and Embedding) applications, such as CorelDRAW! and CorelCHART!, and then moves it around or resizes it until the art is arranged for the presentation.

A presentation can be a computer screen show, where the slides are displayed on the computer screen one at a time, in a timed display. You can set the time that each screen will be displayed. If you want the presentation to ultimately be recorded on slides, overhead transparencies, or paper, you can first preview the show on your computer screen.

The OLE connection is a basic component of CorelSHOW!. (Chapter 15 explains this feature in more detail.) If you want to import a chart created with CorelCHART!, for example, you have two options for bringing it into CorelSHOW!. You can paste a *linked* copy into CorelSHOW!, which causes the contents of the original chart to be mirrored in CorelSHOW!. To make changes to the linked copy, you open CorelCHART! either directly from within CorelSHOW! or from Windows, and modify the original chart. Any changes are reflected in the linked copy. Alternatively, you can *embed* a copy in CorelSHOW!. In this case, if changes are made to the embedded copy, the changes are again made with CorelCHART!, but they are not reflected on the original chart.

CorelSHOW! has some limitations: it cannot import *files* from applications that are not OLE applications. As explained above, if a linked or embedded copy must be modified, this must be done in the OLE application from which it came. CorelSHOW! has no tools to modify its art. Further, if you want to assemble a document, such as a brochure, CorelSHOW! has no word processing capabilities for flowing text around graphics or changing fonts. You must do this in other OLE applications, and link or embed the results into CorelSHOW!. If you must bring in something from a non-OLE application, cut or copy it to the Windows clipboard from the originating application, then load or switch to CorelSHOW! and paste the item. If you need to edit this item, you must leave CorelSHOW!, open the originating application, and, after editing, repeat the copy and paste procedure.

Getting Started With CorelSHOW!

You load CorelSHOW! from within Windows. Once CorelSHOW! is loaded, you have the choice of opening an existing presentation or creating a new one.

Follow these steps to get started:

1. Load Windows, open the Corel Graphics group if necessary, and then load CorelSHOW! by double-clicking on the CorelSHOW! icon.

When CorelSHOW! has been loaded, you'll see the screen displayed in Figure C–1. The dialog box allows you to determine whether to open an

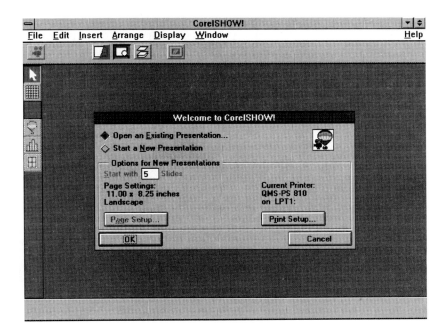

Initial
CorelSHOW!
screen
Figure C–1.

existing presentation or to start a new one. If you choose to open an existing file, and have installed your Corel Graphics sample files, you will find a file called IFONLYX.SHW in your CorelSHOW! SAMPLES subdirectory.

2. Either start a new presentation, or open an existing presentation, by clicking the corresponding option button and clicking OK.

If you open the sample file mentioned above, the screen shown in Figure C–2 will be displayed.

The Screen Elements

On the top of the screen, beneath the title bar, is the menu bar. It contains seven menus: File, which offers various options to manage your files, presentations, and printing; Edit, providing limited editing options such as Cut, Copy, and Paste; Insert, allowing you to insert new pages, objects, files, and animated files; Arrange, which offers several

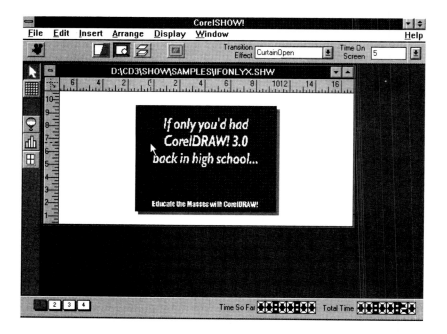

Screen with an existing presentation
Figure C–2.

options for rearranging objects on different levels; Display, which provides rulers, guidelines, and other display aids; Window, which offers a variety of ways to view the presentations on the screen; and Help with the standard Help options.

The tool bar is displayed beneath the menu bar and along the left side of the screen. It will be discussed shortly. The presentation window is under and to the right of the tool bar. It contains the name of the presentation, ruler guides (if specified with the Display menu), and the contents of the current slide.

The bottom of the screen contains the slide number icons on the left, which allow you to switch from one slide to another by simply clicking on the slide number you want. Also at the bottom of the screen, on the right, are the time icons, which assist you in timing your presentation by displaying the Time So Far and the Total Time for previewing the presentation.

The CorelSHOW! Tools and Modes

You can view a presentation in three modes: Background View, which displays art elements common to all slides; Slide View, to view an individual slide (this view is shown in Figure C–2); and Slide Sorter View, to display all slides. The Background View is illustrated in Figure C–3.

The tool bar controls which of the three modes you are in at any time.

The Background View

You can select the Background View by clicking on the Background button found in the top horizontal tool bar. In Figure C–3, the "If only ..." text of the individual slide has been omitted, and you see only the background common to all slides.

The background view is used to create or modify the background of the slides. CorelSHOW! has a series of backgrounds from which you can select, or you can create your own in another application and then assemble it here. Once you identify and insert a background, it will appear in all slides, unless the contents of a slide cover it up.

To insert a background from the CorelSHOW! library of backgrounds, you click on the Background Library icon. A dialog box will display the

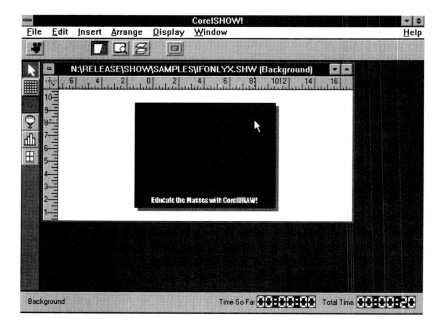

Background
View for
working on the
background of
slides
Figure C–4.

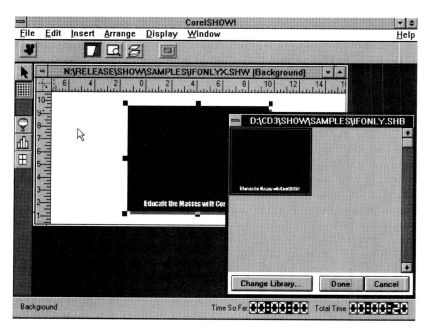

Background
Library with a
variety of
presentations
Figure C–3.

backgrounds that are available, as shown in Figure C–4. You then click on the background you want, and it will be inserted as the background for all slides.

The Slide View

The Slide View is selected by clicking on the Slide View button, beside the Background View button. Use the Slide View to create or modify an individual slide. Figure C–5 shows this view with a slide from the sample presentation.

From this view, you can easily integrate a drawing, chart, or other object from another application. This can be done either by clicking on the appropriate icon, as shown in the table below, or by pulling down the Insert menu and selecting File, then choosing the file to be inserted.

	For CorelDRAW!
	For CorelCHART!
	For other OLE applications

If you click on the icon for CorelDRAW!, CorelCHART!, or other OLE applications, you will be placed within the selected application, but with a link that allows you to easily return to CorelSHOW!. For example, clicking on the CorelDRAW! icon, and then drawing a rectangle in the slide (to identify the area the drawing will occupy), takes you to CorelDRAW!. There, you can create a new drawing or open an existing one, and then copy it to the clipboard. When you return to CorelSHOW! (by choosing Exit and Return from the File menu), you can then paste the drawing onto the slide. The appropriate links with CorelDRAW! are automatically established to insure that changes to the original will be reflected in the copy. Refer to Chapter 15 for more information about how to move from one OLE application to another, and back.

If you insert a file with the File, Object, or Animation commands from the Insert menu, you can select the file to be linked or embedded into CorelSHOW! *without* switching to another application.

C

Slide View for
working on an
individual slide
Figure C–5.

The Slide Sorter View

The Slide Sorter View, shown with the sample application in
Figure C–6, displays the slides in a reduced size. (You can revert quickly
to Slide View by double-clicking on any slide that you want to examine
in detail.)

With this screen, you can manipulate the collection of slides. You can
drag the slides from one position to another, thereby reordering the
slides within the presentation. An alternative way to reorder the slides
is to use the Numbering icon. In this case, you click on the Numbering
icon, and then click on the slides in the sequence that you want the
slides to appear.

If you have more than one presentation open at one time, you can
copy, cut, and paste slides from one presentation to another using
this view. The Tile command in the Windows menu displays two
windows side by side so that you can use the Copy, Cut, and Paste
commands on the Edit menu to move slides between the two
presentations.

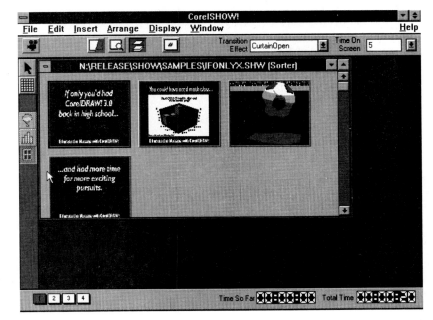

Slide Sorter
View for
working on
slides as a group
Figure C–6.

Transition Effects

The Transition Effects drop-down list box, in the horizontal tool bar,
allows you to apply special effects to the transition between any pair
of slides. To assign a transition effect to a slide, first click on the slide to
select it, then click on the down arrow on the Transition Effects list
box. This causes the drop-down menu to appear, as shown here:

With these options, you can create effects such as a curtain opening to
reveal a slide, or closing to mask a slide. You can zoom in to a slide, or out
from a slide quickly or slowly. Or, you can open a slide with a shutter
effect, in which the shutters of a blind gradually open to reveal the slide.
These are just a few tricks to make a slide presentation more interesting
and animated, without having actual movement in the slides.

Time On Screen

The Time On Screen list box allows you to assign a duration for each slide to be displayed. You click on the down arrow to display a drop-down list of various standard times. Click on each slide, then either select a time value from the drop-down list, or enter a specific time in the entry box.

Previewing a Presentation

To preview a presentation, you can click on the Screen Show button, at the left side of the horizontal tool bar. If you want to first change defaults affecting how the presentation will run, then first choose Presentation Options from the Display menu and make any desired changes in the Presentation Options dialog box. You have the options of advancing to the next slide either automatically or manually, of repeatedly running the presentation until Esc is pressed, of displaying a mouse pointer on the screen, and of generating the slide show in advance, so that the presentation moves from slide to slide more smoothly.

After completing the dialog box, you can click on the Screen Show button, or select Play Screen Show from the File menu.

Introducing CorelPhoto-Paint!

CorelPhoto-Paint! is a multifaceted paint program. It allows you to create bitmap images with an extensive drawing-tool kit, and also enables you to enhance and retouch scanned photos. You can include the resulting images in CorelSHOW! presentations, in CorelDRAW! graphics in word processing or desktop publishing documents, or in other applications.

Getting Started with CorelPhoto-Paint!

To start CorelPhoto-Paint!, first bring up Windows, then double-click on the CorelPhoto-Paint! icon.

After a short time, you will see the screen displayed in Figure C–7.

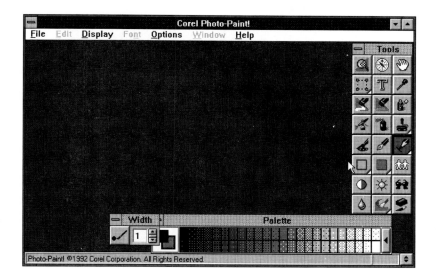

Initial
CorelPhoto-Paint!
screen
Figure C–7.

At this point you can either open an existing picture on disk, or create a new one. If you want to create a new image, select the File menu and choose New; confirm or change the defaults in the Create a New Picture dialog box, shown below. A blank window will open where you can create the picture.

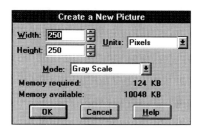

If you want to open an existing picture, select File/Open and identify the file you want. Once you've loaded a picture into CorelPhoto-Paint!, your screen will look something like Figure C–8. In this case, a sample file called BALLOON.PCX has been opened, from the Photo-Paint! SAMPLES directory.

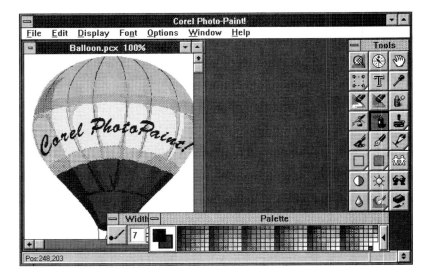

CorelPhoto-Paint! Screen Elements

The CorelPhoto-Paint! window contains many features to help you create pictures or retouch photos.

The menu bar contains seven menus. The File menu contains the file-handling and printing features. The Edit menu offers basic editing features like Undo, Cut, Copy, Paste, and Delete. It also offers filtering features that let you add special effects to a picture or scanned photo, and a Transform option that lets you invert, flip, or rotate a picture, or display it in outline form. The Display menu lets you zoom the on-screen image, and display or hide aids like the workboxes. The Font menu provides a choice of fonts to be applied to text. The Options menu lets you change certain default aspects of the tools' effects. The Window menu offers standard window-display options. Finally, there is a Help menu which has the standard Help options.

Beneath the menu bar is the Photo-Paint! picture window, where you can create or open a picture.

The main Photo-Paint! window contains three other floating windows or dialog boxes: at the right is the Toolbox, containing drawing and retouching tools, at the bottom is the Palette, and to the left of the Palette is the Width and Shape Workbox.

Beneath the Palette and the Width and Shape Workbox is a Status bar. It displays messages, pointer coordinates, and other useful information as you work with a picture. On the right is the Full screen icon, which allows you to remove or restore the title and menu bars on Photo-Paint! window.

The Palette

The Palette allows you to assign colors to a drawing. A selection of 256 colors is provided. The Palette offers an easy way to assign primary, secondary, and background colors to a drawing. The current primary color is displayed in the upper-left box, as shown below. The secondary color is shown in the box beneath it, and the background color is shown in the background.

To select a primary color, click the left mouse button on the desired color. The current primary color will be applied by the painting tools to the outline or border of objects that are drawn. To select a secondary color, click with the right mouse button on a color. Filled shapes will fill with this color. To select a background color, click on it with the left mouse button while holding down the Shift key. The image background will take on that color.

The Palette can be hidden or displayed by selecting the Display menu and choosing Workboxes and Hide Palette or Show Palette. A shortcut key to hide and display the Palette is Ctrl-P.

If you click on the arrow at the right, the Palette will be rolled up, as shown here:

The Width and Shape Workbox

The Width and Shape Workbox, which is to the left of the palette in Figure C–8, is used to control the width of the drawing tools, and the shape of the brush strokes. Pressing the up or down arrows increases or decreases the width of lines drawn. If you click on the Shape button to the left, a dialog box will appear, and offer you several brush effects, as shown here:

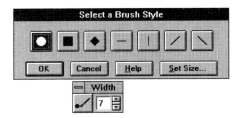

This brief tour of the screen gives you an introduction to the software, but experimenting with the CorelPhoto-Paint! tools is where you will really begin to appreciate the power of the package.

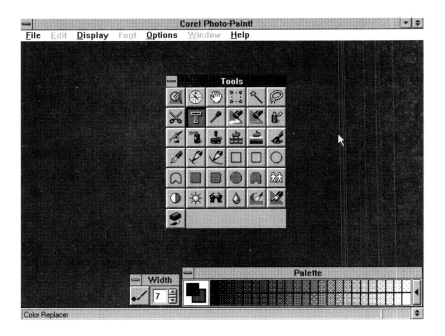

The Toolbox without grouped tools
Figure C–9.

CorelPhoto-Paint! Tools

The CorelPhoto-Paint! Toolbox, as mentioned earlier, is a floating window that you can move around on the screen. Although the Toolbox is displayed by default, you can hide it by clicking on the Control-menu box in its title bar. Its Control menu offers you the options of hiding the Toolbox, or displaying it differently. Once it is hidden, you can later display it when you need it by selecting the Display menu and choosing Workboxes and Show Toolbox. Pressing Ctrl-T is a shortcut toggle which also hides or displays the Toolbox.

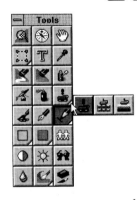

The tools within the Toolbox are arranged according to function. Some buttons represent "groups" of tools; these can be identified by a small white triangle in the lower-right corner of the tool button. When a button with a triangle is clicked on, a fly-out menu displays the tools in the group.

The tools within the Toolbox can be selected by clicking on a tool button, or in the case of group tools, by dragging the cursor on a fly-out menu until the tool you want is highlighted.

Figure C–8 shows the tools grouped into three columns and eight rows of tiles. Each button represents one or more tools, as you have seen. You can display all of the tools without hiding any behind a group button. To do this, click on the Control-menu box of the Toolbox and choose Layout, then Ungroup. Figure C–9 shows the Toolbox with all tools displayed. (This figure was created with a full-screen view, and no pictures showing, and the Toolbox has been moved for easier viewing.)

The Toolbox contains four types of tools: Display, Painting, Retouch, and Selection. A brief summary of each of the tools is provided in the following sections.

Display Tools

Display tools are used to manipulate the display of the picture in some way. There are three display tools:

Hand moves a picture in any direction: up, down, to the side, or diagonally.

Locator displays the same area in any copies of a picture on the desktop.

Zoom enlarges or reduces the size of the image.

Painting Tools

Painting tools are the bread and butter of the Photo-Paint! program. They allow you to create and delete shapes, and add color, texture, or text to a picture. There are 23 painting tools:

Airbrush sprays color into an area, adding shading and depth.

Clone duplicates painting or drawing strokes elsewhere within a picture, or applies them to a duplicate of a picture. As you draw, a clone is produced.

Color Replacer changes one color to another.

Curve lets you create a curve by setting two points, and then dragging the line between them to form the curve you want.

Eraser erases or clears an area of the picture.

Eyedropper picks up a color from a picture so the same shade can be applied elsewhere.

Filled Box creates a square or rectangle with a border of the current primary color, and filled with the current secondary color.

Filled Ellipse creates a circle or ellipse with a border of the primary color, and filled with the secondary color.

Filled Polygon creates a shape having up to 200 sides, with a border of the primary color and filled with the secondary color.

Filled Rounded Box creates a square or rectangle with rounded corners, having a border of the primary color and filled with the secondary color.

Fountain Pen lets you draw smoothly and evenly in a freehand mode.

Gradient Paint Roller fills an enclosed area with a gradient ranging from the secondary to the background color.

Hollow Box creates hollow, unfilled rectangles or squares.

Hollow Ellipse creates hollow, unfilled circles and ellipses.

Hollow Polygon creates hollow, unfilled shapes having up to 200 sides.

Hollow Rounded Box creates hollow, unfilled squares and rectangles with rounded corners.

Line lets you draw straight lines by establishing starting and end points.

Local Undo cancels the last change made since a tool was selected or a command was used.

Paintbrush, using a primary color, lets you draw free hand. The effect is coarser than with the Fountain Pen.

Paint Roller fills an enclosed area with a color.

Spraycan adds a rough pattern to a picture, by randomly spraying a color.

Text allows you to type text onto the picture.

Tile Pattern Paint Roller fills an enclosed area with a tile pattern.

Retouch Tools

Retouch tools are used to refine or retouch parts of a picture (filters are generally used to retouch whole pictures). There are seven retouch tools:

Blend Paintbrush softens the contours of an area.

Brighten Paintbrush adds highlights, or darkens an area.

Contrast Paintbrush intensifies the brightness or darkness of an area.

Sharpen Paintbrush sharpens or adds crispness to an area.

 Smear Paintbrush spreads and smears colors in an area.

 Smudge Paintbrush adds texture to a picture by randomly mixing colors, and spraying a picture with the result.

 Tint Paintbrush adds an overall cast or tint of color to an area.

Selection Tools

Selection tools are used to select, or cut out, an area of a picture. Once selected, an area can be cut, copied, pasted, stretched, rotated, or otherwise manipulated. There are four selection tools:

 Box Selection lets you select an area of a picture by enclosing it in a rectangular box or marquee.

 Lasso lets you select an area by drawing a line around it in Freehand mode.

 Magic Wand lets you duplicate a set of colors from one area or object to another.

 Scissors lets you define an area to be selected by clicking on a spot on the picture, moving the pointer, clicking on another spot, and so on, creating a polygon around the area. The polygon may have up to 200 points.

Summary

CorelPhoto-Paint! contains many more surprises. Continue to experiment with it, and you will be impressed with its capabilities.

This introduction only touches on the capabilities found in CorelSHOW! and CorelPhoto-Paint!. Using the ensemble of Corel products, you can DRAW, TRACE, CHART, PAINT, and finally SHOW presentations in a professional and stunning manner.

INDEX

O

U

V

W

X

Y

Z